D1560118

GERMAN-AMERICAN
LITERATURE

by

Don Heinrich Tolzmann

The Scarecrow Press, Inc.
Metuchen, N.J. & London
1977

Library of Congress Cataloging in Publication Data
Main entry under title:

German-American literature.

   Includes bibliographical references and index.
   1. German-American literature--History and criticism--
Addresses, essays, lectures. 2. Authors, German-American--
Biography--Addresses, essays, lectures. I. Tolzmann, Don
Heinrich, 1945-
PT3903.G4   830'.9   77-21596
ISBN 0-8108-1069-7

FOREWORD

The purpose of this work is to present for the first time an introductory history of German-American literature. The articles selected for this reader were listed in German-Americana: A Bibliography (Metuchen, N. J. : Scarecrow Press, 1975). I have selected articles by recognized German-Americanists, articles from scholarly journals and German-American journals, and also articles which I found useful in the study and teaching of German-American literature.

This reader is, of course, not a comprehensive history of German-American literature. Indeed, this book indicates the immense need for further research. I would like to reiterate some research proposals made by Heinz Kloss:

1. A bibliography of all German books printed in the U.S. since 1830.

2. An anthology of all German ideological writings: Lutherans, Catholics, radicals, etc.

3. An anthology of the German writings of all American-born authors.

To this list, I would add:

4. Histories and bibliographies of German-American literature in each state where there is a substantial German community.

5. Identification and analysis of the several hundred contemporary German-American authors.

6. Name- and subject-indexing of German-American newspapers. A major paper, such as the New Yorker Staats-Zeitung und Herold, should be indexed first.

Map on following page is from Christopher L. Dolmetsch, "Locations of German Language Newspaper and Periodical Printing in the United States: 1732-1976," Monatshefte 68(2):(1976), 91. Copyright © 1976 by the Board of Regents of the University of Wisconsin System.

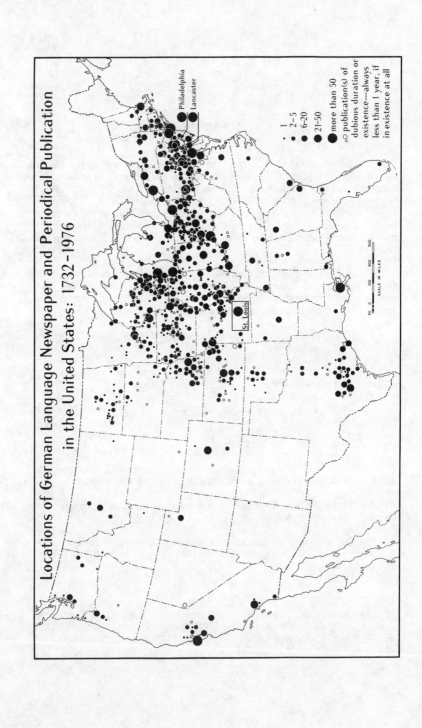

Locations of German Language Newspaper and Periodical Publication
in the United States: 1732–1976

Philadelphia
Lancaster

St. Louis

. 1
• 2–5
● 6–20
● 21–50
● more than 50

○ publication(s) of
dubious duration or
existence—always
less than 1 year, if
in existence at all

50 100 200 300
SCALE IN MILES

CONTENTS

DEUTSCH-AMERIKA

Es ist ein eigen Tun und Lassen,
Das uns're Seele tief bewegt,
Wenn sie zwei Welten muss umfassen,
Vereint als Heimat in sich trägt.

--Maria Raible

PREFACE

Was weiss die alte Heimat, wie wir hier empfinden?
Wird je die neue Heimat es wohl ganz verstehen...
--Friedrich Fiedel

Since the 1690s, when Franz Daniel Pastorius wrote the first
German language poems in America, at least 30,000 volumes of
German-American prose and poetry have been written by 3,000 authors.[1] The German-Americans constitute the largest German element outside of Europe and the largest ethnic element in the U.S.:
35,000,000.[2] It is not surprising, therefore, that the German-
Americans have created the largest body of non-English literature
in America. German-American literature ranks with Austrian,
Swiss and East German literatures as a separate and distinct branch
of German literature. In America it is one of the most significant
of the non-English-language immigrant/ethnic literatures.

The term "German-American" designates "was eigentlich
amerikanisch und deutscher Volksabstammung ist ohne Rücksicht auf
das Land der Herkunft, also Amerikaner, deren Väter und Vorväter
Reichsdeutsche, Volksdeutsche, Österreicher, Tiroler, Schweizer
oder Siebenbürger-, Wolga-, oder Balten-Deutsche waren. Sie sind
alle ethnisch Deutschamerikaner."[3] Estimates as to the number of
German immigrants run as high as twelve million. Their literature
has received scant attention outside of German-America. Between
1856 and 1969, thirty-two anthologies of German-American literature
were compiled, but they only reflect a fraction of the thousands of
poems, novellas, dramas and novels scattered in the numerous
German-American newspapers and periodicals.[4] Heinrich A. Rattermann, the noted Cincinnati German historian and poet, himself
collected the work of five hundred authors for his anthology. Perhaps the finest anthology to date was the last one published: Robert
E. Ward's Deutsche Lyrik aus Amerika (New York: Literary Society Foundation, 1969). It contains the poetry of sixty-six authors
and is supplemented with bio-bibliographical data. Unfortunately,
there is no comprehensive history of German-American literature
available. America's largest non-English-language literature is a
mystery and a neglected dimension of American and German literary
studies.

Several scholars have attempted to define German-American
literature. Linus Spuler describes it as:

ix

Die Gesamtheit der literarischen Erzeugnisse aller jener Dichter, die in den Vereinigten Staaten von Nordamerika als ihrer Heimat (der einzigen oder zweiten) leben und sowohl die amerikanische Welt in all ihren Aspekten als auch alle anderen möglichen Vorwürfe durch das Medium der deutschen Sprache künstlerisch zu erobern und zu gestalten suchen. [5]

Ernst Rose sees German-American literature as "only German literature which became Americanized in form or subject matter. "[6] Ernst Jockers theorized about it as:

... den eigenartigen Ausdruck einer seelischen Grundhaltung, in der Altes und Neues, Deutsches und Amerikanisches in einer Synthese zusammenfliessen und als solche eine bemerkenswerte Bereicherung des Gesamtaspektes des neuen Landes darbieten. [7]

Herman F. Brause, an American-born poet, classifies it as "Heimatdichtung deutschamerikanischer Prägung. "[8] Jockers, in a further attempt to clarify the definition, differentiates between German literature written in America and German-American literature:

Zur deutschen Dichtung in Amerika gehört irgendein poetisches Erzeugnis in deutscher Sprache, das zu seiner Entstehung der amerikanischen Umgebung nicht bedarf. Deutschamerikanische Dichtung aber setzt Amerika als neue Heimat voraus, mit deren Verhältnissen, Menschen und Natur man sich innerlich auseinandersetzen muss, wenn man sich hier einbürgern will. Deutschamerikanische Literatur ist der seelische Niederschlag jener neueingewanderten Gruppe, eine Generationserscheinung... [9]

A basic presupposition is, as Gert Niers writes, "die Bewältigung des (deutsch)amerikanischen Hier-und-Heute in breitem Umfang... "[10] Even the best of German-American authors have been largely ignored and remain unrecognized.

German-American literature is an expression of an intellectual position in which old (German) and new (American) cultural values unite to form a synthesis offering unique perspectives on American life. German-American literature is not "German" or "American" but distinctly "German-American. " It requires an understanding of German life in America. According to Robert E. Ward, a German-American writer is that person who composed literature in the German language while residing in America, or who writes of experiences there.

Many of the three thousand German-American authors, such as Robert Reitzel, edited or wrote for the five-thousand German-American newspapers and periodicals which have been published since 1732. [11] Some, like Konrad Nies, directed, acted or wrote for the German-American stage in various German centers, such

as Cincinnati, Cleveland, St. Louis and Milwaukee. Others, like
Rattermann and Fick, engaged in the professions, but wrote incessantly. Some of their books were published in Europe, but the U.S.
was the major publication center. Authors could turn to middle-of-
the-road publishers such as Ernst Steiger (New York) or Georg
Brumder (Milwaukee); to radical publishers such as the Freidenker
Publishing House (Milwaukee); or to conservative religious publishers
such as the Concordia Publishing House (St. Louis) and the Methodist Book Concern (Cincinnati). Some authors issued their work in
Selbstverlag, advertised them in the press, and sold them from
their homes and through the numerous German-American bookstores
around the country.

German-American literature was and is popular in German-
American communities, although much of it is quite unknown outside
Deutsch-Amerika. The growing interest in ethnic studies and the
interest in German-Americana necessitate the publication of this first
introductory history on German-American literature.

Notes

1. The works of these authors are listed in a soon-to-be-published
    book: Robert E. Ward, Handbook of German-American
    Creative Literature.
2. See my America's German Heritage (Cleveland, Ohio: German-
    American National Congress, 1976) for an introduction to
    German-American history.
3. Austin App, "Deutsch-Amerikanische Sehnsucht. Studie über
    deutsche Dichtung in USA," Klüter Blätter 26 (1975):5.
4. See Karl J. R. Arndt. German-American Newspapers and Per-
    iodicals 1732-1955. Heidelberg: Quelle & Meyer, 1965.
5. Robert E. Ward. Deutsche Lyrik aus Amerika. New York:
    Literary Society Foundation, 1969, p. 5.
6. Cassell's Encyclopedia of Literature. London: Cassell & Co.,
    1973, 1:258.
7. Ernst Jockers, "Deutsch-Amerikanische Dichtung," Der Aus-
    landdeutsche 12(1929):321.
8. Herman F. Brause, "Betrachtungen zur deutschamerikanischen
    Dichtung," Das Mitteilungsblatt des Verbandes deutsch-
    sprachiger Autoren in Amerika 1(1974):1.
9. See my Abschied (Cincinnati: Im Verlage des Verbandes deutsch-
    sprachiger Autoren in Amerika, 1975). This contains a sum-
    mary of German-American literary theory.
10. Gert Niers, "Deutschamerikanische Literatur oder deutsch-
    sprachige Literatur in Amerika," New Yorker Staats-Zeitung
    und Herold (Jan. 24-25, 1976).
11. An excellent recent study of the German-American press is
    Robert E. Cazden, German Exile Literature in America,
    1933-50. A History of the Free German Press and Book
    Trade. Chicago: ALA, 1970.

...viele deutschamerikanische Dichter haben gesungen, aber ihre Lieder sind kaum erhört worden. Ihre Leiden und Freuden, Hoffnungen und Enttäuschungen sind zwar aufgezeichnet und mehr oder weniger aufbewahrt worden, aber auch die besten unter ihnen bleiben zu Unrecht ungelesene, unbekannte Wesen.

--Herman F. Brause

PART I

INTRODUCTION

1. GERMAN-AMERICAN LITERATURE*

Robert Spiller and Willard Thorp

In the work of German-American writers, the most considerable body of non-English writing produced in the United States, many
of the lines of the pattern of development we have indicated [previ-
ous to this reprint] are clearly and easily discernible. Sooner even
than the French in New Orleans, the Germans in colonial Pennsylvania and New York became articulate.

The first exponents of ideas were animated by religious zeal:
Francis Daniel Pastorius, founder, in 1683, of Quietist Germantown,
whose contribution to colonial literature deserves to be better known;
Johann Kelpius, the hermit of the Wissahickon; Conrad Beissel and
his monastic brothers and sisters in the Ephrata Cloister in Lancaster County, Pennsylvania, who composed and edited two large collections of hymns (1739, 1766). Benjamin Franklin printed hymn
books for the Ephrata Dunkers as early as 1730, and Sauer's press,
established in 1738, brought out later editions as well as a complete
Bible in German and a German newspaper which reached four thousand readers scattered from Pennsylvania to Georgia. Henry Miller,
printer to Congress, founded in 1762 the Philadelphische Staatsbote
and published many German books. German presses in the United
States were soon able to handle anything written here except volum-
inous works like the Hallesche Nachrichten (1787) of the Lutherans,
the Nachrichten (1735-1752) of the Salzburgers, the diaries of the
Moravian missionaries, or the travels of Mittelberger (1756), Achen-
wall (1769), and Schöpf (1788). Such books, too elaborate for the
German-American presses, publishers in Germany were glad to
print.

In the second and third decades of the nineteenth century,
when the heavier flow of German immigration set in, a stream of
travel literature began, much of it designed to attract or direct immigrants. Some of these books had considerable literary power;
the immigrants not only studied them before they crossed the ocean
but reread them with pleasure in America.

Critical accounts of the New World began to appear at about
the same time. In the form of essays or fiction they ranged from
extravagant idealization to fierce indictment of everything American,

---

*Reprinted by permission of Macmillan Co., Inc. from Literary
History of the United States by Robert Spiller, Willard Thorp and
others (Fourth ed. New York: Macmillan, 1974), pp. 678-84.

with attempts, by the revolutionaries of 1848, to reshape the United States into something closer to their dreams. Men like Heinzen, Hecker, and Weydemeyer joined with such older liberals as Körner, Weitling, and Münch to form strong German-American blocs bent on reforms which looked to their contemporaries "radical" and "subversive." Others, like Nikolaus Lenau, whose American experience is the basis of Ferdinand Kürnberger's Der Amerikamüde (1855), thought improvement hopeless and contented themselves with denunciation of the "philistines of these hog-besotted States, scoundrels all, who in their horrible vacuity cannot conceive that there can be any gods higher than those struck in the mint." If they had circulated beyond the German reading public, books like Der Amerikamüde, Karl Büchile's Land und Volk der Vereinigten Staaten, and Friedrich Gerstäcker's Nach Amerika! (all published in 1855) would have roused quite as much anger as Dickens' American Notes.

Somewhere between the extremes of delight and disillusion stood Charles Sealsfield, the first important German-American writer to devote himself to fiction. He was an enthusiastic republican, ready to overlook some cultural deficiencies in the United States because he believed in the rugged virtues which he saw pushing on the construction of a new social order. He was also the sworn enemy of oppression in any form, a fiery defender of liberty, who would swing into action his full battery of satire, ridicule, and abuse whenever he encountered human slavery, political corruption, or commercial opportunism.

Sealsfield cloaked his true identity so effectively during his lifetime that he kept the editors and critics of two continents guessing as to his true nationality. When he died in Switzerland in 1864 his last will and testament revealed that "Charles Sealsfield," "C. Seatsfield," and "C. Sidons" were all of them Karl Anton Postl, a runaway monk from a Bohemian monastery. In 1823 he landed in New Orleans as a German immigrant and traveled extensively through the Mississippi Valley region and the Southwest, possibly as far as Mexico City, gathering experiences and impressions which went into a long shelf of books, essays, and stories published in Germany, in Switzerland, and, sometimes simultaneously, in London, Philadelphia, and New York. In the United States, Sealsfield made Kittanning, Pennsylvania, his headquarters; but he shuttled back and forth across the Atlantic, maintaining precarious connections as a newspaper correspondent and a private political agent in London and Paris. Hobnobbing with people as various as Lord Palmerston, Joseph Bonaparte, and Stephen Girard, he had a hand in a variety of picturesque international intrigues. His books were widely translated and reprinted (with and without his permission), adapted, imitated, and plagiarized, and he enjoyed a considerable international reputation before he was much read in America outside German-American circles, where he was popular from the first. He acquired and proudly maintained American citizenship and, while carefully preserving his anonymity, claimed to be "America's Most Famous Author."

His earliest works were The United States of North America
As They Are, published in 1827 in Stuttgart and in London, and a
book on Austria which attacked the reactionary policy of Metternich.
His first novel, Tokeah, or the White Rose (1829), recast in Der
Legitime und die Republikaner (1833), though a rather wooden performance, was a prototype of the genre at which he became so suc-
cessful--the "ethnographic" novel, where the hero is a whole people.
The characters are typical shapers of the new republic, frontiers-
men and pioneers.   They are portraits, Sealsfield insisted, from
life, and they move against a background of magnificent scenery described in realistic detail.

From 1834 to 1841 Sealsfield produced in quick succession a
series of novels based on American themes.   He grouped them under such collective titles as Lebensbilder aus beiden Hemisphären or
Transatlantische Reiseskizzen.   The setting is usually the Southern
or Southwestern states, where he was most at home, and where the
panorama of river and plantation life, racing, fishing, hunting, and
adventures in forest, swamp, and prairie gave his powers of obser-
vation and imagination ample scope.   The best of these collections
is Das Cajütenbuch (1841), stories told by a company gathered at a
retired sea captain's house (built in the shape of a ship's cabin,
hence the title).   The tales are most of them dramatic incidents of
the Texas War of Secession.   "Die Prairie am Jacinto," with which
the book begins, is considered to be Sealsfield's best piece of work.

The later books are inferior to the earlier, partly because,
during his absence from the United States, Sealsfield lost touch with
the rapidly changing American scene, partly because he began to
blur his realism with clouds of romantic phantasmagoria.   He came
to believe that it was impossible to write realistically of a society
that no longer existed; so he burned the manuscript of an autobiography together with all his memoirs and personal papers, and retired to Switzerland, poverty, and seclusion.

In addition to his popularity with readers in Europe and the
United States, Sealsfield put his impress on American letters through
his influence on native American writers.   Longfellow spent entire
evenings reading his "favorite Sealsfield" and reread the Louisiana
portions of the Lebensbilder while he was working on the second
part of Evangeline.   A. B. Faust has shown that William Gilmore
Simms borrowed a telling episode for Guy Rivers from Ralph Dough-
bys Brautfahrt, that Helen Hunt Jackson's Ramona bears striking resemblance to Tokeah, and that the third, and best, part of Mayne
Reid's Wild Life is filched outright from Frederick Hardman's translation of The Cabin Book.

There were other popular novelists who, like Sealsfield, made
literary capital out of their own picturesque adventures in the New
World.   Friedrich Armand Strubberg was a hunter, soldier, rancher,
merchant, physician, and entrepreneur of German colonization ventures before, at fifty-two, he began to turn out, under the pseudonym "Armand," sensational novels with such titles as Sklaverei in

Amerika (1862) and Der Sprung vom Niagarafalls (1864). He was
quite uninfluenced by Sealsfield or anyone else, and his unliterary
straightforward prose gives his wildest tales an air of authenticity.
His Carl Scharnhorst: Abenteuer eines deutschen Knaben in Amerika
(1872) was long one of the most popular German stories for boys.

    Friedrich Gerstäcker, after adventures that led him through
both Americas, produced some hundred and fifty books of travel and
adventure, half fictional, half true, to become, during the fifties, the
most popular of German-American novelists. His best known and in
some respects his best work is Nach Amerika! (1855), a realistic
account of the fortunes of a shipload of German immigrants who land
in New Orleans and make their way up the Mississippi.

    More skillful as a writer--his best Erzählung is Der Pedlar
(1857)--was Otto Ruppius, who came to the United States as a refugee in 1848 and worked as a journalist in New York and St. Louis
until 1861, when the Prussian proclamation of amnesty permitted his
return.

    Heinrich Balduin Möllhausen, sometimes called the German
Cooper, came to seek not political refuge but adventure. He served
as artist and topographer for the Smithsonian Institution on expeditions
charting transcontinental railway routes across the mountains, and
turned his experiences into some fifty novels and travel books which
were translated into English, French, Dutch, and various other languages.

    Though all these writers returned eventually to their native
land, they are to be considered not German travelers but actual German-Americans. They shared the hazards of migration and the hardships of the frontier, and their point of view is always that of the immigrant and settler, never of the European observer merely.

    More brilliant as a writer than any of the adventure novelists
was the German-born polemicist and poet Robert Reitzel. He was
educated for the ministry but turned freethinker. In the United States
he wandered about the country lecturing, writing, and lending a hand
to any agitation fomented in the Midwest by German radicals. He
propagandized for Sozialdemokratie, Weltbürgertum, Materialismus,
Arbeiterbewegung, Turnerei, Freimännerei, defying arbitrary power
wherever he met it and loving truth even to a pose. In 1884 his
friends and admirers set him up in Detroit as editor of a weekly literary paper, which he named Der arme Teufel, and into which he
poured, for the remaining fourteen years of his life, his wit, irony,
and fierce philippic. He recognized revolutionary spirits when he
found them and by excerpt and translation did much to familiarize
readers on the frontier with the ideas of Emerson and Thoreau.

    The nineteenth century German-Americans were of course pro-
lific writers of lyric verse. Thousands of poems chant praise of the
adopted home or sigh for the distant fatherland, and the range beyond these obvious themes is wide. There is a considerable body

also of German-American epic poetry, and there are some interesting poetic narratives based on immigrant and frontier experience.
The poets tried valiantly, too, to familiarize their countrymen with
the poetry which was being read by their new fellow citizens. German translations were made of Evangeline, Hiawatha, "The Raven,"
Snowbound, and Leaves of Grass, as well as of the English poets
most popular in the United States. Chicago was long the poetic capital: at least half the High German poetry written in America was
published there.

The German theater in America began in New York in 1840,
and by 1854 the city had two houses devoted entirely to German
plays. The famous Germania Theater opened in 1872; the Thalia in
1879; and the Irving Place in 1888. Philadelphia, Milwaukee, Chicago, St. Louis, and Cincinnati also had important theaters, and in
at least a dozen other cities with large German populations the drama flourished. With rare exceptions the plays presented were classics of the German stage, for the actors were far more interested
in performing great roles like Wallenstein and Hamlet than in encouraging new playwrights, but there are a few notable instances of
plays by German-Americans reaching and holding the boards. Those
plays that succeeded best had such titles as Ein Lateinischer Farmer
and Der Corner Grocer aus der Avenue A, though, unlike the novelists, most of the playwrights sought to dramatize events of grand
proportions or to tell romantic stories against exotic backgrounds.

After 1870 the use of German in speech and writing declined.
The once popular Erzählungen survived only in the moralized tales
of church periodicals; by 1900 the German theater had almost disappeared; and lyric poetry grew weak and thin. By the twentieth century not more than two or three writers of importance were using
High German. Literature in German dialects, on the other hand,
especially Pennsylvania German, increased steadily as cultural
pride and racial consciousness grew. The dialects lent themselves
readily to humor, and popular verse appeared in Hessian, Swabian,
and Palatinate as well as in Plattdeutsch.

Less defensible linguistically, though amusing to a larger
audience, were Karl Adler's Mundartlich Heiteres (1886) and Charles
Godfrey Leland's Hans Breitmann Ballads (1856-1895), written in a
kind of Kauderwelsch, a mixture of broken English and German dialect, not to be confused with Pennsylvania German. Hans is a huge,
bearded, good-natured rogue, who gorges and guzzles his way
through a roistering and checkered career, speaking a tongue and
portraying a character which German-Americans say is a libelous
caricature. Much later, in the twenties and thirties, Kurt M. Stein
succeeded in amusing both Americans and Germans with the same
sort of linguistic exaggerations.

PART II

REGIONAL LITERATURE

2. PENNSYLVANIA GERMAN POETRY
   UNTIL 1816: A SURVEY*

John Joseph Stoudt

When the thirteen American Colonies declared themselves
free from British rule one-twelfth of their people spoke German.
The largest concentration of these teutonic colonials was in the lush,
fertile, south-eastern Pennsylvania counties where on terrain much
like the Rhineland they developed a fairly homogeneous culture which
already in the eighteenth century was known by the term which President Eisenhower uses to describe his forbears--"Pennsylvania
Dutch." These Rhinelanders, Swiss, Silesians, Alsations and Hol-
landers had accepted William Penn's offer to seek a free new life
in his new-world haven and they came by shiploads to settle next to
English and Welsh Quakers, producing a culture island known as
Pennsylvania Dutch.

Migration began in 1683 when Francis Daniel Pastorius,
friend of Pietist Spener, led some Quakers from Krefeld; it continued throughout the eighteenth century, culminating quantitatively
around 1750. Registration of such non-British immigrants began in
1727 and naturalization of these "foreign Protestants" pursuant to an
Act of 13 George II began in 1740.[1] Thus a "Johann Peder Eisen-
hauer" arrived in Philadelphia from Rotterdam on the Europa on November 20th, 1741, and he was naturalized at Philadelphia Supreme
Court on April 11th, 1752, announcing himself as from Bethel Town-
ship, Lancaster County, Pennsylvania.[2]

In contrast to their Anglo-Saxon neighbours the Pennsylvania
Dutch produced a body of verse, chiefly religious in tone, which
their neighbours could match neither in quantity nor in quality. During the seventeenth century American Puritan verse had sprung but
weakly from the bleak hills of New England to proclaim its grim
kingdom of doom and damnation, and, as far as English verse is
concerned, eighteenth-century America was almost a barren desert.
Most literary historians record only about forty English poets for
the period.

Not so, however, with the Pennsylvania Dutch. A recent anthology by the present writer, Pennsylvania German Poetry 1683-
1830,[3] presents about 300 poems by about 150 poets, or about four
times as many German as there were English colonial writers, and

*Reprinted by permission of the publisher from German Life and
Letters 13 (1960): 145-53.

this collection only skims the surface. Altogether over 350 persons
are known to have written verse during this period; they form the
Pennsylvania German component of American poetry which embraces
three phases, at least five schools, and includes about 10,000 poems.

This German-American verse betrays a different spirit from
that of the English-American verse contemporary with it, on which
issues from the heart of the German baroque[4] and which, as the
eighteenth century progressed, grew to become wholly American. It
reveals the broad road that goes from Pietism (loosely construed)
to American democracy, for the American mind comes not only from
Locke and the French philosophers, not only from Geneva and Edin-
burgh; it has its sources in German Pietism too. The Speaker of
the first and third American congresses was Friedrich Mühlenberg
who, though born in Pennsylvania, had been educated by the Franckes
in Halle. Pennsylvania German poetry shows the roots of democracy in Anabaptism, in the so-called "spiritual reformers," in Sebas-
tian Franck, Jacob Boehme, Johann Arndt, Paul Gerhard, Daniel
Sudermann, Spener, Francke, Tersteegen, and Zinzendorf. And this
German source worked on a different level from British empiricism
and French rationalism.

Pennsylvania German verse, then, started as a poetry of
mysticism introduced into America by the religious sectarian leaders
who had fled an intolerant old world. The mood is clear from Heinrich Danner's Ein Reise Lied, a poem written to justify migration:

> Was hat uns doch bewogen,
> Zu gehen aus von heim?
> Die lieb hat uns gezogen
> Zu suchen die gemein,
> Die Gott der Herr gebauet,
> In einem fremden Land... [5]

Secularize this love theme and the result points towards democratic
brotherhood.

The pioneering patriarch of the Pennsylvania Dutch was also
one of their chief poets. Francis Daniel Pastorius, who came in
1683 at the head of a colony of German Quakers, became one of the
chief literary figures of his time in America, writing more lines of
English verse than had so far been written in America and composing considerable German verse in which a religion centred on this
world was mixed with traditional "inwardness." One of his first poems and thus one of the first German poems written in America was
his protest against negro slavery:

> Allermassen ungebührlich
> Ist der Handel dieser Zeit
> Dass ein Mensch so unnatürlich
> Andre drückt mit Dienstbarkeit.
> Ich möcht' einen solchen fragen,

Ob er wohl ein Sclav' möcht' sein!
Ohne Zweifel wird er sagen:
Ach, bewähr mich Gott: Nein, nein![6]

Pastorius's verse was recorded in common-place books, chief of
which was the celebrated "Bee-Hive," which is still unpublished.

The first school of Pennsylvania German Poets was the group
which came in 1694 on the Sarah Maria led by Johannes Kelpius.
These students and mystics, readers of Boehme, had been gathered
by the Swabian Johann Jakob Zimmermann to go to Pennsylvania and
await there, in a community devoted to the contemplative life, the
end of the age. Zimmermann died on shipboard and forty brethren
came under Kelp's leadership to settle near Philadelphia. At least
seven of them, perhaps more, wrote verse in which baroque imagery,
transcendental mysticism, and overpowering religiosity dominate.
Kelp's musical verse was the best:

Hier lieg ich geschmieget,
    Erkräncket im Schrein,
Fast gänzlich besieget,
    Von süssester Pein,
Ich denke des blühenden lieblichen May'n,
Allwo mich der schönste wird ewig erfreu'n,
Und diese zerbrechliche Hütte verneu'n.[7]

Echoes of baroque imagery appear in the work of Johann Gottfried
Seelig, another of these poets:

Wo bistu mein Täublein!
Mein süssestes Englein?
Ich sehn mich mit schmertzen
Und ruf dich im hertzen,
Wo bistu mein Täublein?
Ach kom doch mein tröstendes Englein![8]

The second school of Pennsylvania German poets are those who belonged to the "Dunkers," "Dompelaars," or new Anabaptists, a
group which arose around 1700 and which came to Pennsylvania in
1719, led by Alexander Mack. Congregations arose in various Pennsylvania communities and each centre had at least one poet. In the
first generation the following wrote verse: Mack himself, Peter
Becker, Heinrich and Jacob Danner, Johannes Preiss and Johann
Naas. Theirs was a world-renouncing mood, wholly ascetic, full of
moral earnestness and ethical strictness. Thus Peter Becker wrote:

Du armer Pilger wandelst hier
    in diesem Jammerthal,
und söhnest dich noch für und für
    nach jenem Freuden-Saal
Wie mancher Feind begegnet dir,
Dass du doch weinest also hier,
    Gedult.[9]

The second generation of Dunkers produced poets of greater skill, including Alexander Mack II, Christopher Saur II, Jacob Stoll, and several skilful anonymous writers.

The most interesting school of Pennsylvania German poets is probably that associated with the name of Ephrata. This place on the Cocalico creek in Lancaster County was a communal retreat on Franciscan lines where a group of several hundred ascetics lived apart from the world for the better part of the eighteenth century. They had fled from what they believed to be a corrupt and declining culture to seek their peace in the American wilderness. They formed the most creative community in colonial America, a community in which art and music, as well as poetry, were produced in quantity and in a spirit in full harmony with their principle of austerity, their religious primitivism. The chief of their many collections of verse is the famous musical manuscript book, <u>Paradiesisches Wunderspiel,</u> [10] (1766) to which nearly sixty writers contributed verse. These mystics had gathered round a gifted man, Conrad Beissel, born in Eberbach near Heidelberg; he was himself the chief American poet of the colonial period in German or English, and produced at least 80,000 lines of verse. His work compares in depth with the prose of Jacob Boehme. Where the Silesian had seen that in all things there was a Yes and a No, the Pennsylvanian knew that "das ewige Nichts will ein Icht sein," anticipating Hartmann's philosophy of the unconscious by a century.

Beissel wrote many forms of verse from alexandrine couplets to long lyric stanzas, the former in imitation of the <u>Cherubinischer Wandersmann:</u>

> Wer sitzt in tiefer still, und ruht in Gottes schoosz
> Vergisset leid und weh, ist aller sorgen losz. [11]

and in a longer strophe:

> Wer Bilder-loss und angeschieden
> Von Sinnen Welt und Creatur,
> Besitzet einen solchen Frieden
> Der höher ist als die Natur...

His most ambitious poem was on the theme of Boehme's "Ungrund," that abyss of undifferentiated reality which was hardly capable of being caught in conceptual image or idea:

> O Ungrund! der gewesen
>   von Ewigkeiten her,
> Mach mich in dir genesen,
>   damit, was mir mich her
> mich ja nicht mehr einführe
>   von deiner Wesenheit,
> noch anderwerts abirre
>   durch einig Ding der Zeit. [12]

Here at Ephrata the goal of selfless surrender was sought by an entire community of brethren and sisters, associated with the married householders who lived in the neighbourhood of the settlement.   The ideal is clear from this stanza by an unknown sister:

> Das kleinste Ich und Mein,
>   Das sich an mir erweiset
> Bringt solche Vielheit ein
>   Die mich von Gott abreisset.

The goal of this eighteenth-century American community is expressed in this verse by an unknown brother:

> Ich kan nun in stillen Frieden
>   Meine Zeit hier bringen zu:
> Weil von allen bin geschieden,
>   Was kan stören meine Ruh.

Here in the Pennsylvania wilderness a forgotten chapter in German literary history was written by exiled Pietists, malcontents who could not find in the homeland the peace and freedom which their spirits sought.

On September 24th, 1734--a day still celebrated as "Gedächtnistag"--about forty Schwenkfelder families landed in Philadelphia under the leadership of Georg Weiss.   They were followed in 1737 by a second wave which settled near the first in Montgomery County, where they continued their Silesian poetical traditions, and thus formed the next school of German-American poets.   These Schwenkfelder housefathers produced large manuscript collections of verse, thus not only preserving their group's poetry but also keeping creative traditions alive.   They brought large quantities of manuscripts with them to Pennsylvania, including the work of German-born poets like Martin John and Cornelius Becker, names still unknown to German literary historians--the lost "fourth Silesian school" which forms the bridge from Silesian verse to Pennsylvania Schwenkfelder poetry of the eighteenth century.   This material is preserved in the Schwenkfelder library in Pennsburg, Pennsylvania, the richest source of Silesian material now available to the western world.

The work of this school of poets was collected in 1762 in the Neu-Eingerichtetes Gesang-Buch which was published by Christopher Saur II.   This work is of historic significance because it is the first collection of this group's verse to appear in print, containing about 300 poems of American origin, and about 600 of German origin.   Sudermann, whose verse was much treasured, is well represented, together with other Europeans, and the dependence of Silesian poetry on the Bohemian writers like Michael Weiss is apparent.   Our interest is in the Americans: George Weiss, Balthasar Hoffmann, Abraham Wagner, Christopher Schultz and several others.   Here in this poetry the influence of Schwenkfeld and Boehme is joined with that of Angelus Silesius and Sudermann.

Not only were the Schwenkfelders adept at making metrical
translations of mystical material, not only did they versify their
doctrine, their sermons, and their prayers, but they also used poetry for controversy.   The sect was divided between strict followers
of Schwenkfeld and those who admitted Boehme and later thinkers to
their hierarchy.   In Pennsylvania a poetical controversy broke out,
in the course of which several parallel poems appeared.   The first,
by Wagner, began thus:

> Wird der Schwenkfeld nicht gelesen,
> Acht man nicht wer Frell gewesen,
> Wird der Crautwald nicht erwegt,
> Eisenmann nicht überlegt...[13]

Balthasar Hoffmann, orthodox champion, answered with:

> Schwenkfeld bekennt Christum reine,
> Frell thuts gross Elend beweinen,
> Crautwald hat uns Gott erkant,
> Eis'nmann zeigt der G'lehrten Tand...[13]

Caspar Kriebel also added his version.

On the whole the Schwenkfelders were less correct technical-
ly than were the other Pennsylvania German schools, and false
rhymes, incorrect metre and other imperfections appeared in their
verse.

By far the most perfect school of Pennsylvania poets, tech-
nically speaking, was the group that is associated with the "Little
Herrnhut" along the Lehigh river--the Moravian settlement of Bethlehem.   Here a homogeneous school of about seventy poets arose who
wrote in imitation, sometimes quite slavish, of their patron, Count
Zinzendorf.   The Count himself set the poetical fashions in imagery
and mood with his mish-mash of bridal figures, with his blood-and-
wound sentimentality, and with his mawkish and sometimes tasteless
religious familiarity.   But the Bethlehem Moravians, fired by their
dream of a new and utopian state of Indians and Pennsylvania Dutch
living in a New World paradise under Moravian religious direction,
were also busy writing in the Mohican and the Delaware languages,
thus introducing European poetry to the American savages.   Indeed,
some of their verse appeared in Delaware translation.   And one of
the strangest experiences for a German ear is to hear the sounds
of American Indian words naturalized in German verse:

> Da is nicht Checkomecko,
> uns hauss Ganassateko,
> nicht eh getröstet, bis
> das stolze Onondago,
> auf ordre Pachkamawo,
> die Frieden räumt vor Mammalkiss.[14]

The extent of Moravian poetry written in America is astonishing.   Of

the seventy known poets before 1830 at least twelve left a solid body
of work, enough to permit thorough judgment as to its quality.   One
of the most interesting of these later poets, now freed from Zinzendorf's sentimentality, was the British-born Moravian John Heckewelder, who came to Pennsylvania in 1754, a brilliant missionary,
linguist, archaeologist and government agent, whose study of the
Pennsylvania Indians is still the standard scientific work.   Most of
his verse has not survived, but the few poems that have show a
competence in strange subjects which must astonish the European
mind:

> Du Heidenkönig; tritt nun herbeÿ--
> Ruf deinem Volck zu und spreche freÿ,
> Nenne ihnen gerne was du für gaben
> Am liebsten von ihnen woltest haben,
>   Sie sind bereit.[14]

Believing that Opitz and the Academies had gone too far in
their standardization of metrics the earlier Moravians had developed
the trick of extemporizing verse in the course of their worship.   As
the musicians played familiar melodies the "Vorsinger" created
words, and the group thus believed that they were returning to pure
and unfettered creative sources.   These extemporized poems, like
the one below, were in dactyls, a metre Opitz did not favour, but
which had been extensively used by the Nürnberg group of poets.   On
Christmas Eve, 1742, a poem of thirty-seven verses was thus extemporized in Bethlehem; it was taken down by a stenographer and
stands as a monument to the creative spirit among these German-
Americans:

> Glücksel'ger ist uns doch keine nacht,
> als die uns das wunder-kind hat gebracht,
> das in einer krippe, (das ist gewisslich
> für eines bettel-manns kind verdriesslich)
> in lümplein lag.[14]

From this tame beginning the poem increases in power and
purity until at the end a persuasive peak is reached which leaves no
doubt that the spirit was then present.

These five major schools, then, form the first phase of Pennsylvania German poetry.   Each school capped its work with the production of a printed collection, although in some cases the work remains scattered and hard to gather up.   The total production of these
five groups amounts to about 5000 poems.

The next phase of Pennsylvania German verse was the broad-
ening of this poetry of high mysticism by joining it with folk-poetry.
In this way a second genre was created in which the traditional folk
forms were charged with new depth.   And in many ways it is in this
mass of mostly anonymous verse, patterned on folk forms and preserved in manuscripts, that the true genius of Pennsylvania German
poetry lies.   Here the old mystical impulses live again.   Here we

find such anonymous treasures as:

> Lieblich, dunckel, sanft und stille,
>   ist die süsse Abendzeit,
> möcht mein Seelen-Grund und Wille,
>   so sich halten allezeit.
> Gottes gegenwart allein
> Macht dass ich also kan seyn. [15]

This anonymous poetry shows a competence, an excellence both in
conception and technique, which sets it apart from the usual folk poetry. So

> Die Liebe kam vom Himmel her,
> Hat uns gebracht die wahre Lehr,
>   Wie wir hie leben sollen;
> Sie leitet uns den rechten Weg,
> Den engen schmalen Lebensteg,
>   Wann wir nur folgen wollen.
>   Liebe, giebe,
>   Ein Verlangen,
>   Zu empfangen,
>   Dich, den Werthen.
> Der da kommt in Knechts Geberden. [16]

This verse retained the poetry of the baroque which lingered long in
the Pennsylvania German culture-island, far beyond its life-span in
Germany. This second genre lasted until the turn of the century,
and as late as 1816 poetry with Boehme's "Ungrund" as its theme
was still being composed here:

> O tiefes Nichts, wer dich einst hat in sich gefunden,
> Der ist fürwahr mit Gott und seiner Lieb verbunden.

    The one abiding theme of Pennsylvania German poetry during
its two first periods was love. At first this was strictly religious
love, but as the century moved on the "brethren" who were to be
loved included not only the small clique who had come in love from
the old world, but, as Pastorius's poem on slavery shows, the Af-
ricans and the red men were to be loved as well. Sectarian love
thus became democratic brotherhood. So Pennsylvania German poetry shows the road that leads from baroque eroticism to democracy.
And the third phase of this poetry, which began to appear with the
American revolution, presents a world foreign to the old world and
its woes:

> Freuet euch, Columbias Brüder
> Stimmet an den Lobgesang;
> Singet muntre Freiheitslieder
> Unter frohem Jubelklang...

Here is a confident, rollicking, swaggering spirit--the spirit of good
fellowship and pride in battles won--which also found expression in

a song which appeared around 1815 entitled 'Die Jäger von Kentucky':

> Wir sind ein herzhaft Volck, und frei,
> Das fremde Macht nicht achtet--
> Im Krieg wie Jagd als Narrethei
> Gefahren nur betrachtet.
> Es eint sich in uns, glaubt es nur,
> Die grösste Kraft der Erde;
> Kentucky's Söhne der Natur
> Sind Aligätor-Pferde. [17]

This chesty confidence, however, was the new frontier, moving ever westwards across the plains, carrying from the Pennsylvania German heartland those values which had come from German Pietism-- a trust in man's abilities, empiricism, a love-ethic centred in this world, and a healthy trust in man's capacity to realize his dreams.

Notes

1. M. S. Giuseppi, Naturalizations of Foreign Protestants, Manchester, 1921, p. 47.
2. Vide R. B. Strassburger and W. J. Hinke, Pennsylvania German Pioneers, Norristown, 1934.
3. J. J. Stoudt, Pennsylvania German Poetry, 1683-1830. An Anthology. Pennsylvania German Folklore Society, 1956.
4. Cf. J. J. Stoudt, Pennsylvania Folk Art, Allentown, Pa., 1948, for relation of baroque verse to folk art motifs.
5. Die Kleine Lieder Sammlung, Ephrata, Pa., 1827, pp. 200-1.
6. Oswald Seidensticker, Bilder aus der deutsch-pennsylvanischen Geschichte, New York, 1885, p. 71.
7. From a MS. in the library of the Historical Society of Pennsylvania, and the Anhang to Der Kleine Kempis, Germantown, Pa., 1795.
8. Cf. S. W. Pennypacker, Pennsylvania in American History, Philadelphia, 1910, p. 324. This verse is still unpublished.
9. Das Kleine Davidische Psalterspiel, Baltimore, 1816, Anhang.
10. Printed on the Press of the Brotherhood, Ephrata, Pa., 1766. This is the greatest collection of American poetry in German.
11. These Poetische Gedichte form the second part of Beissel's Mystische und sehr geheyme Sprüche which Benjamin Franklin printed in 1730 in Philadelphia.
12. From the Paradiesisches Wunderspiel; see note 10 above. This stanza has been badly mutilated by the printer.
13. A. S. Berky, Practitioner in Physick. A Biography of Abraham Wagner, 1717-1763, The Schwenkfelder Library, Pennsburg, Pa., 1954, pp. 141, 143, et seq. On the leaders of the Schwenkfelder group see Howard W. Kriebel, The Schwenkfelders in Pennsylvania: a Historical Sketch, Lancaster, Pa., 1907; also Religion in Geschichte und Gegenwart, Tübingen 1909ff., s.v. Schwenkfeld, Kaspar.
14. These Moravian poems come from the eleventh and twelfth appendices to the Geistliches Gesangbuch der Evangelischen

        Brüdergemein von 1735 zum drittenmal aufgelegt, which was printed in Germany without place or date but contains much poetry by American Moravians.

15. From a MS. in Haverford College Library, formerly in my possession. These poems were heavily dependent upon Tersteegen.

16. Das kleine Blumen Sträussgen, an appendix to Die Aufgehende Lilie, Lancaster, Pa., 1815, p. 180.

17. Der Lustige Sänger, Allentown, Pa., 1856, p. 135.

3. A WISCONSIN GROUP OF GERMAN POETS*

Henry E. Legler

In the making of the social and political life of the United States as found at this day, two notable tides of immigration from Europe have had a part greater than all others. Spanish and French influences were as waves upon the sand; the ideas and customs of the Puritan and Pilgrim forefathers in the early years of the seventeenth century, and those of the German immigrants two centuries later have been graven deep, and in the modifications due to constant contact may be traced the growth of the institutional conditions existing at the dawn of this new century.

New England's radiating influences have been employed as a topic by many able historians, but the importance of German influence as permanently affecting American life has up to this time received but scant mention. That importance must be ascribed primarily to the remarkable contingent termed the Forty-Eighters. Unlike the simple pastoral people who followed Johannes Heckewelder, David Zeisberger, George Heinrich Laskiel, Franz Daniel Pastorius and other religious shepherds of the seventeenth century to a New Canaan, the Forty-Eighters of the nineteenth century were men of rank and education.[1] Among them were many college professors, journalists, men of high literary attainments, university students of noble families, who sacrificed home, fortune, position, brilliant prospects--all the material advantages that men ordinarily cherish, in an effort to bring to their distracted countrymen liberty of thought and action. A hundred thousand of these political refugees and their sympathizers came to America in that stirring period of storm and stress when Die Wacht am Rhein became the expression of nationalist spirit. They were young; they were fired with enthusiasm, with energy; they possessed skill of pen and of speech. In all the leading cities of the United States east of the Mississippi they exerted a potential influence in the educational movements of the time, and naturally their activity soon extended to the significant political movements that foreshadowed the great struggle of the Sixties.

For reasons which it is necessary to mention but briefly here, Wisconsin attracted a large element of the political exiles.[2] In 1844 Moritz Schoeffler established a German printing office in Milwaukee, and his press turned out thousands of pamphlets descriptive of Wisconsin's attractiveness. These were distributed in the

*Reprinted from the Transactions of the Wisconsin Academy of Sciences, Arts and Letters 14 (1904): 471-84.

various provinces of Germany and guided thousands of immigrants hither.[3] The state seconded these efforts a little later on by establishing a bureau of immigration, whose representatives met the newcomers in New York City and encouraged them to proceed to Wisconsin. In Milwaukee, German immigrants arrived by the hundreds every week. German newspapers multiplied; German schools were established; German art, German song, German literature and German social life received an impetus that caused Milwaukee to become known as the "German Athens of America." The Banner und Volksfreund established a department which it called "Wisconsin's Deutsche Dichterhalle" (Wisconsin's German Temple of Poesy), and the ready pens of the Forty-Eighters contributed thereto a mass of literature of great originality, richness and beauty.[4] About the same time Bernhard Domschke issued the initial numbers of the Corsar, and Christian Esselen launched his high-class periodical called Atlantis. The most intellectual and gifted German-Americans were spurred to renewed literary endeavor, and naturally an interesting literary group was formed in Wisconsin. Some of its members have found a permanent niche in the German hall of letters. A curious literary war was waged about this time in the United States, with the storm center in Milwaukee, known as the war of the Grays and the Greens.[5] The former were represented by the old conservative Germans, leaders of the earlier immigration, whose ideas were rooted in religion. The Greens were the Forty-Eighters, chiefly idealists and extreme radicals whose bitter sarcasm and vitriolic humor disturbed, but did not vanquish, the less ready-tongued Grays. Old residents of Milwaukee will recall a favorite tavern on Market Street where the Grays and Greens were wont to forgather to pursue with tongue the arguments begun with pen. The Grays did not lack earnestness and faith, but what they wrote was not literature. The Greens clothed their effusions in form to please the ear as well as to appeal to reason.

It was indeed a notable group of literary writers. Some years ago, under the auspices of the leading Chicago German-Americans, there was compiled a critical anthology of German-American literature.[6] In the period devoted to the Forty-Eighters, thirty-one poets have been deemed worthy of representation. Seven of them were residents of Wisconsin, including Madame Mathilde Anneke, Konrad Krez, Edmund Maerklin, Ernst Anton Zuendt, Augustus Steinlein, Rudolph Puchner and Henricus vom See (Wilhelm Dilg). The heart and soul of this notable group, which included many other members of minor poetic talent, was Madame Anneke. This gifted woman, whose energetic nature and rare sympathies were freely at the disposal of the weary and heavy-laden, exerted an influence upon those who came within her circle that was truly remarkable. Sorrow and disappointment pursued her from childhood, but she faced every succeeding misfortune with cheerful courage, inspiring her associates to like spirit. But in her verses she poured out the feelings of her heart. They are

> Short swallow flights of song
> That dip their wings in tears.

An unhappy early marriage and consequent legal struggle to obtain possession of her child led her to become a warm advocate of equal legal rights for women. She established in Germany what was doubtless the pioneer woman's rights journal--which the government promptly suppressed. Her second husband, Fritz Anneke, was a Prussion officer whose sympathies became enlisted in the cause of the revolutionists of '48. When Anneke was imprisoned at Cologne awaiting trial on the charge of treason, Madame Anneke sold furniture and carpets and replaced them with a printing press, editing a revolutionary newspaper till forced to fly for safety. In the meantime her husband had been liberated, and she joined him in the field. She accepted a place on his staff, of which Carl Schurz was also a member. Madame Anneke served till the end of the struggle, saw many battlefields and was in the thickest of the fray, doing a soldier's duty and sharing all the hardships of her soldier husband. They were forced to flee for their lives, finding haven first in France, then in Switzerland. In 1849 they came to America. Madame Anneke lectured to large audiences in Boston, New York and Philadelphia. In the '50s she began the publication of the Frauenzeitung. The latter period of her life was devoted to educational work.[7]

Interesting as are the careers of the other members of Madame Anneke's circle, the limits of this paper will not permit extended mention. Edmund Maerklin was a member of Franz Sigel's staff in the Revolution of '48. He was a personal friend of such well-known German literary men as Uhland, Gustav Schwab, Justinus Kerner, Nicolas Müller and Herwegh. He was the author of many keen satires. His celebrated poem "Der Deutsche Cavallerist," written when Vicksburg capitulated, is said to have been printed at the time in every German newspaper published in North America.[8]

Konrad Krez was a young exile who left his fatherland under sentence of death at the age of 20, but whose heartstrings remained rooted in German soil to the day of his death--and he lived to nearly the allotted three score years and ten. His exquisite lyric "An mein Vaterland" has been reprinted in every German anthology that has appeared since the day the poem was first published. There is not in the German language a poem that conveys so poignantly the feeling of Heimweh. The chaste and simple words stir one powerfully with the pathos of the exile's cherished love for a fatherland which he can never see again. The verses have been set to music by two composers. One version, by Th. Rudolph Reese, was published in Milwaukee in 1898. The other composition, by Richard Ferber of Eau Claire, was awarded first prize at one of the great sängerfests. At least two translations of the poem into English have appeared. I venture to give one by Wilhelm Otto Soubron. Excellent as this translation is, it fails to express fully the intense fervor and pathetic cadence conveyed by the original tongue.

To My Fatherland

Mine was no tree within thy forests old,
Mine not a sheaf of all thy grain fields gold
And without pity thou didst bid me go,
    The unprotected, to a foreign strand--
Because for thee my soul, and not for self did glow--
    And yet I love thee, O my Fatherland!

Beats there a heart, that of the youthful dream,
Its first sweet love, does not retain a gleam?
Ah! holier was the flame within my breast
    Than lovers e'er with ardor fanned;
Ne'er bride, nor bridegroom e'er so blest,
    Held faith like mine, dear Fatherland!

No "manna" heaven poured on thee, I know,
Yet many were the gifts it did bestow:
I saw the wonders of a Southern clime
    Since last I on thy soil did stand,
Yet fairer seemed to me than palm and lime,
    The apple blossom of my Fatherland!

Land of my fathers! though no longer mine,
If any soil is sacred it is thine!
Thy image, always bright, is in my mind,
    And if no tie were wrought by living hand,
My cherished dead would me to thee still bind--
    Thy holy graves--O thou, my Fatherland!

O, if thy children all, who stayed at home,
Did love thee like the ones thou badest roam,
A Union soon, an empire would have birth,
    And thou wouldst see thy children hand in hand
Make thee the mightiest land on earth,
    As thou'rt the best, my Fatherland!

The story is told that the German emperor chanced upon
Krez's poem in a German publication, and was so affected that he
caused the restrictions applicable to the return of the Forty-Eighters
to be greatly modified. Whether well-founded or not, the story
might well be true. All of these Forty-Eighters poured out their
aching hearts in verse, and naturally what they wrote rang true.
Any of these outbursts stirs the pulses of him who reads:

"Farewell to Germany," by Puchner.
"At Parting," by Maerklin.
"To My Fatherland," by Krez.

Of the few writers who antedated the Forty-Eighters, mention
may be limited to Carl de Haas of Fond du Lac, and Alexander
Conze of Milwaukee. Conze gave promise of a great poetic gift,
but he found a soldier's grave in Mexico when but 28 years of age. [9]

Desire to die on the battlefield, due to personal disappointments, is
said to to have prompted his enlistment in the Mexican War.

The names that most readily occur of the recent school of
German poets are those of Frank Siller, Otto William Soubron and
Julius Gugler.   Mention must not be omitted, in even a brief review of Wisconsin German poets, of the excellent translations which
American poetry has been given at their hands--chiefly by Siller
and Soubron.   Longfellow's poems have been favorites in this particular.   William Dilg translated "Hiawatha," and Frank Siller
"Evangeline."   In the latter, Longfellow recognized the best German
version of his Acadian poem.   It preserves not only the spirit of
the original, but renders in like meter practically a literal translation of the story, with all its idioms and characteristics.   Siller
translated from many languages.   His paraphrases of thirteen quat-
rains from Omar Khayyam (printed in 1889) were the first attempt of
the kind in America. [10]   Among other translations deserving mention
are the following:

"Paradise and Peri" (Moore), by Dr. Max Doerfling.
"Abou Ben Ahdem" (Leigh Hunt), by Augustus Steinlein.
"America" (Smith's patriotic anthem), by Carl Doerflinger.
"Excelsior" (Longfellow), by Franz Siller; also "The Angelus at
Dolores" (Bret Harte); "Laugh and the World Laughs with You"
(Ella Wheeler); "To Maria Clemm" (Poe).
"The Arrow and the Song" (Longfellow), by Herman Ruhland.

Notes

1. "The Germans in Wisconsin Politics," by Ernest Bruncken,
    Parkman Club Publications, No. 9, gives an excellent brief
    sketch of the aims, purposes and characteristics of the Forty-
    Eighters, p. 225-227.
2. Carl Schurz became the most noted among them.   He was a can-
    didate for lieutenant governor on the Republican ticket in
    Wisconsin in 1856.   In 1859 he tried unsuccessfully to secure
    the Republican nomination for governor.   See letters of Carl
    Schurz to Congressman John F. Potter printed in the Milwau-
    kee Sentinel, April 1, 1900 (edited by Henry E. Legler).   See
    also A. M. Thomson's Political History of Wisconsin.
3. Letter of Moritz Schoeffler to the Wisconsin Editorial Association
    at Oshkosh, 1869.   Proceedings, p. 19.
4. Wisconsin's Deutsch-Amerikaner, Vol. 2, p. 5.
5. Wilhelm Otto Soubron in The Sunday Sentinel, May 10, 1903.
6. Zimmermann's Beiträge zur Geschichte der Deutsch-Amerikan-
    ischen Literatur.   Chicago, 1902.
7. A sketch of Madame Anneke's interesting career was printed in
    the Milwaukee Sentinel, No. v 26, 1884.
8. Carl Anneke contributed a long and excellent sketch of Maerklin
    to Im Strome der Zeit, Milwaukee, 1886, p. 4-8.
9. His well-known "Oregon Lied" is reproduced in Milwaukee, by R.
    A. Koss, Milwaukee, 1871, p. 194.   Several others of his

poems are given, p. 224-228.
10. An account of Siller's literary work (by Henry E. Legler) was
     printed in the <u>Milwaukee Record</u>, March 4, 1893.

4. A SURVEY OF GERMAN LITERATURE IN TEXAS*

Selma Metzenthin Raunick

German writings on Texas may be considered as beginning more than a hundred years ago; i.e., about the time (1820) of the Anglo-American colonization by the Austins in Texas. I have divided these writings into three periods or chapters. The first takes us to the middle of the nineteenth century, including the years of the "Masseneinwanderung" (mass immigration), 1844-45, under the auspices of the "Verein zum Schutze deutscher Auswanderer" (Association for the Protection of German Emigrants) at Mainz, Germany, and the immigration of small groups of German radical-idealists and refugees who left their homeland during the "forties," the period of revolutionary thought and revolutionary uprisings in Germany and, for that matter, throughout Europe. The second period extends from the middle to the end of the nineteenth century. This was the time when the German in Texas began to publish newspapers, and to combine into groups for the purpose of organizing churches and schools, as well as political, literary, and musical clubs. The third chapter lists what was written in the present century, after the oldest German pioneers had died and their descendants had intermingled, more or less, with the descendants of pioneer-immigrants of other nations or other states.

As is proved by the innumerable guide-books and other descriptive--often highly exaggerated--writings which came out mainly during the first half of the nineteenth century, Texas was then most popular as a goal for the German emigrant. The poet Hoffman von Fallersleben, though he never saw the Lone-Star state, was so enthused by the glowing descriptions of early romantic writers and travelers that he composed a series of poems[1] on that "land of freedom."

> Hin nach Texas, hin nach Texas,
> Wo der Stern im blauen Felde
> Eine neue Welt verkuendet,
> Jedes Herz fuer Recht und Freiheit
> Und fuer Wahrheit froh entzuendet,
> Dahin sehnt mein Herz sich ganz.
>
> (On to Texas, on to Texas,
> Where the lone star in its glory

*Reprinted from <u>Southwest Quarterly</u> 33 (1929): 134-59.

Prophesies a world of freedom,
Beckons to each heart resounding
To the call for truth and justice--
There alone my heart would be.)

The Earliest Writings, 1820-1850

The earliest German prose writings which, with a few notable exceptions, were confined to official reports, guide-books, and descriptive literature of historical or scientific nature, flourished mainly during the first half of the nineteenth century, for a period of, say, thirty years. Many of the authors of this literature were of the nobility, a circumstance which seems, at first glance, rather unusual. I do not know of a similar condition existing in any other State of the Union. But if we remember that the main colonization movement in Texas was sponsored by nobility and royalty, the "Mainzer Adelsverein" (Association of the nobility of the city of Mainz), the fact stated above seems not at all surprising.

The earliest German books dealing with Texas were, however, written before the activities of the Adelsverein. Of these, Valentin Hecke's Reise durch die Vereinigten Staaten (A Journey Through the United States), was probably the first. It was published in Berlin in 1820. The book is in two volumes. Hecke devotes Chapter 13 of the first book and Chapter 31 of the second to Texas exclusively. In Chapter 13, Book I, he describes the size, location, and climate of Texas, gives a brief historical sketch, and finally points out the advantages of organizing a colony in this promising land. In Chapter 31, Book II, Hecke continues his description of Texas, and characterizes its inhabitants. He bases his information primarily on Pike.

The first book dealing with Texas exclusively is Detlev Dunt's Reise nach Texas, published in Bremen in 1834. This book contains the reprint of a letter from Fr. Ernst, who, in 1831, founded the town of Industry, Texas. Dunt's Reise, on account of its attractive pictures of Texas, is said to have drawn many colonists to this State.

Captain Fr. von Wrede and Lieutenant Oscar von Claren, early Texas writers, were the first Germans to fall victims to Indian cruelty (1845). They were overpowered and scalped when camping near Manchaca Springs on their way from Austin to New Braunfels. Previous to his coming to the United States, Von Wrede, a well-known archaeologist, had made his reputation by books of travel (in Asia). His Lebensbilder aus den Vereinigten Staaten von Nord Amerika und Texas (Sketches of the United States of North America and Texas), published in 1844, in Cassel, Germany, is said to have influenced many wavering Germans to sell their belongings and immigrate to Texas. Among his published letters, "Galveston im Jahre 1838" (see Neu Braunfelser Jahrbuch of 1927) is important. Von Claren published essays on the Texas Indians of 1845.

Some of the most important early documents were written by
Prince Carl von Solms-Braunfels, the chief-commissary of the "Verein zum Schutze Deutscher Einwanderer in Texas" (Association for
the Protection of German Immigrants in Texas) or "Mainzer Adelsverein," and the founder of the city of New Braunfels. But the
prince is the author not only of the valuable reports in connection
with his official position, but of a highly instructive book entitled
Texas; geschildert in Beziehung auf s. geographischen, sozialen und
uebrigen Verhaeltnisse, mit besonderer Ruecksicht auf die deutsche
Colonisation (Texas described in respect to its geographic, social
and general conditions, with special regard to German colonization).
As the title indicates, the book was written with one purpose, i. e.,
to inform Germans contemplating immigration about the natural and
social conditions of Texas, so that they might decide judiciously concerning the advisability of immigration, and that they might be fore-
instructed and forewarned in case they reached an affirmative conclusion.   It was published in Frankfurt in 1846.

Perhaps it might be interesting to hear what the earliest Texas critics, the German pioneers, Roemer[2] and Soergel,[3] have to
say of the prince's Texas.   Both agree that the author shows throughout a genuine desire to give as reliable and helpful information as
possible to the immigrants and that his purpose was accomplished,
with but a few fallacies noted.   Solms-Braunfels had traveled over a
large portion of Texas and, being a highly interested and intelligent
observer, transmitted much valuable, and, on the whole, accurate
information.   His book is written in an easy, readable style.   Roemer, in his Texas, however, modifies somewhat the general praise of
Solms-Braunfels' book by deploring the prince's analysis of the foreign (i. e., foreign to the German) white contingent of Texas population.   In his exceedingly difficult enterprise, the prince had personally met with much opposition, dishonesty, and ignorance.   Besides,
there were some conditions so new to him that he failed to get a
just point of view (note especially his judgment of the religious sects
and their clergy, so unlike the German state-church).

But one must remember that it was the commissary's duty
primarily to acquaint the often too trusting immigrant with imminent
dangers, not only from the unknown natural phenomena, or from Indian tribes, but from tricky strangers of his own race and color.
Nor did the prince neglect to mention the finer qualities of the early
white inhabitants, especially their courage, persistency and deter-
mination, and to exhort the German immigrant to adopt these traits.
In the preface to his book, the prince deplores the ignorance of the
average immigrants concerning the United States, and particularly,
Texas.   He realizes that it will not suffice to learn only generalities
about a country so large that each portion shows differences of climate, soil, and, in the case of Texas in particular, of population.
Solms-Braunfels refers the prospective immigrant to the existing
books on Texas, in particular to one by William Kennedy,[4] translated by Otto von Czarnoski (Frankfurt, 1845) under the title: Naturgeschichte und Topographie von Texas, for which he has words
of high appreciation.   Incidentally, he cites a book by Scherpf,

Entstehungsgeschichte und gegenwaertiger Zustand des neuen amerikanischen Staates Texas (A history of the development and present
condition of the new American State of Texas) as one that "should
be mentioned"; of Kennedy's Texas, however, he says it "should
be emphatically recommended." Prince Solms-Braunfels' book was
published by Sauerlander, Frankfurt, Germany, in 1846.

Freiherr von Schuetz, one of the officials of the "Mainzer
Adelsverein," also published a book, Texas, which he calls a "Rath-
geber fur Auswanderer" (adviser to immigrants). This book, published in Wiesbaden, Germany, in 1847, was endorsed by the "German Association for the Protection of German Immigrants to Texas." Von Schuetz's Texas was severely criticized by Alwin Soergel
in Neueste Nachrichten aus Texas. Soergel claims that von Schuetz's book is entirely misleading, that the author himself lacked
personal experience on which to base his information, and that the
authors of his sources had no more intimate knowledge of conditions
than von Schuetz himself, thus offering the reader pictures of their
romantic imaginations in place of actual information.

A. H. Soergel's Neueste Nachrichten aus Texas, 1847, is
unique in that it is mainly a criticism or mention of early German
authors of Texas, as von Solms-Braunfels, von Schuetz, Bromme,
Czarnowski (who translated Kennedy's Texas), Scherpf and others.
Soergel--as von Solms-Braunfels and Roemer--rates Kennedy very
highly and recommends Czarnowski's German translation. He attempts to correct the flagrant misinformation and inaccuracies of
von Schuetz, Scherpf and other poorly informed "advisers to immigrants." While he has high praise for Prince Solms-Braunfels'
Texas, Soergel calls attention, also, to some errors found in the
book. There is besides--in Soergel's book--some interesting description and information concerning Galveston, Houston, and the
early German settlements on Mill Creek and Cummins Creek, New
Braunfels and Fredericksburg. Soergel concludes his book with an
urgent plea, addressed to the Mainzer Adelsverein, for financial assistance for the German colonists.

A number of the early German books deal in part with the
geology, the flora and fauna of Texas, and with Texas history. The
earliest of the authors of such literature were Eduard Ludecus,
Reise durch die mexikanischen Provinzen Tamaulipas, Coahuila, und
Texas im Jahre 1834 (Leipzig, 1839); V. Wrede, Lebensbilder aus
den Vereinigten Staaten und Galveston im Jahre 1838 (Cassel, 1844);
von Claren, Indianer bei Neu Braunfels im Jahre 1845; Herman
Ehrenberg, Der Freiheitskampf in Texas, Fahrten und Schicksale
eines Deutschen in Texas and Texas und seine Revolution (published
in Leipzig in 1844 and 1845); Victor Bracht, Texas im Jahre 1848
(published in Germany in 1849); Ferdinand Roemer, Texas (Bonn,
1849).

Ludecus in his Reise has interesting reference to the early
relations between Texas and Mexico, including the colonization pro-
jects of the Austins.

H. Ehrenberg, a member of the first company of Texas vol-
unteers in the war for Texas Independence, published (in 1844) a
valuable account of this war in Der Freiheitskampf in Texas (The
Texas War of Independence). In the following year he wrote Fahrten
und Schicksale eines Deutschen in Texas (Journeys and Experiences
of a German in Texas), and Texas und seine Revolution (Texas and
Her Revolution). These articles were published in Leipzig, but were
later reprinted in the German periodicals of Texas.

Victor Bracht divides his Texas im Jahre 1848 into four parts,
The first part includes some descriptive geography, mineralogy,
botany, and zoology, tells of the agriculture and commerce, and,
finally, of the early inhabitants of Texas. The second part acquaints
the reader with the German colonies and offers advice to the immigrant. The third part is composed of letters which relate the author's observations and the conclusions reached by him. Bracht's
criticism of the early inhabitants of Texas is as favorable as that of
Dr. Roemer (Texas). In the fourth part, or conclusion, Bracht
criticises the literature on Texas. He condemns the books by L.
Constant and Hauptmann von Sommers as altogether inaccurate and
full of misinformation, and Marryat's Travels of Mr. Violet as pure
nonsense. He approves, on the whole, the writings of Scherpf,
Ehrenberg, and Kennedy, but considers them somewhat in the light
of propaganda for Texas. Bracht recommends Sealsfield's Kajutenbuch (Cabin Book). For Edward's History of Texas, and for Mrs.
Holley's Texas, Bracht has words of praise only, while he condemns
totally Maillard's History of Texas.

Of all the German writers on Texas, Bracht is probably the
most enthusiastic. He seems to have a deep affection for the land
of his choice, as the quotation at the close of his book illustrates:
"Alles fuer Texas und Texas ueber alles!" (All for Texas and Texas
above all).

Roemer's Texas is one of the most comprehensive works about
the State. The book is divided into three parts. The introduction
deals briefly with the political and physical geography of Texas, with
its plant and animal life, and with its human inhabitants. It also
tells specifically of the colonization by the "Adelsverein," of the errors made by this association of German immigration, and of some
of the Texas writings that might interest the immigrant. The second
part of the book is a detailed description of the author's journey
from New Orleans to Texas, and his travels within the State of Texas
and on its borders. The third part is purely scientific. It deals
with geology, botany, and zoology. There is a topographical-geo-
graphical map of Texas, as well as a list of the geological forma-
tions, the rocks, plants, and animals peculiar to Texas.

Roemer's characterization of the early white population of Texas is
more optimistic than that given by Prince Solms. Roemer has words
of highest commendation for the American-Texan, and very little adverse criticism.

Dr. Roemer also published--in 1849--an account of the German settlements in Texas, in particular those organized by the "Mainzer Adelsverein."

Previous to the publication of his books, Dr. Roemer wrote several essays on the geology of Texas for Silliman's Journal of Science.

In 1850 H. Moellhausen published a German book for the London Emigration Society. Moellhausen came to Texas in 1833 and spent thirteen years here before he attempted to begin his work. Two maps are added to the book, one of Virginia, the other of Texas.

Dr. Ferdinand von Herff, one of the young German radicals who came to Texas during the first half of the nineteenth century and lived in the experimental communistic colony, Bettina, published an unofficial report on the emigration of the German proletarians, Die geregelte Auswanderung des deutschen Proletariats (Frankfurt, 1850). While this publication has value, Dr. Herff's reputation as one of the foremost physicians of this country, well-known also in Europe, quite overshadows his literary work. Dr. Herff spent the latter part of his life in San Antonio, where he died.

Two books warning Germans against emigrating to Texas were published in Germany in or about 1848. One is by F. E. Walther, Texas in sein wahres Licht gestellt (Texas as It Really Is); the other is by L. Constant, Texas. Das Verderben deutscher Auswanderer in Texas unter dem Schutze des Mainzer Vereins (The ruin of German immigrants to Texas under the protection of the Mainz association).

Two early novelists made Texas the background of one or more of their literary productions. One is the internationally known Charles Sealsfield (Karl Postl); the other is the prolific writer, H. E. Belani (Carl L. Haeberlin). Belani's book, Die Auswanderer nach Texas (The Texas Emigrants)--1841--teems with historical allusions of particular interest to Texas; more than that, it tells many complete incidents in the lives of prominent historical characters, as, for instance, Stephen F. Austin, Sam Houston, and the pirate Lafitte.

Charles Sealsfield (1793-1864) is the author of a large number of historical romances, written both in German and in English, and freely translated. He is called the "Writer of Two Hemispheres." Karl Postl (Charles Sealsfield), an Austrian by birth, entered a religious order at the age of twenty-one, although he had no taste for the calling. His position in the order provided him with opportunities of travel and social contact with the Austrian nobility. He became well acquainted with the political situation of his country and voiced his indignation concerning this situation. In his earliest book--published anonymously--Austria as It Is, or Sketches of Continental Courts, by an Eyewitness (Hurst, Chance and Co., London)

he condemned most vehemently the machinations of Metternich.   As
might be expected, the book was blacklisted; no one was permitted
to have a copy in his possession, or aid in its distribution.   The
author himself, if apprehended, was to suffer death.   Of this book
there are only two copies extant, one in the British Museum, the
other in the Library of Philadelphia.

Karl Postl, or Charles Sealsfield, as he called himself from
now on, had left his order in the spring of 1823, as he was not in
harmony with the submissive life demanded by the church of his
calling.   He fled to Switzerland, in slow stages, then to Paris, and
finally embarked at Havre for the North American continent.   He
landed in New Orleans.   Sealsfield traveled extensively in the United
States and Mexico.   In 1826 he took a trip to Europe in order to
publish his book: Die Vereinigten Staaten von Nord Amerika, nach
ihren politischen, religiosen und gesellschaftlichen Verhaeltnissen
betrachtet.   Sealsfield wrote this book under the pen-name Charles
Sidons, a name he never used again.   In 1827 Sealsfield went to
London to find a publisher for his English version, The United
States of North America as they are, in their political, religious,
and social bearings.   The book was published in 1828 by Hurst,
Chance and Co., the publishers of Austria as It Is.   Sealsfield
proved himself such a sympathetic, well-informed and just critic of
American customs and institutions of the early part of the nineteenth
century, that the Southern Review was provoked to remark, "Truly
the Germans are the only peoples who have a comparatively just appreciation of America."

Longfellow, in his diary, mentions in particular Sealsfield's
descriptions of the Southwest, calling these descriptions very striking.   He refers to the author of two hemispheres as "our favorite
Sealsfield."

Sealsfield's first historical novel, Tokeah, or The White
Rose, was written in 1828 in Kittaning, Pennsylvania--in English--
and was published by Carey, Lea and Company, Philadelphia.   Five
years later a revised and enlarged German edition of this book was
published under the title of Der Legitime und die Republikaner. The
novel consists of three volumes.   According to the Sealsfield critic,
Faust, this story is somewhat similar to Cooper's Leatherstocking
Tales in its long, sentimental speeches by the Indians.   On the
whole, Faust considers Sealsfield's books more true to life than
Cooper's.   Faust also compares Tokeah or the White Rose with Mrs.
Jackson's Ramona.   Tokeah and Alessandro, each the last of his
tribe, are irretrievably driven to despair and death by the white
race.   Canondah, the Indian girl in Sealsfield's book, and Ramona,
the heroine of Mrs. Jackson's novel, are made to represent the
ideal of the womanhood of the time and to prove themselves the
"saving angels" of their people.   While the background to the first
part of the novel is found to the east of what is now Texas (Georgia,
Louisiana), Sealsfield chose a stretch of land between the Neches
and Sabine Rivers as the setting of the latter part of the story.   The
Comanche and Creek Indians, in particular the Oconee branch of the

latter tribe, play an important part throughout.   Tokeah himself is
the chief of the Oconees.   El Sol, lover of Tokeah's daughter Canondah, is the chieftain of the Comanches.   Other prominent, more
or less historical, characters are the pirate Lafitte, General Jackson, Major Copeland, and the English cadet, James Hodges, of Her
Majesty's ship, The Thunderer.

During the years 1834-37 Sealsfield published a number of
sketches under the combined title of Lebensbilder aus der westlichen
Hemisphare (Life Sketches from the Western Hemisphere) (Orell,
Fussli and Company, Zurich, Switzerland).   The sketch of most interest to Texans is "Nathan, der Squatter Regulator, oder Der Erste
Amerikaner in Texas" (Nathan, the Squatter Regulator, or The First
American in Texas).   Nathan recalls Daniel Boone.   Both men
were genuine pioneers, pushing ahead ceaselessly, preferring to
brave the dangers of the wilderness rather than remain in the narrow confines and under the restraints of civilization.   Nathan is one
of the most original creations in Sealsfield's works and frequently
called forth various imitations.

According to Faust, Das Kajutenbuch oder national Charakter-
istiken, is the best of Sealfield's historical romances.   It deals with
the Texas War of Independence.   Colonel Morris of Maryland is persuaded to explain his reasons for coming to the wild country of Texas and the circumstances which led him to take part in her War of
Independence.   Morris' reply forms the nucleus of the story.   Sealsfield's description of the San Jacinto prairie is considered one of
the finest passages in his writings.

Sealsfield's importance in American literature lies in the
fact that he preserved for posterity the American characters that
were typical up to 1850, before they faded or disappeared in the
later types.   "The fearless squatter and the honest pioneer, the
Southern planter and patriarchal slaveholder, the avaricious million-
aire and his emissaries, the New York sea captain and the hot-
blooded Kentuckian, the utilitarian alcalde, and the reformed des-
perado--all are being preserved for us in Sealsfield's works.   Like
Bret Harte's Californian gold-seekers, like the daring seamen of
Cooper's romances, like George Cable's creoles or Hawthorne's
New England Puritans, Sealsfield's character-types will ever be as
milestones in the cultural history of America."[5]

It may be interesting to note that Sealsfield was, at one time
(1829-1830) editor of the Courier des Etats Unis, New York, when
Joseph Bonaparte, ex-king of Spain, was the owner.   In 1832 Sealsfield became the friend and confidant of the exiled Queen Hortense
and her son, Louis Napoleon.

Writings Between 1850 and 1900

With the middle of the nineteenth century the official reports
disappear; the Mainzer Adelsverein ceases to exist.   It was left

to Hermann Spiess to close up the financial affairs of the Association. Hermann Spiess, who had come to Texas under its protection, was one of the young radicals of Darmstadt, Germany, who demanded greater political freedom.   Thirty-three of his revolutionary compatriots, disappointed or exiled, left Germany with Spiess and came to Texas, where they became as a leaven to the earlier immigrants, bringing their culture and their enthusiasm to the new country.

After the dissolution of the Mainzer Adelsverein, German emigration to Texas occurred mainly in small groups of friends or families, or of individuals who came on their own responsibility.

After the middle of the century, "Emigranten-fuehrer" (guide books for emigrants) were supplanted by books of travel, sketches of pioneer life, and histories of the settlements. George von Ross' Der Nordamerikanische Freistaat Texas (The North American Republic, Texas), published in Germany in 1851, however, still belongs to the earlier group, in so far as it is devoted primarily to instruction for the emigrant. Ross tells of the history, geography, and conditions in Texas, adding a German translation of its constitution. He also attaches a map showing the counties of the state of Texas.

A few years later the German pioneer Friedrich Schlecht completed his little sketch Mein Ausflug nach Texas (My Excursion to Texas) which was published in Bunzlau, Germany, in 1851.   The preface shows that the author was a man of peculiar modesty, but unusual clarity and independence of thoughts.   The main body of the publication, in which he relates his impressions and tells of his experiences, proves him to be a man of intelligence and insight.   It is interesting to note that the author of this early book was the grandfather of our most productive contemporary German writer in Texas, Clara Palacios.

Rev. Peter August Moelling's Reiseskizzen in Poesie und Prosa (Travel Sketches in Poetry and Prose) seems to be the first German book published in Texas (Galveston, 1857).   For a few years Rev. Mr. Moelling was also the editor of a German Methodist periodical, Der Christliche Apologete.

The most important writer of this period was probably August Siemering. He was born in Brandenburg, Germany, in 1830, and left his native home because of his active sympathies with the revolutionary uprisings of 1848 and 1849. Siemering found many kindred spirits in New Braunfels, and especially in Sisterdale, which was settled by the "Vierziger." Later, Siemering moved to Fredericksburg, where he taught school. When the Civil War broke out, he joined the Confederate Army as a private but was soon made a military officer in his regiment. However, as he was not in sympathy with war of any kind and was opposed to slavery, he was glad when the conflict was ended, even though it meant material loss to him as to others in the South and a victory of the opposing forces.

Siemering was the founder of the German newspaper, the San

Antonio Freie Presse von Texas, which became one of the most
prominent news organs of the day.   In connection with James New-
comb he also organized an English paper, the Daily Express, but
later sold this paper for a mere trifle.   After the publication of his
novel, Ein Verfehltes Leben (A Failure), he went to St. Louis,
where he became the editor of a German daily, Der Anzeiger des
Westens.   A rheumatic malady caused him to return to the warm,
dry climate of Texas.

Shortly before his death Siemering began a comprehensive
history of the German emigration to Texas.   Unfortunately, this
work was never completed.[6]   Siemering, who had lived through the
early storm and stress period of Texas, seemed just the man for
this task--a man of education and superior intelligence.

Besides one or two novels which appeared in German newspapers in New York, Siemering published "Lebensbilder aus dem
Sueden" (Life Portraits from the South), in Deutsche Monatshefte,
1856; "Die Lateinische Ansiedlung in Texas" (The Latin Colony in
Texas), in Der Deutsche Pioneer, Cincinnati; "Texas als Ziel der
Auswanderung" (Texas as Destination of Emigration), by the Harris-
burg-San Antonio Railroad Company, 1882; Ein Verfehltes Leben, a
novel, 1876.   This novel has as its background the Civil War period
and is based on the actual experiences of the Germans in Texas during that period.

About the time Siemering published his Lebensbilder (1856),
a Catholic missionary from France, Emanuel Domenech, wrote his
Erinnerungen an Amerika (Recollections of America), which was published in Germany.   Domenech tells of the hardships he and his superior had to face when visiting their parishioners, who were scattered about the wild and new country.   He relates the story of the
building of the first Catholic church in Texas.

A novel, also entitled Erinnerungen, was published in Leipzig
the same year by George Willrich.   This book was written while
Willrich was being held as a suspect in a political intrigue.   He was
proved innocent and speedily released.   Willrich's Erinnerungen has
both Germany and Texas as background.   It is one of the few outstanding novels in our German Texas literature, although it is not
equal to Belani's Die Auswanderer nach Texas or Sealsfield's Das
Kajuetenbuch), either in artistic or cultural value.

The problems of special interest with which Willrich deals are
the "Woman Question" then taking shape, and slavery.

In 1868 Gustav Duvernoy in his Freude nach Leid oder die
Ansiedler in Texas (Joy follows Sorrow or the Settlers in Texas) relates the experiences of an immigrant family.   The book is well
written and is not as long-drawn-out as the usual nineteenth century
tales of adventure.   A definite plot runs through the story.

Dr. Benno Mathes, traveler, scientist, lecturer, included a

treatise on Texas in his set of Reisebilder (Travel Pictures). Bilder
aus Texas (H. J. Zeh, Dresden, 1861) begins with an explanation of
the name "Texas." Matthes believed the word to signify the land of
plenty and found it very significant. The first picture or sketch in
the little book tells of the great drouth of 1857-1858 and of the ac-
companying changes in the flora and fauna of Texas. The remainder
of the book is devoted to observations and experiences on a hunting
trip. In this connection, Matthes again speaks of the vegetation and
of the animal life of Texas, but also relates significant incidents of
Indian and negro life.

In 1894 Adolf Paul Weber published a book, Deutsche Pioniere
in Texas, which contains the biographies of a number of more or
less prominent German pioneers. Weber's book also gives a brief
synopsis of Texas history, a critical sketch of the work of the Mainzer Adelsverein, and an account of the ideals, the failures and successes, and the cultural contributions of the "Vierziger," those radical German idealists, mostly students or young professional men
who were attracted to Texas by its liberal constitution and the hope
that they might be successful in planting a Utopia in this new state.

In 1894 a series of most interesting "Sittenbilder" were published in Galveston by Hugo Mueller, under the title Aus Deutsch
Amerika. A later collection of sketches, Grand Prairie, was published in 1909 by the same author. In their vivid portrayal of the
life and character of the early settlers, these sketches and short
stories are of decided cultural and literary value.

At the age of eighty-two, Heinrich von Struve, one of the
most heroic and helpful of Texas pioneers, wrote the story of his
long and interesting life. The book, Ein Lebensbild: Erinnerungen
aus dem Leben eines Zweiundachtzigjaehrigen, published in Leipzig
in 1895, is well written; there is nothing tedious or super-reflective
in the Erinnerungen (Recollections), though one would expect this in
an author so advanced in years. The story holds the reader to the
end and leaves him richer for having walked for an hour by the side
of so modest and worthy a man.

Among the writings of the nineteenth century which describe
the founding or development of various settlements we have Mrs.
Ernst Altgelt's notebook (now the property of Mrs. Herman Altgelt,
New Braunfels) on Comfort; Herman Seele's "Ein Beitrag zur Geschichte von Neu Braunfels" and J. Hugo Clauss' "Boerne und das Cib-
olo Thal" (Schuetze's Jahrbuch fuer Texas, 1882; "Die Lateinischen
Ansiedlungen in Texas," published by Siemering, already mentioned,
in Der Deutsche Pioneer; Eichholz, "Die Deutschen Ansiedlungen am
Coletto" (Schuetze's Jahrbuch, 1884); Festausgabe zum fuenfzigjaeh-
rigen Jubilaeum der Stadt Friedrichsburg by Robert Penniger (published in Fredericksburg in 1898); Austin County by W. A. Trenckmann, published in 1899.

Mrs. Altgelt was the wife of the first settler in Comfort; her
notations are interesting and valuable. Herman Seele was the princi-

pal of the New Braunfels Academy. J. H. Clauss was one of the
early settlers of Boerne. Siemering, as we have already noted,
was one of the "Vierziger." Eichholz was the editor of the Cuero
Deutsche Rundschau, and W. A. Trenckmann was the editor of the
Bellville Wochenblatt. Since 1909 Mr. Trenckmann has been editor
of the Austin Wochenblatt.

About the middle of the century German newspapers rose to
extraordinary prominence. The first German paper published in Texas was the Galveston Zeitung. Unfortunately, no files were preserved, but the paper seems to have appeared for the first time in
1846. In 1853 a certain C. W. Buechener was the editor. In 1847
a German pro-slavery paper, Die Union, was published in Galveston.
The first permanent German paper was the Neu Braunfelser Zeitung,
which made its appearance in 1852, with F. Lindheimer as its editor.

Dr. Ferdinand Jacob Lindheimer (1801-1879) was a well-
known botanist. He took part in the Frankfort uprising of 1833 and
was compelled to flee to the United States. After spending a few
years in Missouri and in Mexico, he came to Texas (1836), where
he enlisted as a volunteer in the war against Mexico. At the close
of the war he lived in Houston, collecting and classifying plants, and
adding considerably to the knowledge of Texas vegetation. With the
arrival of the first colonists of the Mainzer Verein, Lindheimer
went to New Braunfels. While he was editor of the Neu Braunsfelser Zeitung (1852-1871), he contributed many valuable essays on his
botanical studies, as well as on general conditions in Texas.

Ludolph Lafrentz, a later editor of the Neu Braunsfelser
Zeitung, and also of the periodical Deutsch-texanische Monatshefte
(published first in New Braunfels and later in San Antonio), was the
author of many valuable essays, a number of which were republished
recently in the Neu Braunfelser Jahrbuecher, "Die Deutschen in Texas vor dem Befreiungskriege" (The Germans in Texas before the
War of Independence), 1926; "Die Deutschen in der unabhaengigen Re-
publik Texas" (The Germans in the Independent Republic of Texas),
1927.

These essays tell of the life and attitude of the earliest pioneers and record the names of the early settlers and of the men
who fought in the Texas War for Independence.

The present editor of the Neu Braunfelser Zeitung, S. F.
Oheim, is the author of many essays and sketches on Texas. Mr.
Oheim also edits the Neu Braunfelser Kalender or Jahrbuch, as it is
now called, which is a true storehouse of information on the past
history of the German pioneers. Here we find extracts from valu-
able books; as Roemer's Texas, Ehrenberg's Der Freiheitskampf in
Texas in 1836 (The Texas War of Independence in 1836), Fahrten und
Schicksale eines Deutschen in Texas (Travels and Experiences of a
German in Texas), and Texas und seine Revolution (Texas and her
Revolution).

From 1853 to 1856 Dr. Carl Adolf Douai, a strong adherent
of the Union and an enthusiastic supporter of the anti-slave movement, edited the Deutsche Zeitung in San Antonio. On account of
his political adherence, Douai became very unpopular even with a
portion of the German contingency. His policy was opposed vehemently by the New Braunfels colonists, who considered Douai's radical stand most imprudent. The greater part of the German population of the early nineteenth century, though they particularly detest-
ed any infringement on "liberty" and were enthusiastic supporters of
personal freedom, believed in state-rights, i.e., liberty for the
states to solve their own problems. They believed, too, that it
would be better for emancipation to develop gradually rather than all
at once.

Douai (1819-1888) was one of the finest minds the German
revolution directed to this country. He took part in the unpopular
movement for political unity and greater personal freedom, especially freedom of speech and of the press and found it expedient to emigrate, arriving in Texas in 1852. Douai was a strong individualist,
aggressive and independent. This was true not only in respect to
his political convictions but his educational ventures as well. While
still in Germany he organized a modern type of school according to
his own personal conception and operated it independently. When in
the United States he again did pioneer work. In Texas he continued
in his profession of teaching on a very humble scale but with excep-
tional results. After he left Texas, his radical stand on the slavery
question compelling him to seek safety in the North, Douai opened
the first Kindergarten in the United States at Boston. In his position as editor, both of the San Antonio Deutsche Zeitung and later of
the New Yorker Volkszeitung, Douai found ample opportunity for the
expression of his many worthy ideals. Olmsted[7] in writing of Douai's San Antonio paper, claimed that he found it to contain more new
and interesting information than any of the Texas newspapers he had
seen up to that time.

The most unique early newspaper was, undoubtedly, Der Bettelsack (The Beggar's Bag). This paper was issued in manuscript,
never in print. Der Bettelsack originated in Comfort and had clever
and well-educated men like S. F. Holekamp, Louis von Breitenbauch,
and Fritz Goldbeck (author of several volumes of verse) among its
literary contributors. Dr. Otto Mehling and Carl Herbst were the
editors.

Carl Herbst was a German pioneer who made Comfort his
home but whose influence was felt over a large area. Herbst was
a teacher and public speaker and, above all, an active friend to
those in need and sorrow. Herbst's speeches have been collected
and, together with an obituary, were published by his appreciative
fellow-citizens.

The Friedrichsburger Wochenblatt made its first appearance
just fifteen years after the earliest issue of the Neu Braunfelser
Zeitung. Its first issue came out in 1867. In 1900, the former

Regional: Texas

editor, Robert Penniger, also published a supplement, Der Sangesfreund, a paper devoted to the German singing societies of Texas.

The Freie Presse fuer Texas was founded in San Antonio by August Siemering. The present editor, Robert Penniger, is well known both as a writer and a speaker. Beginning in the spring of 1929, Mr. Penniger published Eine kurzgefasste Entwicklungsgeschichte der vom Mainzer Adelsverein Gegruendeten deutschen Kolonien in Texas (A Brief History of the Development of the German Colonies in Texas founded by the Mainz Association of the Nobility).

In 1887 the prominent German newspaper of Austin, the Texas Vorwaerts (Onward Texas), was founded by Julius Schuetze, who came to Texas in his early youth. He was one of the foremost of German pioneers. For a long time he worked as a teamster in order to gain a living for himself and his widowed mother and younger sisters and brothers. Later he found opportunity to teach languages and music. Finally he took up the study of law and was subsequently elected county judge of Bastrop county. He also served in the legislature. In connection with O. H. Dietzel he founded, in 1871, a German newspaper, the Vorwaerts (forerunner of the later, more important Texas Vorwaerts), which soon after he took over alone. The Vorwaerts made its initial appearance in New Braunfels in 1870 but a few months later was transferred to Austin (1871) and was issued until 1873. Henry and Albert Schuetze, sons of the pioneer brothers, Julius and Eduard, began the publication of another German paper, the Austin Wochenblatt. In 1885 Henry Schuetze sold the paper to J. P. Duvernaje, who edited it until his death in 1886. In 1883 Julius Schuetze, who had also been connected with the Wochenblatt for several years, launched the Texas Vorwaerts, a daily and weekly, which he edited until the time of his death in 1904, when his son Eduard Schuetze took over the paper. The last issue appeared in 1914, the opening of the World War. In the Texas Vorwaerts there are found many valuable essays and sketches by the pioneer editor himself. R. C. Bardenwerper, C. F. Rumpel, Dr. F. Ilse, and others contributed freely. A number of Julius Schuetze's valuable essays and short stories of pioneer life were reprinted later in Albert Schuetze's Jahrbuch and in the Neu Braunfelser Kalender (Oheim).

There were two other papers published in Austin during the latter part of the nineteenth century, the Texas Staatszeitung (edited by Hugo Heffler), which ran for about four years, and the Texas Stern of even shorter duration.

The Texas Post changed its abode several times. It was begun in Galveston, was moved to Dallas, and then to Austin.

The Deutsche Zeitung fuer Texas made its first appearance in Victoria (1887). Hereafter other German weeklies followed in rapid succession in La Grange (1894), Bellville (1895), Seguin (1895), Waco (1896), Cuero (1896), Dallas (1896), and Taylor (1899). In the twentieth century were added: Lavaca County Nachrichten (1900), Gainesville Anzeiger (1900), and Giddings Deutsches Volksblatt (1904).

At this time there were about twenty-nine German papers in Texas.
About half a dozen other, more or less short-lived, publications
came out within the next four years. After this time no new German papers were founded. The Austin Wochenblatt (1909) was a
continuation of the Bellville Wochenblatt. W. A. Trenckmann, the
editor, had merely changed his place of abode from Bellville to
Austin.

There were a number of periodicals published in connection
with the Lutheran, Methodist, and Catholic churches. Of those the
Protestantische Zeitblaetter (Rev. Eisenlohr, New Braunfels) and
Der Pilger im Sueden (Rev. Wendt, Galveston, 1854) were probably
the earliest. Then followed Der Christliche Apologete, founded by
P. A. Moelling but edited for forty-three years by William Nast,
founder of German Methodism.

A paper, Lutherische Gemeindebote fuer Texas (Lutheran
Churchmessenger) was published in the nineties by the Evangelical
Lutheran Church. In 1894 this paper had more than 1600 subscrib-
ers--a large number for that time. After 1895 the number of subscribers took a great drop, and in 1898 the publication of the paper
was taken over by the Wartburg Publishing House in Iowa. In 1902
the German Catholics founded a paper, Katholische Rundschau, published in San Antonio.

During the activities of the Adelsverein and after its dissolution, criticism pro and con was heard everywhere. Much of this
criticism was published in Germany; a number of critics also used
their pens in Texas. Among these Siemering took an active part,
accusing the German princes and other aristocrats of having been in
league with England in order to reduce the number of slave-holding
states. The majority of the liberty-loving Germans were opposed
not only to social or political dominance of one group over another,
but to the dominance of one race over another. Siemering was rad-
ically opposed to the aristocratic party and therefore had little sympathy with the "Adelsverein," which was composed of noblemen.
Others, as for instance L. Constant and F. E. Walther, also criticized the Adelsverein severely, though but few implied selfish political and personal motives to the Association.

An objective criticism of the Mainzer Verein was published
in Austin as late as 1894 by William von Rosenberg: Kritik,
Geschichte des Vereins zum Schutze deutscher Auswanderer nach
Texas (A Critical Study: The History of the Association for the
Protection of Emigrants to Texas). In this study the author, while
recognizing the errors made, explains their causes and clears the
Association from all ulterior political or mercenary motives. William von Rosenberg was a nephew of Ernst von Rosenberg, one of
the earliest, if not the earliest, pioneer of German descent. Ernst
von Rosenberg, who was a military officer in Germany during the
Napoleonic wars, emigrated in the early part of the nineteenth century and came to Texas from New Orleans. He received a commission as colonel in the Mexican army. When Emperor Iturbide
abdicated, von Rosenberg was shot to death.

Writings Since 1900

The German prose-writings in Texas after 1900 are mainly historical. In the German newspapers and "Kalender" (now generally termed "Jahrbuecher"--yearbooks--since the term Kalender has become antiquated here as abroad) we find reprints of portions of earlier books, of letters and essays telling of the early pioneers and the development of the settlements. There are about half a dozen scattered novels and a few biographies of predominantly cultural and historical value. One author of note, Clara Palacios, who has a number of novels and a volume of poetry to her credit, appears at this time.

Several clergymen wrote on the development of the respective churches in Texas; the most comprehensive and detailed account being J. Mgebroff's Geschichte der Ersten Deutschen Ev. Luth. Synode in Texas (History of the first German Ev. Luth. Synod in Texas), published in Chicago in 1902.

Information on the German conference of the Methodist Episcopal church is found in an official publication composed for the fiftieth anniversary of the conference: Kurze Geschichte der Suedlich-Deutschen Konferenz (A Short History of the German Conference South). The book is edited by the Rev. William Buehrer and five coeditors.

In a booklet published in 1921, on the occasions of the seventy-fifth anniversary of St. Mary's Church in Fredericksburg, Father H. Gerlach tells of the work of the Catholics.

In 1904, the well-known teacher and poet, Ferdinand H. Lohmann, made a valuable addition to the history of the German settlements which had become popular near the close of the nineteenth century. He published an historical sketch of Comfort in connection with the fiftieth anniversary of the founding of that interesting little town. The pamphlet was printed by William Fellbaum, Comfort. Another pamphlet, Die deutsche Sprache, Was Koennen wir beitragen zu ihrer Erhaltung? was published in Chicago in 1912. It exhorts the descendants of the German pioneers to preserve their language, as the disregard of the language might lead to the disregard of those national characteristics and cultural possessions which the forefathers brought to their new home as their highest contribution.

Ed. Schmidt, a pioneer teacher and director of singing societies, is the author of two booklets, each a so-called "Festschrift"; i. e., semi-official publication composed to commemorate a certain event, and designed to be used at an anniversary or other festive day. One of these "Festschriften" (published in 1915 by Penniger, Fredericksburg) was composed in connection with the twenty-sixth anniversary in Comfort of the Texas Mountains Singing Societies. It contains sketches and photographs of leaders and directors of the society and a description of Comfort. The other, Festschrift zur 50 jaehrigen Erinnerungsfeier an das Gefecht am Nueces, den 10.

August, 1862 (published in San Antonio in 1912) commemorates the
tragic skirmish on the Nueces River during which young Comfort
men were killed. A monument was erected to their memory.

A biography similar to von Struve's Lebensbild was written
by Carl Urbantke, a German Methodist pastor. The book, Aus
meinen Lebensfuehrungen, was published in Cincinnati, in 1902.
Urbantke's story, like von Struve's, is written in a simple, modest
but very readable style, in spite of its modesty impressing the reader with its genuine bigness. One cannot help but feel that these
singularly unpretentious men, von Struve and Urbantke, were enormous factors for good in that new country filled with so many undesirable elements and having at that time so little opportunity for culture and refinement.

In supplement to his translation of Edith E. Wiggin's book on
good manners for the home and the school, W. Eilers wrote biographical sketches of a number of pioneer Texans of German descent. Eilers's book was published in 1905 under the title: Edith E.
Wiggin, Anstandslehre fuer Schule und Haus, Uebersetzt von Wilhelm
Eilers, nebst Anhang Geschichte und Biographic prominenter Deutsch-
Texaner.

The Jahrbuch der Deutsch Amerikanischen Historischen Gesellschaft von Illinois (yearbook of the German American Historical
Society of Illinois), vols. XX-XXI, 1920-21, contains an interesting
diary, "Tagebuch ueber meinen Aufenthalt in Texas, 1837-41," written by the well-known German poet, Gustav Dresel. Dresel was at
one time chief agent of the "Mainzer Verein Zum Schutze deutscher
Auswanderer in Texas" (Mainz Association for the protection of German emigrants to Texas). He was a friend of the poet Hoffman von
Fallersleben, whom he inspired to compose the famous Texas-Lieder
(Texas songs).

William Trenckmann, mentioned before as the editor of the
Austin Wochenblatt, is the author also of a novel, Die Lateiner am
Possum Creek (the Latins of Possum Creek), and of a play, Die
Schulmeister von Neu Rostock (The Schoolmasters of New Rostock),
which are valuable "Sittenbilder" of Texas before and during the Civil War. The novel has particular value in its delineation of the difficulties of the Germans of anti-slavery principles and the diversion
of the families and friends on this question and the question of secession.

A Catholic priest, Pater Alto Hoermann, of Fredericksburg,
is the author of an historic romance, Die Tochter Tejas oder Texas
im vorigen Jahrhundert (The daughter of Tejas, or Texas in the last
century). This thrilling story, which is based on the Texas legend
of the Enchanted Rock in Llano County, was published in book form
in 1917.[8]

A number of Texas women are authors of publications in German. Two of these women, Mrs. Ottilie Goeth and Mrs. Louise

Romberg Fuchs, gave accounts of their early experiences during pioneer days. Mrs. Goeth's Was Grossmutter erzaehlt was published in San Antonio, in 1915; Erinnerungen, by Mrs. Fuchs, was published in 1928 in Waco (Baylor University Press). Both Mrs. Goeth and Mrs. Fuchs were aged women when they wrote their narratives.

An interesting manuscript, Die ersten Deutschen in Texas, was written by Caroline von Hinueber, the daughter of Friedrich Ernst, founder of the town of Industry, who was the first German to bring his family to Texas. Caroline Ernst describes the first home of the Ernst family and the primitive conditions in which they lived. This description, written in the early part of the last century, was published in the 1906 edition of the Neu Braunfelser Kalender. It is preserved, also, in the State Historical Quarterly.

Helene Haase, a writer with modern tendencies, who spent several years in Texas, published a summary of her experiences in a novel entitled In Bluffland. The heroine of the story makes her home in New Braunfels and San Antonio. The author presents illuminating character sketches of many well-known citizens, especially those of German descent, and criticizes existing conditions with satirical frankness. In drawing her comparisons between social customs and economic laws of Germany and the United States, Helene Haase shows a growing, sympathetic understanding of conditions and a fine appreciation of whatever she finds of genuine worth. The book was published in 1912 by Egon Fleischel, Berlin.

In 1922 a thesis which was really an anthology of German poetry in Texas was completed in the Graduate School of the University of Texas by the author of this survey. This was the first German literary anthology in the state. The author also published a number of original poems, sketches, and short stories (both German and English) having Texas as their background. The German publications include: "Die Deutschen in Texas" (The Germans in Texas), Taegliche Rundschau, Berlin; "Deutsch-texanische Schriftsteller" (German Writers in Texas), Die Literatur, Stuttgart; "Briefe aus Texas" (Letters from Texas), Die Neue Zeit, Chicago; "Eine Reise in Texas" (A Journey in Texas), Das Wochenblatt, Austin, Texas; "Deutsche Literatur in Texas" and "Das Deutschtum in Texas" (German Literature in Texas and Germans in Texas), in the encyclopedic dictionary on Germans in foreign countries to be published shortly by the Auslandsinstitut, Stuttgart, Germany.

In her book Else, Ein Lebensbild aus Texas von Hedwig Schroeter, einer alten Deutsch-Amerikanerin (Elsie, A Portrait from Texas by Hedwig Schroeter, an old German-American), the author, an old Texas pioneer, tells the simple love story of a young girl living on the Pedernales River. The little book was published in San Antonio in 1926 (Texas Free Press Publishing Company).

The most prolific, the most talented, of contemporary prose-writers in Texas is undoubtedly Clara Palacios. [9]" All of Mrs. Palacios' novels but one, Wer bin Ich? (Who Am I?), which was pub-

lished in Leipzig, appeared in the Austin Wochenblatt. A sketch of
the author (by the writer of this survey) appeared in a German literary review, Die Literatur, and was published in translation for
Bunker's Monthly (now Texas Monthly) by Prof. R. T. House of Ok-
lahoma University.

In her prose writings in contrast to much of her poetry, Mrs.
Palacios is a stern realist. The characters which she portrays
with great vividness are of English, German, and Mexican ancestry,
or they are new-comers from other states, from Europe, or from
Mexico. German and Mexican folklore and national customs play
an important part in her writings. The background of her novels is
laid in Austin County exclusively.

The following novels and short stories by Walter Gray (Mrs.
Palacios) were published in the Wochenblatt:

Teckels Meisterstueck (Teckel's Masterpiece)
Die Sylvesterfeier (The New Year's Eve Celebration)
Die Liese (Lizzie)
"Inseid Informehschen" (Inside Information)
Der Russische Graf (The Russian Count)
Der boehmische Vetter (The Bohemian Count)
Das Ungetuem auf Gummiraedern (The Monster on Rubber
    Wheels)
Das Radio (The Radio)
Herr Naumann (Mr. Naumann)
Der tote Mann von Del Monte (The Dead Man from Del Monte)
Der Compadre (The Compadre)

Der Compadre, which is being translated into the English
language by the author of this survey, is based on the Mexican interpretation of the duties of a "compadre," or, in this specific instance,
on the correct attitude of a compadre toward the mother of the child
to whom he is sponsor (compadre). The hero of the story was asked
to be compadre to the child of friends, a Mexican man and his
American wife. The father dies and the young Mexican feels that
his love for the widow, his compadre, is developing into passion.
Although he realizes that in leaving the home of the widow, who, he
believes, returns his affection, he will cause her great grief and rob
her of the only stay she has, the young Mexican disappears. He
might overcome obstacles or break any statute law in order to gain
his beloved, but the stern traditional law of his race that pertains to
the relationship between "compadre" and "comadre" he dare not
break. It is most sacred. The American widow, knowing nothing
of this powerful unwritten moral law suffers keenly over the apparent faithlessness of one on whom she has come to rely. The development of a happy ending to this seemingly hopeless situation forms
the theme of the story.

Notes

1. See Julius Goebel's "Hoffman von Fallersleben's Texanische Lieder," Yearbook 1918-1919 of the Deutsch-Amerikanische Historische Gesellschaft von Illinois.
2. Texas mit besonderer Ruecksicht auf deutsche Auswanderung und die physisschen Verhaeltnisse des Landes, 1849.
3. Neueste Nachrichten aus Texas, 1847.
4. Texas, its History, Geography, Natural History, and Topography, London, 1840.
5. Faust, Albert B., Charles Sealsfield. I have used Albert B. Faust's Charles Sealsfield, Der Dichter Beider Hemisphäre freely in my delineation of Sealsfield's life and of his writings.
6. Perhaps the most comprehensive work on this subject was done, so far, in a thesis by Dr. Ferdinand Biesele (1928). This is in the English language, however, and is still in manuscript, and therefore does not enter into the scope of this survey.
7. A Journey Through Texas, or A Saddletrip on the Southwestern Frontier (1857), by Frederick Law Olmsted.
8. See "The Enchanted Rock in Llano County," by Julia Estill in Legends of Texas, J. Frank Dobie.
9. Pseudonym, Walther Gray.

PART III

THE GERMAN-AMERICAN PRESS

5. THE GERMAN BOOK TRADE
    IN ST. LOUIS BEFORE 1848*

Robert E. Cazden

   Next to Ohio, the favored destination of Germans moving West
before 1848 was Missouri, particularly St. Louis and neighboring St.
Clair County, Illinois. A German-language press and book trade developed in both states, but in each the circumstances were different.[1] While the early Ohio migration was largely an internal movement of older Pennsylvania German stock, this influence was notice-
ably absent in Missouri.

   German printing, of course, came first to Ohio, with the
elusive Cincinnati German Almanac for 1808 (Teutscher Calender auf
1808), of which no copy survives. From Lancaster, Ohio, came
Der Ohio Adler, founded sometime between 1807 and 1812; and on the
press of this pioneer newspaper was printed, in 1816, the first substantial Ohio German book, a hymnal of more than 350 pages.[2]
About twenty years were to pass before the German book trade
gained a foothold in St. Louis.

   The interest of European Germans in emigrating to Missouri
was greatly excited by publication of Gottfried Duden's celebrated
Bericht... in the year 1829.[3] This glowing report beguiled hundreds if not thousands of Germans into a search for paradise along
the Mississippi. During the aftermath of the Napoleonic Wars, men
like Duden had become concerned with the widespread discontent in
Germany and the growing pressures for emigration. Duden was especially interested in the suitability of the American West for German settlement, and with that in mind had embarked for a prolonged
inspection of conditions in Missouri.

   He purchased roughly 270 acres above Femme-Osage Creek,
close by the Missouri River in Montgomery County, a parcel of land
that later was included in Warren County. Three years of gentleman farming convinced Duden that Missouri was ideal for German
colonization and he returned to Europe in 1829 to publish his findings
in a book that Marcus Lee Hansen called the most important piece
of literature in the history of the German emigration. Duden painted
a provocative picture for which he was later criticized. It must be
stated, however, that he did include certain strictures, but these
were not generally heeded. He urged, for instance, the migration
of moneyed and educated Germans, men of his own class, in organ-

ized groups.   The rural and urban poor, whose plight was largely
the cause of Duden's voyage of investigation, had no allotted place in
his new world. [4]

A number of emigration societies were formed, such as the
Mulhouse Society, which left from Europe in 1831; this group broke
up after reaching Baltimore, though some members did proceed to
Missouri.   On the other hand, a small company of emigrants from
Berlin is said to have settled in St. Charles, Missouri in 1832.   The
following year, a young man of some means and education by the
name of Hermann Steines was sent by his family to examine opportunities in the state.   When word spread that the Steines family was
about to leave for America under the leadership of Hermann's brother Friedrich, other families joined the party and formed the so-
called Solingen Emigration Society, 153 individuals in all, who ultimately settled in Franklin County. [5]

Far better known was the Giessen Emigration Society, founded
in 1833 by a group of disaffected intellectuals and ardent nationalists,
most of whom were veterans of the German student movement.
Guided by Friedrich Münch and Paul Follenius, Karl Follen's brother,
these idealists hoped to create "for German Civilization a worthy
home across the Atlantic Ocean."[6]   Only emigrants with sufficient
means were invited to participate.   The Society was compelled to
ship out of Bremen on two vessels, one landing in New Orleans, the
other in Baltimore.   Petty feuds and ignorance of American conditions had much to do with the demoralization and collapse of the Society once its members were ashore.   Many in the first shipload
made their way to St. Louis, where they scattered.   Follenius and
Münch settled in Warren County near Duden's original farm and their
reputation helped to draw German liberals to the Mound City.

Among the most gifted Germans attracted to St. Louis and
nearby St. Clair County, Illinois, were Gustav Körner, Theodor
Engelmann, his cousin Dr. Georg Engelmann, Dr. Friedrich Adolf
Wislizenus, and the well-to-do businessman Ernst Karl Angelrodt.
Angelrodt had been a wool factory owner in Thuringia with strong liberal views and came over with the Mulhouse Society.   He did not
travel lightly, bringing along 5,000 pounds of baggage including fur-
nishings, tools, farm equipment, pens, ink and paper to last several
years, a copying machine and a library of 2,500 German books. [7]

Other German settlements included the all-German town of
Hermann in Gasconade County, founded in 1835, and Appleton Town-
ship in Cape Girardeau County, which attracted mostly German Catholics from Hanover and Bavaria.   In 1838 a large contingent of Old
Lutherans from Saxony led by Martin Stephan entered St. Louis.
Those Saxons who could find work in the city remained there, while
the others moved to land in Perry County. [8]

St. Louis was the center of German life in the state, with a
German population that grew from about 1,500 in 1840 to 23,774 in
1850. [9]   "You find Germans in every trade now," wrote Theodor

Engelmann in 1836 to his sister in Europe, "as many I think as the
Americans in number. There is no lack of German shops, of inns
and beer houses, and new ones arise daily. The number of German labourers, hired men, and maids far exceeds those of all other
races, no doubt even including the free negroes." In 1838, Engelmann commented, again to his sister, on the social diversity of the
emigrants: "Some occupy a place next to the colored people; Germans are found in all classes of society and, finally, head the
group of those concerned with scientific training and scholarship.
The Americans cannot understand how people from one and the same
country can be so different.... "[10]

        The Germans of St. Louis were notably a factious group.
That city, like Cincinnati, was fast becoming a center of German
Catholicism; and with the opening in 1843 of a Lutheran seminary
(now Concordia College) and publication of Der Lutheraner beginning
in 1844, another conservative religious force asserted itself, the re-
organized Old Lutherans from Saxony, the present Missouri Synod
Lutherans. At odds with the church Germans were both rationalists
and more extreme anticlericals whose critique of organized religion
was presented to German-Americans in newspapers, pamphlets,
books, and public speeches. The German press and book trade in
St. Louis had its origins in this secular camp.

        A clique of educated professional men and merchants[11]
backed the first German newspaper in St. Louis, the Anzeiger des
Westens, founded by Christian Bimpage and B. J. Von Festen in
1835. Type, a printing press, and other necessary equipment were
purchased in Cincinnati by Bimpage.[12] In 1836 Wilhelm Weber was
hired as editor and the Anzeiger soon gained a national reputation.
Weber, whom Gustav Körner characterized as a daredevil idealist,
was a student radical at the University of Jena who exchanged a
Leipzig prison cell for the safety of the Engelmanns' St. Clair
County farm. He joined the Anzeiger after working briefly as Librarian of the St. Louis Library Association[13] and remained as editor until 1850.

        The most abrasive spokesman of German radicalism in early
St. Louis was the watchmaker and journalist Heinrich Koch, a
rough but gifted polemicist of working class origins and not really
socially acceptable to members of the Anzeiger clique, although a
frequent contributor to the newspaper. Born in Bayreuth in 1800,
Koch took part in the Hambacher Fest of 1832, was arrested and
subsequently fled to America. During his fifteen years in St. Louis,
he espoused a variety of causes and published four personal newspapers, the best known being Der Anti-Pfaff.[14]

        Koch's influence is not denied, but he has almost always had
a bad press. The historian of the Saxon Lutherans, Walter O. Forster, portrays him as an irredeemable sinner of "venomous pen and
violent temper ... [and] utter lack of self restraint" ... whose
"rant developed unmistakable cloacal characteristics" ... and who
finally "aroused almost the entire German population against him-

self. " However, the Forty-eighter Anton Eickhoff, whose first job
in America was on a Mississippi river steamer, at which time he
met Koch, recalled him as the finest popular German speaker he
had ever heard, a pitiless fighter against injustice and error. And
finally, students of German-American labor have respected Koch as
an ardent if not always clearheaded disciple of Charles Fourier,
Albert Brisbane, and Robert Owen.[15] All three of these assess-
ments, I would say, can be supported from Koch's own writings.

When the Mexican War broke out we learn from Eickhoff that
Koch recruited a company of 102 Germans from his working class
supporters and equipped them at his own expense. For their war
service, which was nominal, they received government land warrants. Later in 1847 Koch, with the aid of these warrants, was
able to start a communitarian colony in Clayton County, Iowa called
Communia, about fifty miles from Dubuque. After two years and
much squabbling about finances Koch lost all interest in utopian ex-
periments and with his family moved to Dubuque, where he lived
quietly until his death in 1879. A posthumous collection of his poetry was issued by Dr. Karl Brockmann. I have seen only fascicle
one, which is devoted to Koch's version of "the Creation" in 181
stanzas, but perhaps no more was ever published.[16]

If Koch wielded the most pungent pen in St. Louis, it was
scarcely the only one.[17] By the late 1830s the German liberal en-
clave in and around the city began to engage in the literary life.
Worthy of special note was a non-political journal called Das Westland, conceived in 1837 by Dr. Georg Engelmann and several friends,
including Gustav Körner as silent partner. Though edited from St.
Louis the journal was aimed at prospective immigrants and so was
published in Europe by Joseph Engelmann of Heidelberg, the uncle
of Georg and Theodor Engelmann. After three issues the project
collapsed, the logistics of long distance editing proving too daunting.

One article of great interest was Wilhelm Weber's survey of
German-American press.[18] With enthusiasm the author praised his
fellow Germans above all emigrant groups for their ability to maintain schools, Bildungsvereine, library societies and other cultural
institutions like the press. The generation of the 1830s was given
the credit for this resurgence. Weber, a Dreissiger himself, is today remembered as the editor of the Anzeiger des Westens; but he
was also instrumental in bringing the German book trade to St.
Louis.

After 1830, wrote Gustav Körner, almost no cultured German family came West without a small library. It was not uncom-
mon for friends or relations to bring with them from Europe some
desired German books unobtainable in the United States. Hermann
Steines in 1834 gave the following advice to his brother-in-law who
was about to leave Germany: "If you bring with you a selected library of German classics, good theological works (sermons), entertaining and merry tales and novels, you would be doing yourself a
service, since your mouth would water for them once you were

here.   Also for me bring a popularly written German medical work
suitable for a family medical guide ... [and] a sufficient number of
musical instruments, well packed, for our enjoyment.   German
Lieder, songs and sheet music, [Gustav] Dinter's Schullehrerbibel,
philosophical works, etc. , etc.   For me especially a popular anato-
my, a dictionary of pathology and therapeutics; a book on veterinary
medicine would be useful to us all. "[19]

When Wilhelm Weber took over the Anzeiger in 1836 he began
ordering German books from eastern dealers on commission, and
this, as we shall see, led directly to the first German bookstore in
St. Louis.   But Weber also, between the years 1837 and 1841,
printed at least eight German language books.   I suppose you may
call them Missouri German incunabula [see Appendix 1].

The honor of being the first book belongs either to a primer
written by Friedrich Steines and printed in 1837, or to a selection
from the laws of Illinois edited by Gustav Körner, which may have
been printed in 1837 or 1838.   The third Weber publication was part
one only of the laws of Missouri in German, prepared by Theodor
Engelmann and issued in 1838.   I do not know of any copies of
these three books, and only the Steines has ever been bibliographi-
cally recorded.   Happily, Weber's next undertaking, a history of
American political parties translated from the English of James B.
Worden and dated 1839, is definitely not a phantom; nor is the book
Weber printed the following year, the original German edition of
Friedrich Adolf Wislizenus A Journey to the Rocky Mountains in the
Year 1831, an important piece of early western Americana.

We now meet with a most curious publication for that time
and place, Johann Christian Edelmann's notorious Glaubens-Bekennt-
nis (Confession of Faith).   This singular document by one of the
first German disciples of English Deism was originally published in
1746, reprinted in 1748 and publicly burned in Frankfurt am Main
by order of the Imperial Book Commission on May 9, 1750.   No
subsequent edition is recorded until Weber issued the first of four
planned fascicles.   In Germany, almost a century had to pass before
the relaxed climate of 1848 encouraged the radical Leipzig bookseller
Emil Ottokar Weller to attempt a reprint.   (A selection from Edelmann's various works edited by Bruno Bauer did appear a year
earlier under the title--Der neueröffnete Edelmann.)

A reliable contemporary witness tells the fate of Weber's edition: "In December 1839 the first fascicle appeared, sewn, at
37-1/2 Cents each, 4 Dollars the dozen.   Three more fascicles
were supposed to follow, each one consisting of three or four sheets,
and the whole thing to sell for 2 Dollars.   As far as I know, the
second fascicle never appeared, presumably because the first wasn't
bought, and the undertaking foundered on the Christian piety of the
German population. "[20]

Like the Edelmann, the two books printed by Weber in 1841
are unrecorded.   They are: A revised edition of the Steines primer;

and forty-six pages of satiric doggerel, with woodcut illustrations, written by Heinrich Koch in the spirit of Karl Arnold Kortum's Die Jobsiade. Koch's book was apparently the first volume of German-American literature published West of the Mississippi and we may surmise that it infuriated many good citizens of St. Louis, who often expressed themselves vehemently on the subject of Heinrich Koch in the pages of the Anzeiger. These verbal exchanges built to a climax in November 1842, when an anonymous correspondent, while upbraiding Missouri Germans in general for not producing any decent poetry--and naturally his polemic was in verse--referred with undisguised class antagonism to Koch, though not mentioning him by name. Koch replied in kind with one of his stronger efforts and St. Louis Germans could now contemplate their very first Federkrieg [see Appendix II].

I would like now to go back several years and trace the story of St. Louis' first German bookstore, the creation of Wilhelm Weber and Theodor Engelmann. Engelmann's father, Friedrich Theodor Engelmann, was patriarch of the pioneer clan that settled on a farm near Belleville in 1833, a place of refuge for young Theodor, Wilhelm Weber and Gustav Körner, all fellow students at Jena. Theodor Engelmann was not temperamentally suited to farmwork and soon left his parents' household. After a short spell at Mr. Swire's tannery in Belleville, he moved to St. Louis in 1835 to open an intelligence office. As he explained to his sister Gretchen: "... We, that is Körner and myself, figured out that a person might be able to make quite a good living by being the agent in business deals between Americans and Germans, and nothing else; and this induced me to set up an 'Agency and Information Bureau.' "21 To the bureau was added a real estate agency, but for all his efforts Engelmann made little money. Beginning in January 1837, Engelmann also served as Librarian of the St. Louis Library Association for twelve dollars a month plus ten dollars towards the rent. The Library was housed next to the Anzeiger printing office on 33 Pine Street, and Engelmann lived on the premises. 22

The groundwork for Weber and Engelmann's bookstore was laid in 1836. Already in November of that year Weber had announced that German books could be ordered at the Anzeiger office from catalogues supplied by J. G. Wesselhöft of Philadelphia and Schulz & Bleidern of New York. 23 Later in life, Engelmann ruefully recalled how he and Weber tried to eliminate the middleman and open a bookstore of their own:

> In plans of how to remedy the everlasting lack of money,
> we were rich. All of them appeared, however, upon thor-
> ough examination, unattainable, until we came upon the un-
> lucky thought that a book store with German books prom-
> ised success. I had catalogs sent from Uncle Joseph [Eng-
> elmann] in Heidelberg and we made a selection of books,
> which we believed suitable for the taste and needs of the
> German population and ordered them. They arrived at the
> expected time. A catalog was made and printed and the

book store opened.   But the purchasers did not wish to
come in.   They stayed away.   The German public at that
time was still all too busy with its battle for the material
existence.   The need for spiritual nourishment still slum-
bered or the means for its satisfaction were wanting.   The
few books which we disposed of were bought by our close
friends who were living in better circumstances, out of
consideration and kindness and the few dollars which came
in from them were easily and quickly swallowed up by current expenses and the promissory note for $200.00 which
I had given Uncle Joseph instead of payment, could not be
met. [24]

The works of Schiller, Uhland, E. T. A. Hoffmann, and the
Brockhaus encyclopedia were samples of what was offered for sale
in 1837. [25]   Business during 1838 must have been poor, if we take
Engelmann's testimony at face value; yet apparently orders for new
shipments of books were placed with Uncle Joseph.   This we learn
from a diary fragment dated January 3rd, 1839.   By now, as far as
Engelmann's personal affairs were concerned, the wolf was at the
door.

Capt. Bloed[?] came to collect the rent, $75.00 for the
last quarter; I had no money and asked for a week of
grace.   The second day the weather was not much better
and was to have been even worse.   I refused to pay two
promissory notes from my uncle for books which I had received from him which amounted to $800.00.   Had I writ-
ten in time that I could not pay he would have spared me
the promissory notes.   This whole matter, that is the
books and the promissory notes, worries me.   On the
Steamer Belle, which is stuck in the ice 120 miles from
here, there is another shipment of books for me, which
cost $80.00 freight and entrance [duty].   I do hope the ice
will detain the boat for several more weeks!--[26]

By December 1839, Engelmann had moved to 19 Market Street
with some or all of his German books and was now advertising a German lending library of his own.   New acquisitions were noted in the
Anzeiger and ranged from translations of Paul de Kock to Georg Her-
lotzsohn's Hahn und Henne (but also Tieck, Wieland and Jean Paul).
Within a few months, however, Engelmann finally abandoned St.
Louis and returned to Belleville. [27]   Meanwhile, in phoenix-like fashion, the bookstore at the Anzeiger office reopened--certainly by
May 1840--this time under the direction of Arthur Olshausen, younger son of a well-known Holsteiner family. [28]

Book announcements in the Anzeiger during 1840 were more
numerous than ever before.   Besides the older classics, there were
inexpensive books in series, Lieferungswerke, like Joseph Meyer's
Universum and Karl Rotteck's popular world history.   "Young Germany" was well represented, especially the works of Karl Gutzkow.
In general, German political literature was plentiful; but there were

also numerous translations from the French of Hugo, Lamartine and
Béranger. [29] For Gustav Körner, in his history of the German element before the Forty-eighters, these book sales were adduced to
prove the sophisticated tastes of St. Louis Germans. "Missing from
here," wrote Körner, "are the Till Eulenspiegel, the Bairscher
Hiesel, the Heilige Genovefa, the Schinderhannes, which according
to current legend about the German-Americans of that period, were
supposed to have been their exclusive reading matter."[30]

But Körner overstates his case. Olshausen was serving a
very limited clientele by bringing Schleiermacher, Gutzkow and
the latest jungdeutsch polemics to the Mississippi. A bookstore
could not sustain itself on such caviar. Even during 1840 Olshausen
increased his offering of practical texts, grammars and popular religious titles. Sandwiched between Faust and the newest attack on
Metternich were Protestant and Catholic prayerbooks. For Christmas 1841, Olshausen had on hand Sibylla Speranza's Traumbuch,
more prayerbooks, novels, romances and the ubiquitous Ritter-,
Räuber- und Geistesgeschichten. Something for everyone, even a
Christmas gift list for rationalists featuring the fourth edition of
Strauss' Das Leben Jesu. [31]

Perhaps it was an impractical selection of books, or perhaps
the nationwide economic malaise; whatever the reason, when Arthur
Olshausen put his bookstore up for sale on January 15, 1842, he
found no buyers. After waiting a year, he had to sell everything at
public auction "for cash only."[32] [See Appendix III.] St. Louis was
without a German bookstore for about nine months. Then, in September 1843, Johann Georg Wesselhöft arrived from Philadelphia under circumstances that were rather tragic; for this recent widower,
in chronic ill health and with two children to raise, had suffered the
last indignity of unexpected bankruptcy. [33]

Wesselhöft came from a distinguished family. His cousins,
Robert and Wilhelm Wesselhöft, had been leaders of the Burschenschaft movement in its earliest days. Indeed the former composed
and signed the letter of invitation to the celebrated Wartburg Fest in
1817. Both these men later emigrated to America and became prominent physicians. At the age of fifteen, Johann Georg Wesselhöft was
sent to Jena to learn the book trade with his uncles Friedrich Frommann and Carl Wesselhöft. The Frommann house was a center of
cultural life in the Jena/Weimar district, and Goethe himself was a
frequent visitor. In 1824, the apprentice became a journeyman
printer and for a number of years worked and traveled in Europe.
It was during this period that Wesselhöft struck up a close and lasting friendship with the Swiss writer and educational reformer Heinrich Zschokke.

The oppressive political atmosphere in Germany, the tight
government regulation of the book trade, made it difficult for a new-
comer to start his own business and so, in 1832, Wesselhöft decided
to emigrate to the United States. For eleven years he made his
home in Philadelphia. There he founded a very influential newspaper,

the Alte und Neue Welt, engaged in printing, publishing and bookselling. His most profitable specialities were homoeopathic books
and materia medica. By dint of hard work, and using his newspaper as a vehicle for national advertising, Wesselhöft became the
premier German bookseller in the country, and even opened branches of sorts in Baltimore, New York, New Orleans, Charleston,
Washington and Cincinnati. Two other members of his immediate
family settled in the St. Louis area--a younger brother, Carl Friedrich, and a sister who had married a gentleman named F. Frank-
sen. The two men ran a popular German resort in a suburb called
Camp Spring. 34

        In the summer of 1842 J. G. Wesselhöft started out on a
grand tour of the country. He arrived in St. Louis in December
1842 in poor health, and was recuperating at Camp Spring when his
Philadelphia business suddenly failed, though he did not learn of his
misfortune until later. His incompetent partner was apparently at
fault. For the few months he was in St. Louis, Wesselhöft assidu-
ously collected new subscriptions for his newspaper, orders for his
own publications, and for books out of his general stock of over
2,000 titles. He also had brought along a collection of German
books to sell and a list of these was left with almost every tavern
owner and innkeeper in the city. 35 Needless to say, Wesselhöft was
well known to St. Louis Germans when he reentered the city later in
1843 to begin a new career.

        With financial backing from his brother and brother-in-law,
Wesselhöft was installed as manager of a bookstore on Second Street
between Myrtle and Spruce. The new business was announced in October 1843 by the Anzeiger des Westens: "We will stock the most
popular German books and a few English books, together with writing materials, pictures and music.... Our prices are low, but we
only sell for cash. J. G. Wesselhöft of Philadelphia is our manager
and is authorized to accept money for us and to sign receipts in our
name."36 Thus began the first professionally run German bookstore
in St. Louis.

        Wesselhöft had little competition, mainly because the market
for German books in St. Louis was still very tenuous. To the traveler Alexander Ziegler, who was in the city sometime between 1846
and 1847, Wesselhöft seemed a sick and disillusioned man: "Herr
Georg Wesselhöft, who owns the only German bookstore here," wrote
Ziegler, "complained however rather bitterly that the Germans
showed little desire to read books, even less to buy books."37 One
reason for this was the relatively high cost of imported German
books. Wesselhöft's plight was not unique, and presaged what was
to be a dramatic turning point in German-American publishing.

        Despite many eloquent pleas, continental German publishers
were largely adamant in refusing to grant special terms for the
American market; that is, larger discounts on new books, and more
extended credit. The American dealer who imported books from
Germany had to pay shipping and freight costs, customs charges,

transshipment charges to agents in other states, and could not realistically be expected to return unsold books for credit, as was the custom of the European trade. These restrictions, plus the still primitive nature of the German trade in America, resulted in consistently high prices, and a very poor selection of books in German-American bookstores.

The massive German emigration of the late 1840s and 1850s created a large potential reading public for cheap literature. I emphasize the word cheap, for when these newcomers landed they found here a nation in the grip of a publishing revolution. The new printing technology, favorable postal rates, and freedom from any international copyright restrictions, were all exploited to flood the country with extremely cheap reprints of English literature and foreign literature in translation. A spokesman for the German Booksellers' Association (Der Börsenverein der deutschen Buchhändler) who visited the United States in 1845-46 predicted that the great majority of working class German immigrants would quickly become Americanized, and if they read anything at all, it would be those cheap English-language reprints. This otherwise astute observer did not foresee that very soon, cheap reprints of German literature, often published in fascicles as Lieferungswerke, would become a new German-American industry. 38

We can see this new direction in Wesselhöft's advertisements. Religious books had always been a staple of German-American publishers in Philadelphia and other Pennsylvania towns, but now from New York there poured an endless stream of Volksbücher and other colportage production. The same New York publisher, Wilhelm Radde, issued in 1845 a cheap edition of Ludwig Börne's Menzel, Der Franzosenfresser. Very soon, cheap stereotype reprints of German classical literature appeared on the market--Goethe, Schiller, Lessing, Hauff, initially sold by subscription as number publications. In 1846 several novels of Eugène Sue were similarly issued in a Philadelphia and a New York edition; the latter at least was an original German-American translation. How the environment had changed when in 1855 two Philadelphia entrepeneurs could begin issuing competing editions of the collected works of Heinrich Heine, before any authorized edition had appeared in Europe! 39

Wesselhöft's St. Louis bookstore lasted long enough for the old bookseller to experience most of these developments, to see renewed life come to the local German community after 1848. His physical ailments, and the decision of his son to forsake bookselling for farming, finally compelled him to retire in 1854; but by then St. Louis was on the way toward becoming a major midwestern center of the German-American book trade.

Notes

1. See Robert E. Cazden, "The German Book Trade in Ohio Before 1848," Ohio History, LXXXIV (Winter/Spring 1975), 57-77.

2. Herzens Opfer, eine Sammlung geistreicher Lieder, printed in 1816 in Lancaster, Ohio, by Eduard Schäffer for the United Brethren in Christ.

3. Gottfried Duden, Bericht über eine Reise nach den westlichen Staaten Nordamerika's und einen mehrjahrigen Aufenthalt am Missouri (in den Jahren 1824, 25, 26, und 1827)... (Elberfeld, 1829). For a detailed discussion of Duden and the impact of his writings see George Helmuth Kellner, "The German Element on the Urban Frontier: St. Louis, 1830-1860," (unpublished Ph.D. dissertation, University of Missouri-Columbia, 1973), pp. 1-46.

4. Marcus Lee Hansen, The Atlantic Migration 1607-1860 ... Harper Torchbook Edition (New York, 1961), p. 149. See also Paul C. Weber, America in Imaginative German Literature in the First Half of the Nineteenth Century (1926; rpt. New York, 1966), pp. 115-119.

5. On the Mulhouse Society see George S. F. Schrader, ed., Briefe der Familie Schrader aus Amerika an Mutter und Geschwister (aus den Jahren 1832-1835) (n.p., 1912). On the Berlin emigrants see Walter O. Forster, Zion on the Mississippi: The Settlement of the Saxon Lutherans in Missouri, 1839-1841 (St. Louis, 1953), p. 250. Letters and diaries of the Steines brothers have been translated into English by William G. Bek, "The Followers of Duden," Missouri Historical Review, XIV (October 1919), 29-73, (January 1920), 217-232, (April/July 1920), 436-458; XV (April 1921), 519-544, (July 1921), 660-699; XVI (October 1921), 119-145. See also Friedrich Dellmann, ed., Briefe der nach Amerika ausgewanderten Familie Steines (Wesel, 1835).

6. John A. Hawgood, The Tragedy of German-America... (New York, 1940), p. 111. See also Albert B. Faust, The German Element in the United States... (New York, 1927), I, 439-449; Mack Walker, Germany and the Emigration 1816-1885 (Cambridge, Mass., 1964), pp. 66-69; Ralph Gregory, "Paul Follenius," Bulletin of the Missouri Historical Society, XXIII (July 1967), 323-347; Hansen, The Atlantic Migration, pp. 124-126.

7. Schrader, ed., Briefe der Familie Schrader aus Amerika, pp. 55-56.

8. Forster, Zion on the Mississippi, p. 378; Hildegard Binder Johnson, "The Location of German Immigrants in the Middle West," Annals of the Association of American Geographers, XLI (March 1951), 12-16.

9. William Hyde and Howard L. Conrad, eds., Encyclopedia of the History of St. Louis... (New York, 1899), III, 1782-1783; and Theodor Olshausen, Die Vereinigten Staaten von Amerika geographisch und statistisch beschrieben, II (Kiel, 1855), 131. Cited by Kellner "The German Element on the Urban Frontier," p. 101.

10. Theodor Engelmann to his sister Gretchen Hilgard, St. Louis, January 20, 1836, and February 1838. The original letters with English translations are part of the Engelmann-Kircher Mss., in the Illinois Historical Society Library. See also

Martin Timothy Tucker, "Political Leadership in the Illinois-Missouri German Community, 1836-1872," (unpublished Ph. D. dissertation, University of Illinois, 1968).

11. Kellner, "The German Element on the Urban Frontier," Chapter V, provides biographical details on representative members of the clique such as Wilhelm Weber, Wilhelm Palm, Friedrich Kretzschmar, Eduard Haren, Alexander and Heinrich Kayser, members of the Engelmann family, and Arthur Olshausen. See also the excellent if somewhat partisan analysis by Forster, Zion on the Mississippi, pp. 245-277.

12. Johann Gottfried Büttner, Die Vereinigten Staaten von Nord-Amerika: Meine Aufenthalt und meine Reisen in denselben, vom Jahre 1834 bis 1841 (Hamburg, 1844), I, 221. Büttner, who was teaching in St. Louis at the time, claims to have brought Bimpage and von Festen together.

13. Gustav Körner, Das deutsche Element in den Vereinigten Staaten von Nordamerika, 1818-1848 (Cincinnati, 1880), p. 318. The St. Louis Library Association book collection was sold to the St. Louis Lyceum on October 24, 1839 and it ultimately became the core of the St. Louis Mercantile Library. According to John Francis McDermott, a new (unnamed) librarian was appointed by the Association in February 1835; that could have been Weber. McDermott, "Public Libraries in St. Louis, 1811-1839," Library Quarterly, XIV (January 1944), 9-27; and see Eleanora A. Baer, "Books, Newspapers, and Libraries in Pioneer St. Louis, 1808-1842," Missouri Historical Review, LVI (July 1962), 359-360.

14. Koch's St. Louis newspapers were: Der Anti-Pfaff (1843-1845, and possibly published again in 1847), continued as the Vorwärts (1845-1846); Der Communist (1845?-1846?); and Der Reform (1847).

15. Forster, Zion on the Mississippi, pp. 263-264; Anton Eickhoff, "Erinnerungen an einen Freund aus alter Zeit," Der Deutsche Pionier, XII (September 1880), 214; Hermann Schlüter, Die Anfänge der deutschen Arbeiterbewegung in Amerika (Stuttgart, 1907), pp. 19, 27; William Frederic Kamman, Socialism in German-American Literature (Philadelphia, 1917), pp. 21-22, 35; Carl Wittke, The Utopian Communist: A Biography of Wilhelm Weitling... (Baton Rouge, 1950), pp. 240-243.

16. Heinrich Koch, Gedichte ... gesammelt und herausgegeben von Dr. Karl Brockmann (n. p. : Als Manuscript gedruckt, [1880?]. H. A. Rattermann considered the contents, "so subjektiv ultra radikal," unsuitable for republication. A few of Koch's more "acceptable" poems are reprinted in Rattermann, Gesammelte ausgewählte Werke, XI (Cincinnati, 1911), 212-218. Two additional poems may be found in Joseph Eiboeck, Die Deutschen von Iowa... (Des Moines, 1900), pp. 203-205. Most of Koch's radical poetry appeared in sympathetic German-American newspapers. No copies of any of his separate publications seem to have been preserved. As indicated by the following citation of a work banned in Austria, Koch was not entirely unknown in Europe: "Papa"

Koch, der "Antipfaff" und Socialist, die neue, die wissen-
schaftliche Weltanschauung und in dem von H. Komyn ver-
fassten Anhange der kosmopolitisch-sociale Kampf gegen die
theokratisch-barbarische Weltdespotie (Zürich: Selbstverlag
d. Herausgebers H. Ohrheim, 1893). See Anton Einsle, ed.,
Catalogus Librarum in Austria Prohibitorum... (Wien, 1896).
Attempts to locate a copy of this book have so far been
fruitless.

17. Eduard Warrens (1820-1872) was another veteran of the Hambacher Fest who landed in St. Louis, where he practiced law
and cultivated Democratic party politics. Outstanding as a
speaker and writer, Warrens contributed prose and verse to
the Anzeiger and the Alte und Neue Welt. He edited the
Missouri Demokrat from 1843 to 1845, when President Polk
appointed him Consul in Trieste. Warrens remained in Europe as editor of the Journal des Österreichischen Lloyd.
According to Ludwig Salomon, Warrens become "one of the
most gifted journalists ever to have written for the Vienna
press. His brilliant style, his striking dialectic, had been
formed in America..." Geschichte des deutschen Zeitungs-
wesens ..., III (Oldenburg, 1906), 648. (English translation
by the present writer, as are all subsequent translations unless otherwise noted.) On Warrens, see also Rattermann,
Gesammelte ausgewählte Werke, XI, 193-207.

18. Wilhelm Weber, "Die Zeitungen in den Vereinigten Staaten; mit
besonderer Berücksichtigung der in deutscher Sprache ersch-
ienenden Blätter," Das Westland, I (1837), especially pp.
183-211.

19. Letter dated February 1834 in Dellmann, ed., Briefe der nach
Amerika ausgewanderten Familie Steines, pp. 80, 93. Körner,
Das deutsche Element, p. 41. G. F. Dinter was a prolific
writer on pedagogical topics.

20. Büttner, Die Vereinigten Staaten von Nord-Amerika, I, 222-223.
See Walter Grossmann's introduction to Johann Christian Edelmann, Sämtliche Schriften in Einzelausgaben, IX (Stuttgart,
1969), v-xxvi; and Grossmann, "Edelmann and the Silent
Reimarus," in Studies in Eighteenth-Century Culture, IV, edited by H. E. Pagliaro (Madison, Wisconsin, 1975), 195-203.

21. Theodor Engelmann to Gretchen Hilgard, St. Louis, January 20,
1836. Further information may be found in his letters of
December 10, 1833 and July 30, 1834. Engelmann-Kircher
Mss. See also "Reminiscences by Theodor Engelmann 1808-
1889," a collection of material mostly written by Engelmann
and "Copied and typed in German from the original by his
grandson, Theodor Engelmann Kircher in 1921. Translated
by his grandson, Joseph Casimir Kircher in 1950 and 1951."
78 typed pages. In the Missouri Historical Society Library,
St. Louis. Pages 27-51 contain the translation of "Reminiscences Awakened by Koerner's Golden Wedding June 17,
1886," which include a description of Engelmann's life in St.
Louis to 1840. Statements of facts and the chronology of
events should be accepted with caution, as Engelmann at
seventy-eight years of age was recalling events at a distance

of over fifty years. The entire typescript will be referred
to hereafter as Engelmann, "Reminiscences." On the members of the Hilgard family who came to America see, Helmut
Hirsch, Denker und Kämpfer... (Frankfurt a.M., 1955), pp.
1-17, which contain further references.

22. Engelmann, "Reminiscences," p. 48. On January 21, 1837,
Engelmann wrote to Gretchen Hilgard: "Since the beginning
of the year I have taken charge of an additional job which
without giving me much to do will yield about $200 a year for
me. It is the running of the library of an American private
organization. I took this library, which consists of some
3,000 volumes, into my spacious office and have no other duty than to issue books asked for by the members, and to see
that they are returned. There are about two or three calls
a day, and I have the free use of the library, and enjoy having the books around me." Engelmann-Kircher Mss.

23. On Johann Georg Wesselhöft see below. The firm of Schulz
and Bleidern was established in New York City in 1837 to im-
port German books and other merchandise. F. G. Schulz
was then still a partner in the Stuttgart publishing house of
L. F. Rieger & Co., though he resigned that position in 1838.
The original plans seemed to have called for the creation of
a New York agency for Rieger publications. See the New-
Yorker Staats-Zeitung, January 4, 1837. The experiment was
not a success but Schulz and Bleidern did evolve into a pros-
perous currency exchange, commission and shipping agency.

24. Engelmann, "Reminiscences," p. 49.

25. Körner, Das deutsche Element, p. 331, quoting from the Anzeiger des Westens, February 11, 1837.

26. A single sheet bearing diary entries for January 3 and 4, 1839.
Item 98 in the Engelmann-Kircher Mss.

27. Wöchentlicher Anzeiger des Westens, December 28, 1839; January 14 and May 9, 1840.

28. Körner mistakenly credits Olshausen with running the Anzeiger
bookstore in 1838. He supports this by quoting from an Olshausen advertisement in the Anzeiger which, however, did
not appear in 1838, as Körner claims, but in 1840 (Wöchentlicher Anzeiger des Westens, November 28, 1840). Körner,
Das deutsche Element, p. 331. Arthur Olshausen belonged
to a large and gifted family. His brother Theodor later came
to America as a Forty-eighter and became a leader of the
Missouri Republican Party. Another brother, Hermann Olshausen, remained in Europe and won fame as a Protestant
theologian. A third brother, Justus Olshausen, took part in
the Wartburg Fest as a young student and later became an
outstanding Orientalist at the University of Kiel. Arthur Olshausen emigrated to Missouri in 1837 at the age of eighteen
and from 1838 on was associated with the Anzeiger des Westens, first as a compositor, then as a part owner, and from
1846 as sole owner. In 1851 he sold the paper to Heinrich
Börnstein. Armin Tenner, Amerika: Der heutige Standpunkt
der Kultur in den Vereinigten Staaten ... Anhang (Berlin,
1884), p. 67.

29. Wöchentlicher Anzeiger des Westens, November 28, 1840.
    Books for sale included: Heinrich Hoff's Gutzkow die Gutz-
    kowgraphie (1839); Schleiermacher's Vertraute Briefe über
    die Lucinde [of Friedrich Schlegel] with Gutzkow's introduc-
    tion (1835); Joseph Görres' anti-Protestant and grossdeutsch
    polemic, Athanasius (1837) and Gutzkow's rejoinder, Die
    rothe Mütze und die Capuze (1838), both works banned in
    Prussia. Among the more interesting political works offered
    were: F. L. Weidig's Reliquien (1838); Die entlarvten Diplo-
    maten (1836); Der Mucker in der Einsamkeit (1837); Gesch-
    ichte der geheimen Verbrüderungen der neuesten Zeit (1834);
    and J. G. A. Wirth's famous pamphlet, Der Nationalfest der
    Deutschen zu Hambach (1832).

30. Körner, Das deutsche Element, p. 332. The Bairscher Hiesel
    was a famous Bavarian brigand of the eighteenth century, and
    Schinderhannes, of course, the most famous of all German
    robber chieftains.

31. Wöchentlicher Anzeiger des Westens, May 9, 1840; November
    27 and December 18, 1841.

32. Ibid., January 15, 1842; January 7, 1843.

33. This summary account of J. G. Wesselhöft's career is drawn
    from my paper, "Johann Georg Wesselhöft and the German
    Book Trade in America," to be published in Walter Schatz-
    berg and Gerhard K. Friesen, editors, The German Contri-
    bution to the Building of the Americas: Studies in Honor of
    Karl J. R. Arndt.

34. Eduard Warrens celebrated this popular German resort in verse;
    reprinted in Rattermann, Gesammelte Ausgewählte Werke,
    XI, 203-205.

35. Wöchentlicher Anzeiger des Westens, December 10, 1842.

36. Ibid., October 19, 1843.

37. Alexander Ziegler, Skizzen einer Reise durch Nordamerika und
    Westindien (Dresden, 1848), II, 77.

38. Rudolph P. Garrigue, Bericht an die Commission für die Be-
    gründung einer deutschen Buchhandlung in den Vereinigten
    Staaten (n.p., n.d. [1846]), pp. 5, 23-24.

39. Ludwig A. Wollenweber issued Der ewige Jude in 1846 (a copy
    is in my possession). As Wollenweber later recalled: "In
    the autumn of 1846, my business at the office of the Demo-
    krat increased, as we were printing a weekly Demokrat, the
    Wallhalla, and the works of Eugène Sue in parts at the same
    time." Wollenweber, "Aus meinem Leben: Neue Folge,"
    Mitteilungen des Deutschen Pionier-Vereins von Philadelphia,
    Heft 15 (1910), 20. A German translation of The Secrets of
    Paris by Victor Wilhelm Fröhlich was published by Charles
    Müller in New York. In 1855, Friedrich Wilhelm Thomas
    and John Weik published competing Philadelphia editions of
    Heine's Reisebilder in parts. However, only Weik went on
    to produce a collected edition of all Heine's works. The
    first six volumes were ready for press or actually printed
    by the end of 1855. See publisher's statement dated October
    1855, Heine, Sämmtliche Werke (Philadelphia, 1856), VI, 571.
    A seventh volume appeared in 1861.

APPENDIX I

St. Louis German Imprints (1837-1841)
from The Press of Wilhelm Weber

Besides standard sources, the following specialized lists of
Missouriana were consulted: William Clark Breckenridge, "Bibliography of Early Missouri Imprints 1808-1850," in James Malcolm
Breckenridge, William Clark Breckenridge ... His Life, Lineage
and Writings (St. Louis, 1932), pp. 249-299; Historical Records Survey, A Preliminary Check List of Missouri Imprints 1808-1850,
American Imprints Inventory No. 1 (Washington, D.C., 1937); Viola
Andersen Perotti, Important Firsts in Missouri Imprints, 1808-1858
... edited by T. N. Luther (Kansas City, Mo., 1967).

Two omissions from this imprint list must be cited. A subscription notice for an Allgemeines Vieharzneibuch, a book on veterinary medicine written by J. P. Willems of East Frisia, who was
then living in St. Louis, appeared in the Cincinnati Volksblatt for
May 7, 1836. Delivery was promised as soon as two hundred orders
at fifty cents each were received. There is no record that the book
ever was published. Another putative early German imprint is the
sales catalogue reportedly printed at the Anzeiger office in 1837 for
the Weber and Engelmann bookstore (see text).

1. Friedrich Steines. Erstes Uebungsbüchlein für Kinder, welche
   schnell und gründlich lesen lernen wollen. 1837.[1]

2. Auszug aus den Gesetzen des Staates Illinois ... begleitet von
   der Unabhängigkeits-Erklärung ... Zusammengestellt von
   Gustav Koerner. [1837 or 1838.][2]

3. Gesetzbuch von Missouri bearbeitet und herausgegeben von Theodor E. Engelmann. Part I. 1838 [all published.][3]

4. James B. Worden. Kurze Geschichte der föderalistischen und
   demokratischen Partei in den Ver. Staaten. Verdeutscht aus
   dem Englischen ... durch Wm. Weber. 1839. 64 pp.[4]

5. Friedrich Adolf Wislizenus. Ein Ausflug nach den Felsen-Geb-
   irgen im Jahre 1839. 1840. 126 pp.[5]

6. Johann Christian Edelmann. Johann Christian Edelmann's abge-
   nöthigtes, jedoch Andern nicht wieder aufgenöthigtes Glaubens-
   bekenntniss. Aus Veranlassung unrichtiger und verhuntzter
   Abschrifften desselben dem Druck übergeben, und vernünftigen
   Gemüthern zur Prüfung vorgelegt von dem Auctore. Anno
   1746. Part I. 1840. [all published.][6]

7. Friedrich Steines. Erstes ABC- und Lesebuch für Kinder, nach Fr. Steines ersten Uebungsbüchlein Bearbeitet von G. A. Pötter mit vielen Bildern. Arthur Olshausen in meinem Verlag. 1841.[7]

8. Heinrich Koch. Die sonderbaren Jobsen, ein chaldäisches Bruder-Gedicht, nebst geschichtlicher Einleitung oder Commentar-Laterne von Professor Kater. Übersetzt von Heinrich Koch. 1841. [46 pp. with woodcuts.][8]

Notes

1. Listed by Breckenridge as not seen. Advertised in the Wöchentlicher Anzeiger des Westens, December 28, 1839, for twenty five cents. The 1837 publication date is vouched for by W. G. Bek, "The Followers of Duden," Missouri Historical Review, XVI (October 1921), 125. This, or the Abstract of the Laws of the State of Illinois, was probably the first German book printed in St. Louis.

2. Körner himself gave 1838 as date of publication. Das deutsche Element, pp. 332-333. But see Friedrich Schnake's account. "On June 22, 1837, the appearance was announced of the first German book printed in St. Louis, that is: Auszug aus den Gesetzen des Staates Illinois etc. by Gustav Körner. The work, made up of 30 sheets, was given to me for examination and made a good impression with its clear print and tasteful makeup." "Geschichte der deutschen Bevölkerung und der deutschen Presse von St. Louis und Umgegend," Der Deutsche Pionier, III (October 1871), 233. See also the Wöchentlicher Anzeiger des Westens, December 28, 1839.

3. Publication of the Missouri state laws in German had apparently been attempted twice before Engelmann's version, first by Christian Bimpage and then by T. W. Lenz. Our only source for this in Lenz's own account in 1838: "Certainly no one could feel more deeply than I, myself, how ruinous to the immigrant is the lack of knowledge of the law, in a land where so many struggle to gain the advantage for themselves. For that reason, a complete German translation of the collected laws of the state of Missouri was proposed in my name to the owner of the German printing shop in St. Louis. On that occasion, I learned the following: The former publisher of the German paper in St. Louis, by name of Pimhagen [sic] had printed a selection from the Missouri laws in the German language, sale of which was forbidden him, however, on the grounds that the exclusive privilege of dealing with the collected laws was already in the possession of an American bookseller." Lenz, Reise nach Saint Louis am Mississippi. Nebst meinen, während eines vierzehnmonatlichen Aufenthaltes in den Jahren 1836 und 1837, theils im Illinois gemachten Beobachtungen und Erfahrungen (Weimar, 1838), p. 91. In 1838 Wilhelm Weber was able to begin publication of the Engelmann translation though only part one was ever issued.

See Wöchentlicher Anzeiger des Westens, December 28, 1839.

4. Wöchentlicher Anzeiger des Westens, December 28, 1839. A Checklist of Missouri Imprints 1808-1850 records one copy in the St. Louis Mercantile Library, but the entry reproduced appears to be quite ungrammatical. I have not been able to examine an actual copy of the Worden book.

5. Several American libraries own copies of this rare book, including the Library of Congress.

6. Title as given in the Wöchentlicher Anzeiger des Westens, December 28, 1839. It is a transcription, with a few minor discrepancies, of the original 1746 title page. No copy is known. See also the Lichtfreund (Cincinnati), May 12, 1840.

7. A revision of the Steines 1837 primer. Title as printed in the Wöchentlicher Anzeiger des Westens, February 20, 1841. According to this notice, the book was published for Arthur Olshausen who had recently taken over the Anzeiger bookstore.

8. Title as printed in the Wöchentlicher Anzeiger des Westens, June 12, 1841. Published at the expense of the author. No copy known.

APPENDIX II

Pro and Contra Heinrich Koch:
Documents from the Anzeiger des Westens

Scherze[1]

Der Congress von 1841 bis 1842.

A.

Wie der Congress mich gemahnt mit den albernen, langen Debatten,
    Die schier eine Million kosten der armen Nation? --
Stell' an die Krippe den Esel, voll süssen, duftenden Heues,
    Nimmer geht er von selbst willig der wieder hinweg.

B.

Immer gemahnen mich will's an den Spruch des gefeierten Dichters,
    Seh' ich vergeudet die Zeit, seh' ich vergeudet das Geld:
"Einzeln ist noch ein Jeder so leidlich klug und verständig;
    "Sind die beisammen, gleich--wird euch Ein Dummkopf daraus. "

Henry Clay

A.

"Hurra für Clay!" nun schallt's mit Macht aus jeglichem Winkel;
    Rosiger Schimmer verklärt schon das ehrgeizige Haupt.

Ist die ganze Nation denn auf einmal zum Töpfer geworden,
   Dass sie so kneten den Thon, drehen die Scheibe mit Macht?

B.

Parasiten nur sind's, die in der Werkstadt so lärmen,
   Knetend den zähen Thon, drehend die Scheibe mit Macht,
Um sich ein Prunkgefass zu ihrer Lust zu bereiten,
   Daraus dann ihnen zuletzt Milch sich und Honig ergiesst.

C.

Lass sie nur toben, die Heiden und lass die Thoren nur halten
   Stolzen Roth! Das Volk lachet ihrer, und wird--
Kommt die Zeit--ein ernst Gericht dann über sie halten,
   Wird zu Scherben den Thon schmettern mit eherner Faust.

Die harten Zeiten.

H a r t diese Zeiten du nennst?--Breiweich mögt' lieber sie nennen;
   Tragen ja nichts mehr empor, alles geht unter darin,
Unter, wie in den Brei der Papierfabrik, welche verdrängt hat,
   Was dem Ohr jetzt so süss klinget, das harte Metall.

H. K.

K--, Du meinest es gut mit Deiner kräftigen Brühe;
   Nur zuviel Teufelsdreck mengst Du und Knoblauch darein.

Die Gascompagnie.

Gas zu liefern, ja, ja! war unsre wohlthätige Absich[t],
   Licht zu spenden der Stadt während des Dunkels der Nacht.
Aber ein Anderes war im Rath der Götter beschlossen,
   Die auf das grunzende Thier hatten die Absicht gelenkt.
Was als Nahrungsstoff Amerika's Wälder ernähren,
   Jetzt, als Lichtstoff verwandt, hellt es das Dunkel der Nacht,
Hellet den Parlour, den Store, die Strassen, den Markt und die Halle,
   Wohlfeil;--Hart ist die Zeit!--Wunder gebieret die Noth.
Siehe, ein einziges Schwein, an des Schwanzes Spitze gezündet,
   Rennt durch die Strassen der Stadt, spendend sein brennendes Fett.

St. Charles   H. W.

An den Scherzhaften in Nr. 9. des Anzeigers des Westens. [2]

Willkommen.

   Freudig bin ich, Herr Hofrath,
   Und fröhlich, dass Sie noch munter.

Ich habe den Sing-Sang vernommen
Und rufe: Said'r aach hie!--

Scherze.

Nicht Scherze sind es, o Sänger!
Göttlichen Witz nenne ihn;
Der Dir, wie Schweinschwanzesspitzen,
Fliesst von den Lippen breiweich.

Teufelsdreck.

Kanst Du verläugnen dass Rachel,
Die Süsse, Dir schenkte die Hand!
Und dass sie des Burgherrn vom Brocken,
Holdseelige Grossmutter ist?
Teufelsdreck sollt ich drum meinen,
Musste Dir angenehm sein.
Da ihn süss' Rachel Dir spendet
Täglich und stundlich in Fülle.

Knoblauch.

Und Knoblauch dazu; Ei das ist ja
Dein Stamm und Lieblingsgeruch;
Oder sprich, liebst Du alleine
Als Sprössling von David es nicht?

Die Brühe

Soll ich Dir würzen die Brühe
Mit Zwiebeln und Schweinfett?--Nein!
Treve würdest Du werden;
Und die Mämme, gewiss,
Dürfte Dich nimmermehr küssen,
Herr Hoffrath bedenken Sie dies.   H. K.

Unsere Litteratur.[3]

Unsere Litteratur!--O, wir Armen! Wer decket die Blösse?
    Arm und bloss, wie der Sand in der Sahara Gebiet!
Spriesst, wie in der Oase, auch hie und da noch ein Grünes:
    Gleich bedeckt es der Sand, schlingt es Vergessenheit ein.
Kann so lange der Deutsche den trockenen Zustand ertragen,
    Wo die Seele ihm nichts, nichts den Geist ihm erquickt?
Will er geduldig sich mit Dornen und Disteln begnügen,
    Welche der störrische Grund einzig freiwillig ihm trägt?
Ist der Zeitung Posaune der einzige Weg zu den Ohren
    Dessen was Publicum heisst? wo Du durch Kaffee und Thee,
Zucker und Wein, und Bier und Taback, durch Kleider und Hüte
    Durch Martin'sches Hurrah, tothen Lott'riestore's Geschrei,
Hader polit'scher Parteien, langweilige Stadtrathsgeschichten

Mühsam hindurch Dich quälst, um aus verschüttender Spreu
Endlich ein Korn zu erspähn. --O warum schweigen die Geister?
Blieb denn gänzlich der Geist dort in der Heimath zurück?
Haben Jahrzehende noch des Leibes Bedarf nicht gesättigt?
Ziehet denn Pegasus noch immer im drückenden Joch?
Oder soll ich Gekreisch von des Pöbels Auswurf hinnehmen
Für der Lyra Getön, wie sie Unsterblichen klingt?
Ist die Leier verstummt, die mit anmuthigen Tönen
Winkelried's Heldenthat sang, klagt' um Follenius Tod?
Du auch, edeler Kämpe in Warren County, warum nicht
Schwingest die Geissel Du noch die so erbaulich Du schwangst?
O, so sammelt euch denn und regt euch, ihr edleren Geister,
Wirket auch hier und schafft deutsche Litteratur!

[anon.]

Epigrammatischer Aufruf im Anzeiger. [4]

An die edel veredelt unsterblichen Geister der deutschen Literatur
dahier zum ästethischen Feldzug gegen "des deutschen Pöbels Auswurf."

"O, sammelt euch den und regt Euch, veredelte Geister,
Wirket auch hier und schafft deutsche Literatur,
Oder soll ich Gekreisch von d e s P ö b e l s A u s w u r f
h i n n e h m e n?"

Blättlein, beschützt und gehegt von den Deutschen dahier,
Sage, wer ist es, der wagt zu sprechen von P ö b e l s A u s w u r f?
Elender, wer du auch seiest, der deutschen Pöbel hier sieht,
Und ruft so brünstig um Hülfe den Sänger von Winkelrieds That,
Und ruft um Hülfe den Bauern, den edlen, von Warren County,
Dass er noch einmal die Geissel schwinge erbaulich als Fuchs!
Ist die Leyer verstummt, klagt er mit zärtlichen Thränen,
Muss ich stat Anmuth und Geist "des Pöbels Auswurf hinnehmen?"
Wohlan, so ruf die Herren, o ruf die gewaltigen Barden!
Ja, "sammelt euch denn und regt euch, veredelte Geister,"
Rufe zum Kampfe sie auf, dass sie den Pöbel hier geisseln,
Stelle zur Rechten die Geissel, zur Linken Follenius Tod,
Schmeichle Winkelrieds Leyer, besinge das Fressen mit Löffeln,
Lobhudle edel dem einen, noch edler dem andern Töffel,
Dann komm' in veredeltem Triplo, die Larve will ich dir lüften,
Dass du, veredelter Pöbel, ob deines Bildes erzitterst.
"Pöbels Auswurf?" Ha, zeigst du so schon die Klauen,
Verächtliches vornehm Gewürm, giftiges Lyra-Geschmeiss,
Kommt ihr unsterblichen Sänger, die ihr stets edler euch preist,
Kommt und singt ihr Helden, singt von "des Pöbels Auswurf!"
Und ich will es euch zeigen, dass ihr selbsten es seid.

H. Koch

Notes

1. Wöchentlicher Anzeiger des Westens, November 5, 1842. The lines headed H. K. are of course directed at Heinrich Koch.
2. Ibid., November 10 [i. e. 12], 1842. The antisemitic content of Koch's polemic called forth the following letter to the editor in the issue of November 19, 1842.

   Herr Redakteur!

   Ich bitte Sie im Namen vieler Freunde um Antwort auf folgende Fragen:

   1) Ist der H. K., der die saubern Verse der vorletzten Nummer ihrer Zeitung unterzeichnet hat, der nämliche, welcher hier ein Blatt herausgibt, welches, wie es heisst, der Vertheidigung allgemeiner Menschenrechte und Herrschaft der Vernunft und Sittlichkeit gewidmet ist?

   2) Welche Zwecke glauben Sie selbst zu fördern, indem Sie ein Produkt in ihre Zeitung aufnehmen, was an Engherzigkeit und Pöbelhaftigkeit seit der glucklicher Weise beinahe vergessenen Hep-Hep Geschichte in Deutschland, nicht erreicht worden ist?

   Anmerkung der Redaktion. Indem wir die Beantwortung der ersten Frage dahin gestellt sein lassen, bemerken wir zur zweiten folgendes: Wenn wir gelegentlich, der Curiosität halber, die Ergiessungen eines oder das andern unserer hiesigen Dichter abdrucken, so thun wir es natürlich in der Erwartung, dass das Publicum uns nicht für etwaige darin genommene Freiheiten verantwortlich macht, und verwahren uns ein für allemal gegen den, wie es scheint, von obigem Einsender gehegten Irrthum, dass wir derartige Gedichte, wie sie öfters in unserm Blatte erschienen sind, als Muster eines guten Geschmacks, oder gar als Ausspruch unserer Gesinnung unsern Lesern vorlegen.--Für den gegenwärtigen Fall müssen wir hinzufügen, dass wir uns zur Aufnahme der fraglichen Verse um so mehr verbunden hielten, da der Verfasser derselben der angegriffene Theil, durch einige andere Verse in einer frühern Nummer dieses Blattes war.

   On the Hep-Hep anti-Jewish rioting of 1819, see especially Elenore O. Sterling, "Anti-Jewish Riots in Germany in 1819: A Displacement of Social Protest," Historia Judaica, XII, Part 2 (October 1950), 105-142. The nationalist ideology of many early Burschenschafter and their professors was also mixed with a deep-rooted antisemitism. See Uriel Tal, "Young German Intellectuals on Romanticism and Judaism--Spiritual Turbulence in the Early 19th Century," in Salo Wittmayer Baron Jubilee Volume on The Occasion of His Eightieth Birthday. English section Volume II (Jerusalem, 1974), 919-938.
3. Wöchentlicher Anzeiger des Westens, November 26, 1842. "Martin'sches Hurrah" refers to President Martin Van Buren, who had the strong backing of the Anzeiger.
4. Ibid., November 26, 1842.

APPENDIX III

Auction Sale of Arthur Olshausen's Bookstore
(Wöchentlicher Anzeiger des Westens, January 7, 1843)

Auction von Büchern

Am Dienstag, den 10ten Januar 1843, Abends 7 Uhr, werde ich in der Expedition dex "Anzeigers" den Rest meiner Bücher an den Meistbietenden gegen gleich baare Zahlung in Specie verkaufen. Die meisten derselben sind deutsche, einige englische, französische und lateinische Werke: eine Partie Stahlstiche, Lithographien u. s. w. Ein vollständiges Verzeichniss ist in dieser Expedition aufgelegt, wo dieselben auch in Augenschein genommen werden können. Wer noch vor der Auction Bücher zu kaufen wünscht, erhält sie billiger, als er künftig je wieder Gelegenheit haben wird.

Es sind unter andern noch vorräthig: Schillers, Langbeins, Zschokkes, Kloppstocks, Thümmels, Gessners, Gleims Werke;-- Chamissos, Geibels, Körners, Seumes, Mathisons, Fouques, Höltys, Salis' Gedicht. --Heine's Reisebilder, Le Petit's Sittengallerie der Nationen, Wirth's Culturgeschichte und dessen Vertheidigungsrede, Schaffroth's Critik der Urtheile gegen Theilnehmer an der Burschenschaft, Geschichte der geheimen Verbindungen neuster Zeit, aktenmässige Darstellung der im Grossherzogthum Hessen stattgehabten Hochverrätherischen Unternehmungen, Welker's Gefahren des Vaterlands, Böttigers deutsche Geschichte, Neyfelds Geschichte der poln. Revolution, Geschichte unserer Zeit in Memoiren, 17 bde., Dr. Robertson's Geschichte Karls des 5ten, Roscoe's Lorenz von Medici, Geschichte der Ver. Staaten, Riemer's Mittheilungen über Göthe, Schillers Album, E. Schulze's bezauberte Rose, Wieland's Oberon, Aufzeichnungen eines nachgebornen Prinzen, Engelhards Verfassungen aller Ver. St. , Gutsmuths Turnbuch, Eschenburg's Handbuch der klassischen Litteratur, Blanc's Erdbeschreibung, Volger's Geographie, Cannabich's Geographie, Meyer's Schulatlas, Heyse's Lehrbuch der deutschen Sprache, englisch-deutsche und deutsch-englische Dictionairs, Grammatiken und Gespräche, Thibaut's französisches Dictionair, Kohloff's Schilderungen von Paris, Lehmann's geschichtl. Gemälde von Rheinbaiern.-- Schleiermacher's Predigten (4 bde), Dräseke's Predigten, Olshausen's bibl. Commentar, 3 bde., Strauss's Leben Jesu, 2 bde., Scrivers Gleichnissandachten, Starks Gebetbuch, Hundeiker's häusliches Festbuch, Der Mensch nach den Forderungen der Vernunft und des Herzens, Hempel's Rede über Christenthum und Civilisation, Röhrs Reformations-Predigt.-- Naturgeschichten mit Abbildungen, --Erzählungen vom Verfasser der Ostereier, u. dergl. Bilderbücher und Bilderbogen. --Feines deutsches Postpapier.

Karten der Ver. Staaten und von Missouri, Illinois und Iowa. --Amerikanischer Pferdearzt.

An Stahlstichen, Lithographien &c. &c. habe ich noch:

Panorama der Säugethiere von Reichert und Giradet, in 40 vol.
Blättern. Die ausgezeichneten Israeliten, lith. von Eugen Breza,
Text v. O. Spazier. Meyer's Universum.

Varietes nationales polonaises, par Antoine Oleszezynski, in 32 der
herrlichsten Stahlstiche.

Der Rittersaal im Schlosse zu Erbach, in aqua tinta geätzt, 19 Blätter Schiller's Fridolin in 8 Zeichnungen, nach Retzsch.

Guttenberg's Monument in Mainz.
Ansichten von Hamburg.
Portraits von Jackson, Van Buren, Webster.
Memoiren Washington's in Bildern.
Militärisches Bilderbuch für Kinder.   Fibeln mit Kupfern.   Heiligen-
  bilder.
Diverse Kupfer, Ansichten &c.

Die noch vorhandenen Exemplare von Steines' ABC Buch, so
wie von dem Gemeinschaftl. Gesangbuch, --beide Werke sind in
allen resp. Schulen und Kirchen hiesiger Gegend eingeführt und er-
freuen sich eines starken Absatzes, --werden vor der Auktion äuss-
erst billig im Ganzen abgegeben; ebenso Kiderlen's Geschichte der
Ver. St. und Schade's deutsche Grammatik für Amerikaner.

Arthur Olshausen

Exped. dies. Bl. No. 44 Pinestrasse, Südseite, 5te Thür
  oberhalb der 2ten.

6. NOTES ABOUT THE GERMAN PRESS IN THE MINNESOTA RIVER VALLEY*

LaVern J. Rippley

Any comment on the German Press in Minnesota must take
into account that there are only three areas in the state where the
German population between 1850 and 1900 amounted to 15% or more
of the total population. These three areas have two things in common: they border rivers and they were once at least partially covered with hardwood forests. The three areas I am referring to are:
1) the two counties of Winona and Wabasha adjacent to the Mississippi in southeastern Minnesota, 2) the two counties of Stearns and
Benton, both of which are adjacent to the upper Mississippi, west
and east respectively, and 3) the counties of Ramsey, Dakota, Carver, Scott, Sibley, Nicollet, Blue Earth and Brown, all of which
edge the Minnesota River. To the latter block, which by all considerations comprises the major lode of German settlers in Minnesota,
must be added several counties situated one-county removed from the
Minnesota River, which also had a near 15% German population up
to 1900, namely, McLeod, La Sueur, Waseca, and Martin.

Excluding the first two areas from consideration for this essay, we are concerned with a territory extending basically from the
mouth of the Minnesota River at St. Paul in the east central part of
the state to just west of the southernmost elbow of the Minnesota
River in the south central part of the state. Within this general region are many German place names such as New Trier, New Ulm,
Gotha, Hamburg, Heidelberg, Cologne, and St. Bonafatius.[1] Viewed
in terms of both cultural and numerical importance, the German influence in the area stacks up as a barbell configuration in which the
two major concentrations were heavy at opposite ends, namely in the
City of St. Paul in the northeast, and in the City of New Ulm in the
southwest. Essentially, the Minnesota River served as the dorsal
artery of this trunk.

Germans do not, however, predominate in either the towns or
on the lands immediately adjacent to the river except in the major
towns of St. Paul, Shakopee, Chaska, Mankato, and New Ulm. The
main reason for this is that they arrived on the scene at a time
when the easily accessible lands had already been preempted by yankee "immigrants" who consequently furnished most of the place
names. This meant that Germans who arrived en masse between

*Reprinted from the Report: A Journal of German-American History
35 (1972): 37-45, by permission of the publisher.

1860 and 1870 had to move inland.   Also, they acquired more farms
west of the river than east, making Carver and Sibley Counties with
Brown County the three most German, proportionate to the total population of all counties in the state as late as 1900. [2]

Several factors impelled Germans to gravitate to this area of
Minnesota.   In the first place, this area of the state represented excellent soils which attracted the German peasantry.   Moreover, inasmuch as some yankee farmers had already taken up homesteads,
their experiences furnished raw data from which records on crops
and productivity could be established.   This was important because
Minnesota was set on luring German immigrants to the state, and
the more data immigrant agents had to work with, the better they
could fulfill their missions.

Minnesota enacted its first law calling for a territorial Commissioner of Emigration in 1855[3] and subsequently developed an
elaborate State Board of Immigration with substantial funding and immigrant agents not only in New York, Quebec and Montreal, but in
Sweden, Denmark and, notably, Germany. [4]   Certainly one of the
most fascinating commentaries ever written on the recruitment of
German immigrants within Germany is contained in an official report
made by Albert Wolff to Minnesota's Governor Horace Austin on September 7, 1850. [5]   Earlier, Minnesota's State Commissioner of Emigration for Germany, Albert Wolff, had distinguished himself in
Minnesota by his role in German-language journalism in the area under discussion.   After leaving his duties with the Board of Immigration, he once again returned to German-language journalism in Minnesota.

There is some question as to where Albert Wolff started publishing a German newspaper in the United States, but seemingly it
was in the town of Chaska, a flourishing German settlement on the
Minnesota River in territorial times.   At any rate, an early history
of the area reports that "the Minnesota Tallboat [sic] printed in German, was the first newspaper published in the county [Carver].   It
is established in 1857 at Chaska by Fred Ortwein and Albert Wolff.
After one years' issue, it was removed to St. Paul. "[6]

From a published collection of Wolff's creative writing in
German, it is evident in the editor's introduction that Wolff was for
some time indeed the editor of what is referred to as the Carver
County Minnesota Thalbote, as noted by Neill. [7]   Before coming to
Minnesota, Wolff was a theology student at the University of Göttingen until in May, 1849 when he took part in a revolution in the City
of Dresden for which he was arrested and sentenced to death, though
the penalty was commuted to ten years in prison, and eventually to
pardon in 1852.   In November of the same year he came to the
United States, arriving shortly thereafter in St. Paul.

Before he died on November 25, 1893, Albert Wolff had lent
his services generously to the State of Minnesota and the cause of
German-language publishing.   Perhaps most significantly in 1865, he

edited, translated, and published the first official booklet on Minnesota in German, Minnesota als eine Heimath für Einwanderer.   Actually this first of an annually updated edition was the result of an
1864 Minnesota law offering prizes for the two best essays describing Minnesota in a truthful but promotional way. [8]   After Minnesota
officially established its State Board of Immigration in 1867, it was
a routine matter that the annual booklet was translated and published in German by Wolff's presses of the St. Paul Staatszeitung.
As a rule the German versions are somewhat abbreviated from the
English publications, and it would make an interesting study to an-
alyze exactly what was considered superfluous and excisible by the
German editors.

In addition to German-language publications, another factor
influencing the movement of German immigrants to the lower Minnesota River region is a geographical one.   That is, the counties under discussion were once extensively covered by a tract of trees
known as "The Big Woods" (from the French le bois grand).   A lecture given by N. H. Winchell in 1875 pinpoints this tree-covered region of Minnesota: "In general, the Big Woods may be thus bounded: Beginning a few miles west of Minneapolis the eastern edge of
the Big woods crosses the Minnesota in a line toward Lakeville in
Dakota County.   Continuing in a southerly direction, it passes about
a mile east of Canon City, and Owatana, when it takes a short bend
to the west and northwest, passing about four miles north of Waseca, ...   About six miles south of South Bend, it turns north and
crosses the Minnesota.... Running along the west side of the Minnesota ... it begins to bear off toward the northwest at St. Peter,
and passes five miles west of Henderson."[9]

In considering where Germans settled outside of the urban
areas in Minnesota, it is important to know that, for reasons not always explicable, they showed preference for forested regions over
prairie lands.   One of their considerations was that the woods provided fuel and could also be sold to city dwellers to heat their
homes, thus affording the immigrant farmer an economic cushion
until his crop production could be expanded.   This preference partially explains why there were heavy concentrations of Germans in
the counties east and west of the lower Minnesota River.   It does
not account for the most singularly German settlement in the state,
New Ulm, being essentially a German city on the prairie, although
even in this case it is clear that in pioneer times a spur of the Big
Woods did run parallel to both sides of the Minnesota northwestward
beyond the present city of New Ulm.   Early plat books of the region
indicate that as available land in the wooded regions became exhausted, Germans tended to move onward slightly west of the wooded
regions to the available prairie soils.

A final factor in the immigration of Germans to the lower
Minnesota River region lies with another German journalist and distinguished Forty-eighter, Eduard Pelz.   This well-educated Saxon,
born in 1800, acquired an almost fanatical conviction that Minnesota
was destined to become the greatest state in the world and he ex-

pended bursts of energy to entice his countrymen to share his
dream.[10] Pelz came to Minnesota by the round about route of an
active literary career in Halle, Copenhagen, Breslau and St. Peters-
burg, with many travels including that as official representative of
Silesia to the 1848/49 German Parliament in Frankfurt. For his
publications supporting the cause of the weavers' uprisings in Silesia
he was imprisoned and subsequently released to take part in the liberal revolutions going on in various cities, especially the one in
Karlsruhe in March, 1848. Seeking a better country for the future
of German culture, Pelz arrived in America in 1850 and eventually
in Minnesota in 1858. His first significant book fostering emigration to the United States was Kompass für Auswanderer nach den
Vereinigten Staaten Nordamerikas (Kassel: J. C. J. Raabe, 1853)
followed by his Nachrichten über Minnesota (Bamberg: Buchnersche
Buchhandlung, 1858) which went through three editions and sold over
150,000 copies.

These items were followed by two others, Die Auswanderung
mit besonderer Beziehung auf Minnesota (Hamburg: Hoffman und
Campe, 1866) which was a translation by Pelz of a book by Thomas
Rawlings, and Vier Hauptfragen in der Auswanderungsangelegenheit
(Hamburg: Hoffman und Campe, 1869); these were followed in 1870
by Pelz's own monthly journal Der Pfadfinder with the subtitle "A
Monthly for the Evaluation of German Emigration and Immigration. "
The explicit purpose of the latter was to promote Minnesota and to
advertise the lands available for colonization from the Northern Pa-
cific Railroad, whose agent at that time was Pelz. The focus of
publications in the journal is not specifically on the lower Minnesota
River region, but it is obvious that one of the side effects of Pelz's
efforts was to bring German immigrants to this area as well.

Although a personal friend of Albert Wolff, Pelz was never
editorially involved with the German Language press in Minnesota.
He did contribute, however, to the Bremen-based Auswanderer Zeitung. Praising the advantages of Minnesota, particularly its climate,
Pelz made a strenuous effort to correct the then popular myth, still
believed, that Minnesota is America's Siberia.[11] Other states and
in particular the railroad agents from states farther south distributed
adverse information which many a writer as well as Pelz found it
necessary to counter.[12] Thus, it was frequently mentioned that the
growing season was longer in Minnesota than in the middle tier of
States, and, according to a certain Dr. Anderson of Minneapolis, it
was even claimed that in Minnesota the temperature could fall as low
as 20° with the right conditions and there would be no severe dam-
age to crops. One writer put it more encompassingly, "The atmosphere in Minnesota in winter is like a wine, so exhilarating is its
effect on the system. "[13] In the final analysis, the best place to
counter false information continued to be advertisements in the emigrant newspapers in the country of origin of which there were at least
five in Germany and two in Switzerland in 1855.[14] Some effort was
also made to advertise in the German-language papers in America's
eastern states, among them the Schnellpost of New York, the Tele-
graph of Buffalo, and Der Ohio Correspondent of Chillicothe.[15]

Investigating the role of journalists in bringing Germans to
Minnesota reveals an occasional opinion that a few of them may have
actually dissuaded certain groups from coming, particularly the
Catholics and those Protestants who were not sympathetic to freethinkers. Alexander Berghold, for example, wrote that the New
Ulm Pionier, through its "misconception of the idea of freedom
brought great discredit upon the city of New Ulm, especially among
religious people. The same feelings were entertained toward all
who were not Germans, especially toward those whom they called
'Americans'."[16] Similar qualms existed in regard to the Minnesota
Staatszeitung, whose editor was Samuel Ludvigh.

Picking up essentially where the Deutsche Zeitung by Wolff
and Orthwein left off in 1858, Ludvigh began publishing the Minnesota Staatszeitung on July 24, 1858 with an editorial reminding his
readers that he was a materialist of the extreme left, one who was
very well known to the German public of North America, and one
who was simultaneously very loved and very hated by everyone. He
proclaimed that he had come to beautiful Minnesota after twenty-
eight years of travels (Lust- Irr- und Geschäftsfahrten) on three
continents. Immediately he took up the torch of the Republicans in
Minnesota, declaring in 1859 and 1860 that very few intellectual
Germans any longer belonged to the Democratic Party.[17]

After considering thus far the reasons why German immigrants came to the Minnesota River Valley and what influence German-language journalists had in their coming, it would be well now
to make some general remarks about the influence of the German-
language press on the regions. To do so it would be appropriate to
have some idea of the composite circulation of German-language papers in the area between the representative years of 1870 and 1910.
In the compilation, the figures used are given in the book German-
American Newspapers.[18] A casual glance at this volume shows that
those Minnesota German-language newspapers with large circulations
in the specific time period were distributed much more widely than
to the German population of the Minnesota River Valley.

In particular, the Minnehaha which was a Sunday insert of
the St. Paul Tägliche Volkszeitung was credited as having a circula-
tion of 28,403 in 1905 but there is grave doubt that the Tägliche
Volkszeitung was indeed published as a daily after the year 1871.[19]
As a matter of fact, it is doubtful whether a daily German-language
newspaper was ever really successful. The St. Paul Volksblatt
tried it unsuccessfully in 1859 and again from 1867-1871.[20] The
Minneapolis Herold achieved it for less than a year in 1884; Die
Presse briefly in 1885; and the St. Paul based Minnesota Staats-
Zeitung managed a three-times weekly edition for a time after 1868.
Thus, there is reason to doubt whether the Minnehaha ever achieved
such a high circulation as is reported in Arndt/Olson. There is no
evidence, for instance, that it was distributed with any other German-language paper anywhere in the Northwest. Yet the Minnehaha
continued after World War I on its own as a semi-weekly paper.

Another paper that enjoyed a wide circulation was Der Wanderer, a Roman Catholic weekly that began in 1867 with a circulation of about 3,000 and passed the 10,000 mark shortly after 1900. Bearing a subtitle of "Glaube, Hoffe, Liebe," the Wanderer stated editorially at its inception that it was called into being in the interests of truth and uprightness, primarily because there was no other like-minded German-language newspaper published in the whole of the Northwest, and none along the Mississippi with the exception of the Herold des Glaubens in St. Louis. Claiming approval of Bishop Grace, the paper promised to be a weekly visitor in Catholic homes in support of Catholic spirituality. Accepting ads from various areas of Minnesota and even Iowa, the paper seemed to have fulfilled its goals admirably, at least in the earlier years. [21]

Finally, the National Farmer und Familien Journal, began in 1902, had a circulation as early as 1910 of 31,589 which grew steadily until 1924, but it is evident in its very title that this publication had a large audience. In summary, then, it is unlikely that the Minnehaha enjoyed as large a circulation as is credited to it. Regarding the latter two publications, it appears that their circulations went far beyond the target region, if not to the whole nation.

Excluding these three, therefore, a tally of the composite circulations of German-language newspapers in 1870 would amount to a mere 8,750. In 1880, the figure failed to remain constant, dropping to about 7,000. If we carry forward the 1880 figures for the two Twin Cities papers whose circulations in 1890 are not available, we find a nearly constant figure again of about 7,500 for the 1890 distribution. Moving to the year 1900, composite circulations bounded to nearly 25,000. However, this leap is deceptive inasmuch as the two most prominent St. Paul papers, the Minnesota Volksblatt and the Minnesota Staats-Zeitung had by this time merged with the Tägliche Omaha Tribüne, thus greatly swelling the potential subscriptions. The Minneapolis Freie Presse-Herold, however, enjoyed a circulation of 5,000 on its own in 1900. Begun in 1869 by the distinguished German journalist, Lambert Nägele, founder of the New Ulm Pionier, [22] the Presse-Herold continued to thrive until 1924, enjoying in 1920 a circulation over 10,000 although by that time many of its facilities had been merged with the Westlicher Herold Publishing Company of Winona, Minnesota. [23] In other words, it cannot be assumed that the circulation of 10,000 refers to the Minneapolis edition alone. The possible audience for 1910 German-language newspapers in the Minnesota River Valley, therefore, is not necessarily above the 8-10,000 figure that prevails for earlier decades.

The conclusions that result from these data are that the Minnesota River Valley territory supported between eight and ten thousand families where a German newspaper was read regularly over the entire spread of 1870 to 1910, after which date the Germans were no longer the most populous foreign-born nationality in Minnesota, being then superseded by the Swedish. [24] Looking forward from 1910, the conclusions that can be drawn are: First, that the

demise of the German press in Minnesota did not result on a massive scale as a result of America's involvement against Germany in
World War I, as tends to be the pattern elsewhere.[25] Secondly,
German-language newspapers were founded and faded from the Minnesota scene with seeming regularity from November 19, 1855 on,
with a few still publishing.   Thirdly, the period between 1880 and
1910 witnessed a kind of heyday in the number of independent German-language papers,[26] while the years after 1920 saw the most
substantial decline of publications and circulations.   Finally, as for
the three mainstays of the Minnesota Valley, the Minneapolis Freie
Presse-Herold capitulated in 1924, having earlier moved operations
to Winona; the New Ulm Post continued almost a decade longer, dis-
continuing finally in 1933 after nearly seventy years of service; and
back at the opposite end of the German-settled barbell, the St. Paul
Tägliche Volkszeitung, having merged with the Omaha Tribüne in
1937, provided an overall circulation in 1935 of over 16,000 and
continues today as the St. Paul Volkszeitung-Tribüne.

        Evaluating the political or cultural impact made by the Ger-
man press on the life of the Minnesota Valley is more difficult.
However, a general survey of all the available papers permits a few
generalizations.   One is that the everyday life of the area formed a
kind of cultural unit.   Secondly, that the two German cultural centers at opposite ends of the barbell were some eighty miles apart
did not seem to be a negative factor.   The advertisements, for example, indicate that local merchants in towns within the area valued the patronage of customers throughout the region.   One is struck
by the heavy advertising of the German-American Bank of St. Paul,
placed continuously for decades in most of the German papers of the
target area.[27]   Thirdly, it is clear that Minnesota also had its share
of Männerchöre and many a Sängerfest.   Ample attention was given
in the press to the Club life of the Germans and, in fact, the St.
Paul Volksfreund proclaimed that one of its primary functions would
be to cover news of the German organizations in the area.

        Theater performances in German were also common, draw-
ing praise and criticism in the Twin Cities and New Ulm papers. Like
German stages throughout America in the nineteenth century, however,
a great many authors unknown today were played to rather undis-
criminating audiences.   To Minnesota's credit, perhaps, August von
Kotzebue was staged less in the region than in many other German-
American cities[28] while Friedrich Schiller was by far the most-often
staged classical German writer.   Goethe's Faust enjoyed some
prominence and surprisingly Shakespeare's Hamlet, Othello, and Merchant of Venice did run in German with considerable interest shown
by the major German papers.[29]

        Over the years, of course, German plays appeared on many
city stages in the target region, among them Mankato, Chaska, Os-
seo, New Rome, Young America, Waconia, Carver, Faribault, Jor-
dan, St. Peter, Shakopee, and Waseca.[30]   Surely the best playwrights as well as the finest German theatrical performances in the
region were those offered in the City of St. Paul.   Building on a

long tradition from the first Thalia group which existed already in
1858 to a kind of climax in the years after 1920, the St. Paul German Theater was usually good and often distinguished. It resulted
eventually in the construction of Das deutsche Haus, which was completed in 1921 and thereafter served all the German organizations of
St. Paul, offering along with its other facilities a large hall with a
fine stage. 31

An item of national scope that interested the Valley German
editors was of course the temperance movement. As elsewhere,
the Germans dealt with the issue partly through the ballot box and
partly through ridicule. John P. Mueller, editor of Shakopee's
Minnesota Post, wrote, for instance, that the Catholic University in
Washington, D.C. planned to establish a Chair on Temperance. But,
he said, the professor would have as many students in attendance as
the Sanskrit professor who at that particular time was on leave at
the University of Göttingen. But if attendance were made manda-
tory, "then the students will flee as if from a medieval torture
chair, and the temperance professor will become the University's
student-scarecrow. "32 To many Minnes ta editors of German papers, the "English water-preachers" were a kind of public enemy
number one. A feeling permeating editorials of the time is that the
anti-alcohol advocates were the enemy because in condemning liquor,
they were really attacking the German language and thus the very
German identity in the United States.

Opposition to temperance and by association to the Republican
Party was widespread among the German papers. On the issue of
public v. private schools, there were attacks, for example, by the
Minnesota Post on the New Ulm Post, though usually such opinions
depended on whether a paper represented a Catholic, Protestant, or
Freethinking clientele. 33 More often than not, internecine conflicts
hinged on whether one editor had strong political feelings as opposed to another. In Minnesota, as elsewhere in the United States,
the German-American hero, Carl Schurz, enjoyed legendary acclaim. 34

Minnesota Germans also were, for years, aware of the Indians. Ever since the Sioux uprisings at New Ulm which wiped out
the New Ulm Pionier in August 1862, German papers in the target
area were concerned about Indian affairs. Mostly, it appears, the
Germans wanted to render the Indians into an agriculturally self-
sufficient people. As the problem evolved from the level of physical threat into innocuous curiosity, editors became less opinionated.
In 1891, for example, stories were serialized on how Sitting Bull
actually died. On the broader subject of ethnic minorities, a few
editors feared that ill effects might accrue to the German element
on the coat tails of anti-Chinese laws which they believed to be the
products of "nativists" and "puritans. "35

In the final analysis, it must be maintained that no matter
how strong the German-language press was in the Minnesota River
Valley, it was never by itself an influential cultural force. This

coagulant force must be ascribed to the churches, either Lutheran
or Catholic, and in the case of New Ulm, Freethinkers. [36] Political boundaries, German state of origin, shopping areas, and the
German-language press all seem secondary in the face of the over-
riding cohesive cultural forces of the churches. Important as the
press was, its influence was never a paramount force in Minnesota's
German element.

Notes

1. See Warren Upham, Minnesota Geographic Names: Their Origin
    and Historic Significance (St. Paul: Minnesota Historical So-
    ciety, 1920). For a description of the Undine region around
    Mankato and its German significance, see p. 65. There are
    many more German place names outside the target area:
    Hanover, Friesland, Potsdam, Danube, Flensburg, New Mun-
    ich, Nassau, Humboldt, Elba, and even "Prosit." Some
    township names include Germantown, Germania, Posen, Augs-
    burg, Berlin, Bismarck, Fanconia, Sigel, Frankfort, New
    Germany, North Germany, etc.
2. U.S. Censuses, 1860-1910. See also the maps and graphs
    showing percentages of German stock in Minnesota in Hilde-
    gard Binder Johnson, "The Distribution of German Pioneer
    Population in Minnesota," Rural Sociology, 6 (March, 1941),
    30-31. Additional information is available in official state
    descriptions of Minnesota such as Minnesota As It Is in 1870,
    Its General Resources and Attractions for Immigrants, Inval-
    ids, Tourists, Capitalists and Business Men [partial title] ed.
    J. W. McClung (St. Paul: Press Printing, 1870).
3. Livia Appel and Theodore C. Blegen, "Official Encouragement of
    Immigration to Minnesota During the Territorial Period,"
    Minnesota History, 5 (1923), 177.
4. Theodore C. Blegen, "The Competition of the Northwestern
    States for Immigrants," Wisconsin Magazine of History, 3
    (1919-1920), 3-29, and Theodore C. Blegen, "Minnesota's
    Campaign for Immigrants," Yearbook of the Swedish Histori-
    cal Society, 11 (1926), 3-28.
5. Preserved in the Governor's files #608, the document is re-
    printed in the Yearbook of the Swedish Historical Society
    (1926), 55-64.
6. Rev. Edward D. Neill, History of the Minnesota Valley (Minne-
    apolis: North Star Publishing Co., 1882), p. 355, John
    Massmann, "Friedrich Orthwein: Minnesota's First German
    Editor, American-German Review, 26 (April-May, 1960), 16-
    17, and Karl J. R. Arndt and May E. Olson, German-Amer-
    ican Newspapers and Periodicals 1732-1955 (Heidelberg:
    Quelle and Meyer, 1961), 220, who refer to the Thalbote as
    originating in 1855 in the town of Carver (whereas in fact it
    began in Chaska in 1857) but do not associate Wolff's name
    with it.
        Further evidence linking the name of Albert Wolff with the
    paper is available in Samuel G. Ludvigh, "Nach dem Westen;

von St. Louis nach New Ulm in Minnesota," Die Fackel, 11
(1858), 217.   Ludvigh tells of stopping in Chaska where he
spoke to a small gathering of Republicans and of debating
with the Democrat Wolff, editor of the local Thalbote.   It
should be pointed out at this point that Arndt/Olson include
in their bibliography, p. 790 the following reference: Herman [sic] E. Rothfuss, "Copies of German Language Newspapers printed in Minnesota preserved in the Archives of the
Minnesota Historical Society, St. Paul, Minnesota." The Society's archivists are unable to identify such a collection.
Furthermore, in a personal letter to me, dated November 17,
1971, Hermann Rothfuss wrote: "I cannot give you any information concerning the item on page 790, Arndt/Olson.   In
fact this is the first time I heard of it, but I can say that I
do not possess any copies of old German language newspapers. "

7.   See Poesie und Prosa aus dem literarischen Nachlass von
Albert Wolff (St. Paul: Volkszeitung Druck, 1894), 216 pages,
available in the Minnesota Historical Society.   For a brief
description of the Nachlass, see Lynwood Downs, "Albert
Wolff," Minnesota History, 27 (December, 1946), 327-329.
For additional particulars about Orthwein and Wolff and other
early German journalists in Minnesota, see Daniel S. B.
Johnston, "Minnesota Journalism in the Territorial Period,"
Collections of the Minnesota Historical Society, 10, Pt. 1
(St. Paul: Minn. Hist. Society, 1905), 286-289 and 317-318.
See also John C. Massmann, "Friedrich Orthwein: A Case
Study in Historical Investigation" (unpubl. M. A. Thesis, Univ.
of Minn. , 1959).

8.   The first essay was written by Mary J. Colburn, the second by
William R. Smith.   Copies of the German pamphlets are
available in the Minnesota Historical Library.   See also
Carlton C. Qualey, "A New El Dorado: Guides to Minnesota,
1850's-1880's," Minnesota History, 52 (Summer, 1971), 215-
224.

9.   See "Notes on the Big Woods," Transactions of the Minnesota
State Horticultural Society (1875), 47-48.   See also Rexford
Daubenmire, "The 'Big Woods' of Minnesota: Its Structure,
and Relation to Climate, Fire and Soils," Ecological Monographs, 6 (April, 1936), 225-268.

10. For biographical data, see Der deutsche Pionier, 8 (Cincinnati,
1876), 213-227 and 282.   See also Hildegard Binder Johnson,
"Edward Pelz and German Emigration," Minnesota History,
31 (December 1950), 222-230.

11. See, for example, Pelz, Über Auswanderung, with subtitle "Besonderer Abdruck aus der deutschen Auswanderer Zeitung"
No. 47-49 in the Minnesota Historical Society.

12. See the many official State of Minnesota publications on "Minnesota as a Home for Immigrants," as well as Philip D. Jor-
dan, The People's Health: A History of Public Health in
Minnesota to 1948, especially Chapter I, "Salubrious Minnesota" (St. Paul: Minnesota Historical Society, 1953).   Also
Blegen in "Minnesota's Campaign," op. cit. , 6 quotes from

Hans Mattson, Minnesota's Immigrant Agent who reports
that "a prominent newspaper writer in Kansas accused me of
selling my countrymen to a life not much better than slavery
in a land of ice, snow, and perpetual winter, where if the
poor emigrant did not soon starve to death, he would surely
perish with the cold."

13. Ledyard Bill, Minnesota: Its Character and Climate (New
York: Wood and Holbrook, 1871), 71.

14. See Appel and Blegen, "Official Encouragement ... During the
Territorial Period," op. cit., 186.

15. See Cardinal Leonidas Goodwin, "The Movement of American
Settlers into Wisconsin and Minnesota," Iowa Journal of History and Politics, 17 (July, 1919), 420. See also La Vern
J. Rippley, "The Chillicothe Germans," Ohio History (Autumn, 1966), 217 ff.

16. A prolific writer on many subjects, Berghold was the Catholic
pastor at New Ulm and is quoted in Louis A. Fritsche, ed.,
History of Brown County, Minnesota, Its People, Industries,
and Institutions, Vol. I (Indianapolis: B. F. Bowen, 1916),
452.

17. Samuel Ludvigh was born in Grünz, Austria-Hungary in 1801 and
traveled widely in Turkey, Greece, and the Balkan countries
until 1833 when his writings about the "Metternich System"
brought censorship and embitterment followed by departure
for the United States. After working on German papers in
Philadelphia and Baltimore, he initiated Die Fackel in 1849,
a Baltimore-based quarterly which for the most part vented
Ludvigh's own radical opinions. See Alexander Schem,
Deutsch-Amerika isches Konversationslexikon, 6 (New York:
Steiger, 1872), 657. For an overview of the German Press
in Minnesota in 1872, see Schem, VII, 369-370.

As regards Die Fackel, see Der Deutsche Pionier, ed.,
Heinrich Rattermann, 1 (1869), 358. See also Dieter Cunz,
The Maryland Germans (Princeton: Princeton University
Press, 1948), 261-262. The Minnesota Historical Society has
volume 7 (1853) and volume 11 (1858) of Die Fackel.

18. See Arndt and Olson, 220-237.

19. Ibid., 228-229.

20. For information about the Volksblatt's founder, Philip Rohr, see
Lynwood G. Downs, "Music Moves West," Minnesota History,
20 (December, 1951), 239-242. Rohr was also linked with
the German edition of the Emigrant Aid Journal, the official
paper of the now famous Minnesota ghost town of Nininger.
See Dudley S. Brainard, "Nininger, A Boom Town of the
Fifties," Minnesota History, 13 (June, 1932), 131.

21. Der Wanderer, November 16, 1867 and ff.

22. For details on the career of Lambert Nügele see Hermann E.
Rothfuss, "Westward with the News," The American-German
Review, 20 (February-March, 1954), 22-25.
See also Isaac Atwater, ed., History of the City of Min-
neapolis, Minnesota (New York: Munsell, 1893), 377. "The
Freie Presse Herold is a weekly newspaper published in the
German-language, and is the only German newspaper in the

city. The Freie Presse was founded in the year 1869 by
some German-American citizens of Minneapolis, mostly be-
longing to the Harmonia Society, the West Minneapolis, St.
Anthony-Turnverein and Lodges." In its early years the paper was edited by Dr. A. Ortman and Anthony Grethen, lawyers who gave their services without pay. The first salaried
editor was Theodore Hielcher. In December, 1890 the paper
merged with the Minneapolis Herold, a German weekly which
was established in 1882. In 1892 the officers of the new
Minneapolis Freie Presse Herold are listed as: Otto E.
Naegle, president, Arthur W. Schlichting, secretary and manager, Adolph Duevel and Charles Baehr, directors, and
Charles Bachr, editor. The paper was said to be democratic
in politics, and enjoying a circulation of nearly 10,000, a
good reputation and offices in the Evening Journal building.
Some of this information augments and varies from what is
furnished in Arndt/Olson, 223. See also a file of clippings
and manuscripts entitled "Lambert Naegle and Family Papers" in the Minnesota Historical Society, and a feature story
in the Minneapolis Tribune, August 17, 1952.

23. The story of the Westlicher Herold Company at Winona has not
    yet been told. This company was involved in the production
    of countless German publications throughout the upper Mid-
    west, including Minneapolis papers, many from Wisconsin,
    North Dakota and even Ohio.
24. See U.S. Census, 1910 and Johnson, "The Distribution of the
    German Pioneer Population," 19.
25. See Carl Wittke, The German Language Press in America (Lex-
    ington: University of Kentucky Press, 1957).
26. Most of these had short lives, were bland with opinion, skimpy
    on news of local interest and ill-equipped to receive major
    news stories. For the most part they are detailed in Arndt/
    Olson to whose compilation little new information can be add-
    ed. Regarding the Minnesota Staats Anzeiger, however, it
    could be included in Arndt/Olson, 228, that Julius Stackemann
    was editor from April 26-July 26, 1889.
27. Headed for years by the brothers F. and G. Willius, the bank
    offered every possible financial service for the German Amer-
    ican. Currency transactions as well as business and finan-
    cial dealings in either country were available, even the serv-
    ices of a Prussian Consul, who for a time was F. Willius.
    In later years, the ads announced that the bank existed for
    the general public, but for the German public especially. See
    e.g., Minnesota Staats-Zeitung, January 4, 1877. Later in
    the century the bank is proclaimed as the "German Bank"
    with officers Wm. Bickel, President, and P. M. Kerst,
    Cashier. See St. Paul Volksfreund, September 22, 1894.
28. See, for example, La Vern J. Rippley, "German Theater in
    Columbus, Ohio," German-American Studies, 1 (1970), 78-101.
29. Hermann E. Rothfuss, "Criticism of the German-American The-
    ater in Minnesota," The Germanic Review, 27 (April, 1952),
    124-130, and "Early German Theater in Minnesota," 32 (Sum-
    mer and Autumn, 1951), 100-105 and 164-173.

30. Ibid., "Plays for Pioneers: German Drama in Rural Minnesota," Minnesota History, 35 (Summer, 1955), 239-242 and "Theodore Seidle, German Theater Pioneer," American-German Review, 17 (February, 1951),17-19.
31. Oscar H. Rudnick, Das Deutschtum St. Pauls in Wort und Bild (St. Paul: n.p., 1924). Pp. 69-107 cover the history of German Theater. Other chapters deal with the Vereine, etc.
32. Minnesota Post, April 13, 1893.
33. During this time Archbishop Ireland of St. Paul had become controversial in Minnesota and beyond state borders for his Faribault Plan, which was an accommodation by which state monies were funneled to Catholic Schools through an arrangement for the leasing of Catholic facilities by local school districts.
34. The evidence derives from many papers. See also Hildegard Binder Johnson, "The Election of 1860 and the Germans in Minnesota," Minnesota History, 28 (March 1947), 28 ff.
35. Minnesota Post, August 3, 1893.
36. See Esther A. Selke, "Pioneers of German Lutheranism in Minnesota," Minnesota History, 14 (March, 1933), 45-58, and Sister Grace McDonald, "Father Francis Pierz, Missionary," Minnesota History, 10 (June, 1929), 106-125. See also Hildegard Binder Johnson, "Intermarriages Between German Pioneers and Other Nationalities in Minnesota in 1860 and 1870," The American Journal of Sociology, 51 (January, 1946), 229-304.

PART IV

THE GERMAN-AMERICAN THEATER

7. THE BEGINNINGS OF THE GERMAN-AMERICAN STAGE*

Hermann E. Rothfuss

For a great number of years German-Americans supported German-language theatres, both amateur and professional. Many factors, among them the gradual Americanization of German groups, the first World War, the reduction of immigration, and the decline of the American legitimate stage as a whole, brought about the virtual disappearance of these theatres, so today only the Players from Abroad in New York, German departments in colleges and high schools, and an occasional amateur group present German performances. Many persons interested in the German language never have a chance to attend a play. Yet not much more than one hundred years have passed since the German theater established itself firmly on the East Coast and gradually spread into the interior, so that finally it was found from Texas to Minnesota and from the head of navigation on the Mississippi to its mouth. While before 1840 German performances were certainly few and far between, not more than twenty years were needed to spread the German stage throughout the quickly developing interior of the nation.

Not only the German, but also the English drama had been slow in coming to the territory that is now the United States. While a Spanish comedy was given on the Western bank of the Rio Grande, now New Mexico, as early as 1598,[1] a century and a half went by before plays were also seen by audiences in the original thirteen colonies. On December 6th, 1732, the first recorded play in New York, entitled "The Recruiting Officer," was performed.[2] Charleston, S.C., and Williamsburg, Va., are next on record. In the latter city Addison's CATO was shown on September 10th, 1736.[3] This play is perhaps the first on American soil to be of interest to the historian of the German drama, since it was one of the sources for Gottsched's tragedy Der Sterbende Cato.

Ten years later the appearance of a figure destined to become famous in German literature was announced in the New York Evening Post of September 14, 1746, when it advertised The Curious and Surprising Magic Lantern, with Friar Bacon, Doctor Faustus, and other entertaining figures.[4] This was three years before Goethe's birth, but it seems to have taken exactly fifty years more before Dr. Faustus actually appeared in America as a stage character. On June 3rd, 1796, he made his debut in a harlekinade as

*Reprinted from German Quarterly 24 (1951): 93-102, by permission of the publisher.

The Necromancer or Harlekin Doctor Faustus. [5]

     Before this latter event occurred, however, the first play by
a German author actually had been performed in the United States,
for on February 18, 1795, Lessing's Minna Von Barnhelm was given
on the Charleston, S. C. , stage. It bore the strange title The Dis-
banded Officer or The Baroness of Bruchsal. Soon after, the north
also saw German plays, beginning with a performance of Schiller's
Die Räuber in New York on May 14, 1795. [6] It was the forerunner
of a veritable flood of German plays descending upon the American
stage, most of them from the pen of one author: August von Kotzebue. His early, if rather brief prominence on the English-language
stage foreshadowed his popularity on the early German-American
stage half a century later, although it should not be supposed that
even then his triumphs were unmarred by criticism. The performance of his plays was defended by the statement that Kotzebue was
now "the favorite playwright not only of Germany, but of England
and France. "[7] There was, however, a second very persuasive reason, for it appears that Kotzebue's plays were very remunerative.
William Dunlap, one of the mainstays of the American theatre at the
turn of the eighteenth century, actually learned the German language
in order to translate Kotzebue plays into English and to have them
performed on the American stage. [8] He adapted no fewer than seventeen plays from the German. [9] The translations, rather free, to be
sure, proved a financial lifesaver for him. This Kotzebue craze
was not restricted to New York, for in Philadelphia no less than
twenty-eight performances of nine different plays by Kotzebue were
given during the 1799-1800 season. [10]

     However, no evidence exists that any stage productions were
given in the German language up to this time. Philadelphia, the
metropolis of a region with a large German-speaking population,
would have been the logical center for German plays, but American
German-language newspapers printed in the eighteenth century do not
contain any news bearing on this point. These papers, circulating
among the pious and frugal Pennsylvania Germans, on the contrary
attack various forms of amusements, such as "dancing, theatrical
performances, and the celebration of New Year's Eve by the shoot-
ing of firearms. "[11] The condemnation of theatre performances,
however, was much more general than attacks on dancing. When a
playhouse was built in Philadelphia in 1766, the Staatsbote joined the
English-language papers in a determined opposition to the project.
An announcement was made from the Lutheran and Reformed pulpits
that the various religious denominations, both German and English,
had united to send a protest against the playhouse to the provincial
governor, [12] thus reenforcing a stand taken in 1759 when a petition
from ministers, church wardens and elders of the German Lutheran
congregation of Philadelphia was presented, "praying that a law be
enacted to prevent the building of a playhouse or a theatre in or near
the said city. " One Lutheran clergyman declared in print that the
yellow fever was a visitation sent by God to punish the admission of
a company of stage players. Philadelphia, in spite of this opposition, did become the most important theater center in the colonies,[13]

but as late as 1789 a Lancaster County German paper showed its
disapprobation of plays when it reported that young boys in Germany
had formed a band of robbers after reading Schiller's Räuber.
Samuel Saur may have represented the general Pennsylvania-German
mood when he asserted that tragedy and comedy were written for the
purpose of entertaining vain people.[14] If this was the opinion of
church people it may be added that the German element outside the
church, if not opposed to the theater, was wholly indifferent to it.

In short, no documentary evidence can be brought forward to
show that any plays were given in the German language during the
eighteenth century.[15] Nor is much material available for the first
third of the nineteenth century. The year 1807 seems to be the
first giving evidence that theatrical entertainment of a sort was presented to a German-language audience in the United States. On July
2nd of that year it was announced that Der Zwergeltantz would be
given in the Old Theater in Philadelphia, to be concluded with a
"magic chamber" entitled Das Schattenspiel. This program was re-
peated on August 7, and on September 16th a farce was announced
which bore the title Die Alte Jungfer[16]--the first actual evidence of
a German stage play in the United States.

The evidence is meager indeed, doubly meager if one considers that nothing more can be added for the next twenty-three years.
In September, 1830, a company of German amateurs appeared for a
few evenings in the Washington Theater on Old York Road in Philadelphia and performed a German play each night.[17] The German
Amateur Theatrical Society of Philadelphia indeed became so ambitious that the New York Staatszeitung announced its intention of giving four performances in New York City.[18] Whether this intention
was carried out cannot be established, and thus New York is deprived of the honor of being the second American city with authenticated German stage performances.

This honor is bestowed upon a city in what was then still
considered the West. In 1838 a German amateur theater, "unques-
tionably the first amateur stage in Ohio and in the far-flung West,"
was founded in Canton, Ohio, and during the same fall Schiller's
Räuber and Weber's Der Freischütz were performed there. To
judge by these undertakings, the society must have possessed no
mean ambition. It even attracted the attention of the New York
Staatszeitung whose editor chided his New York Germans for being
outdistanced by "backwoodsmen" and for not yet having properly organized a German theater society of their own.[19] This remark will
perhaps permit the conclusion that German plays had been given in
New York before, though perhaps not by a "properly organized theater society."

However, this deficiency was soon overcome. On January 6,
1840, the first fully authenticated German language performance was
given in New York, when Körner's Hedwig, Die Banditenbraut and
Kotzebue's Der Gerade Weg, Der Beste were performed by the German Dramatic Society.[20] The choice of pieces reflects the reper-

toire of many a German stage in America in its beginnings. In contrast to the performances reported so far these plays no longer remained isolated events. The number of German language plays given
in New York grew by leaps and bounds, till in 1854 a permanent
professional stage came into being. [21]

    Soon the performance of German plays no longer was con-
fined to a few cities, but spread far into the South, the Middle
West, and the Southwest. During this very year of 1840 a German
stage seems to have existed at New Orleans, the first on the long
course of the Mississippi. In 1828 Charles Sealsfield (Postl) had
written that two theaters, one English and one French, gave performances there, in which German operas were represented. "Karl
Maria von Weber would not have been very pleased if he had attended a performance of his Freischütz," he said. "It was metamor-
phosed into The Wild Hunter of Bohemia. Six violins bringing forth
all kinds of noise except music, and some voices, which did not
seem to come from human beings, presented the opera, and it was
applauded. The Kentuckians expressed their enthusiasm by a huzzah
that made the walls tremble. "[22] Unfortunately, the German stage of
1840 also left something to be desired, for it was housed "in a
board structure in the suburb of Lafayette, where it was not very
effective "[23] This theater, however, must actually have existed before 1840, for on April 22, 1840, the first guest actor appeared on
the New York stage in the person of Herr Icks, who was called stage
manager of the German stage in New Orleans. A week later he appeared as Karl Moor in Die Räuber, "the first classical play of the
New York German stage. " He stayed in New York at least until the
end of 1842. [24]

    This man, Icks, may be considered one of the first profes-
sional pioneers on the German stage in the United States in general
and in the Mississippi Valley in particular. In a manner of speaking, it was he who inaugurated the German language stage in St.
Louis, for on September 21, 1838, he had appeared before the foot-
lights of the old St. Louis Theater and during an intermission of the
English language play recited the monologue from "Wallenstein's
Tod. " This undertaking was successful enough to be repeatedly scheduled. Icks at this time called himself a member of the Berlin
Königstädter Theater. [25] It may be assumed that he travelled from
St. Louis to New Orleans, there managed (or perhaps even founded)
the German stage, and then went on to New York. As fate would
have it, the man who actually inaugurated German plays in St. Louis,
Rudolph Riese, first was in New Orleans, travelled up the river to
St. Louis, and finally also ended up in New York. The travels of
both illustrate the importance of waterways, and particularly of the
Mississippi, for the itinerary not only of English language, but also
of German language actors in America. It finally had its influence
also upon the German stage in Minnesota, at the head of navigation.

    Riese calling himself former manager of the German Opera
in Philadelphia, and manager of the German theater in New Orleans,
during the summer of 1842 was stranded in St. Louis, but succeeded

in interesting a number of young Germans in taking part in a German theatrical performance. According to one source,[26] the performance took place on August 22, 1842, and featured the farce Der Eckensteher Nante im Verhör; according to another,[27] Riese and his amateur company actually performed Schiller's Räuber during the summer of 1842.[28] Eighteen years passed, before the first professional season, under Heinrich Börnstein, was opened in St. Louis.[29]

The development of the German-American theater in the interior of the continent ran somewhat counter to that of the English stage. Instead of coming down the Ohio Valley to St. Louis, the German stage went up the river. During the winter of 1843 the first German plays, the forerunners of many, were given in Cincinnati, where the first German singing society had been founded in 1823.[30] The pioneer in this city was the teacher of Trinity Parochial School, Meis, who with his school children performed two religious plays, Die Lauten-Schlägerin and Genoveva. The very same stage was taken over and enlarged by a newly organized amateur group which within four weeks gave four different performances, beginning with Eckensteher Nante on February 23.[31]

By 1849 a second city in the Ohio Valley, Louisville, Ky., also had a flourishing German stage under the management of Julius Bötzow.[32]

Meanwhile the German Theater had further developed in the Central States. Early in 1848 a theater group was founded in the Swiss colony of Highland, Illinois, which shortly after was headed by Heinrich Börnstein,[33] later one of the most famous German-American actors, theater managers, and journalists. Even the Missouri Valley was invaded by German Thespians. In Hermann, Missouri, home town of Fr. Münch (Far West), one of the most famous of the so-called 32ers, dramatic activity began in 1848,[34] and in St. Joseph, Missouri, then on the extreme edge of the frontier, an amateur theater had come into being by 1850.[35]

But the awakening of the German theater was by no means confined to the Mississippi Valley and its tributaries. The German stage also began to appear in Texas, and on the shores of the Great Lakes. At Fredericksburg, Texas, a German Dramatic Club was formed in the early fifties; and this was also the period when the theater obtained a foothold on the shores of Lake Michigan, where perhaps it flourished longer than anywhere else. The first Wisconsin community where German amateurs banded together to perform a play was Manitowoc, where the omnipresent Eckensteher Nante appeared on the stage on December 25, 1848.[36] Finally, on February 11, 1850, a number of journeyman printers in Milwaukee inaugurated German plays in the city that became more famous as a home for the German drama on the new continent than any other. These amateurs also selected Kotzebue plays as their initial offering, putting the two comedies Der Hahnenschlag and Die Barmherzigen Brüder upon their very primitive boards. When two weeks later another amateur society also appeared on the scene, Körner's comedy Der Vetter aus <u>Bremen</u> was shown to the Milwaukee German public. [37]

During this decade from 1850-60, the German drama quickly conquered new fields. In Chicago, where in 1843 the first meeting of German citizens had taken place and where in 1845 the first German newspaper had appeared, [32] plays were being given in the early fifties, though the exact date can no longer be established, since all Chicago German papers up to 1861, and many later issues, were lost in the great Chicago fire. [39] In 1853 a German Theater Society was founded in Detroit for the presentation of comedies and drama. [40] Even in Charleston, South Carolina, where the first German drama (in the English language) had been presented in 1795, a German-language stage was founded in the fifties, with bi-weekly performances being given. [41]

Finally the German theater pushed its way up to the head of navigation on the Mississippi river, and even beyond. An important step was the opening of a flourishing German theater in Davenport, Iowa, on the direct steamer route from St. Louis, Missouri, to St. Paul, Minnesota. This event happened on December 1, 1855, when Wilhelmi's one-act comedy, <u>Einer Muss Heiraten,</u> was presented, followed by another play. [42] Almost exactly two years later, on November 14, 1857, the German drama made its debut on Minnesota soil at St. Paul, and again two months later, on January 17, 1858, before Minnesota had even become a state, it had advanced to New Ulm on the Minnesota River, literally on the outermost frontier of white civilization. Be it accident or be it the outcome of river transportation problems: Davenport, St. Paul and New Ulm all included <u>Einer Muss Heiraten</u> among the offerings of their opening days. [43]

The final step in the advance of the German theater in the Mississippi valley before the Civil War was taken on March 2, 1859. On that date Schneider's <u>Der Reisende Student</u> was performed in St. Anthony, now a part of Minneapolis. Thus the German theater was established from New Orleans to the Falls of St. Anthony, [44] along the entire navigable length of the river. [45]

Notes

1. Odell, <u>Annals of the New York Stage</u>, Vol. I, p. 2; quoting H. H. Bancroft, History of Arizona.
2. Ibid., Vol. I, p. 11.
3. Ibid., p. 20.
4. Odell, <u>op</u>. <u>cit</u>., p. 18.
5. Chas. Brede, "The German drama in English on the Philadelphia stage," in <u>German-American Annals</u>, New Series, Vol. X, p. 100.
6. Odell, <u>op</u>. <u>cit</u>., p. 42.
7. Brede, <u>op</u>. <u>cit</u>., p. 135, quoting Letter No. 3 from American Resident Abroad, in <u>Portfolio</u>, Philadelphia, 1801.
8. Odell, <u>op</u>. <u>cit</u>., vol. II, p. 43.

9. Ibid., p. 220.
10. Brede, op. cit., p. 106.
11. Jas. Owen Knauss, Jr., Social Conditions among the Pennsyl-
    vania Germans in the Eighteenth Century, as revealed in the
    German Newspapers published in America, p. 125.
12. Ibid., p. 126.
13. Brede, op. cit., p. 3.
14. Knauss, op. cit., p. 126. An interesting letter written from
    Dayton, Ohio, in the Pennsylvania-German dialect in 1872 and
    contained in the Deutsche Pionier of March, 1872 (vol. 4, 1,
    p. 9), would indicate that the Pennsylvania-German attitude
    toward the theater did not change much during the 19th cen-
    tury. It reads as follows: "I wees gut, dass es Plätz geba
    muss, wo d' Mädel sich z'amma finna, und dass, weil in de
    Städte d' Kircha nimme fashionable sin, se de Opernhäuser
    erfunne hen, aber des isch grad's g'fährliche an der Sach.
    Mer denk emol nach, was gworre wär, wenn der Washington
    sei Martha hätt in Opera House suacha müsse.... Der alte
    Kunradt."
15. Dr. Knauss, in conversation with the writer, expressed the
    opinion, however, that members of a Mosheim'sche Gesell-
    schaft in Philadelphia actually did give plays as early as 1790.
16. Brede, op. cit., p. 243.
17. Brede, op. cit., p. 17.
18. The German Theater in New York, by Fritz A. H. Leuchs, p. 20.
19. Der Deutsche Pionier, Feb. 1872, 3/12, p. 375.
20. E. Zeydel, "Das Deutsche Theater in New York" (D. A. Geschichts-
    blätter, 15/1915), p. 256; Leuchs, op. cit., p. 20.
21. Leuchs, op. cit., p. 75.
22. Sealsfield-Funde, von Otto Heller (in D. A. Annalen, 1911, IX/1-
    2, p. 21, quot. Das Ausland, July 1, 1828.
23. "Texanisches Tagebuch," von Gustav Dresel (D. A. Geschichts-
    blätter, 1920-21, vol. 20-21, p. 466.
24. Leuchs, op. cit., p. 26.
25. "Geschichte der deutschen Bevölkerung von St. Louis und Unge-
    bung," von F. Schnake (Der Deutsche Pionier, Nov. 1871), p.
    275.
26. Schnake, op. cit., 3/X, Dec. 1871. See R. Wood, Geschichte
    d. deut. Theaters von Cincinnati, Ithaca, 1932.
27. Alfred H. Nolte, "The German Drama and the St. Louis Stage"
    (German-Am. Annals, Vol. XV, 1-2, 28 following Börnstein's
    account).
28. In 1843, Riese, "but recently come from New Orleans," opened
    a German season in New York, where among other plays he
    also offered Wilhelm Tell and Die Räuber. His career as a
    manager lasted only three months, however, though he had
    received great praise. (Leuchs, op. cit., p. 44) Under the
    name of Benedetti he sang in Italian opera for several years
    in New York, Philadelphia, Boston, and other cities, until he
    lost his voice. Finally, a broken man, he died in the Poor
    House on Blackwell Island, N. Y., in 1859 (Nolte, op. cit.,
    p. 32). His life typifies the vagaries of a German-American
    actor's existence.

29. Nolte, op. cit., p. 5.
30. Carl Wittke, We who Built America, p. 199.
31. H. A. Rattermann, "Das 1. Deutsche Theater in Cincinnati"
    (Der Deutsche Pionier, 6/1, March 1874, p. 26).
32. Der Deutsche Pionier, I/2, April 1869, p. 48.
33. Highland, Ill., von A. E. Bendelier (Der Deutsche Pionier, II/7,
    Oct. 1879, p. 265).
34. Wittke, op. cit., p. 262.
35. Schnake, op. cit., p. 333.
36. Wisconsin's Deutsch-Amerikaner, p. 140.
37. "Die literarische Geschichte des Milwaukee Deutschen Bühnen-
    wesens von 1850-1911," von J. C. Andressohn (G. A. Annals,
    X, 1912, p. 68).
38. Gustav Körner, Das deutsche Element in den Ver. Staaten, p.
    278.
39. Esther Mary Olson, "The German-American Theater in Chi-
    cago," D. A. Geschichtsblätter, 1937, vol. 38, p. 72.
40. Warren Washburn Florer, Early Michigan Settlements, p. 43.
41. J. A. Wagner, "Die Deutschen von Südkarolina," in Der Deutsche
    Pionier, Sept. 1871, 3/7, p. 212.
42. Joseph Schick, The Early Theater in Eastern Iowa.
43. St. Paul Deutsche Zeitung, Nov. 21, 1857; Neu Ulm Pionier,
    January 22, 1858.
44. Minnesota National Demokrat, Feb. 26, 1859.
45. Thirty years later the German stage also reached the head-
    waters of the Missouri. In April, 1889, the German Volks-
    theater in Harmonia Hall, Helena, Mont., was opened with a
    performance of Das Fest der Handwerker (Minneapolis Freie
    Presse, April 27, 1889). This performance was not the first
    German performance in Montana, however. Six years earlier
    the St. Paul Volkszeitung (Nov. 2, 1883), had contained the
    following report from Fort Keogh, Mont.: "The Schurz Club,
    consisting of German soldiers, is held in great respect. The
    officers are very much in favor of it and like to attend the
    theater on many an evening. Every Wednesday we give per-
    formances for non-members, while on every Sunday we per-
    form for our own members. Our hall is always full."
        But even earlier performances may have been given. A
    letter from Virginia City, Mont., gold mining camp and ter-
    ritorial capital, appearing in the St. Paul Volksblatt on March
    18, 1865, contains the following interesting statement: "No
    German paper is published here as yet, but it would be well
    supported by Germans and Americans alike. The number of
    Germans is estimated at 2,500.... A few days ago a Ger-
    man Turner Society was called into being. To judge by the
    list of officers it ought to be good. The German Singing So-
    ciety will reorganize in a few days in order to work jointly
    with the Turners." It would be strange if this joint activity
    had not also included theater performances.

8. SOME CHARACTERS OF THE
    GERMAN-AMERICAN STAGE*

John J. Weisert

In 1858 Samuel Ludvigh's Die Fackel published an essay, "Ueber Liebhaber-Theater," which is basic to a consideration of the primitive German-American theater in the Midwest. In twelve pages the unidentified author tellingly summarized the problems and aims of our semi-professional German-language stage. In view of contemporary editorial practice, and the fact that about five-sixths of it were reprinted early in the first volume of the Minnesota Staats-Zeitung founded by Ludvigh the next year at St. Paul, the indications are that he was the author. Since the article deals with those transitory organizations which flourished throughout mid-America during the 'fifties rather than the metropolitan houses of the eastern seaboard, its significance is evident. The following are biographical details of a few of the people involved in the initial proliferation of the immigrants' stage.

Of outstanding importance to the infant German theater of the whole central valley was Julius Boetzow. His origin is unknown, as is also his death; but with a fittingly histrionic effect, he probably died in Williamsburgh, New York, whither the popular comedian, stricken with blindness, had retired before 1867. Carl Anneke, author of a rhymed survey of the local German theater for the Milwaukee Theater-Kalender of 1864, states:

> Herr Boetzow, der kleine komische Mann,
> Kam also von Louisville hier an,
> Er konnte das Theater dort nicht mehr hueten,
> Weil grausam die Nichtwisser dort thaten wuethen.
> Von Natur war er aeusserst ruhig und milde,
> Und fuehrte durchaus keine Intriguen im Schilde.

He first comes into view in Cincinnati, thwarted by intrigue from working with either of the two dramatic groups active there in 1850, but directing a theater the next year. The Cincinnati Volksblatt of April 24, 1851 urged its readers to turn out for Boetzow's benefit night. The succeeding season he made his debut as impresario in Louisville. He and Ernst Magius rented the facilities on the second floor of Washington Hall, where they inaugurated Kentucky's most successful non-English theater. However, monthly expenses of $250 were barely made during that autumn.

*Reprinted from American German Review 24:4 (1958): 12-15, by permission of the publisher.

The hall was chosen, probably, because the previous year it
had witnessed the birth of the German theater in Louisville, an
event effected by the Strasser family. This aggregation originally
consisted of Xaver, the father, Josephine and Sophie, his daughters,
Mrs. Strasser, and a step-son. Strasser's name appears initially
in 1847, when he managed a new theater in Cincinnati. The following year he offered for sale 1500 German plays, with the roles written out. If not a bit of blague, this advertisement indicates at least
a passing acquaintance with an impressive amount of the repertory.
The Strassers stayed in Kentucky from October until March, 1851,
then moved to the deceptively greener fields of St. Louis. This
ephemeral venture was enlivened by Xaver's intoxications, but was
financially disappointing for the same reason. In the autumn, some
of the family wandered to Evansville, Indiana, where they opened its
first Liebhabertheater, an organization still functioning two years
later under the original direction.

At New Year, 1852, Boetzow and Magius rented the larger,
more professional Apollo Hall. Here the German theater flourished
until the frosts of August 5, 1855, the day of the election riots inspired by the Know Nothing party of the town. A casting of accounts printed in the Louisville Anzeiger of April 1, at the very
time when the coming political disturbances had already overshadowed
the boxoffice, discloses that during the preceding season Hensler's
Das Donauweibchen had been given nine successive performances and
Nestroy's Lumpaci Vagabundus four, frequently to houses unpleasant-
ly crowded. In all, ninety pieces were produced. Of the dramas,
ten out of twenty-six were new to the local public. Eleven new
comedies or farces were given from a total of twenty-six. Of other
types of productions, seven out of thirty-eight were novelties. This
record was made on a schedule that called for three performances
a week, with an outlay of between $800 and $900 a month. Writing
of these golden days four years afterwards, a correspondent of the
Westliche Blätter recalled that Boetzow allowed himself to be cheated
financially "from pure good nature and phlegm." For this reason,
or because the gathering clouds of Nativism foretold that conditions
would not improve, Boetzow embarked on an exploratory trip after
his benefit on June 2, 1855. He visited Indianapolis, Chicago, Milwaukee, St. Louis, and Burlington, then returned to Milwaukee,
there to be joined by his family. A contemporary tells us that he
undertook the job of director in "Deutsch-Athen" at $24 per month,
this modest salary being eked out by earnings as factotum for the
theater, poster of announcements, and wardrobe tailor.

Alas, intrigue again dogged his path. As a sympathetic historian puts it: "Boetzow had been kicked out in an extremely tact-
less manner...." And soon the little comedian's family was again
on the move, to come to rest at last in Williamsburgh under the sad
circumstances mentioned.

Boetzow's partner, Ernst Magius, was a different type. He
and his wife, Sophie Strasser Magius, are discovered in Milwaukee,
where both were active in starting the German theater. Rehearsing

the incidents of November, 1850, connected with a would-be charity
performance which turned into a series of bitter recriminations,
Rudolf H. Koss relates in his history of Milwaukee that the Magius
couple received $3.34 for writing out the roles and "for salary."
Before these unpleasant as well as unremunerative events, Mrs.
Magius had gathered her laurels as a singer and actress.

In Louisville she was soon described on benefit nights as a
woman dependent upon her own talents for her livelihood. The marriage ended formally on August 1, 1857, Ernst, during that summer,
having entered into what the press called a "romantisch ritterliches
Verhältnis" with Louisa Ehrler, while both were working at a small
summer theater operated in connection with his saloon by Franz
Ehrler, the lady's husband. The latter left town in haste for St.
Louis, when a heavy fine was imposed upon him for playing on Sunday. Apparently he expected his wife to follow at leisure. She
chose to travel with Magius in the opposite direction. In Cincinnati,
the confrontation of injured husband and romantic seducer then took
place, ending in a brawl. These and similar details made up what
the Anzeiger characterized with an inky leer as the "Chronic scan-
daleuse" of the year.

Although Magius had no less a man than Friedrich Hassaurek
for his lawyer, he was found guilty, jailed for thirty days on corn-
bread and water, and fined twenty dollars and costs. His former
wife later married Philipp Horwitz, an actor. By 1864 she was
back in Milwaukee enjoying the praise of the Wisconsin poetaster already quoted.

The chief rivals of Boetzow in Louisville had been the Thiele-
manns and the notorious Wilhelm von Adlersberg. Like Strasser,
Christian Thielemann brought his family down the river from Cincinnati. Louise Ehlers Thielemann, his wife and mentor, had belonged to a theatrical troupe at Cassel, Germany. By his alliance
with her, the husband had forfeited his career in the army of Hesse.
In New Orleans, on May 11, 1842, they enter the records. For the
next two years they acted in and directed (occasionally, Louise even
wrote) the German drama in the Crescent City. In 1844 they were
in Cincinnati, where their efforts established a professional German
playhouse. They played engagements in New Orleans, St. Louis,
and intermediate towns, and even as far west as Fort Leavenworth,
during the second half of the 'forties.

Unfortunately, at a later date (May 25, 1852) they were par-
takers in a ruction, a partial account of which is preserved. Mrs.
Hacke, a thespian in Thielemann's company, was discharged by von
Adlersberg, the stage manager, because, in an uncontrollable attack
of laughter, she had left the stage and would not return when ordered to do so. A week after her dismissal, Mrs. Hacke charged
the stage manager with assault. At the trial von Adlersberg took
offense at some of the testimony of Mrs. Thielemann; the offense
was carried from the courtroom to the theater, where Mr. Thielemann became involved. In the altercation he was stabbed by his

Theater: Characters   95

employee, who was then arrested. The press becoming perversely
reticent, the promised "rich developments" at the trial were lost.

Driven from Cincinnati by public indifference, the Thiele-
manns came downriver and re-opened Louisville's Washington Hall
theater, presenting classics and serious popular plays. Boetzow
negotiated a brief amalgamation of the companies. In 1856 Thielemann directed and acted in Baltimore. The next year he and his
wife were in Chicago, which proved to be the end of their extended
peregrinations. Christian resumed his military career as a Federal cavalry officer in 1861. His wife soon managed her own theater,
an institution of such vigor that it could be revived from the ashes
of the great fire, on Chicago's near north side.

Wilhelm von Adlersberg, the second party in the fracas in
Cincinnati, was a man of many and violent passions on stage and
off. For his use of the knife in the instance cited, he was sentenced to one year in jail; but a second trial resulted in his freedom, which he could enjoy with his wife, the former Miss Henriette
Fenner, the marriage having been performed in the jail.

An admirer has remarked that Adlersberg was often given
the sobriquet "Büffel-Fritz," not because he "büffelte" too many
roles, nor yet because of his marksmanship, but because a buffalo
hide was always the main prop in his wardrobe, whether it was actually worn, as in the title role of Halm's Der Sohn der Wildnis,
or simply used to recline upon in the Bohemian forest of Die
Räuber.

About this last piece, a further anecdote is told. During the
course of one of his guest appearances in New Orleans, Adlersberg
quarreled with the director, Adolph Icks, when the latter refused to
give up the role of Karl Moor, insisting that the guest play Franz.
The insulted actor cried: "If I must play Franz, I'll play Karl,
too!" which he proceeded to do. Since the excitement of this tour
de force brought on a hemorrhage, the performance was not repeat-
ed for reasons of health, not from artistic scruples. Further dam-
age to health is recorded in a dispatch from Baltimore during May,
1855, announcing that Adlersburg had been painfully burned by an ex-
ploding rocket, part of a too realistic portrayal of Faust's damnation.

Writing from Berlin in the eighteen-eighties, Wilhelm Müller
describes a tiny stage in Indianapolis upon which "gigantic Adlersberg, gifted with a powerful voice," had executed Tell's fateful shot
at the apple. Later in the drama, being ashamed to shoot his cross-
bow at such a short distance as the stage allowed, this Tell struck
down his enemy by a blow from the shaft of his weapon, which satisfied the spectators just as well.

Adlersberg was, indeed, in Indianapolis in February, 1856,
there earning the condemnation of the Freie Presse when he attempted to draw patronage away from the local Theaterverein by present-

ing Körner's Hedwig, die Banditenbraut two days before the Verein's
scheduled performance. When that failed to diminish their support,
he turned in a fire alarm while the amateurs were on stage, which,
as the newspaper commented, "obviously must have caused a dis-
turbance."

Before his death at Belleville, Illinois in 1859, Adlersberg
had served as a constable in Evansville, Indiana for six months and
then resigned; had been accused of murder, albeit unjustly, in Milwaukee; had been arrested in Cincinnati for beating his fifteen-year-
old sister-in-law; and had been arrested in Evansville for using
threatening language to an actress.

Of refreshingly different character were Mr. and Mrs. Heinrich Kenkel who came to Louisville in 1852 at Boetzow's invitation
after an unsuccessful concert there the previous year by Mrs. Kenkel alone. In Germany, Albertine Kenkel had been engaged at the
Hoftheater in Oldenburg. New York audiences learned to know and
appreciate her talents, as did those of the western towns. After the
political debacle in Kentucky, she and her husband joined the company in Milwaukee, whose poetic historiographer noted:

> Boetzow hat sich verdient gemacht,
> Dass er Herr und Frau Kenkel hat hergebracht.
> Frau Kenkel war der Buehne Stern,
> Und jeder im Publikum sah sie gern;
> Sie spielte sehr lieblich mit grosser Gewandtheit,
> Und es fehlte ihr durchaus nicht an
>   Buehnenbekanntheit.

Certainly she was a favorite of the press in Louisville. Even the
Daily Democrat of February 21, 1854 wrote about her performance:
"Madame Kenkel, the principal actress, was very happy in the rendering of her part. Besides being a very pretty woman, she is an
accomplished actress and excellent vocalist." This was praise indeed, as the English-language newspapers did not generally review
the German productions.

The only intimation of anything but enthusiastic appreciation
crowning her later efforts is found in a letter to the Westliche
Blätter of May 29, 1859. The writer bemoans the fact that Mrs.
Kenkel's unwillingness to mix with the local society leaders and exchange the chitchat of domesticity had abruptly terminated her stay
in Milwaukee.

While Heinrich Kenkel appeared on the stage in most of the
productions with his wife, his acting never rose above average. He
has left a valuable account of the founding of the German theater in
the Windy City. At Christmas, 1861, he entered the Union army.
His military career was a short one, he was back on the stage, after being wounded in action, when his daughter, Miss Clara Kenkel,
made her theatrical debut in Chicago some months later.

In 1863 Kenkel retired to devote his time to an insurance business. His wife continued to act until 1867, when she, too, withdrew to private life. It is the subsequent life of Clara Kenkel which provides the Cinderella-like aura to the ending of their story. She married Louis C. Huck, a wealthy brewer of Chicago. Their third child, christened Albertine, married Marshall Field II, a merchant prince, and became the mother of Marshall Field III.

In a devil's dictionary published in the Louisville Anzeiger under "Theater, deutsches in Amerika," the entry gives the cross-reference: "siehe unter Kinderbewahranstalt." The foregoing details indicate that the German American theater of the hinterland was less innocuous than that. They strengthen the suspicion that the lives of its personnel were more interesting than most of the plays which they tried to vivify.

9. CRITICISM OF THE GERMAN-AMERICAN THEATER IN MINNESOTA*

Hermann E. Rothfuss

Today it is hardly possible any longer to see a German theater performance anywhere in the United States, aside from an occasional college play, and yet it was not much more than one hundred years ago that German amateur theaters began to spring up wherever immigrants from German-speaking lands had settled in their new country. From the East Coast these stages began to spread into the interior, and soon they were found along the reaches of the Mississippi, in the Ohio soon they were found along the reaches of the Mississippi, in the Ohio valley, on the banks of the Missouri, in Texas, and on the shores of the Great Lakes.[1]

In the course of time a number of these theaters developed into professional stages; others at least employed professional managers; while again others remained largely or completely on an amateur basis, with now and then a professional actor, director, or group appearing upon the scene. The German stage in Minnesota belonged in the last-named category. The first German-language performance in St. Paul was given late in 1857, six months before Minnesota became a state. In January, 1858, the long-flourishing amateur theater in New Ulm was opened, and barely a year later another one was in existence at St. Anthony, now a part of Minneapolis. During the following twenty years German amateur stages came into being in more than twenty Minnesota communities. German newspapers, however, appeared at first only in three cities. In St. Paul a German newspaper began to appear in 1855, in New Ulm early in 1858, though Minneapolis, with a much smaller German population, had no paper until 1869. Their editors frequently were men of vigorous opinions. At least four of the early German editors in Minnesota had left the old country because of revolutionary activities, and a fifth one had been in the French Foreign Legion. Thus it is possible to gain an insight into early theater conditions, though even these men of strong opinion always had to watch their step very carefully as soon as they ventured into theater criticism. Because of their limited number of subscribers they could rarely afford to offend any of them to the point where they cancelled their subscriptions. Now and then an exasperated editor even let it be known that to spare the sensitivities of amateur actors and actresses his paper would refrain altogether from publishing critiques.

*Reprinted from the Germanic Review 27 (1952): 124-30, by permission of the publisher.

Samuel Ludvigh, a well-known German-American in his day, a man who had left Austria in the thirties because of his liberal convictions and who had published a number of German-language newspapers before he finally founded the Minnesota Staatszeitung in St. Paul, was averse to this silent treatment. In the very first issue of the new paper he started to impress the idea upon St. Paul theater lovers that an amateur stage was confronted by peculiar difficulties. He stressed the fact that amateur actors are not yet real artists. "But," he continued, "the amateur stage can be a school of art if it is headed by an efficient manager to whom the members of the ensemble owe obedience."[2]

This idea that theaters, even amateur theaters, are educational institutions, is brought out again and again. After the first performance in New Ulm it was expressly stated "that the New Ulm stage is an educational institution and will be strictly maintained as such."[3] This aim was also clearly, if somewhat haltingly, expressed in the dedication written for the opening of the second St. Paul season. Undoubtedly composed by a disciple of Schiller, it reads as follows:

> Wenn der Mensch durch dieses Lebens Sorgen,
> Schmerz und Mühen sich bedrücket fühlt;
> Wenn die rauhe Wirklichkeit des Geistes
> Und des Herzens Flügelschläge lähmt:
> Sind es Wissenschaft und Kunst, die ihn
> Durch die Zauberkraft des Wahren und
> Des Schönen in das Reich der Ideale
> Und des geistigen Genusses führen.[4]

Two years later, after an amateur ensemble had begun to play in St. Anthony, the German residents of the community were praised "for preparing the soil for real progress, open-minded endeavors, and interest in art."[5]

Ludvigh, who seems to have considered himself an expert in the field of the theater and even claimed that he had been introduced to it by Adolf Bäuerle, a famous Viennese theater director, was fully in sympathy with these aims, but he could clearly see the obstacles in their path. Therefore he first wanted to establish the right of newspapers to criticize amateurs:

> The fact that mistakes are made even on the best stages and by the most excellent actors demonstrates that criticism is an absolutely necessary tool for the protection of art.... But those people who are of the opinion that criticism is justified only in the case of professional stages seem to assume that the artistic value of a performance is dependent upon whether the playing is for pay or not.... We must insist that amateur theaters are in duty bound to perform as well as possible or else to close the show if the players are no good....[6]

A year later the Staatszeitung published even more incisive
remarks, this time undoubtedly from the pen of Albert Wolff, who
had taken part in the barricade fights in Dresden. After he had
spent some time in prison, with a death sentence over his head, he
was permitted to depart for America. When reviewing a performance of Die Räuber in 1860 he criticized it unusually sharply for
three reasons. First, he said, no part in a classical drama, not
even the smallest, should be played by a person who cannot fill it
satisfactorily. Secondly, a completely correct interpretation of characters like Karl and Franz Moor requires not only considerable talent but also an amount of study and rehearsal time which simply
cannot be given by people who do not concentrate upon acting as a
profession. Thirdly, if a masterpiece like Die Räuber is to be performed in a worthy manner it is necessary to have stage equipment,
decorations, and wardrobe in quantities rare in an amateur company. It could not possibly be expected of a new organization such
as the St. Paul German theater.

When Ludwig Bogen, editor of the New Ulm Post, wrote, a
few years later, about a performance of the same drama, he accepted the realities of the situation with a more resigned attitude. Bogen, who had been a member of the Frankfurt parliament and like
Wolff had spent some years in prison before coming to America,
stated quite frankly that he was not attempting to review amateur
performances regularly: "The reason is ... that we have not yet
discovered a criterion for evaluating a dramatic personnel deserving
greater praise for their endeavors than for their accomplishments as
actors."[7]

Finally the day came when the amateur players themselves
made it clear that they were not professionals and therefore did not
want to have a strict criterion applied to themselves. This was
brought out in a letter by St. Paul players to a Minneapolis paper:
"The German Society gives its performances for the purpose of nur-
turing dramatic art; for the instruction of its members in a field
that is still alien to them; and for the entertainment of the public.
For this the players are entitled to the forbearance of their fellow
citizens, not to criticism such as was directed against them."[8]

Sometimes the papers directed their criticism not only
against the players, but also against the public itself. At one time,
for instance, the audience was sharply attacked for not acting as a
sounding board:

> The actor, the speaker, and the author must consider the
> public as an indispensable cooperator. Without its under-
> standing, its participation, its appreciation, their force
> and their enthusiasm are broken and their labor is lost.
> But the public in America and especially here in the West
> has its head so full of the almighty dollar, or at best of
> politics ... that its understanding of the elevated, noble,
> and grand ideals of the classical drama is cold and dead
> .... Only a few ... show that they are really moved by

the play.... In the faces of others we see only too clearly an expression of 'I don't care' or 'None of my business. '
Pity the actors if they observe it, too![9]

Even the public that did not attend was attacked for this very
reason. When some professional actors came to St. Paul and did
not draw satisfactory audiences the reviewer indulged in bitter ac-
cusations. "What about the reputation of the Germans of St. Paul
will acquire if excellent German actors do not find better support
than they did yesterday?"[10] he concluded. Finally, to cite just one
more example of criticism directed against the public, we also must
ponder the distich composed by a thoroughly aroused theater critic
when the attendance did not measure up to expectations:

> Nennen sich prahlend auch noch ein Volk der Dichter und
>   Denker,
> Steht doch die Literatur hinter dem Biere bei ihm.[11]

Inevitably the question must be asked whether the critics
sought to influence the type of plays offered by the amateurs. There
is evidence to show that they did. When Schiller's Kabale und Liebe
was played in New Ulm the players were reminded that they had
striven for heights that were too steep for their powers. Not long
afterwards, on the other hand, the editor expressly gave his approval to pieces of the lighter genre: "Comedies with a lively action,
an interesting dialogue, and a quick development are splendidly
suited for relatively small amateur theaters such as ours."[12] It is
a matter of record that for years afterwards the New Ulm theater
concentrated almost exclusively upon comedies, farces, and tableaux.

The German-American paper in Minneapolis originally also
was in favor of light offerings. At one point the reviewer considered it his duty to remind the amateurs that severely classical
pieces were not suited for the Minneapolis stage. "They are understood only with difficulty and therefore are not appreciated according
to their real value," he commented. "Dramas of the extraordinary
length of Kabale und Liebe are perhaps least suited of all, because
they are too much of a test for the patience of the public....
Lighter pieces will always produce a more favorable effect."[13]

However, after the paper was headed by a new editor, who
was personally greatly interested in directing and playing, its attitude changed and the presentation of classical dramas was vigorously
defended. "We do not have to be told that amateurs cannot perform
these dramas in an exemplary manner," the paper commented. "Yet
we believe it is of great value to have them put before the public in
a country where the majority of Germans is not familiar with even
the most prominent works of our German authors."[14] The article
concludes with the interesting statement that a performance of Don
Carlos in St. Paul had resulted in the sale of forty copies of the
drama by the German bookstore in that city. Whether the article
had anything to do with it or not, the fact remains that after years
of theatrical fare composed almost entirely of light pieces, the

Minneapolitans were now given an opportunity to see in relatively
short succession five dramas by Schiller, including Wilhelm Tell,
Die Räuber, Wallensteins Lager, Maria Stuart, and Don Carlos
(some of them repeatedly); Goethe's Faust; Shakespeare's Othello
and Hamlet (in German); and plays by Bauernfeld and Gutzkow.

So far the attitude of the critics towards the duties of the
stage, towards the players, toward the public, and toward the various genres has been discussed. What was their attitude towards individual writers? Today the names of the authors of many of the
plays performed in those days are barely known to the specialist.
But even a number of dramatists whose names are not completely
eclipsed yet are hardly ever represented on the stage any longer.
Kotzebue, once more famous in the United States than Goethe and
Schiller; Theodor Körner, once one of the favorites in German-
American playhouses; Mosenthal, Brachvogel, Raupach, Holtei--who
considers them prominent today? Not to speak of the once omnipresent Birch-Pfeiffer!

It is interesting to see their stars wane even in the pages of
German-American newspapers between 1860 and 1880. Kotzebue,
to be sure, was condemned from the beginning. Ludvigh branded
his products as having almost no literary value. In Minneapolis
some years later the idea was repeatedly expressed that Kotzebue
"belonged to an older generation" and "need not be drawn upon."[15]
Körner also was the recipient of early barbs. His characters were
accused of walking "partly on stilts and partly in slippers."[16]

Samuel Raupach, a writer of many plays, also was consistently rejected. When his drama Der Müller und sein Kind oder Die
Totenschau in der Weihnachtsnacht was shown in 1861, the Minnesota critic remarked that "the subject matter of the play was alien
to the spirit and the philosophy of the present.... It is no wonder
that the spectators finally no longer ask 'How is it going to end,'
but 'When is it going to end?' Thank Goodness our public has out-
grown this kind of horror and emotion." Ten years later we read
again that Raupach's dramas "belong to a theater period that per-
ished with the generation that produced it. His language, his emotions, his effects, affectations, and views no longer enjoy the appreciation of our more practical days."[17]

Charlotte Birch-Pfeiffer, once extremely popular, loses her
dramatic reputation before our eyes. In 1860 her play Hinko der
Freiknecht was called "a drama of powerful effects, boldly developing action, and superb diction ... full of beautiful sentiments."
The author was called "one of the most famous writers of modern
times." But sixteen years later a review contains the following
judgment: "Good Birch-Pfeiffer delivers endless explanations about
what already happened instead of showing us red-blooded natural
controversies."[18]

Holtei, also once a prominent playwright, was praised and
condemned within a very short time. In 1861 one of his plays was

called "a magnificent product of talented Holtei's pen, worthy of his
Leonore," but barely a year later it was admitted that the latter
play had disappeared from the stage in Germany long ago. The reviewer also considered it somewhat unwise to transplant this drama
to Minnesota, since it had been written only to glorify Frederick the
Great.[19]

Brachvogel's Narciss, long considered a drama of great literary merit, also fell into popular disfavor. In 1872 it could still
be called "the most outstanding dramatic production of our days."
But in 1877 the point was reached where the audience concluded that
Narciss was a fool, and gave vent to its feelings, so that some fine
points of the performance were lost.[20]

Mosenthal also was a bright star whose rays became quickly
dimmed. When his drama Deborah, die edle Jüdin was played in
1861, it was proclaimed "a masterwork of German culture by an author who in the opinion of the best critics is almost the equal of
Schiller." Later, however, when one of his village plays was given,
there was a lack of enthusiasm on the part of the spectators which
the reviewer explained by saying that "the peculiarities of Westphalian peasants ... cannot arouse great sympathy in the hearts of our
free-thinking native-born people."[21] This, by the way, seems to indicate that German plays were also attended by members of the second generation.

It is perhaps no injustice to say that in the lean years between the middle of the century and the coming of the Naturalists
only one dramatist appeared upon the German scene whose fame has
survived the years. This man was Anzengruber, and it is a pleasure to report that he was immediately applauded in Minnesota. "The
piece with all its details and in the broad dialect of Upper Austria
enters irresistibly into the heart of the listener," said a St. Paul paper of Der Pfarrer von Kirchfeld. "The part of the priest is a mon-
umental masterpiece "[22]

Generally speaking, the literary value of classical plays was
taken for granted, though only works by Schiller, and perhaps
Goethe's Faust, were played more than occasionally. Kleist, Grillparzer, and Hebbel were hardly ever performed, although in justice
to German-American theaters it must be said that theaters even in
Germany had a tendency to neglect these authors. Kleist's Käthchen
von Heilbronn drew only the comment "that the profoundest expectations were satisfied. The play was good, the costumes were magnificent." Fifteen years later Hebbel's Genoveva was described as
being based on a story "that has been dear to the German people for
centuries.... No villain was ever more despised than Golo, and
thus the piece finds many admirers again and again."[23]

Occasionally, though perhaps hesitantly, criticism is actually
directed against Schiller, by far the most popular of the classical
authors. One writer carefully called Wilhelm Tell "the beautiful
work of a great poet" and then went on to subject not only the players

but also the play itself to an unfavorable review: "The title role is
by no means the main role ... the famous monologue is too long by
half."[24] He also believed that the feminine sex was neglected in
the plot and the loving couple was added only because the public tra-
ditionally had the right to expect that at least one couple in a play
made love to each other.

After a performance of The Merchant of Venice (in German)
Shakespeare fared even less well, and here the criticism sounds
strangely modern. "Among comedies 'Shylock' is undoubtedly one
of the best," said the reviewer. "But it is unfortunate that Shakespeare here gave vent to the hatred of Jews which in his days was
very pronounced.... The story of the pound of flesh actually did
happen in Venice, but it was a Christian who wanted to cut, and a
Jew who was to lose his flesh...." The critic humbly ended his
review by describing himself as "one who can criticize but cannot
do better."[25]

We have now seen, by means of a few examples selected out
of many, how critics dealt with the German-American stage in Minnesota. If they failed to lift the theater to a higher level they suffered a fate that befell greater critics before them. We need only
think of Lessing and his Hamburgische Dramaturgie. At least they
did their duty as they saw it.

Notes

1. Hermann E. Rothfuss, "The Beginnings of the German-Ameri-
       can Stage," The German Quarterly, XXIV (1951), 93-102.
2. Minnesota Staatszeitung, July 28, 1858.
3. New Ulm Pionier, Jan. 22, 1858.
4. Minnesota Staatszeitung, Dec. 18, 1858.
5. Ibid., July 14, 1860.
6. Ibid., Nov. 27, 1858.
7. New Ulm Post, June 19, 1866.
8. Minneapolis Freie Press, Sept. 15, 1877.
9. Minnesota Staatszeitung, July 7, 1860.
10. Ibid., June 7, 1870.
11. Minneapolis Freie Presse, Oct. 21, 1875.
12. New Ulm Post, Oct. 14, 1864; Dec. 3, 1864.
13. Minneapolis Freie Presse, Dec. 4, 1875.
14. Ibid., Feb. 14, 1880.
15. Minnesota Staatszeitung, Dec. 31, 1859; Minneapolis Freie
       Presse, Oct. 18, 1873; March 15, 1879.
16. Minnesota Staatszeitung, June 22, 1861.
17. Ibid., Dec. 23, 1861; April 2, 1872.
18. Ibid., Feb. 11, 1860; Volksblatt, Oct. 12, 1876.
19. Minnesota Staatszeitung, Oct. 19, 1861; Dec. 27, 1862.
20. Ibid., June 22, 1872; Volksblatt, Dec. 4, 1877.
21. Minnesota Staatszeitung, Sept. 7, 1861; Minneapolis Freie Presse,
       April 10, 1878.
22. St. Paul Volkszeitung, June 20, 1879.

23. Minnesota Staatszeitung, Oct. 15, 1872; St. Paul Volkszeitung,
        Nov. 1887.
24. Volksblatt, Dec. 21, 1876.
25. Minneapolis Freie Presse, March 14, 1881.

PART V

GERMAN-AMERICAN AUTHORS:
AN OVERVIEW

10. JOHANN CONRAD BEISSEL, COLONIAL MYSTIC POET*

Dennis McCort

Anyone who has read Thomas Mann's novel, Doktor Faustus, could not fail to be impressed by the austere but charismatic figure of Conrad Beissel, the eighteenth-century founder and patriarch of the Ephrata cloister in Lancaster County, Pennsylvania. In the novel, the musicologist Kretzschmar mentions in one of his lectures that his father had often heard the entrancing church music at Snowhill, a sister community of Ephrata. Comparing it with European opera, Kretzschmar's father had said of the latter, "das sei Musik für das Ohr gewesen, die Beissels aber ein Klang tief in die Seele und nicht mehr noch minder als ein Vorgeschmack des Himmels."[1] If Conrad Beissel composed music for the soul, it can also be said that he never wrote a poem which did not in some way depict either the plight of the soul in this life or its beatified existence in the next.

Beissel has often drawn the interest of scholars as a mystic, a theosopher, a musician, and a religious organizer. As a poet he has received scant recognition. The few critics who have read Beissel's poetry have read it superficially and then have usually dismissed it as being too long and too much. However, if the sensitive reader allows himself to look beyond the common afflictions which Beissel's lyrics share with most Pietistic poetry--the occasional run-on hymn, the stock image, the banal rhyme--to the panoramic soul-scape spun out in his hundreds of hymns, each hymn another strand in a meticulously wrought spiritual tapestry, he will find himself in the presence of a mystic imagination rivalling that of Jakob Böhme and Meister Eckhart. It will be my purpose here to survey the corpus of Beissel's religious poetry from three perspectives: first, to elucidate its general content and form; then, to flesh out this explication with a much-needed outline of some of Beissel's artistic and intellectual links with the past; finally, to consider his mystical-poetic vision of America, the New Zion.

Born in Ebersbach in the Palatine region of Germany in 1690, Beissel grew up in circumstances of extreme poverty, which proved to be excellent conditioning for the life of severe asceticism he was to pursue later on.[2] A baker by trade, he was largely self-taught and gained familiarity with the various separatistic religious move-

*Reprinted from German-American Studies 8 (1974): 1-26, by permission of the publisher.

ments from his wanderings through Germany. Shortly after 1715 he
settled in Heidelberg where he rose to the position of treasurer of
the Baker's Guild and moved with ease among Pietistic circles. His
most notable acquaintance there was a Pietist by the name of Haller
who was a friend of Johann Georg Gichtel, a zealous student of
Böhme. [3] Beissel's inflexible honesty as treasurer of the Baker's
Guild moved the members to search for a pretext by which to dis-
pose of him. Using his extremist Pietistic leanings to that end,
they promptly succeeded in getting him banned from the city. [4] He
wandered through the areas of Wittgenstein, Berleburg, and Büdin-
gen, all havens for separatistic sects at that time. [5] However, his
impoverished condition and his disillusionment with the organized
churches soon led him to set his sights on America, the new land of
religious toleration.

        In 1720 Beissel arrived in Boston and immediately made his
way to Germantown. [6] His first association in the New World was
with Johannes Kelpius' monastic community on the outskirts of Germantown. But the community was by that time in its dying stages
and Beissel severed his connection with it after a short time. [7] In
1725 he became pastor of a German Baptist congregation at Cones-
toga. [8] Continually at odds with the headquarters congregation in
Germantown, he resigned his pastorship in 1732 and retired in seclusion to the village of Ephrata on the banks of the Cocalico. [9]
Beissel's reputation for piety and asceticism soon gained him many
followers and the embryonic community rapidly developed into a
thriving religious institution.

        Under Beissel's spiritual inspiration and creative leadership
Ephrata became and remained one of the most important colonial
centers of artistic activity until well after its founder's death in
1768. The more gifted of the brothers and sisters excelled in the
composition of hymns, the illumination of manuscripts, and the
printing of important theological works. According to John F. Watson, the Ephrata press printed more original literary works than
any other in the union at that time, and many families in the Philadelphia and Baltimore areas sent their children to Ephrata to be educated. [10]

        Beissel himself was a prolific musician-poet who wrote, as
nearly as I can estimate, about seven-hundred hymns. Perhaps the
most consistent theme in the vast body of his poetry is that of renunciation of the world and its material allurements. Particularly
in his early hymns, such as the collection Jacobs Kampff- und Ritter-Platz (1736), this theme is expressed in vigorous, robust metaphors portraying the heroic nature of the struggle to overcome one's
involvement in the world. The believer is the knightly warrior on
the battlefield of earthly existence whose mission it is to storm and
conquer the fortress of self-will and wordly attractions:

                Kommt ihr glaubenskämpffer,
                Und ihr sünden-dämpffer,
                Kommt und sehet eure kronen!

Es ist euch gelungen,
Weil der feind bezwungen,
Nun da habt ihr euren lohne. [11]

The terse, staccato trochaic verses sonorously reflected the ferocity
of the battle and highlight the boldness of the faithful warriors whom
the poet summons to their reward. The poem is a typical example
of Beissel's extensive use of martial images to express an inner
spiritual process or activity. To Beissel the process of cutting
oneself off from the world in order to achieve the proper receptive
disposition for the in-dwelling of the Divine Spirit is an inward-going one that entails entering into the self and ridding the consciousness of all material images and ties. In the above poem, as in
many others of the Jacobs Kampff- und Ritter-Platz, Beissel employs the imagery of external social conflict--the battlefield, wrestling with the enemy, soldiers of the spirit, deeds of valor--in order to dramatize and make comprehensible to his charges at Ephrata
this internal process of self-purgation:

Wo die helden thaten
Einmal sind gerahten,
Da kan man es weiter wagen.
In dem kampffe ringen,
Seine feind bezwingen,
Biss sie alle sind geschlagen. [12]

When the believer has totally withdrawn into himself, he is
in the state of Eingekehrtheit, a condition of perfect inner calm affording spiritual rejuvenation much akin to the yogi's meditative
trance. Beissel often compares tranquil spiritual state to the satisfaction of a physiological need:

Dann wann mein Hertz ermüdet auf den Wegen
so führ mich Gott in meine Kammer ein:
und speiset mich mit reichem Trost und Segen,
und träncket mich mit seinem Guten Wein. [13]

At other times he uses the metaphor of the isolated garden:

Ich bin ein verschlossner Garten,
Achte nicht, was ausser mir. [14]

But the poet does not always fall back on the external to represent
the internal. Occasionally he attempts to describe this inward-going
process directly, without the aid of concrete, mediating images:

Drum thu ich täglich in mir spüren,
Dass er [God] mich thut hinein werts führen,
Da ich genie verborgne krafft,
Die meinem hertzen leben schafft. [15]

Although Beissel did not hold with the practice of self-inflicted
bodily pain as a means of purging the flesh (a grim tactic of many

mystics of the past) he did demand of himself and his charges at
Ephrata the cultivation of an extremely severe asceticism.   The
world is an obstacle to the soul in its quest for God, and one must
therefore strive to blot it out of one's awareness completely.   The
consciousness is always to be directed either inward or upward,
never outward:

> Mein Leben ist zwar ausgeleert
> von Bildern und von Weisen;
> doch ist mein Hertz zu Gott gekehrt,
> lässt sich von nichts abreissen. [16]

The theme of renunciation finds its most compelling expression in the concept of the mystical death, a figurative dying to this
world as a precondition for attaining the next:

> O Wol! wer hier bey Zeit der eitlen Welt absaget,
> der wird alldorten nicht vom andern Tod genaget. [17]

The poet sometimes imagines himself as existing in a state of frus-
trating transition between the earthly and the divine realms.   He
has forsaken the former but can only anticipate the latter.

> Die alte Welt ist hin, die neu hat noch zu werden:
> drum bleib in beyden arm, so lang ich leb auf Erden[18]

Beissel's poetry is replete with melancholic verse lamenting
the inadequacy of earthly existence to fulfill man's deepest needs:

> Die Tage gehen hin, die Zeit kan mir nicht geben,
> Was mich vergnügen kan alldort in jener Welt. [19]

Particularly in the Theosophische Gedichte (1752) he lapses into a
morose introspectiveness, wistfully brooding over the trials and
tribulations of one who travels die enge Bahn.   Only the hope of a
higher and better existence can provide some measure of peace to
the troubled soul:

> Ich muss zwar stetig schweben
> In vielem Weh und Leid;
> Doch wird die Hoffnung geben
> Den Frieden nach dem Streit. [20]

It is this sustaining hope that enables the poet to perceive the salu-
tary effects of suffering and to view human suffering as a positive
good:

> Meine Schmertzen, die ich leide,
> Tragen mich zu Gott dahin:
> Sind des Geistes süsste Weide,
> Enden sich mit viel Gewinn. [21]

Viewed in this light, self-denial and suffering become a kind of

spiritual currency. The more we can amass in this life, the higher
will be our reward in the next:

> Trage ich schon manche Lasten
> Auf dem Weg zu Gott hinan:
> Werd ich so viel süsser rasten,
> Wann sich öffnet Canaan. [22]

  The opening hymn of the Turtel-Taube (1747), the first great
hymnal of the Ephrata press, incorporates most of the themes and
images discussed above. The progression of thought and feeling in
this poem of ten stanzas points up the didactic tendency in much of
the Ephrata-patriarch's religious poetry. The first four stanzas
comprise a discouraged lament in which the poet bewails the cease-
less hardships and temptations that assail the soul as it gropes its
way along the narrow path:

> Ach Gott! wie mancher bittrer Schmertz
> durchdringet meinen Geist und Hertz,
> hier in dem Leib der Sterblichkeit,
> auf meinem Weg zur Seligkeit. [23]

The hopeful outlook and clarity of vision often become clouded as
the spirit vacillates between peace and turmoil, confidence and
doubt:

> Der enge Weg ist zwar gebahnt,
> worzu uns Jesus angemahnt:
> doch ist so vieler Drang dabey,
> als ob er zugeschlossen sey. [24]

In the fifth stanza the emotional fluctuation begins to diminish as the
tone becomes firm and positive. The poet marvels at the simul-
taneous dwindling of sensory attachments and expansion of spiritual
awareness as the soul is purified:

> Wie klein und niedrig wird der Sinn,
> der auf demselben [engen Weg] gehet hin!
> Wie rein und sauber wird der Geist,
> der diesen Weg zu Gott hinreist. [25]

Having described in stanza five how the senses and the soul are in-
versely affected in the process of purifying transformation, Beissel
assumes the tone of the spiritual pedagog in the next four stanzas
and tells us what we must do to effect this transformation:

> Wo gantz ertödet die Natur,
> da findet man erst diese Spuhr
> zum Himmelsreich....[26]

Here Beissel has named the second formidable enemy of man in his
quest for God--Natur. If man's first great enemy is the world and
its material seductions, his second is his own nature which, in Beis-

sel's view, is essentially weak and corrupt.   Unillumined human nature is identical with self-interest and individual desire, which is
the source of evil.   A man who allows himself to be dominated by
the self lives in Finsternis.   Conversely, when the soul is filled with
God's love, "so gehet ... ein Licht in dem Menschen auf, da sein
verfinsterter Verstand erleuchtet wird."27   Just as even in this life
man must die to the world in order to be saved, so too must he
transcend his own depraved nature and his enslavement to self-interest.   Beissel asserts this in stanza eight:

> Ein Geist, der rein, wie Gold bewährt,
> und lauterlich Gott zugekehrt,
> erstorben allem Ich und Mein,
> der geht zur engen Pforte ein.28

It is in this sense that Beissel consistently uses expressions in his
poetry like "meiner selbst entladen" and "mir selbst entwerden."
The poem ends on a typically triumphant note, the poet asserting his
own freedom from the self:

> Drum freue dich mein müder Geist,
> der du bist aus dir selbst gereist.29

        By undergoing the mystical death man attunes himself to the
Divine.   Those who are uninitiated in the mystical experience have
extreme difficulty in grasping Beissel's conception of the Divinity.
Experienced by the expanded mystical consciousness as a noumenal
being, God is beyond the grasp even of metaphoric language.   He is
simply das Unaussprechliche.   Nevertheless, Beissel attempts to
convey his experience of God and his longing for union with the Infinite Being in hymn number 298 of the Paradisisches Wunderspiel
(1766), the last and largest Ephrata hymnal.   The sweeping continuity
of rhythm and the internal rhyme contribute to a mood bordering on
ecstatic anticipation of the poet's wish-fulfillment:

> O Ungrund! der gewesen
> von Ewigkeiten her
> mach mich in dir genesen,
> damit, was um mich her
> mich ja nicht mehr entführe
> von deiner Wesenheit,
> noch anderwerts abirre
> durch einig Ding der Zeit. 30

God is the Ungrund, the Abyss, the Infinity, defying all attempts at
description or definition.   Still, the poet feels compelled to share his
vision and, as always, must resort to those material images which,
by virtue of their sheer colossal breadth, bear the closest phenome-
nal resemblance to infinity.   In stanza four Beissel likens God to a
boundless sea and expresses his longing for union in terms of complete submersion into its depths:

> Drum lasse dich erbitten:
> o bodenloses Meer!
> bring mich in deine Mitte,
> da du seyst um mich her. [31]

In stanza five the poet acknowledges God as the source of all material creation and implies in the maternal invocation that sexuality
is a meaningless material distinction when applied to the Infinite Being:

> O Mutter aller Dinge!
> Kleid mich in dich hinein;
> und in dein Wesen bringe,
> es wird bald anders seyn. [32]

Scholars such as Walter Klein[33] and E. Ernest Stoeffler[34]
have well established the influence of Jakob Böhme on Beissel's
theosophical writings. Undoubtedly, Beissel's mystico-poetic conception of God as the Ungrund and many of the images he uses in
his poetry to represent this abstraction stem from Böhme's theosophy. In discussing Böhme's concept of the Being that exists outside
of time, Rufus Jones says:

> This infinite Mother of all births, this eternal Matrix, he
> [Böhme] calls the Ungrund, 'Abyss,' or the 'Great Mys-
> tery,' or the 'Eternal Stillness.' Here we are beyond be-
> ginnings, beyond time, beyond 'nature,' and we can say
> nothing in the language of reason that is true or adequate
> .... It is an absolute Peace, an indivisible Unity, an un-
> differentiated One--an Abysmal Deep, which no name can
> adequately name and which can be described in no words
> of time and space, of here and now. [35]

Beissel must have realized that these highly rarefied verbal
symbols of God were too cold and abstract to provide the less mystically inclined brothers and sisters of Ephrata with the necessary
spiritual nourishment. For most of the members there was little
sense of communion to be gained from contemplating the vague, neb-
ulous Abyss. It appealed to the intellect and the intuitive sense but
not to the heart. A much more concrete and comprehensible being
was needed, one that would have greater human appeal as an object
of religious devotion. We find this being in Beissel's poetry in the
figure of die göttiche Sophia, often referred to as die himmlische
Weisheit.

A detailed account of Sophia's place in Beissel's theosophy
would take us too far afield, since my primary concern here is
with her dominant position in his poetry. Nevertheless, a brief
word of explanation will help greatly to clarify her meaning. For
Beissel Sophia is a virgin of divine stature who occupies a position
equal in rank to the Persons of the Trinity. As Beissel explains in
his theosophical treatise, Urständliche und Erfahrungsvolle Hohe
Zeugnüsse... (1745), Adam had been united with Sophia as long as

the harmony of his androgynous nature remained undisturbed. But
his Fall caused a breach in the male-female balance and a separation from Sophia which man has been trying to repair ever since.
Sophia hovers near every human being, hoping to win him for herself, but man cannot effect the reunion by his own power. Only by
mystically uniting himself to Christ, who is the perfect embodiment
of the male-female principle and is both Son and Bridegroom of Sophia, does man become spiritually capable of reunion with Sophia,
his original Bride. [36]

Beissel composed innumerable hymns in which Sophia appears
as the focus of all his longing for transcendence. His anticipation
of reunion with his Bride sustains him in the midst of his earthly
ordeal:

> Mein Glück wird schon erscheinen
> auf meinem Hochzeit-Tag,
> muss ich schlon oft jetzt weinen
> bey so viel Ungemach:
> nach vielem Schmertz und Quälen,
> und so viel bittrem Leid,
> wird sie sich mir vermählen
> in jener Ewigkeit. [37]

In Beissel's theosophy Sophia is a goddess and as such commands man's highest esteem and reverence. In many hymns the poet invokes her as a transcendental force capable of elevating his
spirit above the material world to her own sphere of cosmic harmony:

> O Sophia! du reines Licht
> und Glantz der Ewigkeiten:
> wer dir vermählt, kan ewig nicht
> mehr fallen oder gleiten.
> Dein Adel hat mich dir verwandt,
> weil ich verliebet worden
> dass aller Welt wurd unbekant
> durch deinen hohen Orden. [38]

Just as often, however, the paradoxical relationship between the
erotic and the spiritual in the mystical temperament is revealed as
the poet describes his intimate communion with Sophia in erotic language befitting the most earthly of lovers. Devotion to her pre-
cludes natural marriage, and all the libidinal energy which the poet
has learned to suppress in his cultivation of the celibate life becomes sublimated and directed toward Sophia, his Divine Beloved:

> Der weiszheit liebeström erquicken meine sinnen
> Tränckt mich an ihrer brust, zieht meinen geist von hinnen. [39]

The figure of Sophia has a long history in the Western mystical tradition extending back to the book of Proverbs in the Old Testament. There she is called "Wisdom" and is the personification of

justice, righteousness, and understanding, which men have forsaken.
John Joseph Stoudt traces the history of Sophia in the Christian era
from Philo and the Neo-Platonic tradition through such medieval
mystics as Bernard of Clairvaux to Böhme and Gottfried Arnold.[40]
Beissel's own concept of Sophia is probably derived from Böhme.
According to Hans Lassen Martensen, Böhme regards Sophia as the
Bride of Adam before the Fall to whom he became unfaithful.[41]
She is also indissolubly wedded to Christ, who is the Second Adam
and is to restore her to man.[42]   Theosophically, Beissel's concept
of Sophia is identical with Böhme's so that it seems not out of place
to regard Beissel's Sophia-hymns as to the lyrical expression of
Böhme's prose.

I have enumerated what appear to me to be the dominant
themes in Beissel's poetry: renunciation, asceticism, and human
suffering; the necessity of attaining the state of Eingekehrtheit; the
evil inherent in the self; God as he is conceived in the abstract and
represented in the concrete; and the cult of Sophia.   A few words
now on Beissel as a stylist will round out my survey.

As a poet-craftsman Beissel was quite versatile.   He was
adept at most of the traditional lyrical forms and metrical patterns.
His verse ranges from terse, clipped iambic dimeter to Langzeilen
of up to seven accented syllables; from the elevated Alexandrine
quatrain to the simple folksong strophe; from the short, pregnant
epigrammatic couplet to the long lyric stanza.   In his chronicle,
Ephrata. Eine amerikanische Klostergeschichte, Oswald Seidensticker hurls the following charge at Beissel as a stylist: "Beissel,
der bei weitem die meisten Lieder lieferte [among the Ephrata breth-
ren], schrieb zu viel und zu handwerksmässig.   Der ehemalige
Bäcker knetete seine Verse als stände er am Backtroge und schob
Strophe an Strophe, als gälte es so viel Laib Brod zu machen."[43]
There is no denying a degree of truth in Seidensticker's accusation.
Beissel's meters are at times forced and contrived, and he uses certain standard rhymes with such frequency that they become all too
predictable: e.g., "das keusche Lamm ... der Bräutigam," "die
Gottesfülle ... die ewige Stille," "die Schmertzen im Hertzen."
One searches in vain for a thread of unity in some of the longer
hymns which contain more than thirty stanzas.

However, certain mitigating factors might be mentioned which
partially explain, if not vindicate, Beissel's stylistic flaws.   He had
had very little formal schooling and probably had little more than a
rudimentary knowledge of the prescriptive poetic of his day.   His
foremost purpose was always to communicate his mystical vision to
those who believed as he did, and he was not averse to forcing a
metrical pattern or using a hackneyed rhyme to achieve his end.
The phenomenon of Ephrata's longevity as a vital religious community is proof of his admirable success.   Furthermore, Beissel was
also a gifted composer and a unique one, having invented his own
system of musical notation.   His unorthodox theories of harmony,
which he explains in detail in the preface to the Turtel-Taube, are
doubtless at least partially responsible for the unbending rigidity of

his meters. [44] In any case, most of his poems are also hymns of
his own composition, which means that the musical factor must be
taken into account in any comprehensive evaluation of Beissel as an
artist.

Moreover, one should not let Beissel's shortcomings as a
stylist blind one to his strengths in the same area.   Examples of
bland imagery and humdrum meter can be countered with bursts of
true poetic inspiration.   Numerous lyrics can be cited in which language, meter, rhythm, and idea evolve as an inextricable unity.
Consider, for example, the first stanza of hymn number sixteen in
the Paradisisches Wunderspiel, in which Beissel consoles the brethren by pointing to the imminent end of their time of suffering:

> Bald gehen zu ende die traurige Stunden,
> betrübete Seelen, die Gott sich verbunden;
> die öffters gesessen in mancherley Drang,
> und vielen Weh-Tagen statt Lobens-Gesang. [45]

The tripping amphibrachs and feminine endings in the first two verse-
es establish the joyful anticipatory mood of a rapidly approaching
end to the hours of sadness, while a sudden, contrasting static effect is achieved in verses three and four through the heavy masculine rhyme Drang and Gesang, emphasizing the seemingly endless
suffering of the past.   Consider how the poet's apocalyptic rapture
is so contagiously conveyed by the high-pitched vowel sounds and by
the rhythmic flow of liquids and sibilants in hymn number seven,
stanza one, Paradisisches Wunderspiel:

> Ach verzeuch doch länger nicht,
> meine Seel, erheb dich wieder:
> siehe wie das Dunckle bricht,
> darum singe deine Lieder. [46]

Notice finally, how the poet elsewhere makes the fullest use of
dizzying amphibrachs and liquid sounds to express the dynamic, bit-
ter-sweet vacillation of the spirit between this world and the next:

> Wir loben Freuden, und lieben in Leiden:
> und leben auf Erden in himmlischer Freud. [47]

It should be clear from the foregoing discussion that, although
Beissel spent almost half his life in the contemplative seclusion of
the Ephrata community, his thinking and creative work were by no
means carried on in intellectual isolation.   Unfortunately, the dearth
of biographical evidence makes it difficult to single out specific influences of other poets on Beissel.   As far as I can ascertain, neither the Chronicon Ephratense, which is the most authentic account
of Beissel's life, nor Beissel's prose writings yields any information as to his poetic models.   Nevertheless, internal evidence alone
leads one to suspect that Beissel patterned the Alexandrine couplets
in the collection, Mystische und sehr geheyme Sprueche (1730), on
those of another mystic and devotee of Böhme, Angelus Silesius. [48]

A comparison of Beissel's <u>Sprueche</u> with those in Silesius' Cherub-
inischer Wandersmann reveals several arresting parallels in theme
and style.   Both poets proclaim the paradoxical mystical death as
the way to eternal life:

> S. : Indem der weise Mann zu tausendmalen stirbet,
>   Er durch die Wahrheit selbst um tausend Leben wirbet. [49]

> B. : Wilt leben du in Gott, so much du erst verderben,
>   Der beste glantz u. schein, musz gantz in der ersterben. [50]

Complete withdrawal into the self enables one to establish closer
contact with God:

> S. : Wer in sich selber sitzt, der höret Gottes Wort,
>   Vernein es, wie du willst, auch ohne Zeit und Ort. [51]

> B. : Geh in der seelen grund, aus allen weltgetümmel,
>   So findest du in dir den stillen Gottes-Himmel. [52]

We must break the chains of enslavement to the self; possession of
God and love of self are mutually exclusive:

> S. : Wer sich verloren hat und von sich selbst entbunden,
>   Der hat Gott, seinen Trost und seinen Heiland, funden. [53]

> B. : Wer Gott besitzen will, der musz sich selber lassen,
>   Dann wer sich selbst besitzt, kan Gott nicht in sich fassen.[54]

Both poets delight in exploiting the contrapuntal qualities inherent in
the structure of the Alexandrine couplet.   Half-lines stand poised
against each other in the tense interplay of verbal paradox:

> S. : Die Armut ist ein Schatz, dem keine Schätze gleichen.
>   Der ärmste Mensch im Geist hat mehr als alle Reichen. [55]

> B. : Das ist der Reichste mensch, der ärmste von begehren,
>   Wer sich darinnen find't, den kan kein ding beschweren. [56]

Although both poets are mystics within a general Böhmian
orientation, there were also certain deep-rooted differences in outlook and temperament that should be acknowledged in any comparison between them.   For example, although the themes of renunciation and worldly vanity crop up repeatedly in the epigrams of both
poets, Silesius' pantheistic tendencies enabled him to view external
reality as a positive good and to see in it the signature of its Divine Author:

> S. : Die Schöpfung ist ein Buch; wers weislich lessen kann,
>   Dem wird darin gar fein der Schöpfer kund getan. [57]

Beissel, on the other hand, never spoke approvingly of external reality except when using some aspect of it as a metaphor of the soul.

Otherwise, he viewed the world with grave suspicion and believed
that its natural function was to seduce man from his eternal destiny:

> B. : O Welt! du trügerin, mit deinem eitlen schein
> Ich bin dir nun entflohn, geh nimmer in dich ein. [58]

Moreover, Silesius firmly believed in the total interdependence of
God and man:

> S. : Ich weiss, dass ohne mich Gott nicht ein Nu kann leben;
> Werd ich zunicht, er muss von Not. den Geist aufgeben. [59]

Such a notion must surely have struck Beissel as blasphemous, feeling as he did that man could never be quite sure of his standing
with the Creator:

> B. : Hast du noch nicht gesehen das thal der nichtigkeit,
> So baue ja kein nest ins Hauss der Sicherheit. [60]

The theosophical ideas and the attitudes toward the religious
life that find expression in Beissel's poetry did not come to him in
the form of revelation from on high, even if he did not discourage
his followers from believing so. I have already alluded to Böhme's
influence on his conception of God and his cult of Sophia. Beissel's
idea of the Ich or self-will as giving rise to evil probably derives
from Böhme as well. [61] Moreover, much of Beissel's specialized
vocabulary of mysticism, including such terms as magia, Tinctur,
centrum, and Temperatur, can be found scattered throughout Böhme's writings. But the question of whether Beissel knew Böhme's
works directly or through his interpreters cannot be answered with
certainty. It seems likely that he read both Böhme and his interpreters.

Two of these interpreters were Johann Georg Gichtel and
Gottfried Arnold. Beissel probably became familiar with their writings through Haller's encouragement while in Heidelberg. He may
have understood Böhme's concept of self-will and individual desire as
the origin of evil (Finsternis) through Gichtel's mediation. [62] Arnold's tract, Das Geheimnis der Göttlichen Sophia (1700), could also
have contributed to Beissel's understanding of the Heavenly Wisdom [63]--although, according to Stoudt, Arnold conceived of Sophia as
the threefold body and blood of Christ, an idea that would not be
consonant with Beissel's theosophy. [64] It seems much more likely
that Beissel's position on Sophia came directly from Böhme. Beissel's glorification of virginity and celibacy could have been influenced by Arnold, who was vehemently against natural marriage, [65] as
well as by Ernst Christoph Hochmann von Hochenau, who preached
union with Christ as the only pure marital state. [66] Beissel knew of
Hochenau through Alexander Mack and his Dunker sect, with which
he came in contact during his wanderings in Wittgenstein. [67]

In any outline of probable and possible influences on Beissel's
thought, the English Philadelphian movement should not be omitted.

The Philadelphians were a society of mystics in the Böhmist tradition founded in London in 1670 by John Pordage and Jane Lead.[68] Their espousal of separatism and their ideas on the formation of religious communities with the designation of members as "brother" may well have been a contributing stimulus to Beissel's founding of Ephrata.[69] If this is so, then the Philadelphians may also have been the mediators for some of Beissel's knowledge of Böhme. Since Beissel had almost no knowledge of English, it is doubtful that he had any direct association with the Philadelphians. But he probably gained a familiarity with their ideas through the German Philadelphian sect in Wittgenstein before coming to America.[70] It is also possible that he later renewed this indirect contact through the members of Kelpius' monastic community near Germantown. Before setting sail for America in 1694, Kelpius had lived in London and had made the acquaintance of Pordage and Lead. While in Pennsylvania he maintained a lively correspondence with them.[71]

Finally, it is possible that even Rosicrucian mysticism did not escape Beissel's interest. Julius Sachse, the well-known chronicler of Ephrata, identifies Beissel as one of the revivers of Rosicrucianism in Pennsylvania.[72] Sachse refers to the Ephrata community as the successor to Kelpius and his chapter of "true Rosicrucians" on the Wissahickon and says that at Ephrata "the secret rites and mysteries of the true Rosicrucian philosophy flourished unmolested for years."[73]

Influences come from the future as well as the past. Although Beissel's intellectual links with the religious poets and thinkers of his native Germany were deep and durable, the visionary temperament of the mystic could not help but be profoundly shaped by the promise of spiritual rebirth held out by the New World to which he had come. One could easily be led to infer from Ephrata's situation of relative isolation from its environment and from Beissel's strong inclination to the solitary life that his only interest in America was as a refuge from repressive ecclesiastical authority. However, his prophetic, if ungrammatical, words in the fifth "Theosophical Epistle" reveal a much grander, chiliastic vision of the New World:

> Asia ist gefallen u. seine Leuchter ist verloschen.
> Europa ist die Sonne am hellen Mittag untergangen.
> America siehet eine Lilie blühen, ihr Geruch wird
> unter den Heiden erschallen. Abend und Morgen wird
> wieder einen Tag machen. Das Licht gegen dem Abend
> wird einen Schein setzen gegen dem Morgen: und der
> letzt verheissene Abend-Regen wird dem Morgen zu
> hülf kommen, und wird das Ende wieder in seinem
> Anfang bringen; alsdann wird Jacob fröhlich seyn,
> und Israel sich freuen.[74]

The full significance of these cryptic utterances can be decoded without undue difficulty. Beissel first refers to the crumbling of the old ecclesiastical order in Asia and Europe. He then says America will

bear witness to the blooming of a lily. The rich symbolism of the
lily in Christian mystical literature has its origins in the Song of
Songs in which Christ, the Bridegroom, woos the lily, which is the
church, or, as the mystics would have it, the individual soul.[75]
Beissel's prophecy of the blooming of the lily is thus meant to sym-
bolize the regeneration of the Christian spirit in the New World.
This vision of the gradual westward movement of religion and of
America as the new kingdom of God has deep intellectual roots in
the medieval historical concept of the translatio imperii, the belief
based on Old Testament prophecies that Rome's abuse of secular and
religious authority had forced God to transfer the earthly seat of
power to the Germanic peoples.[76] Beissel, along with other Pennsylvania German separatists, viewed his own forced exodus from the
oppressive religious atmosphere in Germany and his journey to
America as the beginning of still another phase in the westward migration of God's kingdom on earth. The remaining metaphors in the
oracular passage quoted above are also rooted in the Old Testament.
The image of evening and morning forming one day derives from the
account of the creation at the beginning of Genesis. It would seem
that Beissel envisioned this imminent spiritual regeneration as ana-
logous to God's act of material creation. The promised evening
rain is probably based on the innumerable Old Testament metaphors
depicting rain as the beneficent, fertilizing shower. The references
to Jacob and Israel imply that America is the New Canaan, the land
of spiritual plenty where the descendants of the twelve tribes of Israel will flourish. Beissel thus expresses his vision of America in
sweepingly apocalyptic style as a utopian land which was to witness
a profound revolution of the Christian spirit.

The following passage from the preface to the Paradisisches
Wunderspiel, anonymously written by one of the brethren, expresses
the similar sentiments of the entire Ephrata community:

> Erweckung über das grosse Welt Meer in America
> begleiten. Wer wolte noch zweifflen, das nicht Penn-
> silvanien von Gott darzu bestimmt, des sich darinnen
> die Nachkommen der Zwölf-Sämmen unsers himmlischen
> Jacobs solten ausbreiten als in dem Land ihres Erb-
> teils.[77]

Using Beissel's prose as a conceptual key, one can delineate
a lyrical Amerikabild in the first, second, and fifth poems from
section one of the hymnal, Vorspiel der Neuen-welt (1732), the title
of which is itself significant. The first poem presents an expansive,
euphoric vision of the New World in terms of its lush natural beauty,
which inspires the poet to identify it with the Garden of Paradise.
In the first stanza Beissel makes effective use of tropological imagery to represent America as the land of spiritual fertility with unlimited potential for the flowering of the soul. Also implied is the
notion of a new era of religious freedom which is metaphorically con-
trasted with the former era of discrimination and persecution:

Ich sehe die pflantzen im Paradies feld
Vom lieblichen frühling sehr herrlich aussprossen,
Nun wird wieder sanfte was vor war verstellt,
Durch herbe und kälte im winter verschlossen.
Da stehen die bäume mit lieblichem grünen,
So dass es zur freude und wollust muss dienen. [78]

That Beissel is actually describing America as an earthly paradise
and not merely entertaining visions of an afterlife becomes clear in
the first two lines of stanza seven, in which he refers to the sisters
of Ephrata:

Da gehen die Töchter sehr prächtig einher,
In diesem gefilde der Paradies-erden. [79]

The second poem also abounds in tropological imagery, beginning with a triumphal proclamation of the end to Old-World strife
and the imminent reunion of the Bridegroom with his Bride:

Der frohe Tag bricht an, es legt sich nieder,
Der harte Jacobs-dienst, es wird ihm wieder,
Gegeben seine Braut die ihm vermählet,
Und sich beym lebens-bronn, zu ihm gesellet. [80]

In stanza three the poet exhorts men to bear witness to America as
die neue liebes-welt and prophecizes the worldwide spread of the
spiritual revolution:

Der neuen liebes-welt, die sich thut zeigen,
Mit ihrem vollen pracht, wer solte schweygen,
u. es nicht zeigen an, was er thut sehen,
Weil es bald aller welt, wird offen stehen? [81]

The fifth poem is the shortest, consisting of only ten stanzas.
Its relative brevity enables the poet to achieve a pleasing structural
symmetry and thematic integration. The first four stanzas are earthbound and portray the blossoming of spring in the landscape of the
New World, which, as always, is also the landscape of the soul.
That Beissel intends his landscape to contain these two levels of
meaning is evident from the following verses in stanza one:

Im geist man sieht,
Wie alles blüht,
Und breit't sich aus zur fruchtbarkeit. [82]

In the second stanza the poet alliteratively affirms the unfettered
growth of the spirit in the New World and deplores its former
smothered existence in the Old:

Der kalte winter geht zu ende,
Es rückt herebey das frohe jahr,
Drum hebet auf hertz, haupt und hände,
Weil nun wird hell und offenbar,

> Was lang verdeckt,
> Und war versteckt. [83]

Stanza four reveals that this renaissance of the spirit is not limited to the confines of Ephrata. Even the infidels will be engulfed in its wave:

> Die blätter dieser fruchtbarkeiten,
> Die dienen auch zur artzeney,
> Und zum genuss der wilden heyden. [84]

In the fifth and sixth stanzas the New Jerusalem is significantly set in the middle of the landscape, and in the middle of the city are assembled the priests and Levites of the Old Testament. Stanzas five and six, then, are the pivotal stanzas of the poem both structurally and thematically, since they form a transition from the earthbound description of the first four stanzas to the transfigured vision of the last four.

As the poem moves into its final stanzas it becomes increasingly difficult to discern whether the scene of events is still the greening utopia of America or whether we have been transported to the Eternal Kingdom. Occurrences seem no longer to be rooted in time and space: a sacrificial offering is made to the Lord at his golden altar (st. 8), and the soul-bride takes her place beside her King and receives the golden crown (st. 9). Subtly, imperceptibly the poet has blended the one realm with the other. The New World, the New Jerusalem, and the Kingdom of Heaven have become one. In the final stanza the two realms of reality resume their separate modes of existence as the poet realizes he has allowed his imagination to be seduced by the fertile promise of his new earthly environment:

> Ich freue mich schon in dem geiste,
> Ob ich schon noch auf erden bin. [85]

Conrad Beissel's lapse into obscurity among the German poets and writers on the early colonial scene is an undeserved fate. Few of his colonial contemporaries could match the range of his religious thought or the breadth of his poetic vision. Although it is certainly easy to fault him on esthetic grounds, such fault hardly diminishes the monument of his poetry as a profound probing into the depths of the human soul, combining the homely simplicity of biblical wisdom with the all-embracing mystical vision of an Eckhart or a Böhme.

I have had to work with a microprint reproduction of the original editions of the Ephrata hymnals. A complete lack of dating of individual hymns makes it most difficult to trace Beissel's development as a poet within a chronological framework. Clearly, much remains to be done even in the area of preliminary scholarship. To my knowledge, no comprehensive survey of Beissel's poetry has yet been made and there is no edition of selected poems. The few critics

such as Stoudt and Stoeffler who have touched on Beissel as a poet
have not really distinguished him from the many members of the
Ephrata community who composed verse. No effort has been made
to sort out Beissel's poetry from that of the cloister as a whole.
Also, a much more thorough investigation of the sources of Beissel's
mysticism is needed. As the leader of a thriving and influential religious community entrusted with the education of many of early
Philadelphia's young people, Beissel was an important connecting
link in the transmission of religious culture from the Old World to
the New. His relationship to some of the great religious poets and
writers of the German baroque, such as Daniel Czepko, Paul Ger-
hardt, Quirinus Kuhlmann, and Gottfried Arnold, is still virtually
unexplored. I have dealt with only a few of the most obvious strains
of Böhme and Silesius in his poetry; if Sachse is correct in asserting that Rosicrucian rituals were carried on at Ephrata, there may
well be traces of Rosicrucian mysticism and symbolism in Beissel's
verse that I have not managed to uncover. A more intensive scrut-
iny of the theosophical writings than I have been able to make might
help to bring some of these connections to light.

Notes

1. Thomas Mann, <u>Gesammelte Werke</u> (Berlin, 1956), VI, 93. In
    an informative article, "Conrad Beissel and Thomas Mann,"
    <u>AGR</u>, XXVI (1959-60), 24-25 and 38, Andres Briner identifies
    as Mann's factual sources for his account of Beissel a letter
    by Jacob Duche, an Anglican priest, written in 1771, and
    William Fahnestock's "An Historical Sketch of Ephrata" in
    <u>Hazard's Register of Pennsylvania</u>, XV. 11. Both sources de-
    scribe the moving effect of Beissel's music on the listener.
       For an extensive analysis of Beissel's function as a char-
    acter in Mann's novel, see Theodor Karst, "Johann Conrad
    Beissel in Thomas Manns Roman 'Docktor Faustus,'" Jahr-
    buch der deutschen Schillergesellschaft, XII (1968), 543-585.
2. Walter C. Klein, <u>Johann Conrad Beissel: Mystic and Martinet</u>
    (Philadelphia, 1942), p. 2. Hereafter cited as Klein.
3. Klein, p. 26.
4. Klein, p. 27.
5. Klein, p. 29.
6. Klein, p. 34.
7. Klein, pp. 40-41; 198.
8. Oswald Seidensticker, <u>Bilder aus der deutsch-pennsylvanischen
    Geschichte, Geschichtsblätter, Bilder und Mittheilungen aus
    dem Leben der Deutschen in Amerika</u>, II, ed. Carl Schurz,
    2nd ed. (New York, 1886), p. 188. Hereafter cited as
    Seidensticker.
9. Seidensticker, p. 194.
10. John F. Watson, <u>Annals of Philadelphia and Pennsylvania, The
    Olden Time...</u>, II (Philadelphia, 1850 ed.), p. 110. The
    later edition was not available.
11. Conrad Beissel, <u>Jacobs Kampff- und Ritter-Platz...</u> (Philadel-

phia, 1736), p. 13, no. 5, st. 1. Hereafter cited as JK.
According to Eugene E. Doll and Anneliese M. Funke, The
Ephrata Cloisters: An Annotated Bibliography (Philadelphia,
1944), p. 41, no. 182, Julius Sachse claims that Beissel is
responsible for twenty-eight of the thirty-two hymns in the
collection.
12. JK, p. 13, no. 5, st. 4.
13. Conrad Beissel, Das Gesang der einsamen und verlassenen Turtel-Taube Nemlich der Christlichen Kirche... (Ephrata,
1747), p. 7, no. 7, st. 4. Hereafter cited as TT. According to Doll, p. 92, no. 374, two-thirds of the hymns in the
Turtel-Taube are by Beissel, the remaining hymns having
been contributed by sixteen brothers and twenty-three sisters.
The style and thematic development of hymn no. 7 indicate
Beissel's authorship.
14. Conrad Beissel, "Theosophische Gedichte," in Erster Teil der
Theosophischen Lectionen... (Ephrata, 1752), p. 407, no. 39.
Hereafter cited as TG. Doll, p. 96, no. 380, says the
"Theosophische Gedichte" are to be attributed to Beissel.
15. Conrad Beissel, Vorspiel der Neuen-welt. Welches sich in der
letzten Abendroethe als ein paradisischer Lichtes-glantz unter
den Kindern Gottes Hervor gethan... (Philadelphia, 1732), p.
18, no. 8, st. 2. Hereafter cited as Vorspiel. The authorship of hymn no. 8 is uncertain, but the mystical images and
concepts it contains suggest that it may have been Beissel's.
16. TT, p. 15, no. 18, st. 3. The style of the hymn indicates
Beissel's authorship.
17. TT, p. 4, no. 5, st. 1. Again, authorship is uncertain, but
the didactic tone points to Beissel.
18. TG, p. 403, no. 25.
19. TG, p. 401, no. 18.
20. TG, p. 409, no. 49.
21. TG, p. 412, no. 60.
22. TG, p. 418, no. 82.
23. TT, p. 1, no. 1, st. 1. Authorship is uncertain, but the progression of thought and feeling indicates Beissel. Moreover,
it was customary to print Beissel's hymns first in the Ephrata hymnals out of deference to his position before printing
those of the other brothers and sisters.
24. TT, p. 1, no. 1, st. 4.
25. TT, p. 1, no. 1, st. 5.
26. TT, p. 1, no. 1. st. 6.
27. Conrad Beissel, "Die 1. Gemüts-Bewegung," Urständliche und
Erfahrungsvolle Hohe Zeugnüsse Wie man zum Geistlichen
Leben gelangen möge (Ephrata, 1745), p. 2. Hereafter cited
as UZ.
28. TT, p. 1-2, no. 1, st. 8.
29. TT, p. 2, no. 1, st. 10.
30. Conrad Beissel, Paradisisches Wunderspiel, Welches sich...als
ein Vorspiel der neuen Welt hervorgethan... (Ephrata, 1766),
p. 1997, no. 298, st. 1. Hereafter cited as PW. The first
section consists of 441 hymns by Beissel.
31. PW, pp. 197-198, no. 289, st. 4.

32. PW, p. 198, no. 298, st. 5.
33. Klein, pp. 188-197.
34. E. Ernest Stoeffler, Mysticism in the German Devotional Litera-
    ture of Colonial Pennsylvania, The Pennsylvanian German
    Folklore Society, 14 (Allentown, 1949), pp. 43-65. Hereafter
    cited as Stoeffler.
35. Rufus M. Jones, Spiritual Reformers in the 16th & 17th Centu-
    ries (London, 1928), pp. 174-175. Hereafter cited as Jones.
36. Stoeffler, pp. 50-51.
37. PW, p. 224, no. 331, st. 10.
38. PW, p. 194, no. 293, st. 1.
39. Conrad Beissel, Mystische und sehr geheyme Sprueche, Welche
    in der Himlischen schule des heiligen geistes erlernet...
    (Philadelphia, 1730), p. 19, no. 53. Hereafter cited as MS.
40. John Joseph Stoudt, Consider the Lilies How They Grow, The
    Pennsylvania German Folklore Society, II (Allentown, 1937),
    pp. 127-131. Hereafter cited as Lilies.
41. Hans Lassen Martensen, Jacob Böhme: His Life and Teaching,
    or Studies in Theosophy, trans. T. Rhys Evans (London,
    1885), p. 234. Hereafter cited as Martensen.
42. Martensen, p. 265.
43. Seidensticker, p. 222.
44. Conrad Beissel, "Vorrede über die Sing-Arbeit," in TT, 2nd
    preface, pp. viii-xxi. This is Beissel's treatise on the basic
    rules of harmony peculiar to the choral music of the cloister.
45. PW, p. 13, no. 16, st. 1.
46. PW, p. 6, no. 7, st. 1.
47. TT, p. 8, no. 9, st. 4.
48. John Joseph Stoudt, Pennsylvania German Poetry 1685-1830.
    The Pennsylvania German Folklore Society, XX (Allentown,
    1955), lxv-lxvi. Stoudt mentions the connection between Si-
    lesius' Cherubinischer Wandersmann and Beissel's Alexand-
    rine couplets, but does not pursue the subject.
49. Angelus Silesius, Sämtliche Poetische Werke, ed. Hans Ludwig
    Held, 2nd ed. (Munich, 1924), III, bk. 1, 15, no. 27. Here-
    after cited as Silesius   Silesius is abbreviated "S." and
    Beissel "B." to save space.
50. MS, p. 17, no. 35.
51. Silesius, bk. 1, 24, no. 93.
52. MS, p. 15, no. 8.
53. Silesius, bk. 2, 65, no. 61.
54. MS, p. 17, no. 38.
55. Silesius, bk. 5, 188, no. 80.
56. MS, p. 15, no. 11.
57. Silesius, bk. 5, 189, no. 86.
58. MS, p. 18, no. 41.
59. Silesius, bk. 1, 12, no. 8.
60. MS, p. 15, no. 13.
61. Jones, p. 178. Jones discusses Böhme's concept of the light
    and dark worlds: individual desires and aims sever a being
    from the totality of divine goodness, thereby creating the
    realm of darkness. This idea seems to conform closely to
    Beissel's notion of Finsternis in his theosophical prose and

his notion of the evil I̱c̱ẖ or M̱e̱i̱ṉ in his poetry.

62. Klein, p. 201.
63. Stoeffler, p. 40.
64. Lilies, p. 127.
65. Klein, p. 199.
66. Stoeffler, p. 42.
67. Klein, pp. 30-31.
68. The Encyclopedia Americana (New York, 1963 ed.), XXI, 734-735.
69. Stoeffler, pp. 39; 48-49.
70. Seidensticker, p. 176.
71. Brothers Lamech and Agrippa, Chronicon Ephratense, Enthaltend den Lebens-Lauf des ehrwürdigen Vaters in Christo Friedsam Gottrecht [Beissel], Weyland Stiffters und Vorstehers des gestl. Ordens der Einsamen in Ephrata... (Ephrata, 1786), p. 11. According to Doll, p. 117, no. 427, the Chronicon Ephratense contains a history of the Ephrata community of Seventh-Day Baptists since its foundation, including the background, customs, struggles, and accomplishments of the brothers and sisters, as well as the biography of the founder, "Friedsam Gottrecht." It is the chief source of information on life in the cloister and was used extensively by both Klein and Seidensticker.
72. Julius Friedrich Sachse, The German Pietists of Provincial Pennsylvania (Philadelphia, 1895), p. 198. Hereafter cited as Sachse.
73. Sachse, pp. 4-5; 7. Sachse makes much of Rosicrucian mysticism in Beissel's thinking and in the religious ceremonies at Ephrata, but, unfortunately for us, he neglects to support his assertions with documented evidence.
74. Conrad Beissel, "Die V. Theosophische Epistel," in UZ, p. 98.
75. In Lilies Stoudt traces the history of lily-symbolism in Christian mysticism beginning with the Old Testament. On pp. 113-122 he quotes numerous passages from Böhme's writings in English translation (Bath, 1775 ed.) to illustrate the meaning of the lily for Böhme: essentially, it is the true reflection of God since it is an image of the new-born or regenerated soul. It is quite possible that the stimulus for Beissel's use of this symbol in his fifth theosophical epistle is to be found in Böhme.
76. See Ernst Robert Curtius, Europäische Literatur und lateinisches Mittelalter, 4th ed. (Bern and Munich, 1963), pp. 38-40.
77. "Vorrede," PW, p. 5.
78. Vorspiel, p. 5, no. 1, st. 1. Beissel is most likely the author of all seven poems in section one of the Vorspiel.
79. Vorspiel, p. 6, no. 1, st. 7.
80. Vorspiel, p. 7, no. 2, st. 1.
81. Vorspiel, p. 8, no. 2, st. 3.
82. Vorspiel, p. 13, no. 5, st. 1.
83. Vorspiel, p. 13, no. 5, st. 2.
84. Vorspiel, p. 13, no. 5, st. 4.
85. Vorspiel, p. 14, no. 5, st. 10.

11. RECENT SEALSFIELD DISCOVERIES*

Karl J. R. Arndt

Due to the world situation during the past decade some very important new Sealsfield material discovered either shortly before or during the war has remained hidden from the eyes of American scholars. Part of this material is presented here in the form of eleven Sealsfield letters. In themselves they constitute a kind of autobiography of the author, touching important high spots of his various lives: his arrangements for flight under the name of Postl, his first contacts in America as Sidons, his early struggles as Sealsfield, his later comfortable social life as Sealsfield, and the last painful months when he is convinced that "it cannot last much longer."[1]

The first letter, for which I am indebted to Herr Albert Kresse of Stuttgart, is probably the last one which Sealsfield wrote and signed as "Postl." It shows us the manner of his escape from the monastery. The second, likewise from the Sealsfield-Archiv of Herr Albert Kresse, is the earliest Sealsfield letter found dated from our country. It is of great importance because it establishes a definite time and place for Sealsfield in this country soon after he had begun his second life, and it also proves that he then used the name Sidons, under which he also published his first German book.[2] It shows us that Hofrath André was an important link in Sealsfield's escape to a new life from the very beginning of his flight. The mention of von Bonnhorst and Dr. Eberle in this letter is further indication of his excellent early connections in this country; for, as we will show in the notes to the letter, both of these men were men of great prominence in America at that time.

The importance of the third letter, which I obtained during the war from Sealsfield's London publisher, lies in the new light which it sheds on the genesis of Sealsfield's anonymously published and internationally discussed Austria as It Is.[3] The letter was written in February 1827 and tells of a hitherto unknown trip to Paris which might help explain why the Paris publisher A. Bossange brought out an anonymous French edition of Austria as It Is (L'Autriche telle qu'elle est) in 1828, the same year that the London publishers Hurst, Chance, and Company first published the work which in this letter is being offered to Murray. The mention of interviews with Prince Esterhazy would indicate that at least this noble-

---

*Reprinted from JEGP 52(1954): 160-71, by permission of the publisher.

man was a partner to the secret of the authorship of the book on
Austria. It is important to remember this when we consider that,
soon after publication, Austria as It Is caused an international incident and was banned in all areas under Austrian control. In view
of the vigor with which the Austrian secret police moved against
this work, one must conclude that the failure to expose Sealsfield as
author at this time could be due to only one of two causes: either
he had powerful protection in strategic places, or the secret police
was very ineffective. 4 Murray knew that Sealsfield was the author
of Austria, and when Hurst, Chance, and Company in 1828 also published Sealsfield's The Americans as They Are, they did not give
his name but identified the author of this work as the "Author of
Austria as It Is." In his letter of 3 January 1828, written from
Kittaning, Pennsylvania, to Cotta, Sealsfield twice mentioned that
Austria was to be published in London, and the work itself proclaimed that it was by an eye-witness and a native of the Austrian
Empire.   The Kittaning letter was signed "Sealsfield" (Faust, p. 210);
so Cotta now knew Sealsfield by that name, as "Sidons"--and probably also as "Postl." How careless Sealsfield was at this time
about covering up his past is further seen from the following information about him which I found in the certified passenger list of the
ship "Stephania" for the voyage from Havre to New York (arrival
August 16, 1827): "Chas. Seafield, age 31, sex male, occupation
Gentleman, native country Austria." As this third letter reveals
Sealsfield's early interest in political intrigue, so it also gives the
real explanation for his break with Cotta. That this is the case is
substantiated by a letter from the historian B. G. Niebuhr, written
on behalf of Cotta to F. Lieber and offering him the post of American correspondent for the Cotta papers. Niebuhr gives this warning:
"One thing I cannot sufficiently recommend to you,--you must not
take it amiss, for I do not mean to cast reflections on you, but to
point out the rock on which most newspaper-correspondents wreck,--
no political dissertations and generalities, but facts, simply and con-
cisely told. "5

        Sealsfield's fourth letter, made available to me for publica-
tion through Herr Kresse, is actually signed "Charles Sidons Sealsfield" and thus establishes by Sealsfield's own hand that he used the
two names. Moreover it is the first letter we find dated from a
point in Louisiana. This should assist in the clarification of the
question of Sealsfield's Louisiana plantation. Sealsfield is looking for
a new publisher and in effect admits that he has learned about the
dangers of which Niebuhr had warned Lieber.

        I obtained the fifth letter, addressed to Heinrich Faesi, from
the Archiv der Hansestadt Hamburg, and the ninth from the Preussische Staatsbibliothek in Berlin, both shortly before the war began.
These letters show us Sealsfield as a well established and respected
citizen and give a hitherto undocumented picture of his interest in social activity. Since he has often been pictured as a monk lacking social graces, it is amusing to see this demonstration of his interest
in the dance, to which he invites guests in the fifth letter. It is undated but was probably written about a week before November 22,

1837. Sealsfield had just returned to Switzerland from a short trip
to the United States. The New York Evening Post of July 27, 1837,
as I have been able to determine by a search of this paper in the
American Antiquarian Society, announced his arrival from Havre on
the ship "Great Britain," spelling his name "C. Sarsfield." The
same paper on October 10, 1837, lists his departure for Havre on
the ship "Charlemagne" and gives his name then as "Chas Searls-
field."

Letters five, six (obtained shortly before the war from the
Stadtbibliothek of Vienna), and nine give us further light on Sealsfield's friendships. The persons to whom they are addressed are
men of social importance or of intellectual interests. Dorer Egloff
was well known as a "Goethekenner," and Johann Lukas Schönlein,
to whom the sixth letter is addressed, was a famous German physician. He was also an outspoken democrat, and for that reason had
left his native land and was teaching at the University of Zürich
when Sealsfield addressed this letter to him. It is for this reason
that Sealsfield speaks of him as a German of whom his and any nation might be proud.

The seventh letter was obtained from the Preussische Staatsbibliothek in Berlin before the war, the eighth is taken from my own
Sealsfield collection, and the tenth from the T. O. Mabbott collection in the New York Public Library. These three letters were written to Sealsfield's publisher Erhard. The seventh reveals Sealsfield's closeness in financial dealings, a trait in his character which
prevented a more successful publication of his works. It is probable that it was this disagreeable trait in him which, more than other reasons, kept his last works from being published. The tenth
letter is a farewell letter to his publisher, written on his way to
Havre, where he embarked on the ship "Humboldt" on September
28th and--after a delay of two days, due to low water which held the
big ship at the dock--sailed for New York. The "Humboldt" arrived in New York after a rough crossing on the evening of October
14, 1853, and its arrival was hailed in the New York papers by long
articles bringing "the latest" from Europe. It was her last trip to
New York, for she was wrecked off Halifax on her next return trip,
a coincidence which caused Sealsfield to think that fate still was
keeping him for some important further work. The New York Weekly Herald of October 15, 1853, gives his name in the list of passengers as "C. Sealsfield," marking the first time, to my knowledge,
that the American papers spelled his name correctly.

The eleventh letter, obtained from the Kresse Sealsfield-Archiv, was written the day before Sealsfield signed his will and reveals some of the fortitude with which he was very consciously
awaiting the end. It came less than three months later.

Through the kindness of Herr Kresse I have a photograph of
Sealsfield's sketch for his tombstone. It reveals his desire to have
his first self united with his last self on the stone which was to
mark the head of his grave, for above the name Charles Sealsfield

are inscribed the initials "C. P." Above this sketch Sealsfield's
hand wrote in English two verses from the Psalms which, on the one
hand, seem to reflect a sense of guilt because he had broken his
priestly vows, and on the other a sense of calm confidence in the
justice of his God. His grave at Sankt Nikolaus in Solothurn,
Switzerland, today still shows that his directions were faithfully executed. The headstone of that grave bears the following inscription:

C   P
Charles Sealsfield
geboren den 3 März 1793
gestorben den 26 Mai 1864

Psalm 143 And enter not into judgement with thy servant,
for in thy sight shall no man living be justified.
Psalm 51 Have mercy upon me my God, according to thy
loving kindness, according to the multitude of thy tender mercies blot out my transgressions.

The texts are given only in English, and on the stone slab
covering the full grave are inscribed the six words:

Charles Sealsfield
Bürger von
NORD AMERIKA.

Only after his true identity was discovered could men realize
why he chose these verses to mark his last resting place. Probably
his full and complete break with his name and existence as Postl is
best explained by the fact that in this manner he kept his priestly
vows to the end--to the end of Postl's existence. The Sealsfield who
became famous as an author was another man. This is one of several explanations, but the tombstone inscriptions show that in his inner-
most heart he was concerned about his actions to the very last.

I

Dem Hochwürdigsten Herrn Leopold Stöhr des ritterl. Kreuzherre-
nordens mit dem roht. Stern Commandeur etc. Wohlgeboren zu
Eger.
Hochwürdigster Wohlgeborener Herr Commandeur!
Sehr dringliche und wichtige Aufträge rufen mich morgen in
die Gegend von Pilsen. Ich bin so frey, Euer Wohlgeboren um Ihren
Wagen und Pferde bis Plan, bis wohin mir die Pferde entgegengesch-
ickt werden, höflichst zu ersuchen Da die Sache nicht mich bet-
rifft, und unaufschiebbar ist, so bin ich der zuversichtlichen Hoffnung dieselben werden diese Bitte nicht abschlagen, die ich übrigens
bis dahin, wo ich nochmals persönlich die Ehre zu sehn haben werde
mit aller Achtung geharre.
Euer Hochwürden Wohlgebor.

dero
ghsmst Dr.
Postl--Sekretair.

(?) Priesen Franzenbad den 10. May/23.[6]

II

Envelope marked: Pittsburgh, Penns.

A Monsieur   Monsieur Cotta noble de Cottendorf etc.
                  Stuttgardt
                  Royaume Wirtemberg

Euer Wohlgeboren!
        In der Voraussetzung, dass die Ursachen noch bestehen, die
Sie zu den gütigen mir durch Herrn Hofrath André7 gemachten An-
trägen veranlassten, bin ich so frey Ihnen hiemit meine Dienste zur
Einsendung von monatlichen Berichten für Ihre Zeitschriften und
öffentliche Blätter ergebenst anzubieten. Sie würden demzufolge reg-
elmässig jeden Monat einen Bericht erhalten, der das öffentliche
Leben und Treiben in den V. St. v. Nordamerika nach kräften dar-
stellen soll. Haben Sie etwas besonderes bei der Auswahl der ein-
zusendenden Materien zu erinnern so bitte ich dieses in Dero Antwort
gefällig zu thun. Die Bestimmung des Honorars überlasse ich Ihnen,
ersuche jedoch selben nach Erhalt der ersten Nachrichten gütig fest-
zusetzen.
        Genehmigen Sie die Versicherung meiner besonderen Hochach-
tung mit der ich die Ehre habe zu seyn

                                        Euer Wohlgeborner
                                        und gehorsamster Dr
                                        Sidons

Pittsburgh den 20 Sept 1824[8]

P. S. Ich brauche nicht erst zu bemerken, dass Sidons nicht mein
eigentlicher Name sey. Diesen werden Sie in Verbindung mit Herrn
Hofrath André und bei Zurückrufung des jungen Mannes dem Sie bei
seinem Erscheinen in Ihrem Hause so viele Theilnahme erwiesen,
leicht errathen. Meine Addresse kann lauten Mr. Sidons with von
Bonnhorst Esq.[9] in Pittsburgh Pennsylvania.
        Addressieren Sie jedoch Ihre Antwort nach Philadelphia so bitte
ich Sie an M. Dr. Eberle[10] daselbst zu addressieren. Beyde sind
meine Freunde und werden sich möglichst beeilen mir selbe mitzuth-
eilen.

III

John Murray Esq.
        Mr. Sealsfield presents his compliments to Mr. Murray & de-
sires to know whether he thinks a work upon the present state of
Hungary with engravings representing the settings of the Diet, castles,
etc. as well as the most interesting particulars respecting this nation
of sufficient importance to be published.
        Being obliged to delay his return the undersigned has arrived
before yesterday from Paris, having in the meantime taken all the
necessary steps to further the progress of the said work, for which

purpose he had several interviews with Prince Esterhazy. The undersigned wishes an interview as soon as possible and begs Mr.
Murray to send him word if it can be to day.   It is unnecessary to
observe that the strictest secrecy respecting P-e Esterhazy is desired as his certain political or rather diplomatical bearings would
not allow a premature participation--.
        The undersigned[11] resides at Grosvenor place Chester Street
19--

                              IV

Respected Sir!
        I have some years since published a work, (: Die Vereinigten
Staaten von Nordamerika mit einer Reise durch Ohio Indiana Illinois
etc. :) by Cotta in the year 1827, which as I understand, has made
an impression, sufficiently favorable to warrant the publication of
another, to be entitled "Hülfsbuch für Auswanderer in die Ver.
Staaten oder Uebersicht derselben in ihrem gegenwärtigen Agrikul-
tural &c, Zustande"--This work, which I have finished chiefly from
my own experience, and that of men of common sense, is of a nature which might become very valuable if not indispensable to Emigrants.   It shows where they best embark in Europe, their means,
necessary for this purpose, the precautions, which they have to
take, according to these means, they are in possession of; what city
they embark; or have to embark for, what they have to furnish or
to provide themselves with.   The modes of getting the best information according to their various trades.--The precautions they have to
take when arrived.   The manner in which they have to travel to the
western states, if they are agriculturists, (farmers), where they
best settle, if they are artists, mechanics, merchants etc.   In short,
everything, which may be necessary, to conduct an honest German
properly to the place of his destination.   The states and countries,
which are best suitable for Germans, are minutely described, and
the means enumerated and mentioned, which they must have if willing or desirous to begin business of any description--.
        There is no work of this description existant yet, which in
one view gives a complete picture and prospect, of what an emigrant
has to hope, to expect, to do and to evite.   It would be necessary
at the same time to make this book by a moderate price accessible
to everyone, the sale would then be the larger.   It contains from 25
to 28 printed sheets with the most perfect map (Tanners newest map
of the United States 1829 Philadelphia.) as a guide.   I have nothing
to say more, than that I wish a liberal publisher for this work and
that I take the liberty of addressing myself to You--.
        The work Die V. St. v. N.A. in ihr. polit. relig. Verh. men-
tioned above, was the first ever written by me, it contains many
crude and rough attacks, these have been omitted of course--but at
the same time it will be seen, that every thing said in this work respecting political parties has verified itself literally--Jackson has become President in short the whole has turned out as predicted in
these pages.   The work has been translated into the English but the
translator did not follow its spirit but rather that of a political an-

tagonist   It has found many adversaries, but even among these
there has often been justice done to it.   The fact is that the English
notwithstanding the frequency of their intercourse with the U S. of
N.A. have less real knowledge about them, than any nation, their
heads and brains are so obscured by prejudice that they never see
objects in their true light, but always through the dampy Atmosphere
of their nationality or rather national prejudice--That the German
has more correct sense to value things and objects, is manifest
from the circumstance, that they among all nations of Europe, if
properly guided, thrive best in America--.   I thought it necessary
to give these few explanations in candour and frankness, in order to
lay things before You in proper point of view--.   My request therefore is--You may be pleased to fix the price which You would be
willing to give for the work, or the single sheet--In this case, that
is if You have shown any desire or willingness to enter into any con-
nexion with me, I would transmit to You the work.

A second request which I take the liberty of making to You is
to send the following two works immediately after the receipt of this
letter.   I Allgemeine Geschichte der Welt von Eichhorn the last and
best edition if I am not mistaken published 1817.

II Allgemeine Geschichte der Völker u Staaten von H. Luden
third or fourth edition.   You are civilly requested to address these
works Ch. S. Sealsfield--to the Care of Messrs Carey Lea &
Carey Publishers & Booksellers, Philadelphia.

The amount for the works will be paid at the delivery of the
works into the hands of the Undersigned, either to Messieurs Carey
Lea & Carey a very respectable house and the first publishing concern in the U.S., or whomever You are pleased to assign.   The Undersigned requests You to send these works immediately, and relies
in this respect on your kindness.   The present letter is forwarded to
You honoured Sir, by Messieurs Carey Lea & Carey, who have received the necessary instructions on this point--.

I conclude with expressing my desire of entering with Your
respectable firm into the above mentioned business, and I am so
free to add, that I am fully convinced it will turn out to our mutual
satisfaction--.

In the meanwhile I avail myself of this opportunity of expressing to You the high esteem with which I have the honour to be
                                    Respected Sir

Below St. Francisville La the 28 of march 1829
                             Your most humble obdt servt
                             Charles Sidons Sealsfield--

Letters or the packet addressed to me,
as above please to direct simply
to Ch Sealsfield Esq.,
Care of Messrs Carey Lea & Carey
Publishers & Booksellers Philadelphia

H. Brockhaus. Esq. Publisher & Bookseller at Leipsic Germany.

V

Mein lieber Herr Faesi:[12]
    Ihre Tanzlust wohl kennend--glaube ich Ihnen eben keinen
sehr grossen Verdruss zu erwecken, wenn ich Ihnen zu wissen thue,
dass künftigen Mittwoch über act Tage am 22 des Monats und dem
Caecilia Feste hier in Baden--der neue Saal des neuen Caffeehauses
durch einen Ball sowohl als Concert eingeweiht werden soll--auf
welche beyden sich die Badener grosse und hohe Welt sehr freuen--
Da ich nun Ihre Ankunft und die Ihrer lieben Elise erwarte--Ihrer
werthen und geehrten Frau dürfte die Witterung jetzt wohl zu rauh
seyn und Sie sich Ihren Besuch bis Frühjahr aufheben--so hielt ich
es für gut Sie von diesem Balle wissen zu lassen--um es Ihnen
wohl zu überlassen, ob Sie Sonntags oder Samstags--oder Mittwoch
darauf kommen wollen? Kommen Sie Mittwoch, so würde ich rathen
entweder Dienstag vorher zukommen, oder es so einzurichten, dasz
Sie den Mittwoch hier ganz zubringen können--Thun Sie jedoch wie
Sie wollen, kommen Sie Sonntags oder Mittwoch--Sie werden immer
willkommen seyn
                        Ihren ganz
                        ergebenen
                        Sealsfield

VI

Herrn Dr. & Prof. Schönlein Wohlgeboren[13]
Theuerster Herr Professor--
    Ich war willens Ihnen gestern eine Art Abschiedsbesuch ab-
zustatten da ich auf einige Monate zu rusticiren gedenke in einer
espece involuntary exile von Ihren lieben Zürich zu leben--. Sie
sind jedoch in Bern zerbrochene Diplomatie restaurirend, und so
muss ich mich denn darauf beschränken Sie statt mündlich schriftlich
in diesen meinen Zeilen zu begrüssen--Nehmen Sie also einstweilen
meinen herzlichen & innigen Dank für die Stunden die Sie mir so
köstlich versüsst, meinen Wunsch diese Stunden noch oft wiederkeh-
ren zu sehen--und erhalten Sie in freundlichem Andenken Ihren Sie
hochschätzenden Sealsfield--der sich wirklich gefreut hat in Ihnen
wieder einmal einen Deutschen zu sehen auf den seine und jede andere
Nazion stolz seyn darf.--Ich hoffe Sie jedoch bald zu sehen das Ver-
gnügen zu haben, denn wie gesagt ich rusticire bloss 8 Stunden von
Zürich in einer Art unwillkührlichen Exiles mir verschafft durch
einen jener Freunde von denen das spanische Sprichwort gilt: Gott
behüte uns vor Solchen Freunden--vor Feinden wollen wir uns schon
selbst bewahren--Herrn Burgm. Hess und übrigen Freunden habe ich
noch vor meiner Abreise meinen Abschiedsbesuch abgestattet und Sie
ersucht Ihnen mündlich zu versichern wie sehr ich bin
                        Theuerster Herr Professor
                        Ihr Sie hochachtender
                        Sealsfield
Den 10 Juny 1839--

VII

Herrn H. Erhard Wohlgeboren
Stuttgart

Euer Wohlgeboren--
    Am 31 März übersandte ich Bogen 8 und 9--mit Manuscript
Bogen 20--bis 32 u 33 1/2 inclusive--Sollten Sie diese Sendung nicht
erhalten haben, so bitte ich mir es sogleich wissen zu lassen--Es
wäre das eben fatal--

Mit aller Achtung
Euer Wohlgeboren
ergebener
Diener
Sealsfield

Den 6 April 1842
    Noch muss ich bemerken dass ich diese Correctur nicht
frankiere--und auch nicht in Briefformat und zwar deshalb nicht sende
weil mir der hiesige Postbeamte sagte das Paquet werde vierfaches
Briefporto bezahlen müssen--also 64 Kreuzer--Haben Sie die Gefälligkeit mich wissen zu lassen wie viel Sie bezahlten. [14]

VIII

Herrn Heinrich Erhard etc etc
Wohlgeborn
Stuttgart

Euer, Wohlgeboren
    Habe ich zugleich das Vergnügen Band VI in der neuen Auf-
lage Band V wieder zurück zu senden. [15] Wie Sie ersehen werden
so sind einige Veränderlungen in dem Arrangement vorgenommen
worden. Es sind nämlich etwas über 2 Bogen nämlich von pag 1 bis
35 oder das Capitel VI noch zu Band vier gezogen und von Seite 36
fängt erst pag 1 des V Bandes an. Es sollte dies bereits in der I
Auflage geschehen syn, denn diese 2 Bogen gehören noch zum Pflanzerleben und die Farbigen, erst mit pag 36 fängt der eigentliche Nathan an. Auch wäre ohne diese Aenderung der V Band zu stark im
Verhältnisse zu den andern. Ich ersuche jedoch höflich darauf zu
sehen, dass beim Drucke ja keine Confusion Statt findet. Sehr gut
wäre es, wenn ich die Endbogen von Band V und Anfangs Bogen sehen
könnte, und Sie mir selbige zusenden möchten. Doch bis dahin hat
es noch Zeit und ich verbleibe mittlerweile

Euer Wohlgeboren
Ergebenster
Sealsfield

Den 29 Sept. 1842.

IX

Herrn Landammann Dorer Egloff[16]
    Wohlgeboren
    zu Hause

Herrn Landammann Dorer Egloff Wohlgebohren
Werthester & Geehrtester!
    Herr Ziegler zum Egli reist heute nach Zürich ab, und ich
musste ihm versprechen, zu Mittage im Stadthofe Sein Gast zu seyn.
Haben Sie nicht etwa Lust gleichfalls da zu essen, und wenn nicht,
würden Sie nicht wenigstens nach dem Mittagessen statt in den Engel
in besagten Stadthof kommen? Mit der Bitte--das eine oder das
andere gefällig beschliessen zu wollen,--hochachtungsvoll wie immer
                            Ihr
                    ganz ergebenster
                        Sealsfield
Den 30 7br 1846

X

                        Arlesheim bei Basel den 24 7br 1853
Geehrtester Herr![17]
    Ich habe gestern Ihr werthes durch Passavant[18] erhalten und
danke Ihnen verbindlichst für Ihre Güte und Mühe. Es its ganz so
recht wie Sie gethan haben. In eine förmliche Verbindung und Verp-
flichtung mit C. würde ich eben aus 100 Gründen nicht mehr einge-
hen--und zwar aus der sehr begreiflichen Ursache weil eine solche
Verbindung mir hoechst lästig werden müsste. Sollte sich eine
oder die andere Gelegenheit ergeben Herrn C. in dieser oder jener
Beziehung gefällig zu seyn so werde ich es schon deswegen thun:
weil eine Hand die andere wäscht.
    Ich bin gestern früh 7 Uhr in Basel angekommen und gedachte
mit dem 4 1/4 Uhr Bahnzuge nach Strassburg--allein ein Freund
hinzwischen, Obergerichtspresident Gutzweiler[19] von Arlesheim, der
um Lebewohl zu sagen nach Basel kam--überredete mich den Abend
--Nacht bei ihm zuzubringen. Wollten Sie wohl die Gefälligkeit
haben ihm ein Exemplar der Gesammtausgabe in 15 Bänden (wohl-
feilen) durch einen der Basler Buchhändler mit der Fuhre zukommen
zu lassen--Die Kosten des Transports und Eingangszolles versteht
sich birgt er--
    Nun ein bestes herzlichstes Lebewohl--Dank für Ihre Freund-
schaft und hoffentlich sehen Sie bald
                    Ihren Ergebenen
                        Sealsfield

XI

Unter den Tannen bei Solothurn,
den 6. März 1864.

Theuerster Verehrtester Herr & Freund[20]

Erst heute haben meine Augen wieder soviele Sehkraft erlangt,
dass ich Ihren so gütigen Brief lesen und beantworten kann. Seit
vier Wochen war dieses nicht mehr der Fall, ich musste H. Gutz-
weilers Brief mir vorlesen und von einem anderen beantworten lass-
en.

So wie die Sehkraft bei dem ewigen Blutverluste abnihmt, so
die uebrigen Kräfte, sodass das Ganze nicht mehr lange dauern kann.
Um Ihre Lecture beneide ich Sie, seit Wochen liegt Post hier[21] auf
meinem Tische, aber mit 7 Siegeln verschlossen.

Ich arbeite jetzt an meinem Testamente und werde so bald es
fertig ist, ein Dupplikat mit mehreren Werthpapieren übersenden.
Es ist das wichtigste das mir am Herzen liegt. Meine achtungs-
vollsten Empfehlungen Ihren Damen--Herrn Pfister bitte ich zu
grüssen, und

God bless you my dear friend
Der Ihrige
Chls Sealsfield

Notes

1.   For the period up to 1939 the most complete Sealsfield bibliogra-
     phy is: Otto Heller and Theodore H. Leon, Charles Seals-
     field (Bibliography of His Writings), Washington University
     (St. Louis) Studies--New Series, Sept. 1939. Many important
     studies shedding new light on Sealsfield have been published
     since in this country and in Europe.--The most complete col-
     lection of Sealsfieldiana belongs to Herr Albert Kresse of
     Stuttgart, Germany. I am deeply grateful to him for allowing
     me such generous use of his materials. I also wish to thank
     the following libraries and institutions for permitting me to
     publish material from their archives: New York Public Li-
     brary, Murray Archives in London, Archiv der Hansestadt
     Hamburg, Stadtbibliothek Wien, and the old pre-Soviet Preuss-
     ische Staatsbibliothek in Berlin.--A completely new field of
     Sealsfield research was opened by Professor Krumpelmann of
     Louisiana State University through his studies of Sealsfield's
     Americanisms, by which he has made historical lexicography
     indebted to him. Cf. John T. Krumpelmann, "Charles Seals-
     field's Americanisms," American Speech, February 1941,
     April 1941, October 1944. Also, James B. McMillan, "Lexi-
     cal Evidence from Charles Sealsfield," American Speech, Ap-
     ril 1943.
2.   C. Sidons, Die Vereinigten Staaten von Nordamerika, Stuttgart,
     1827.
3.   Karl J. Arndt, "Sealsfield's Early Reception in England and
     America," Germanic Review, October, 1943.
4.   Gustav Winter, "Einiges Neue über Charles Sealsfield," Beiträge

zur neueren Geschichte Österreichs, Wien (May) 1907, pp. 1-23.

5. T. S. Perry, Life and Letters of Francis Lieber, Boston, 1882, pp. 78-79.

6. Another hand wrote on the envelope: "Postl Sekretair verlangt Gelegenheit nach Plan--und verschwindet aus dem Orden."

7. The references to Hofrath André in this letter show that he was a partner to the secret from the start. This link to his past worried Sealsfield, as we see from his letter to Cotta dated November 7, 1826: "Ich ersuche abgeredetermassen das Werk unter dem Titel Charles Sidons abzudrucken, Herrn André zu sagen im Oesterreichischen darauf aufmerksam zu machen, übrigens aber sich in keine kleinlichen Details einzulassen, was ich sehr von demselben zu vermuthen Ursache habe" (A. B. Faust, Charles Sealsfield, Weimar, 1897, p. 183).

8. Under this date another hand has written the dates "20 Dec." and "10 Merz 1825," presumably the date the letter was received and the date it was answered.

9. Charles von Bonnhorst was a prominent Pittsburgh lawyer. He handled legal matters for the Harmony Society at Economy, about which Sealsfield wrote.

10. Dr. John Eberle (1787-1838) was a Philadelphia physician, medical writer, and one of the founders of Jefferson Medical College and professor there.

11. On the outside of the letter is written: "1827 Feb.," but the top of the letter is cut off. This might explain the missing signature. Under the date is written "Mr. Sealsfield." On January 29, 1827, Sealsfield had signed his contract with Murray for the publication of The United States of North America etc.

12. Opposite this address another hand wrote "Heinr. Fäsi." Baden is in Kanton Aargau. Since the "Caecilia Fest" is on November 22, which in this letter comes on a Wednesday, the letter was probably written a little more than a week before November 22, 1837. Sealsfield often went to Baden and was there in 1837. In that year November 22 came on Wednesday. This did not happen again until 1843, the second possibility.

13. This letter was addressed: "Herrn Dr. & Prof. Schönlein etc. etc. Wohlgeboren zu Hause." It was sent to Basel and returned on June 11th with the note "Vermutlich in Zürich selbst." The letter was hastily written and all Umlauts given here were omitted in the original letter.

14. Notation below: "49 Kr." Notation on outside of letter: "Sealsfield Baden 6 April 1842." Since Sealsfield at this time was working on Süden und Norden, this letter probably concerns the manuscript of that work.

15. This letter refers to the first edition of the Lebensbilder aus der westlichen Hemisphäre, to be published in Germany by Sealsfield's new publisher. The new edition was to bring order into the previous confusion of his works, a confusion caused in part by a change of publishers and in part by the

publication of the Lebensbilder aus beiden Hemisphären in
six volumes (Zürich, 1835-1837; I-III Orell, Füssli und Compagnie, IV-VI Friedrich Schulthess) before the completion of
the series Transatlantische Reiseskizzen (Zürich: Orell,
Füssli und Compagnie, 1834).

16. Notation in another hand above text of letter: "Baden, 30. Sept.
1840. 7br then was commonly used for September. Dorer
Egloff had a very fine Goethe library and was known as a
"Goethekenner." Cf. Allgemeine Deutsche Biographie,
XLVIII, 27-29.

17. On the other side of the letter in another hand: "Sealsfield,
Arlesheim, 24. Sept. 1853." From the context of the letter
it is clear that it was addressed to his publisher Erhard.
The "C" refers to Cotta. Obviously, Sealsfield was on his
way to America. Faust publishes a letter from New York,
dated April 25, 1854, in which Sealsfield says: "Herrn B.
Cotta oder seiner Allg. Zeitung zu schreiben, fand ich nach
reiflicher Ueberlegung nicht gerathen. Es würde curios
ausschen, wenn ein so alter Republicaner, der mehr denn 30
Jahre im Weinberge des Volkes gearbeitet, nun in seinen
alten Tagen für die Monarchien anfangen wollte zu arbeiten."

18. A Swiss banking house through which Sealsfield bought stocks.

19. One of the few close friends of Sealsfield. He was a man of
means.

20. Addressed to Nationalrat Peyer, executor of Sealsfield's testament.

21. "Post hier" is very difficult to read, it could also be "Vischer."

12. TWO PENNSYLVANIA-DUTCH POETS*

George Allen

I. HENRY HARBAUGH

For the past eighty years a most interesting literature has been growing in Pennsylvania, written in the Pennsylvania-Dutch dialect, and having, for the most part, no connection with the literary movement of either the United States or Germany. Works have been composed both in prose and verse by extremely facile writers. While the prose writers have remained almost solely concerned with the humorous, dialect poetry of a singularly high order and varied subject matter has been flourishing continually. Of the dialect poets the two most popular have been Henry Harbaugh and Henry Lee Fisher, the first writers of importance in their field.

The task which these men set themselves in order to mould a rather despised dialect into a language capable of poetic expression is perhaps worthy of discussion. By the time of Harbaugh and Fisher the Pennsylvania-Dutch dialect had reached a comparatively high state of homogeneity, through the fusion which had taken place in the course of the preceding two centuries. While the poet knew, however, that he could make himself understood by all his readers, his great difficulty was to find sufficiently lofty diction to maintain the level of poetry. When the early Germans began settling this country, they failed to furnish a means of supplying new words for new ideas or things which they would find here, a problem which could be met, and then only partially, by maintaining constant communication with the fatherland through reading the newspapers and the literature of Germany. Accordingly they had to invent new words, some of them indeed curious. For instance, when the railroad came into their daily life, they formed the words Rigelweg and Schteam for "railroad" and "steam," in one case by translating the words "rail" (Rigel) and "road" (Weg) into their language and in the other case by Germanizing the English word "steam." The latter example would seem to be the result of intellectual inertia, for they could have used the German word Dampf. "Radio" and "Movies," on the other hand, have been taken over exactly as they are in English.

The result is that poets, besides being limited to an everyday vocabulary much smaller than that brought over by the original

*Reprinted by permission of the publisher from American-German Review 8 (1942): 10-12, 34; and 9 (1942): 10-13, 37.

colonists, have had to adopt very un-Germanic and odd words into
their verse or do without the words altogether, the latter being the
choice wherever possible. Now the original vocabulary of the immigrants was in the first place inclined to be rather small, at least as
far as poetical expression was concerned, and when we consider the
added difficulty of being unable to represent modern ideas in writing
without making the work appear ludicrous, it is not surprising that
true dialect poetry began to develop at a rather late period.

William Cowper, in the introductory remarks to his translation of the Iliad, observes, "It is difficult to kill a sheep with dignity in a modern language, to flay and to prepare it for the table,
detailing every circumstance of the process." Cowper's situation,
in regard to expressing in another language ideas which are themselves poetical only if the tongue of the translator permit, was much
like that of the dialect poet. Thinking modern ideas and having a
modern outlook on life which, in conception, might be very poetic,
he simply cannot, in writing, touch on many of the usual subjects of
poetry and treat them with becoming dignity. Bryant's Thanatopsis,
translated some years ago into the dialect, develops into somewhat
of a farce because of the limitations of the vocabulary at the translator's disposal. On the other hand, domestic scenes can be made
unusually effective, since so many familiar words from the German
have been retained in the dialect.

With such limitations on the composition of serious poetry,
writers in the dialect were bound to develop rather late. In fact,
it was not until the second half of the nineteenth century that there
was any sustained effort to write dialect poetry.

While much verse, mainly of a theological strain, had been
written previously in High German by men like Francis Daniel Pastorius and Conrad Beissel, and there had been two sporadic attempts to compose verse in the dialect earlier, Henry Harbaugh is
the first dialect poet worthy of the name.

Henry Harbaugh was born near Waynesboro, Franklin County,
Pennsylvania, on October 28, 1817. Of Pennsylvania-Dutch ancestry on both sides of the house, he was brought up in the center of
a very German community. In his youth he showed a tendency towards study, but, at the insistence of his father, he learned farming. He went to school in the winter, beginning to work in the
fields as soon as the weather permitted, as was the custom at that
time. Later he decided to practice carpentry, in order to earn
enough money to go to theological school. After doing this for a
period, he went to Ohio, where he worked as a farmer and attended
school at the same time. Then he became a student at Marshall
College, and later at the Theological Seminary of the Reformed
Church at Mercersburg, Pennsylvania, though he did not finish his
courses because of lack of money.

After 1843 and for the greater part of the remainder of his
life, he was pastor of various Reformed churches, first in Lewis-

burg, later in Lancaster, and finally in Lebanon. His last position
was that of Professor of Theology in the Seminary at Mercersburg.
On December 28, 1867, he died, apparently of overwork.

During his short life Harbaugh published many books, both
theological and historical, several hymns which are said to be sung
to this day, some English poetry and some in the dialect, the latter
being printed in the Guardian, a church magazine which he founded
and edited. It was this poetry which, in after times, brought him
the most fame.

After his death it was suggested that it be made available in
book form. The poems were accordingly published in 1870, under
the title of Harbaugh's Harfe, by the Reformed Church Publication
Board and edited by the Reverend Dr. Benjamin Bausman, who, in
the preface in High German, begs the reader " 'die Harfe' nicht an
die Weiden zu hängen, sondern recht oft ihre schönen Klänge im
Kreise der Familie ertönen zu lassen." Several editions have since
been printed, so that the book, with its quaint illustrations, is quite
well known.

The first poet to apply himself seriously to the composition
of dialect poetry, Harbaugh found his task exceedingly difficult. His
knowledge of the language, as well as of High German, was of
course excellent. He then had to find subjects which would permit
of translation into an as yet untried dialect. For this purpose he
chose poems of the reminiscent, moral and humorous types, as well
as nature poetry, the first group being his largest. Harbaugh realized that the language he intended to use had great limitations, being considered eminently unsuitable for poetic expression. But with
the pioneering spirit that is characteristic of his people, he both
wrote and published his compositions.

It is unfortunate that Harbaugh's muse did not have the versatility that is usually the sign of a great poet. Of the four classifi-
cations of his poems, there are perhaps ten examples of reminiscent, two each of moral and humorous, and one poem dealing with
a nature subject. The latter, entitled "Der Pihwie," is in most respects his best. The author's great love for nature, which is seen
in all his poems, is best shown in this delightfully intimate and
quaint poem of ten stanzas on the return of a phoebe.

> Pihwie, Pihwie, Pihwittitie!
>   Ei, Pihwie, bischt zerick?
> Nau hock dich uf der Poschte hi'
>   Un sing dei' Morgeschtick.
>
> Hoscht lang verweilt im Summerland,
>   Bischt seit Oktower fort;
> Bischt drunne ordlich gut bekannt?
>   Wie geht's de Vegel dort?

Harbaugh's most representative and best known poem, per-

haps because it is first in the collection, is "Das alt Schulhaus an
der Krick."

> Heit is 's 'xäctly zwansig Johr,
>   Dass ich bin owwe naus;
> Nau bin ich widder lewig z'rick
> Un schteh am Schulhaus an d'r Krick,
>   Juscht neekscht an's Dady's Haus.

He goes on to tell how he has knocked about in the world,
but finds "Es is all Humbuk owwe draus," and then begins to remi-
nisce about his youth at the old schoolhouse, the lovely trees, the
birds, the schoolmaster, whose picture he paints with the words:

> Dort war der Meeschter in seim Schtuhl,
> Dort war sei' Wip, un dort sei' Ruhl,--
> Ich kann's noch Alles seh'.

He continues to give an excellent description of a country
schoolhouse of the early part of the nineteenth century, the instruction, the passing of "lofletters," the playing of games during lunch,
the ceremony of locking the teacher out, which was faithfully observed each Christmastime, and concludes:

> Oh horcht, ihr Leit, wu nooch mir lebt,
>   Ich schreib eich noch des Schtick:
> Ich warn eich, droh eich, gebt doch Acht,
> Un nemmt uf immer gut enacht,
>   Des Schulhaus an der Krick!

The simple charm and affectionate longing for home expressed
in his "Heemweh" is somewhat reminiscent of Goldsmith's "Deserted
Village."

> Ich wees net was die Ursach is--
>   Wees net, warum ich's dhu:
> 'N jedes Johr mach ich der Weg
>   Der alte Heemet zu;
> Hab weiter nix zu suche dort--
>   Kee' Erbschaft un kee' Geld;
> Un doch treibt mich des Heemgefiehl
>   So schtark wie alle Welt;
> Nor'd schtärt ich ewe ab un geh,
>   Wie owe schun gemeldt.

He continues to describe, in a passage undoubtedly reflecting
his own experience, pausing on the hill near the family home, the
view through the trees, and his emotions on first seeing the house.
Suddenly he notices that

> Alles is schtill--sie wisse net,
>   Dass epper fremmes kummt.

He recollects, in a very touching scene, how he left his home and saw his mother for the last time. This makes him pause, he realizes that it is no longer the home that he knew, for his parents are now dead. Then he becomes philosophical, and considers that this is his home for only a short while, and that he soon will go the path his parents trod. The theological element, which is never repressed in Harbaugh's poems, inevitably comes out in the last three stanzas, when he reflects on the "ew'ge Heemet," and what is in store for all.

Among his best poems are "Will widder Buwele sei'," "Die Scholfschtub" and "Der alte Feierheerd," all on the days of his youth which the author thinks could not be duplicated. They all show an enduring love for the days when he was a child.

In his poem "Lah Bisness" (Law Business), usually regarded as his poorest, Harbaugh shows that the Pennsylvania-Dutch dialect has a capacity for a reasonably subtle brand of humor, besides the lustier type for which it is perhaps too well known. This piece is without a doubt the best piece of poetry in a lighter vein in the dialect. In "Busch un Schtedtel" the author sings the praises of the country, to the obvious disadvantage of the city (where, it might be mentioned, he went whenever he had the opportunity). In addition to these poems, Harbaugh wrote a number of others relating childhood experiences and much in the manner of Robert Louis Stevenson.

The esteem with which Harbaugh's poetry has been regarded can be shown in no better way than in the number of imitators he has had. From Fisher, his near contemporary, Harter, Brunner, Rachel Bahn and many others down to the present day, dialect writers have been greatly influenced by his poetry.

II. HENRY LEE FISHER

Of the number of poets who followed Henry Harbaugh, Henry Lee Fisher (Fischer) had by far the most ability. He was born in 1822 in a section of Franklin County, Pennsylvania, known by the unofficial and probably superfluous name of the Dutch Settlement, at that time one of the more remote and less thickly settled parts of the county. There he acquired an education, and then taught school, both in Pennsylvania and Ohio. Later he took up law, and was admitted to the bar in Chambersburg. He then moved to York, Pennsylvania, where he lived for the greater part of his life, becoming a member of the York County bar. After over fifty years of practising law, he died in 1909.

Fisher was quite proud that among his ancestors was one who was also Harbaugh's. The life of the latter, along with his poetry, was a frequent source of inspiration to Fisher, a fact which is obvious immediately on reading his poetry. As a poet, however, Fisher is in some respects better than his predecessor. For, although the

latter occasionally wrote poems which were not childhood reminiscences, he did not have command over such a varied field of poetry as his part-time imitator.   Fisher could write nature poems
and ballads, humorous, anacreontic, descriptive and mourning verse,
as well as excellent translations and adaptations from English, German, and German-dialect poetry.   And while his poems do not always have the polish and charm of Harbaugh's, the varied selection
of topics on which he can write is so much greater as to balance
this.

In 1875, when confined to bed by an illness, Fisher worked
out a group of verses based on the old Market House in the square
of York, Pennsylvania.   Later he wrote another batch of verses on
the "olden times," and published them, in 1879, under the title 'S
Alt Marik-Haus Mittes in d'r Schtadt, un die Alte' Zeite'.   E'n Centennial Poem in Pennsylfanisch Deutsch.   In the introduction he is
careful to explain that they were not printed through his wishes, but
at the request of a number of friends who had heard them recited,
and who wished to possess copies of them.

Since they actually took form the year of the Centennial Exposition at Philadelphia, Fisher decided to stretch out the first poem
into a hundred stanzas, in honor of the occasion.   To this poem
was added "Die Alte Zeite," another series of verses strung together.   The first stanza of the first work is quite characteristic of the
whole production.

> Die Kerich isch schö, d'r Thurn isch hooch
> Un zielt 'm Himmel zu;
> Die Glock leit traurich in d'r Höh,
> Die Orgel schpielt 'n Liedli schö,
> Un all isch Fried un Ruh;
> Doch hen m'r nie so schönes g'hat,
> Wie's Marik-haus mittes in d'r Schtadt.

There is no bond of unity holding together the entire work,
except that " 'S alt marik-haus mittes in d'r Schtadt" is the center
of all the rhymed pictures.   We are told what we can buy at the
market, about the church, the courthouse, the prison, the cat who
keeps the mice away,

> Ich schtimm for selle braaf alt Katz
> For Head-Policeman nau...

and every other conceivable creature or thing that had any connection, however remote, with the neighborhood of the Market House.

"Die Alte Zeite," a congeries of verses built on quite the
same principles, was added to complete the book.

> Ich kan's net helfe, nem m'rs net
> For üwel, wan ich's sag;
> Ich sing nau fon die alte Zeite,
> Un henk mei Harf' nord uf die Weide
> 'N Mancher, Mancher Dag;

> Die Weide, die, die weil ich Sing,
> Die schteene noch dort an d'r Schpring.

It is occupied with descriptions, often interesting and entertaining, of intimate scenes and quaint customs of the Pennsylvania
Dutch. We have verses on their frolics, corn-huskings, apple butter
bees and quilting parties, threshing, flax-gathering, weaving, life in
a country school and a rural church, and many other scenes of extraordinary interest.

Now while these poems with their original orthography and
amazing illustrations, are particularly important to us because of
their antiquarian interest, the descriptions they give us of life in the
70s and earlier, they deserve the name of poetry only in that they
are usually found to scan. In talking about an old water mill, Fisher says:

> So mahlt a'h mei Gedichte-mühl,
> Was zu m'kummt zu mahle...

and this is precisely how the poem took form. Any scene, story,
or character that suggested itself to the author was immediately
twisted into rhyme and lined up along with the rest of the verses,
regardless of whether or not there was a connection with what pre-
ceded or followed. If we had to judge Fisher solely on the basis of
these two poems, our opinion of him would not reek with compli-
ment. Fortunately we know that he published them only at the insistence of his friends, and that his own opinion of them was not as
favorable as theirs.

By far Fisher's most important contribution to dialect poetry
is Kurzweil un' Zeitfertreib, Rührende un' Launige Gedichte in
Pennsylfanisch Deutscher Mundart, first published in York, Pennsylvania, in 1882 and republished in 1896. Here he wrote poetry with
more of the romantic and less of the reminiscent about it. The author displays the various sides of his own nature as well as his own
ability to express them in a much more convincing manner than in
his earlier book.

Fisher, in a footnote, tells us that the first poem he wrote,
in 1842, was "Jugendzeit," quite in the Harbaugh tradition (though
before he could have been influenced by Harbaugh), consisting of
reminiscence and longing for the days when he was young.

> Ach, wie fergnügt die Jugendtägen!
> Der Abend und der Morgen war;
> Wie frei fon alle Sindeplagen,
> Das herrlich, frölich, Jugendjahr!

This type of poetry, consisting of recalling the days of one's
youth, is most characteristic of the Pennsylvania Dutch. The genius
of the people, as well as the vocabulary, seem most suited to this
genre. It is fortunate, however, that Fisher soon gave it up to

write other kinds, because his poems with rural settings are decidedly the best of his original work.

Of his poems dealing with nature "Frühjohrs Lied" is outstanding. The author tells us his reaction to the coming of spring much in the manner of Friedrich von Spee in his "Der trübe Winter ist vorbei."

> Der Winter isch fort un' ich bin so froh--
> Wan er kumm't un' a'h wan er geht;
> Die Wolke sin weis un' der Himmel isch blo,
> Un' lieblig isch 's wu mer sich dreht;
> Die Hinkel, die, gaxe,
> Die Zwiwle, die, wachse,
> Un' die Amschel, die, baut sich e' Nescht.

Although Harbaugh shows a great appreciation of nature, no dialect poet before or since Fisher has written such a charming poem on spring and the delight he feels at its approach. With its sprightly meter and its charming one-line portraits of all the barnyard animals and the change that spring makes in their lives, we can feel with the writer that spring on a farm, apart from the additional work, is most delightful.

Although it begins with an unfortunate line, "Der Schnee" gives us an excellent picture of another time of the year.

> Der Schnee! der Schnee!   der schneeweisz Schnee!
>   Guck wie der Wind 'n bloost,
> Mer hen a'h drei sort Wetter, heut,
>   Es regert, schneet un' schloost.
>
> Die Luft isch dunkelfoll mit Schnee,
>   Guck, wie die Flocke danze;
> Der Wind, der, isch Drillmeschter, heut,
>   Un' macht die Flocke ranze.

These two poems, and "Der Einsiedler," with the exception of imitations and perhaps one or two others, are the author's only poems dealing with nature alone, but they show, with their excellent vocabulary for the sounds and actions of animals and for description of the country, that Pennsylvania Dutch is particularly adapted to this genre of poetry. Unfortunately too few poets have cared to develop it, perhaps because the temperament of the people is suited to feeling, rather than reading about, the out-of-doors.

Fisher was the first to mention the praises of women or drink in dialect poetry, in the type known as anacreontic, usually a very popular classification. Of this type he wrote two poems, quite in the tradition of the wandering scholars of the Middle Ages.

> Haet ich nix as mei Lisli mei Peif un' mei Wei,
> Es weer mer doch alles so hibsch un' so gut;

       Un' wan ich die hab, bin ich luschtig un' frei--
       Sie schtärke mer, immer, mei Herz un' mei Muth.

This poem and "Der Wei erfreut des Mensche Herz" are Fisher's
only two along another line which is well adapted to the dialect vocabulary.

      The only ballad that Fisher wrote is "Hesse Dhal," a medi-
ocre tale based on the Hessian army at Princeton on Christmas eve
of 1776 and later excesses.

      The author, in common with many other persons, took great
delight in such occupations as sitting home by the fire and feeling
the security from cold which only a warm fire can bring so efficient-
ly. "Wan's Feuer schö im Oefli brummt" and "Owet-Lied" are just
such poems, in which the poet expresses that peculiar feeling of
safety and peace with the world which we feel best when our work
is finished, and we know that all is well with the world.

      Fisher had a lively sense of humor. More of his poems can
be placed in the category of humorous verse than in any other.
Some six or seven of his works are humorous and occasionally, like
"Der Pessimist: oder, Wan alles in die Zeitung Kummt," they have
a touch of cynicism, which is apt to be the bedfellow of humor.
The Pennsylvania Dutch have always regarded lawyers and the law
with eyebrows somewhat raised, and even though the author was a
lawyer by profession, he indulged in a little fun at his own expense
in "Der Bauer Hans un' Der Advokat" and several others, especially with a liberal use of legal Latin, a most curious component of
dialect poetry. "Zu Grosz For Sei Hosse" is another humorous poem on the law.

      Certainly Fisher's most touching poem is "Mei Büwli," in
which he gives a heart-stirring lament for his little boy, who,
though long since dead, appears before his eyes at all times of the
year.

      Fisher also wrote occasional poetry, such as "Küchler's
Ruuscht," about a famous eating place no longer in existence, not
far from the city of Reading, Pennsylvania, and "Der Ehrlich Fritz,"
dedicated to a farm worker who had rendered faithful service for
many years and was now retiring.

      Not the least of Fisher's work consisted in translations of
many writers like Hebel, Nadler, Longfellow, Burns, Poe, and
many others. One of his best is a translation of Poe's "The Raven"
("Der Krab"), which is singularly close to the original in content as
well as meter. Translations of Burns's "Auld Lang Syne" and Longfellow's "A Psalm of Life" are among the group of more well-known
works he translated, though adaptations of Hebel and Nadler, the
German poets, are frequently nearer to the genius of the language
than the poems originally written in English.

Fisher is accordingly to be commended on his ability to tune his lyre to other themes besides reminiscence, and he has done a pioneer task in showing that the Pennsylvania-Dutch dialect is also adapted to the ballad, and the other types he used so skillfully, as well as the kinds of poetry to which Harbaugh confined himself.

Since the days of Harbaugh and Fisher many writers have written dialect poetry, so that the field is ever becoming richer for the occasional reader, as well as for the student. The occasional reader can revel in a delightful and extremely interesting literature, while the student has what Professor Albert B. Faust has called "one of the few original notes in American lyrical poetry," and a type which should, on historical grounds, be given equal rank with the plantation lyrics of the South.

13. FRANCIS LIEBER (1798-1872): GERMAN-AMERICAN POET
     AND TRANSMITTER OF GERMAN CULTURE TO AMERICA*

Thomas J. Kennedy

Francis Lieber was a nineteenth century liberal, as the title
of Frank Freidel's biography of him indicates.[1] He was known
chiefly for his contributions to the fields of history and political science. At South Carolina College (later the University of South Carolina) and Columbia University he had a reputation as a lively and
informative lecturer and teacher. Lieber led a feverishly active life
which brought him into contact with many eminent Americans. In
this brief study, it is my intention to indicate some neglected areas
of investigation which might prove to be valuable sources for new
researches in the field of German-Americana.

The story of Francis Lieber's youth reads like the pages of
an adventure novel. An impetuous young Berliner in the second
decade of the nineteenth-century, he marched in the ranks of the
Turnverein under the leadership of Ludwig Friedrich Jahn, whose
goals included a free and united Germany. He fought patriotically
against the armies of Napoleon at Waterloo and elsewhere, once re-
ceiving a wound which nearly cost him his life. After the defeat of
Napoleon, Lieber's attention was directed towards Greece where a
civil war was in progress. He joined the Philhellenic movement in
1821, only to have his romantic notions about Greek nobleness and
heroism crushed by the reality of the situation. He wrote later in
his diary: "... the cowardice and incapacity of the Greeks made
them unfit to defend or free their country."[2] The enthusiasm and
idealism which marked Lieber's participation in these youthful undertakings were qualities which were to endear him to the hearts of his
students and friends during a long and distinguished career in this
country.

Lieber studied at the Gray Friar's Cloister Gymnasium in
Berlin, "where he attended classes primarily in Latin, Greek, and
the antiquities."[3] Because of his radical political activities he was
refused permission to continue his studies at a Prussian university.
Defiantly, he matriculated as a student of theology at Jena, where
in August of 1820 he received his Doctor of Philosophy degree. He
had plans to enter upon a career in teaching, but was told by the
Prussian ministry that he would never be allowed to teach in Prussia.
Especially important for Lieber's intellectual development were the
lectures he attended in Berlin at the university which had been

*Reprinted by permission from German-American Studies 5 (1972):
28-50.

founded there in 1809, and which was under the directorship of Wilhelm von Humboldt. A remarkable faculty had been assembled. Fichte was professor of philosophy, Friedrich Schleiermacher lectured in theology, and Barthold Niebuhr and Friedrich Wolf taught history and archeology respectively.

Lieber's social life in Berlin brought him into contact with many important personalities. Through his acquaintance with Henriette Herz, a person of great charm and intellect who had become the warm friend of many of Germany's leading intellectuals and artists, he met the Humboldt brothers.[4] At the home of Julius Hitzig, a highly respected and influential lawyer, he entered into stimulating discussions with E. T. A. Hoffmann, Adalbert von Chamisso, and Friedrich de la Motte Fouqué.[5] With little hope of attaining any distinction in Germany, however, Lieber left for England with the intention of obtaining a professorship in German at the London University. He was bolstered by a warm letter of recommendation from his historian friend Niebuhr.

It is interesting to note that at this point Lieber may have attempted to obtain a letter of recommendation from Goethe, using the influence of Goethe's grand-nephew, Alfred Nicolovius. In a letter to Nicolovius of April, 1827, Goethe writes: "Verziehen sey mir gleichfalls wenn ich Bedenken trage ein Attestat für Lieber auszustellen, da ich seine Persönlichkeit gar nicht kenne und sein Talent nicht zu beurtheilen weiss."[6] Before any decision was made regarding Lieber's application for the professorship, he sailed from England to Boston, Massachusetts, where he taught physical education at a gymnasium and founded a swimming school. Turnvater Jahn had recommended him for the post.

During Francis Lieber's forty-five years in the United States, he came into contact with countless distinguished Americans. President Gilmann of the Johns Hopkins University once said: "... of the Americans devoted to public affairs, from 1840 to 1870, it may be said that Lieber knew every one of them."[7] Despite his German background, Lieber must not be thought of as being a zealous advocate of introducing German institutions and values into American life. He was clearly against the "Germanizing" of America. His attitude in this regard was expressed in a letter written April 23, 1847:

> I love my country ... but when they talk of Germanizing
> America, I spurn the idea.... What, Germanize Amer-
> ica and draw out of our country the Anglican institutions
> as the bones of a turkey, and leave a lump, fit only to be
> dispatched? No, no--modern liberty, people may say
> what they like, is ... essentially Anglican liberty; develop,
> modify, change, trim, improve, but keep the backbone.[8]

Thus, it was not through any programmatic effort, but rather because of his German intellectual training and his admiration for German literature and scientific method, that Lieber became a vehicle for transmitting German culture to America. Pochman states that he was "the first scholar of note widely to introduce the German scientific methods of research into American colleges and universities."[9] Lieber is characterized as one whose "influence was exerted through periodicals, in the classroom and lecture halls, and in books."[10]

In his large works in the field of political science, which display a Kantian influence,[11] Lieber documented his quotations and sources thoroughly. This care in documentation was not popular in America at the time, and Lieber appears to have been chided by some for being pedantic. In a letter to his friend, George Hillard, a lawyer and author to whom Lieber sent a fifty-five volume set of Goethe's works for his assistance in preparing a manuscript for publication,[12] he explains the reasons for his care in the use of footnotes:

> One word to you on the charge of pedantry.... The making acquaintance with a considerable part of literature, even outwardly, only by passages or titles, seemed to me not unimportant. One thing leads to another. I owe thanks to many authors for faithful citation; it has led me on. If I effect nothing by my quoting than that I aid, perhaps, some chap in Michigan, I consider myself already rewarded for what, you know well, is after all not pleasant in writing.... I knew very well that this way of quoting is not relished by French, English, or Americans. I did it, however, as a matter of conscience....[13]

It was this kind of care which critics praised in Lieber's most ambitious enterprise, the first edition of the Encyclopaedia Americana.

Francis Lieber signed his name to the preface of the final volume of the Encyclopaedia Americana on February 1, 1833. "In a little less than five years he had completed the task of editing an encyclopedia which was to remain standard in America until the time of the Civil War."[14] Cheap in price, the Americana sold phenomenally. Lieber himself later estimated the total sales to have reached one hundred thousand sets.[15] The work was based on the seventh edition of the Brockhaus Conversations-Lexikon.[16] But this served only as a basis. "Almost all the significant articles were new or rewritten--and from an American point of view ... Lieber had striven almost to the point of error to make the Encyclopaedia timely."[17] The work received very favorable reviews. In the influential North American Review appeared the comment: "This work ... deserves to be recommended to the great body of our people, as a library of itself:--cheap, comprehensive, exceedingly well executed, and of the highest authority."[18]

The project had been given backing by many of Lieber's distinguished New England acquaintances, among them Edward Everett, classics scholar and later president of Harvard, George Bancroft, Massachusetts statesman and scholar, Charles Follen, the first instructor of German at Harvard, and George Ticknor, instructor of

modern languages and literatures at Harvard.   Everett promised to
prepare articles on classics, and Ticknor on modern languages. 19
Both of these men had studied in Göttingen which makes their contributions to the Encyclopaedia of significance to Germanisten.

     An interesting incidental effect of the Americana's success
was the praise heaped upon the Brockhaus work as the reference
work most suitable to be used as the basis for the first American
encyclopedia.   German scholarship received wide acclaim.   One reviewer said of the Conversations-Lexikon:

>   It is free from all the narrowness of English prejudice,
>   it contains many important and interesting details which
>   can be found in no English production, and is a work
>   which could be written by none other than German schol-
>   ars.... 20

     In the Americana there was an emphasis on German civiliza-
tion which was lacking in early English-language encyclopedias.   "Infinite and incalculable as the effect of this emphasis may have been,
the wide circulation of this work served as a means by which a
strong element of the German spirit was injected into the American
mind, leading to a fuller understanding and appreciation of German
arts, sciences, and institutions. "21   In the Americana there are at
least 265 individual articles on German writers, artists, composers,
scientists, philosophers, theologians, and philologians. 22   In addition there are numerous articles on German geographical locations,
historical personages, and the like.   There is an article on Germany which has the sub-headings: "German Language, " "German
Literature and Science, " "German Prose, " "German Poetry, " and
"German Criticism. "

     In this rather long essay Schiller is viewed particularly as a
follower of Klopstock.   His ideas are as holy and as elevated as
Klopstock's, "but they appear clothed in reality and truth. "23   It is
noted that Schiller's poetry has been objected to as being too philosophical, but in German drama he is "undoubtedly the first. "24
Goethe is compared to Wieland.   Grace and fullness are found in the
poetry of both.   These qualities are attributed to Wieland because of
his continual study of Greek and French models.   But Goethe's excellence is due to the "strength with which his bold and penetrating
spirit pervades the unlimited variety of nature and the hidden re-
cesses of the human heart. "25   The author continues, however:
"One thing ... is wanting in Göthe's productions.   He does not set
forth strongly the moral dignity of man.... "26   Ludwig Tieck is said
to possess "poetical resources hardly inferior to Göthe's; and his
productions, moreover, are distinguished for virtue and purity as
well as for poetical spirit. "27   Novalis, "to whom the whole world
was one great poem, wrote sacred hymns of the most intense feeling and the highest spirit. "28   In evaluating the works of Goethe and
Schiller, the author exhibits a typically mid-nineteenth century concern for man's "moral dignity. "   I believe, however, that such high
praise for Tieck and Novalis was as yet rather unusual in America in

a survey of this kind. This emphatic endorsement of their talents
may have influenced the reputations of both poets on this continent.
All in all, the article contains hundreds of names and facts, and
presents the reader with a satisfactory synopsis of the course of
German literature.

Lieber himself is known to have contributed at least twenty-
three articles to the Encyclopaedia.[29] These cover a wide range of
topics from cookery to the immortality of the soul. The essay on
cookery reveals Lieber's informal manner and is very entertaining
reading (he recommends a German work on the subject "which
should be glad to see a translation"[30]). His articles concerned with
German culture are: "Dresden," "Goethe," "Haller," "Hegel,"
"Kant," the "Nibelungenlied," and "Karl Sand." The articles on
Kant, the Nibelungenlied, and Goethe are well done. The one on
Hegel is poor and reveals, perhaps, Lieber's personal dislike for the
man.[31]

Lieber exhibits a good grasp of the details of Kant's life, and
shows an admirable ease in handling a brief exposition of Kant's
philosophy. He maintains that "a man can hardly hope to acquire a
good idea of Kant's philosophy without reading him in the original."[32]
Kant's categories are enumerated, and two bibliographies of the philosopher's works are recommended. The Nibelungenlied is described as "an ancient German epic, little known to American and
English readers, but ranking, in our opinion, among the noblest
works of the imagination."[33] A brief account of the plot is then giv-
en and the historical background of the work is explained, noting,
rather interestingly, that August Wilhelm Schlegel considers the author to be either Klingsohr of Hungary or Henry of Ofterdingen. The
epic is then compared to the Iliad. "The language of the Iliad, is,
in our opinion, superior to that of the Nibelungenlied, both as to the
idiom itself and the mastership with which the Greek poet wields it,
though the German epic has a childlike and venerable simplicity....
On the other hand, the plan of the latter appears to us vastly superior to that of the former."[34]

Lieber calls Goethe "the greatest modern poet of Germany."[35]
Goethe is looked upon as the universal artist, having made significant contributions to practically every literary genre. Although his
dramas are not as great as Shakespeare's, and his epics and novels
have certain shortcomings, Goethe is the preeminent poet of philoso-
ophy.[36] "It is the philosophy of life and of individual characters,
pervading his works, which places them among the first ever produced.... His greatest production is his Faust, emphatically a philosophical poem."[37] Despite the mislabeling of Goethe as a poet of
philosophy, Lieber displays an intimate knowledge of Goethe's works.
Such unequivocal, high praise of Goethe was not common in the
United States at this time. In his work on German literature in
American magazines prior to 1846, Goodnight states:

> ... in 1832 the Goethe cult was as yet very young in
> America.... And it must not be forgotten that Charles

> Follen, who, by virtue of his position in Harvard, was
> perhaps the greatest of the forces then at work in the in-
> terests of German culture in America, and Franz List in
> Pennsylvania, were political refugees, intense admirers of
> Schiller, and, as former associates of Wolfgang Menzel,
> allies of the latter in his hostility toward Goethe.... it
> need excite no wonder that not many champions of Goethe
> appeared among the Harvard graduates in the early years
> of Dr. Follen's labors there....[38]

Among Lieber's other writings there are several short pieces
which are pertinent to his role as a transmitter of German culture
in America. In his Miscellaneous Writings[39] there is an essay on
Barthold Niebuhr, his historian friend, in which Voss, Schiller,
Klopstock, and Goethe are mentioned.[40] The collection also contains an address on Alexander von Humboldt given before the American Geographical Society in 1859.[41] Lieber once said of Humboldt,
"If it were allowable to use the term for any mortal, he, more than
any other, would lead me to call him Humboldt Divus."[42] In 1835,
Lieber translated the life of Caspar Hauser, a famous feral child,
into English from the German of Anselm Feuerbach, one of the foremost writers on criminal law in Germany. The translation passed
through several editions.

A thorough evaluation of Lieber's contributions to American
periodicals has never been made. It is known that Lieber contributed anonymous articles to several American reviews.[43] An investigation of this area of Lieber's activities may yield profitable
results. As an example of what one may find, consider Lieber's
article on "Turkey"[45] in the North American Review. It is a discussion of German works on this subject, one of them by Ranke,
with whom Lieber corresponded.[45] Ranke is praised highly for his
thorough research and his use of source material. In another article, entitled "German Association of Naturalists and Physicians."[46] Lieber uses the occasion to quote and translate selections
from Goethe and Schiller, while he promotes a literary and scientific union between Germany and the United States.

Besides corresponding with Ranke, Lieber carried on a correspondence with Wilhelm von Humboldt, whose works he read with
great interest. He exchanged information with Humboldt on a number of topics, chief among them being the North American Indians,
one of Lieber's favorite interests. Lieber had planned to establish
a society for the promotion of the study of Indian languages. He
asked Humboldt for advice concerning the project.[47] He also was
acquainted with the writings of the Grimm brothers and Franz
Bopp.[48] On one occasion, Lieber assisted Albert Gallatin, retired
Secretary of the Treasury, in preparing a work on Indian languages
by translating extracts from German manuscripts written by early
missionaries to Pennsylvania.[49] It is difficult to assess the depth
of Lieber's knowledge of the science of linguistics. He studied it
for a while in Rome with Niebuhr.[50] Perhaps Freidel underesti-
mates Lieber's importance in this field when he states that "Lieber

never became more than a dilettante who helped to introduce Americans to a little known study. "[51]

No survey of Lieber's influence would be complete without taking into account his many acquaintainces and friends. I would like to suggest some personalities whose relationship with Lieber may have led to a furthering of German culture in America.

One of these was Mrs. Elizabeth Ellet, the wife of chemist William Ellet. The Ellets met Lieber in South Carolina, when he arrived there to assume his responsibilities as professor of history and political science in 1835. Mr. Ellet became known for her translations of German works, and wrote a whole series of essays on the works of Schiller. Goodnight states that she "... did more than anyone of her sex to make Schiller known and appreciated in America. "[52] In addition to these well known writings, Mrs. Ellet translated a poem of Lieber's which was published in 1844. [54] Goodnight suggests that Lieber may have been influential in arousing Mrs. Ellet's interest in German literature. [54] In 1835 the Ellets occupied the other half of a duplex assigned to the Liebers, and in the following years they continued to live in close proximity to the Liebers on the campus. A chronology of Mrs. Ellet's works shows that her first publication appeared in 1836, a year after meeting Lieber. Even if Lieber didn't initiate in her this interest in German literature, the exchange of ideas between the two might have focused her attention upon it at the time.

Julia Ward Howe, American author and reformer famous for her "Battle Hymn of the Republic," met Lieber when she was a student in New York. They engaged in long conversations about German philosophy, among other things. Their friendship lasted a great many years, and it is quite possible that Lieber's animosity toward Hegel and admiration for Kant influenced her own opinion of these men. In a tribute to Lieber, she recalls:

> He [Lieber] had heard Hegel lecture, and had been impressed by his harsh dialect and unpleasant manner. I asked him whether Kant was not the greater of the two. He thought so, and thought, as many do, that Hegel in his cumbrous way of expressing himself had aimed rather at obscurity than at clearness of diction. [55]

Mrs. Howe, as well as her friend Theodore Parker, an intellectual associated with the Dial and its transcendentalist philosophy, had read Lieber's Manual of Political Ethics. [56]

Lieber's friendship with Henry Wadsworth Longfellow, Charles Sumner, and Joseph Story is rather well known. Lieber and Longfellow spent much time together and criticized each other's poetry. Longfellow even translated one of Lieber's poems. [57] Charles Sumner, whom Lieber referred to as Don Carlos, might never have learned German had it not been for Lieber's constant urging. In a letter to Sumner, Lieber mentions Hillard as well:

> Ah my friend if you knew German ...! Now I charge you
> and Hillard to say to each other every morning when you
> first meet, 'O Sumner,' or 'O Hillard, remember thou
> knowest not German ..!'[58]

Sumner replied: "Your friendly address to me I appreciate, and under your advice shall hasten to learn German."[59]

It was through Lieber's influence that both Sumner and Judge
Story, who contributed articles to the Americana, became acquainted
with Karl Mittermaier, professor of criminal law at Heidelberg.
This contact resulted in an exchange of legal thought across the Atlantic, which eventually led to the inclusion of an article by Story
in a German legal publication, and to the publication of articles by
Mittermaier in the American Jurist.[60] Once Lieber supplied Sumner with letters of introduction when Sumner traveled abroad.[61] In
1835 Lieber had done the same for Ticknor, "to introduce him to
Mittermaier, Ranke, Thiersch, Menzel, Förster, and Hitzig."[62]
The results of this kind of activity have never been thoroughly investigated.

Two other people whom Lieber might have influenced are
Ralph Waldo Emerson and James Freeman Clarke, a Unitarian
clergyman and Transcendentalist. Emerson makes rather frequent
mention of the Encyclopaedia in his journals, and once quotes Lieber, identifying the latter's sentiments with his own.[63] James Freeman Clarke, a person with whom, to my knowledge, no one has
connected Lieber, recalls meeting Dr. Lieber and discussing Schleiermacher with him. After they parted, Clarke writes: "I received
some letters from this new friend, one of which contained a poem to
Niagara."[64] This meeting took place in 1832, before Clarke began
to publish his many translations of German literature.

Other persons whose connection with Lieber should be investigated are Edgar Allan Poe, William Cullen Bryant, and Nathaniel
Hawthorne. It was Poe who invited Lieber to contribute articles to
the Southern Literary Messenger.[65] Bryant and Hawthorne are
named as contributors to the Americana, and further research may
bring to light unknown works by these authors.[66] There is an impressive list of contributors to the Americana whose work for the
Encyclopaedia and whose connection with Lieber have not been fully
explored. This list includes: Josiah Quincey, president of Harvard
while the Encyclopaedia was in progress; William Ellery Channing,
Transcendentalist and Unitarian religious leader; Cornelius Felton,
translator of Wolfgang Menzel's German Literature (1840); Sylvanus
Thayer, head of the West Point Military Academy; philologian Peter
S. Duponceau; historians Bancroft and Prescott; Zoologists John
James Audubon and Johann Bachmann; the botanist Nuttall; Henry
Wadsworth Longfellow; the ex-king Joseph Bonaparte; and some of
Lieber's earliest backers in the undertaking, Charles Follen, Ed-
ward Everett, and Moses Stuart.

Francis Lieber's poetic writings constitute another area for

investigation which has never been adequately treated.   Concerning
a small volume of verse, Wein- und Wonnelieder (Berlin, 1826),
which Lieber wrote in prison under the pseudonym Arnold Franz and
dedicated to Karl Maria von Weber and Karl Friedrich Zelter,
Goethe's composer friend, Lieber says:

> Genuss ... was one of the elements of my intellectual life
> at this period.   Goethe was not inactive in all this.   Asi-
> atic poetry; Goethe; patriotism; serious reading; stern view
> of my opinions and convictions; Italy, as if I were in Rome;
> philosophy; history; disesteem for my fellow prisoners;
> everything as active within me as if it existed alone at the
> time....   I now plunged ... into the idea of the day, of
> the hour, of wirklich sein wirklich haben, of Genuss in der
> Gegenwart; yet all my Goethic ideas or feelings were al-
> ways tinged with additional glow and fervor.   Hence these
> Wine-Songs. [67]

Lieber also wrote a tragedy during this period, "Die beiden
Hedwigs," which he took to Holtei for his critical opinion.   It never
appeared in print. [68]   In addition, he sent a play and some poems to
Jean Paul, asking him for comments.   Lieber received no reply.
Not until eighteen years after the fact did he discover that Jean Paul
had indeed sent him a reply which never reached him.   Mrs. Elizabeth Lee, the American biographer of Jean Paul, discovered the letter in the course of her research and notified Lieber.   Jean Paul
had some encouraging words for the young poet: "Ihrer Muse werde
Musse und Segen. "[69]

The number of poems written by Lieber before he left Europe
is difficult to ascertain.   On several occasions in his diary he mentions writing poems.   He is also known to have written several doz-
en poems dedicated to Matilda Oppenheimer, his future wife whom
he met in London in 1826.   These are still among the unpublished
Lieber papers. [70]

Lieber's wife tells us that during his career in America he
often composed poems: "Bei den ernsten Arbeiten, erholte er sich
öfter auf diese Weise."[71]   To my knowledge, less than thirty of his
poems have appeared in print in this country.   Lieber wrote poetry
in both English and German.   The poems were printed, for the most
part, in small groups in German-American periodicals.   Only one
small volume of Lieber's verse was published separately in the
United States, The West (New York, 1848, pp. 31).   The first small
group of poems to appear here was published in translation in 1847.
The translator was Rev. Charles Timothy Brooks, whom Lieber described as a man "with a delicate and sensitive soul panting for the
food of literature and poetry,--a real character for Jean Paul to
dwell upon."[72]   Other poems were not published until after Lieber's
death in 1872.

Lieber was a versatile poet.   He wrote sonnets, lyric poems
in varying rhymes and rhythmic patterns, metrical epistles, long

descriptive poems, and several poems in free verse. The recurring
themes are love, nature, patriotism, America, brotherly love, and
trust in God. Lieber was a sincere American patriot and expressed
in some of his poetry a heartfelt attachment and pride in his adopted
country. He viewed America as a refuge for fleeing Europeans, a
haven for law and order, and a country of tremendous wealth and
potential where hard work and respect for the rights of others were
woven into the fabric of society.

The following is a selection (3rd stanza) from "An Champollion," a long poem written as a tribute to Jean Francois Champollion (1791-1832), a French archeologist and Egyptologist who was a
friend of Niebuhr and Lieber. The poem is of interest since it is
probably one of the very earliest poems written in free verse on this
continent.

An Champollion (Boston, den 7. Mai 1832)

Verschlossene Pforten,
Vor denen Jahrtausende
Wundernd vorüberzogen,
Sprangen auf vor dem Zauber
Deines entriegelnden Scharfsinns
Du heissest die starren
Basaltenen Bilder
[Uns näher treten.
Und uns erzählen]
Saulen und Bogen
Und Obelisken,
Unermässliche Wände
Und Pyramiden,
Bedeckt mit geheimer
Schrift verflossener,
Längst entschwundener
Thätiger Völker--
Räthsel die Keiner gelöst,
Wie Viel' es versuchten,--
Sie wurden von dir,
Wie entsiegelte Bücher,
Beredte Kunden
Grauer Vorzeit.[73]

All of the observations made in this article were based on the
relatively small amount of material available on Francis Lieber. No
use was made of the Lieber papers in the Henry E. Huntington Library.[74] This collection contains tens of thousands of items and
would aid inestimably in arriving at a fuller view of Lieber's contributions to the advancement of German culture in America.

To my knowledge, no one has compiled a comprehensive list
of Lieber's contributions to American periodicals. Lieber's connection with the whole group of Transcendentalists affiliated with the
Dial would be worth investigating. And finally, the relationship be-

tween Lieber and Mary Baker Eddy, and the claim that she utilized a Lieber manuscript as the basis for significant passages in her Science and Health, have not been considered here, since the matter is still open to some doubt.[75]

Notes

1. Frank Freidel, Francis Lieber, Nineteenth-Century Liberal (Baton Rouge: Louisiana State Univ. Press, 1947).
2. Thomas Sergeant Perry, The Life and Letters of Francis Lieber (Boston: James R. Osgood, 1882), p. 14.
3. Freidel, p. 19.
4. Ibid., p. 41.
5. Ibid., p. 41.
6. Johann Wolfgang von Goethe, Goethes Werke (Weimar: Hermann Böhlaus Nachfolger, 1907), IV. Abteilung, 42. Band, 131.
7. Henry August Pochmann, German Literature in America (1600-1900), (Madison: Univ. of Wisconsin Press, 1957), p. 570, n. 538.
8. Ibid., pp. 569-570, n. 537.
9. Ibid., p. 126.
10. Ibid., p. 491.
11. Ibid., pp. 125-126.
12. Freidel, p. 165, n. 55.
13. Perry, pp. 134-135.
14. Freidel, p. 76.
15. Ibid., p. 80.
16. Allgemeine deutsche Real-Encyclopaedie für die gebildeten Stände (Conversations-Lexikon), (Leipzig: F. A. Brockhaus, 1827-1829).
17. Freidel, pp. 77.
18. John Neal, "Encyclopaedia Americana," North American Review, 34 (1832), 262.
19. Freidel, p. 68.
20. Francis Lieber, Letters to a Gentleman in Germany (Philadelphia: Carey, Lea & Blanchard, 1834). This review appeared two pages after page 356 in the left hand column.
21. Pochmann, p. 125.
22. I arrived at this figure by checking through the indices to the 13 volumes. All German-sounding names were investigated.
23. Encyclopaedia Americana, ed. Francis Lieber, (Philadelphia: Carey, Lea & Carey, 1832-1835), V. 474.
24. Ibid., V. 474
25. Ibid., V. 474.
26. Ibid., V. 474.
27. Ibid., V. 474.
28. Ibid., V. 474.
29. The articles are: "Common Law," "Constitution," "Cookery," "Cousin," "Dresden," "Greece," "Goethe," "Grotius," "Gymnastics," "Haller," "Hegel," "Immortality of the Soul," "Kant," "Macchiavelli," "Memory," "Montesquieu," "Mutual Instruction," "Napoleon," "Niebelungenlied," "Niebuhr,"

"Prisons," "Prison Discipline," and "Sand."

30. Americana, III, 512.
31. See text to note 55.
32. Americana, VII, 305.
33. Ibid., IX, 276.
34. Ibid., IX, 277
35. Ibid., V, 543.
36. Ibid., V, 545.
37. Ibid., V, 545.
38. Scott Holland Goodnight, German Literature in American Maga-
    zines Prior to 1846, in Bulletin of the University of Wiscon-
    sin, No. 188, Philology and Literature Series, Vol. 4, No.
    1 (Madison: Univ. of Wisconsin Press, 1907), p. 73.
39. Francis Lieber, Miscellaneous Writings, ed. Daniel C. Gilman,
    2 vols. (Philadelphia: J. B. Lippincott, 1881).
40. Ibid., I, 82-148.
41. Ibid., I, 389-410.
42. Lewis R. Harley, Francis Lieber, His Life and Political Phi-
    losophy (New York: Columbia Univ. Press, 1899), p. 173.
43. Frank Luther Mott, A History of American Magazines, 1741-
    1850, 2 vols. (Cambridge, Mass.: Harvard Univ. Press,
    1957). See indices under "Lieber."
44. Francis Lieber, "Turkey," North American Review, 31 (1830),
    291-308.
45. Perry, p. 89.
46. Francis Lieber, "German Association of Naturalists and Physi-
    cians," North American Review, 31 (1830), 84-95.
47. Perry, p. 81.
48. Freidel, p. 178.
49. Lieber, Miscellaneous Writings, I, 499.
50. Freidel, p. 178.
51. Ibid., p. 178.
52. Goodnight, p. 100.
53. Ibid., p. 299.
54. Ibid., p. 100.
55. Julia Ward Howe, "Dr. Francis Lieber," The Critic, 2 (1832),
    352.
56. Francis Lieber, Manual of Political Ethics, 2 vols. (Boston:
    C. C. Little & J. Brown, 1838). See Howe, The Critic, 2
    (1832), 352.
57. Freidel, pp. 243-244, n. 43.
58. Perry, p. 106.
59. Edward L. Pierce, ed., Memoirs and Letters of Charles Sum-
    ner (Boston: Roberts Bros., 1893), p. 144.
60. Mortimer L. Schwartz and John C. Hogan, ed., Joseph Story
    (New York: Oceana, 1959), pp. 80-81.
61. Pochmann, p. 577, n. 558.
62. Perry, p. 105.
63. Ralph Waldo Emerson and Waldo Emerson Forbes, ed., Jour-
    nals of Ralph Waldo Emerson (Boston: Houghton Mifflin,
    1912), VII, 459.
64. Edward Everett Hale, James Freeman Clarke (Cambridge,
    Mass.: Riverside, 1891), p. 64.

65. Karl Goedeke, Grundriss zur Geschichte der Deutschen Dichtung aus den Quellen, 2nd ed., herausgegeben von Herbert Jacob (Berlin: Akademie-Verlag, 1964), XV, 584.

66. Heinrich Armin Rattermann, "Franz Lieber," German American Annals, 2 (1904), 711.

67. Perry, p. 59.

68. Ibid., p. 60.

69. Jean Paul Friedrich Richter, Jean Pauls Sämtliche Werke, Historisch-kritische Ausgabe, ed. Eduard Berand (Berlin: Akademie-Verlag, 1955), 3. Abteilung, 8 Band (Briefe 1820-1825), 270.

70. Freidel, p. 47.

71. "Nachgelassene Gedichte von Franz Lieber," Der Deutsche Pionier, 11. Jahrg., Heft 9 (December, 1879), 330

72. Perry, pp. 176-177.

73. Heinrich Armin Rattermann, "Franz Lieber," German American Annals, 3 (1905), 6. Lines 8 & 9 were published in reverse order.

74. Freidel, pp. 418-421.

75. Ibid., p. 420.

14. FRIEDERICH GOLDBECK*

Robert Govier

Among the writers of poetry in New Braunfels, none has left a more complete historical record of the times than Friederich Goldbeck. He was born in Itzingen-Verden in 1830[1] and died in San Antonio, Texas on April 11, 1899.[2] He was one of the first to emigrate under the auspices of the Adelsverein. He arrived in Texas in 1844 at the age of fourteen. In 1846 he was a member of the first confirmation class accepted into membership by The First Protestant Church of New Braunfels.[3] He served as Justice of the Peace and Tax-Collector,[4] and was Mayor of New Braunfels from May 12, 1867 to November 8, 1872.[5] Goldbeck's poetry is collected in two volumes under the title Seit fünfzig Jahren.[6] His verse is "rustic" by literary standards. He himself sub-titles his work "Prosa in Versen." A later commentator says she would like to call his poems "Bilder in Versen."[7] Concerning his poetry Goldbeck says:

> Ich bin kein Studiosus,
> Kein Mann der Wissenschaft,
> Was thut's? Natur, die Mutter,
> Gab mir Empfindungskraft
>
> Ich las in ihrem Buche,
> Ich schaute ihre Pracht,
> Und brachte dann in Reime,
> Was ich gefühlt, gedacht.
>
> Ob diese mir gelungen,
> Wag ich zu hoffen kaum,
> Sie gleichen wilden Rossen,
> Die nie gefühlt den Zaum.
>
> (Vol. II, p. 3)

Using rhymed couplets almost exclusively, he tells of the arrival of the first immigrant ships, the overland trip to the grant, the founding of New Braunfels, Friedrichsburg, and Boerne, and the building of the Sophienburg. In all, his two volumes contain some one hundred and forty poems.

*Reprinted from Robert A. Govier, "German Poetry Written in New Braunfels, Texas." University of Texas: M.A. Thesis, 1962, pp. 10-20. By permission of the author.

One of Goldbeck's most poignant poems is "Die Leiden der
ersten Einwanderer." In it he pictures the plight of the immigrants
who, having contracted the plague during their stay on the coast,
drew near to New Braunfels but were destined not to succeed in
their plans. His stanza form is ABCB with masculine rhyme
throughout. The meter is iambic trimeter.

Im dunklen Waldesschatten,
Im Sumpf, auf grüner Flur,
Im weiten Prärielande,
Sucht ihrer Gräber Spur.

Die Sonnenstrahlen glühten,
Die Luft war dumpf und schwül,
Da fuhr ein kleiner Wagen
Durch dichtes Staubgewühl.

Ein kleines Maulthier schleppte
Ihn durch den tiefen Sand,
Das kleine Fuhrwerk mahnte
An's deutsche Vaterland.

Ein Mann, sein Weib, vier Kinder
Die folgten wohlgemuth,
Im Wagen war geborgen,
Ihr bischen Hab und Gut.

Die guten Leutchen zogen
Dem Städtchen Braunfels zu.
Zwei Tage noch, dann fanden
Sie die ersehnte Ruh.

Der Wagen aber leider
Hielt nicht mehr lange Stand,
So lagen denn die Armen
Hilflos am Waldesrand.

Dumpf rollte schon der Donner,
Gewitter zog daher,
Den schutzlos so Bedrängten
Ward wohl das Herz recht schwer.

Die bösen Wetter tobten
Mit ungeschwächter Wuth,
Der Regen floss in Strömen,
Den Armen sank der Muth.

Es schützte sie nur wenig
Das wilde Waldgerank,
Bald lagen, Frost durchschüttelt,
Sie Alle siech und krank.

Es fand sie drauf ein Farmer,
Die Meisten waren todt.
Ein Knäblein wurd' gerettet
Aus jener Schreckensnoth.

Kennt ihr den grossen Nussbaum
Der in Dors Prärie steht?
Dort ist ihr Grab zu finden,
Wenn nicht von Sturm verweht.

So Mancher, heute glücklich,
Die Frucht der Zeit geniesst,
Der nimmer daran denket,
Dass sie aus Gräbern spriesst.

                                    (Vol. I, pp. 16-17)

Besides poems dealing with the arrival of the Germans and
their colonization activities, Goldbeck has poems dealing with typically Texan figures such as the Squatter, Farmer, Hunter, and Cowboy. He also pictures more universal characters, sometimes in a
tragic vein. In "Ein Tramp" he tells of a uniquely happy family
that comes to grief because of drink:

Es war ein nett und freundlich Haus,
Glückselig drin die Leute,
Manch köstlicher Geburtstagsschmaus
Mich dort als Gast erfreute.

Der Herr des Hauses und sein Weib,
Zwei Menschen brav und bieder,
Bei ihnen fand ich Zeitvertreib,
Verkehrte hin und wieder.

Des Hauses frohe Kinderschaar,
Ein Knabe und zwei Mädchen,
Der Eltern grösste Freude war,
Beliebt im ganzen Städtchen

So lebten sie in Einigkeit
Manch liebes langes Jährchen,
Doch Eintracht und Zufriedenheit
Hängt oft am schwachen Härchen.

Der böse Feind kam in das Haus,
Der Trunk mit einem Worte,
Die guten Geister flohn hinaus,
Der Unhold blieb am Orte.

Vertrieben hat er dort das Glück,
Die Herzen all geschieden,
Der Greis zog fort, kehrt nicht zurück,
Wo fand er Ruh und Frieden?

Zur Brücke geht er, steht dort lang,
Die Wasser unten rauschen,
Er mag wohl auch dem trauten Klang
Des Abendglöckleins lauschen.

Denkt er an die Vergangenheit
Mit ihren schönen Stunden,
Die sind für alle Ewigkeit
Verloren ihm, entschwunden.

Er neigt das Haupt, beugt sich hinab,
Sein Herz ist am verbluten,
Hier findet er ein kühles Grab
In heimatlichen Fluthen.

Man findet, doch erkennt ihn nicht,
Der Tramp wird still begraben;
Das ist die letzte Menschenpflicht,
Wer mag wohl um ihn klagen?

                                        (Vol. I, pp. 86-88)

(For the sake of brevity, only selected stanzas are quoted above.)

Goldbeck also alludes to the antagonism between the Germans
and native Americans in respect to slavery and secession.   The
Germans were by disposition and training opposed to slavery.   They
considered it an evil and felt that it lessened the value of their own
labor.[8] Still, the great majority of the Germans, in spite of their
leanings, cast their lot with the Confederacy during the Civil War.
One group, however, formed a military organization with the object
of marching to Mexico and joining the Union Army from there.
They were met and attacked by a large body of Confederates at the
Nueces River on August 10, 1862.   Of the seventy, thirty-two were
killed.   Some of the others were taken prisoner and later shot; only
seven escaped.[9]   This incident is celebrated by Goldbeck in the poem "Das Monument der am Nuces [sic] Gefallenen zu Comfort":

Auf Comforts Eichenhügel
Steht heut ein Monument,
Zu künden später'n Zeiten
Lojaler Leute End.   4

Dort ruhen arme Opfer
Der grossen Secession,
Dem Eid getreue Bürger
Der freien Union.   8

In ihres Lebens Blüthe,
Der schönsten Jugendkraft,
Hat blinder Fanatismus
Sie einst dahin gerafft.   12

Politische Gesinnung,
Das freien Mannes Gut,
Fand damals keine Duldung
In der Empörungsgluth.   16

Von Comfort hin nach Westen
Zum fernen Rio Grand,
Dehnt sich ein Felsbesätes,
Zerrissenes, wildes Land.   20

Bedeckt mit Cederwäldern,
Wo noch in mancher Schlucht
Die schwarzen Bären hausen,
Vom Jäger ungesucht.   24

In jenen wilden Bergen
Sind Wolf und Pantherthier
Die ungestörten Herren,
Durchstreifen das Revier   28

Eintönig, melancholisch,
Der Taube Ruf erschallt,
Sonst herrschet Todtenstille
Im weiten öden Wald.   32

Durch die sterile Wildness,
Die damals Pfadlos war,
Zog nach dem Rio Grande
Beritten jene Schaar   36

Der armen Conseribirten,
Die schliesslich in der Flucht
Vor dem verhassten Zwange
Ihr einzig Heil gesucht.   40

Wo unterm Ufer rieselt
Ein Quell am Waldessaum,
Liegt in den dunklen Cedern
Ein weiter offener Raum.   44

Wild gab es dort in Fülle,
Der Ort lud ein zur Rast,
Nicht leicht fand jene Stelle
Ein ungebetener Gast.   48

Die jungen Leute wähnten
Sich endlich einmal frei,
Gesichert und geborgen
Vor jeder Tyrannei.   52

Bald knallten ihre Büchsen
Im Walde ringsumher,
Ja leider, sie versäumten
Die Vorsicht täglich mehr.   56

So schlich denn das Verderben
Auch über Nacht heran,
Sie wurden überfallen,
Ein wilder Kampf begann.   60

Bald lagen da die Meisten
Von Kugeln arg zerfetzt,
Nur wenige entkamen.
Gesund und unverletzt.   64

Verschont hat man nicht Einen,
Der da verwundet lag.
Das war für jene Sache
Ein blutger Opfertag.   68

Man hat dann nach dem Kampfe
Den Schlachtplatz rings umstellt,
Wo die Gefall'nen lagen
Auf blutgetränktem Feld.   72

Verderben drohte Jedem,
Der sich den Ort mocht nahn,
Noch mancher fiel zum Opfer
Dem blinden Rückschrittswahn.   76

Der letzte Schuss verhallte,
Der Bruderkrieg war aus,
Des Südens Heere kamen,
Enttäuscht, zurück nach Haus.   80

Sie hatten brav gestritten
Für and'rer Leute Gut,
Die unterdessen blieben
Zu Hause, wohlgemuth.   84

Da Ordnung wieder herrschte,
Nicht mehr die Raserei,
So zogen auch die Freunde
Der Todten bald herbei.   88

Was von den theuren Resten
Da noch zu finden war,
Das sammelte mit Schmerzen
Die tiefbetrübte Schaar.   92

Im kleinen Heimathstädtchen,
Am grünen Waldessaum,
Ruhn friedlich die Gebeine
Vereint, im engen Raum.   96

Ein Stein bedeckt nun Alle,
Die einst in schwerer Noth

Treu zu einander hielten,
Bis sie ereilt der Tod.   100
(Vol. I, pp. 25-27)

The above poem is quoted in full because it is, to a high degree, typical of Goldbeck's output. The lines are numbered for
quick reference, and all line-references in the following discussion
relate to the above poem.

Note must be made of the relative purity of Goldbeck's language. Only in treating Texan types such as Squatter, Farmer,
Hunter and Cowboy are non-German words found. This is not to
say that Goldbeck's diction is flawless, for in line 4 we would expect "Loyaler" rather than "Lojaler," and in line 37 we see "Conseribirten" rather than "Sonscribierten." Also, in line 74 we find
"den Ort" when we would expect "dem Ort." Attention must be
drawn to the possibility of these inconsistencies being printer's errors (especially "conseribirten") inasmuch as, in the volume before
this commentator, some punctuation marks seem to be added mistakenly, as at the end of line 63. Other punctuation marks are
seemingly neglected. A period was supplied by this writer after
line 44, where it is called for by both sense unit and line unit.
Note also the misspelling in the title.

Not only does Goldbeck hold to a relative purity of language,
but he is well-meaning and has an enthusiasm for his subject. He
doubtless felt his subject matter to be more important than his style
or the poetic quality of his verse. Thus, his verses are chatty and
their poetic tension is low. Certainly Goldbeck is successful in his
undertaking, and especially so in the eyes of the unsophisticated
reader. This does not, however, necessarily make him a good poet.

There is very little variety in Goldbeck's verse. Occasionally one finds a poem in six-line stanzas (p. 73, Vol. I). Already
mentioned were his narrative poems in rhymed couplets, but the
great majority of his poems are in four-line stanzas utilizing iambic
meter. The rhyme scheme is for the most part ABCB or, perhaps,
ABAB. The second and fourth lines usually exhibit masculine
rhyme, while the first and third lines, if they rhyme, will more
than likely incorporate feminine rhyme or feminine slant rhyme (as-
sonance). The last mentioned arrangement is seen in lines 25 and
27.

The lack of variety is seen in Goldbeck's diction also. In
lines 34 and 36 the words "war" and "schaar" form the masculine
rhyme. These same two words, in the same order, form the
rhyme in lines 90 and 92. Another case of duplication of diction is
seen in lines 42 and 44 when compared with lines 94 and 96. The
same words, "Waldessaum" and "Raum," are used for rhyming pur-
poses.

It is evident that Goldbeck endeavored to maintain a very
strict iambic meter. This in itself leads to dullness. It would be

far better to vary the meter in such a way as to emphasize a certain word or thought. This he has done with success in line 99,
where the word "treu" must be accented, and, in disrupting the
meter as it does, receives the added stress which it deserves.
More often than not, however, he seems to vary the meter only because he isn't able to force the thought into the accustomed iambic
mold. In short, the meter seems to manipulate the poet, rather
than vice versa. Line 67 incorporates correct meter, but the result is an unpoetic line. Lines 35 and 43 exhibit variety in meter,
but do not do so in such a way that they contribute to the total effect of the poem.

Goldbeck's images sometimes lead to confusion. In lines 75
and 76 we are told that many a one still fell, a victim to blind
"Rückschrittswahn." But there is some doubt as to who this "many
a one" was. We have already been told in lines 64 and 65 that none
of the wounded were spared, thus "mancher" may refer to some
prisoners who had been taken. Of this we can't be sure, however.
Perhaps some of those who had escaped tried to return, as is perhaps suggested in line 74.

The tone of the poem is well chosen. There can be little
doubt concerning Goldbeck's sympathies. Witness the very effective
characterization of the Confederates as "das Verderben" in line 57.
Yet his account creates a certain feeling of objectivity. Goldbeck
does not insist upon a stronger response than what the situation
calls for.

Notes

1. "Kirchenbuch der Protestantische Gemeinde Neu Braunfels, Texas," I, p. 6. A transcription of this work was made in the
   nineteen-thirties under the direction of R. L. Biesele, and is
   located in the Archives of The University of Texas.
2. Personal interview with Miss Edna Goldbeck of San Antonio and
   Mrs. Edith Goldbeck Frost of Bulverde, both of whom are
   granddaughters of Friederich Goldbeck.
3. Oscar Haas, The First Protestant Church, Its History and Its
   People 1845-1955 (New Braunfels, 1955), p. 118.
4. Selma Metzenthin-Raunick, Deutsche Schriften in Texas (Austin,
   1935), p. 16. This work will hereafter be referred to as
   Raunick, with page number.
5. The names and terms of office of all Mayors of New Braunfels
   are given on a plaque which is located on the south wall of
   the Sophienburg Memorial Museum at New Braunfels.
6. Fritz Goldbeck (San Antonio, 1895).
7. Raunick, p. 17.
8. G. G. Benjamin, The Germans in Texas (Philadelphia, 1909),
   p. 90.
9. Alexander T. Schem, Deutsch-Amerikanisches Konversations-
   Lexicon, X (New York, 1873), p. 694. Article, "Texas."

15. MATHILDE FRANZISKA GIESLER-ANNEKE*

Albert B. Faust

The histories of the German element in the United States have
done but scant justice to the career and personality of Mathilde
Franziska Anneke, undoubtedly the most heroic figure among the
many noble types of German womanhood who have come to this country, and whose achievements have so largely remained unrecorded.
The founder of radical journals, she did not have the genius for
business which distinguished Anna Behr Ottendorfer and allowed the
latter to follow the bent of her heart in founding institutions of charity; she did not command the social prestige of the talented Therese
v. Jakob Robinson (Talvj), or Marie Hansen Taylor (wife of Bayard
Taylor), whom she equalled or surpassed in literary ability, and re-
sembled in their devotion to husband and children. But Madam Anneke, as she was generally called in this country, was above all
others the champion of human liberty, social, political, and intellectual, and was surpassed by neither man or woman of her generation in her ardent and fearless advocacy of freedom and justice.

At the present time, when the legislature of every state and,
in fact, every home throughout the country is concerned with the
question of equal political rights for women, it is fitting to call to
memory the career of Mathilde Giesler-Anneke, for she belonged to
a small group of pioneers in the woman's suffrage movement at its
very beginnings, about the middle of the last century. Susan B. Anthony mentions her repeatedly as her faithful colleague, who always
untiringly responded to the call, year after year, in the unequal
struggle for woman's rights, and even twenty years after the death
of Mathilde Anneke recalled the services of her co-worker. This
was on the occasion of the International Woman's Congress, held in
Berlin in the summer of 1904, when the venerable suffrage leader
spoke to the astonished German delegates of the commanding figure
of Madam Anneke, the Westphalian woman, "almost six feet high,"
who in the earlier decades braved with her the violence of popular
prejudice and shared the initial successes. In the pages of the History of Woman's Suffrage,[1] frequent reference is made to the work
of Madam Anneke, the "German lady, of majestic presence and liberal culture." She usually spoke in the German language, because
she had greater freedom and power of expression in her native
tongue. In the first woman's rights convention, held in New York
City in September, 1863, her remarks were translated by Mrs.
Rose, but only through the heroic appeal of Wendell Phillips could

---

*Reprinted from German-American Annals n. s. 16 (1918).

a hearing be gained for her. [2]   Whether her personality aroused
curiosity, or sympathy was stirred by Wendell Phillips' reference
to her part in the revolutionary movement in 1849, the noisy crowd
restrained itself long enough for her to make a brief speech, a part
of which was as follows:

> Before I came here, I knew the tyranny and oppression of
> kings; I felt it in my own person, and friends and coun-
> try; when I came here, I expected to find that freedom
> which is denied us at home.   Our sisters in Germany have
> long desired freedom, but there the desire is suppressed
> as well in man as woman.   There is no freedom there,
> even to claim human rights.   Here they expect to find
> freedom of speech; here, for if we cannot claim it here,
> where should we go for it?   Here, at least, we ought to
> be able to express our opinions on all subjects; and yet,
> it would appear, there is no freedom even here to claim
> human rights, although the only hope in our country for
> freedom of speech and action, is directed to this country
> for illustration and example.   That freedom I claim.   The
> women of my country look to this for encouragement and
> sympathy, and they, also, sympathize with this cause.
> We hope it will go on and prosper; and many hearts
> across the ocean in Germany are beating in unison with
> those here.

Madam Anneke's method of argumentation appears to advantage in the following extract from a subsequent address, delivered
in 1869:[3]

> That which you cannot longer suppress in woman--that
> which is free above all things--that which is preeminently
> important to all mankind, and must have free play in every
> mind,--is the natural thirst for scientific knowledge,--
> that fountain of all peacefully progressing amelioration of
> human history.   This longing, this effort of reason seek-
> ing knowledge of itself, of ideas, conclusions, and all
> higher things, has, as far as historical remembrance goes
> back, never been so violently suppressed in any human
> being as in woman.   But so far from its having been ex-
> tinguished in her, it has under the influence of this en-
> lightened century become a gigantic flame, which shines
> most brightly under the protection of the star-spangled
> banner.   There does not exist a man-made doctrine, fabri-
> cated expressly for us, and which we must learn by heart,
> that shall henceforth be our law.   Nor shall the authority
> of old traditions be a standard for us--be this authority
> called Veda, Talmud, Koran, or Bible.   No.   Reason,
> which we recognize as our highest and only law-giver, com-
> mands us to be free.   We have recognized our duty--we
> have heard the rustling of the golden wings of our guardian
> angel--we are inspired for the work.   We are no longer
> in the beginning of history--that age which was a constant

struggle with nature, misery, ignorance, helplessness,
and every kind of bondage. The moral idea of the state
struggles for that fulfillment in which all individuals shall
be brought into a union which shall augment a millionfold
both its individual and collective forces. Therefore, don't
exclude woman, don't exclude the whole half of the human
family. Receive us--begin the work in which a new era
shall dawn. In all great events we find that woman has a
guiding hand--let us stay near you now, when humanity is
concerned. Man has the spirit of truth, but woman alone
has passion for it. All creations need love--let us, therefore, celebrate a union, from which shall spring the morning of freedom for humanity. Give us our rights in the
state. Honor us as your equals, and allow us to use the
rights which belong to us, and which reason commands us
to use. Whether it be prudent to enfranchise woman, is
not the question--only whether it be right. What is posi-
tively right, must be prudent, must be wise, and must,
finally, be useful....

As this extract shows, Madam Anneke made an appeal not only for equal suffrage rights, but for the higher education of women.
With this principle in view she founded a school for young ladies in
the city of Milwaukee, which had a memorable influence far beyond
the community in which it was located.

A champion of social and intellectual liberty in her adopted
country, she had been in her fatherland a revolutionist in the cause
of political freedom. Mathilde Franziska Anneke, daughter of coun-
cillor Karl Giesler, was born April 3, 1817, on the estate of her
grandfather at Lerchenhausen, near Blankenstein, in Westphalia.
She had the advantage of spending her youth amid beautiful natural
surroundings and living much out of doors. She was brought up a
devout Catholic, and dutifully allowed her native spirit of inquiry to
be constrained by her faith. At the age of nineteen she was married to a nobleman named v. Tabouillot, but the marriage proved a
very unhappy one, and was dissolved before the end of a year. The
struggle for the possession of her daughter for the first time brought
her to a realization of the injustice of certain then existing man-
made laws, and of the necessity of fighting for human rights. Still
she found consolation for a time in the teachings of her church, and
gave evidence of her firm religious faith in the prayer-books which
she published: Des Christen freudiger Aufblick zum himmlischen
Vater, and a second one, which was warmly endorsed by the Bishop
of Münster, called Der Meister ist da und rufet dich, with the subtitle that well describes the purpose of the book, "Ein vollständiges
Gebet- und Erbauungsbuch für die katholische Frauenwelt." Other
literary efforts rapidly succeeded these, a collection of her own writings in prose and verse, called Heimatgruss, containing also a selection of poems of love and liberty from poets as Petrarca, Byron,
Kathinka Schücking, Levin Schücking, Freiligrath, Lenau, and others.

In 1842 appeared the Damenalmanach, with contributions from

contemporaries, and three years later a story, "Michelangelo," under the influence of Alex. Dumas. In 1846 appeared Produkte der roten Erde, a collection of the writings of Westphalians as Freiligrath and Droste-Hülshoff, among them two contributions of her own pen: "Wilhelm Kaulbach," and "Eine Reise im Mai 1843." Her most ambitious work of this period was the drama in verse completed in 1844, entitled Oithono, oder die Tempelweihe. Oithono is an architect, who has constructed a wonderful temple. A rival undermines the structure, and even Oithono begins to become doubtful of his own skill. He goes into banishment, where a youthful basketmaker cares for the helpless stranger. With her he returns, when the malicious intrigues of the rival are revealed and the temple is saved in time. But the close is tragic, Oithono dies at the feet of the princess Mechthilde, who had once inspired the hero to his great work. The drama was successfully performed a number of times; first at Münster, by the troupe of the prince of Lippe-Detmold. In 1882 the play was performed in Milwaukee, in honor of the author. A translation into English was made under the auspices of the actor, Charles Fechter, but it was never staged, owing to his early retirement.

In this play there was noticeable a change in the inner life of its author. Oithono has become a doubter, an inquirer. Similarly the author was beset with doubts on religious and social questions. There was no lukewarmness or half-way repose in the character of Mathilde Giesler, and the devout believer rapidly changed to the radical free-thinker. On the great social question of woman's position, her independence of judgment was disclosed in the essay, "Das Weib im Konflikt mit den sozialen Verhältnissen," a bold venture at that time, exposing its author to ridicule and scorn. A period of free-thinking was dawning, soon to be directed toward political affairs. The revolution of 1848 drew near, following the disappointment felt at the attitude of Frederick William IV. In 1847 Mathilde Giesler had become the wife of the young Prussian artillery officer Fritz Anneke, whose outspoken liberal views had got him into difficulties and caused his dismissal from the service. Their union was a happy one, and they established themselves at first in Cologne, where Karl Marx established the Neue Rheinische Zeitung, and revolutionary spirits gathered from far and near. At the Anneke home the poet Freiligrath was a constant guest, and Gottschalk, Willich, Beust, Emma Herwegh and others were frequently seen. Frau Anneke founded the Neue Kölnische Zeitung and edited it in the interests of the Revolution. It was soon suppressed. In the meantime Anneke was implicated in a trial for treason, together with Gottschalk and Willich,[4] and was confined in prison for eleven months. Frau Anneke founded a woman's journal, Frauenzeitung, advocating equal rights, and the widening of woman's sphere of work, one of the earliest attempts of the kind in the history of the woman's equal rights movement of the nineteenth century. The Frauenzeitung was also suppressed, but a few years afterwards was revived by the editor, in the United States (1852).

The revolutionary epoch, particularly as seen by Frau An-

neke, is described in detail in her Memoirs, which are reprinted in
the succeeding pages. [5] Fritz Anneke assisted in organizing the artillery forces of the Revolutionary Army, and retreated with the latter into Baden. His wife followed him into the field and served under him as a mounted orderly (Ordonnanz) to the end of the campaign. Colonel Anneke was in command at the battle of Ubstatt,
near Karlsruhe, having four cannons and 1200 men in his charge,
and made a brave defense. Driven back upon Rastatt, Anneke was
appointed inspector of the war materials of the fortress. He fled
with his wife before the surrender of Rastatt, escaping in time over
the Swiss border, and then by way of France to America.

The Memoiren einer Frau aus dem badisch-pfälzischen Feld-
zuge were printed in a limited number of copies for private circulation by the press of Fritz Anneke in Newark in 1853, and were once
reprinted in the early seventies by the Westliche Post, under the editorship of Preetorius. They are, however, practically inaccessible,
and their historical interest justifies their being again brought to
light. The war pictures are vividly sketched, and between the lines
we can easily discover the causes of the failure of the campaign in
the lack of organization and other equally serious faults. The Memoiren einer Frau are a valuable companion-piece to the description
by Carl Schurz of the campaign in Baden of 1849, contained in the
first volume of his Memoirs. [6]

The Annekes arrived in the United States toward the end of
the fateful year of 1849. They first lived in Milwaukee, where Madam Anneke, as early as 1850, appeared as a very successful speaker before large audiences, addressing them on the subject of the
Revolution, or at other times on literary subjects. The Deutsche
Frauenzeitung, revived in Milwaukee in 1852, she soon took to New
York, and then to Newark, N.J., where her husband founded and
published the Newarker Zeitung. [7] Her subscribers at the period are
said to have reached the number of two thousand. After the suffrage
meeting in the Tabernacle, in New York City, in September, 1853,
Madam Anneke made many trips throughout the country in the cause
of woman's rights, and was one of the most noted speakers, sought
for wherever the German population was large.

From 1860-1865 she was in Switzerland, accompanied by her
literary friend Mary Booth, who translated into English many of the
poems of Mathilde Anneke. The latter was not idle, for in 1863 she
published in Jena Das Geisterhaus in New York, and in the same
period wrote Die gebrochenen Ketten, Als der Grossvater die Grossmutter nahm, and Uhland in Texas. She was also a contributor to
the Belletristisches Journal (N.Y.), and to the Illinois Staatszeitung,
and her letters were very well received on this side.

She returned to the United States in 1865, and then began her
last period of activity, not in the least less useful. She founded an
academy for young ladies in Milwaukee, which she continued till her
death in 1884. The following paragraph was written by one of the
students of the school, while it was still in existence:

In 1866, shortly after her return from Switzerland, Madam
M. F. Anneke together with a highly educated pedagogical
lady, Caecilie Kapp, who had accompanied her abroad,
founded a young ladies' academy, having been requested to
do so by many people in Milwaukee. This academy has
since been called the Milwaukee Toechter Institut. About
a year after the founding of the school, Miss Kapp accepted a call to teach in Vassar College, and Mrs. Anneke,
laying aside her literary labors, continued the institute under many difficulties, and has ever since devoted herself
to educating her own sex. The academy is conducted in
quite a free religious way, and educates not only pupils
from Milwaukee, but also young ladies from distant states.
Her school maintains a high standard among educational
institutions of its kind, pupils being instructed in all the
important branches in the English, German and French
languages. The greatest number of pupils has been fifty,
and the teachers employed are experienced educators.

Undoubtedly Madam Anneke taught more by example than by
precept, more through the inspiration of her personality than her
learning, and impressed the deep lessons of life out of her own rich
experience. Her last score of years she spent in the school-room,
devoting herself more than ever to the elevation of women, a fitting
close to an heroic and eminently useful life. [8]

Notes

1. History of Woman's Suffrage, Vols. I-II. Edited by Eliz. Cady
    Stanton, Susan B. Anthony and Mathilda J. Gage. Volume IV,
    by S. B. Anthony and Ida Husted.
2. This first stormy meeting was finally forced to adjourn by the
    mob-like behavior of the vast audience. Very few speakers
    gained as much of a hearing as Madam Anneke. When Wen-
    dell Phillips was suppressed shortly after, he cried out:
    "Go on with your hisses; geese have hissed before now; if it
    be your pleasure to argue this question for us by proving that
    the men here, at least, are not fit for exercising political
    rights."
3. Supra, Vol. II, pp. 393-394.
4. Willich came to the United States, and distinguished himself in
    the Civil War. Cf. Kaufmann, W.: Die Deutschen im ameri-
    kanischen Bürgerkriege (1911), pp. 472-475.
5. I am indebted for a typewritten copy of the Memoiren einer Frau
    aus dem badisch-pfälzischen Feldzuge to the surviving son and
    daughter of Mathilde Giesler-Anneke, Mr. Percy S. Anneke,

of Duluth, Minn., and Mrs. Hertha Anneke Sanne, of Los
Angeles, Cal. They have kindly permitted the Memoirs to
be republished, observing that it should not be forgotten, that
the Memoirs were originally intended only for circulation
among a few friends, and that they describe personal observations only. Mrs. Anneke Sanne is in possession of the literary legacy, in large part unpublished, of her distinguished
mother. I wish to acknowledge my obligations to both Mrs.
Anneke-Sanne and Mr. Percy Anneke also for their putting
into my hand valuable biographical materials and giving full
answers to my numerous questions, aiding me greatly in the
preparation of this sketch.

6. The passages in the Memoirs of Carl Schurz, that contain references to Colonel Anneke are contained in Volume I, pages
115, 171, 179, 188, 191, 196-197, 203, 239, 240. Carl
Schurz served in the same artillery regiment with Colonel
Anneke, as his aide-de-camp. A glowing tribute to Madam
Anneke is found on page 197: "In the appreciation of this
(the romantic aspect of the night-march) I found sympathetic
response with the wife of my chief, Mathilde Franciska Anneke, a young woman of noble character, beauty, vivacity,
and fiery patriotism, who accompanied her husband on this
march."

7. Colonel Fritz Anneke took part in the Civil War, as colonel of
artillery in McClellan's staff, subsequently colonel of the
Thirty-fifth Wisconsin Regiment. He had difficulties with
certain of his superior officers, whose incompetence he exposed and whose revengeful spirit finally brought about his
dismissal from the service. (See Kaufmann, supra, pp.
478-479.) Anneke's correspondence with the Augsburger
Allgemeine Zeitung on certain battles of the Civil War is
noteworthy. He died in Chicago in 1872, after many vicissi-
tudes of fortune.

8. Biographical sources not already named are the following: C.
H. Boppe, Lebensbild. Mathilde Franciska Anneke, Freiden-
ker, Milwaukee, 1885. Wilh. Hense-Jensen und Ernst
Bruncken, Wisconsins Deutsch-Amerikaner, Milwaukee, 1900-
1902; 2 Vols. Schem, Deutsch-Amerikanisches Conversations-
Lexikon, Bd. I. Regina Ruben, Mathilde Franziska Anneke,
die erste grosse deutsche Verfechterin des Frauenrechts,
Hamburg (R. Ruben).

16. KARL HEINZEN'S GERMAN-AMERICAN WRITINGS: SOME LITERARY ASPECTS*

Katherine and Gerhard Friesen

> ... setzt mir einen Leichenstein mit folgender Grabschrift,
> die meinen Verbrechen bei den kommenden Geschlechtern
> zur Entschuldigung dienen wird: 'Hier ruht ein Teutscher,
> der das Unglück hatte, im 19ten Jahrhundert ein freier
> Mann zu sein.'[1]

In the eyes of his contemporaries Karl Heinzen stood pre-judged as "der Lange,"[2] "der grosse radikale Streiter,"[3] "der gefürchtete Redacteur des 'Pioniers,'"[4] and "das Krokodil."[5] Today he is remembered, if at all, primarily for his lectures, journalistic pursuits, and for his consistently radical and outspoken nature. This study intends to focus on a few lesser known literary aspects of Heinzen's work. In an attempt to rectify some errors made by previous Heinzen scholars, it will concentrate on his role as a German-American author, with particular emphasis on the literary and documentary value of the only one of his satirical comedies set in America, Die teutschen "Organisten der Bildung" in Amerika (1859).

Heinzen was born in Grevenbroich near Düsseldorf on February 22, 1809 as the son of a forester. He attended the Gymnasium in Cleve and later the University in Bonn. Relegated from the university for allegedly bad conduct, he joined the Dutch military service and spent 1829 to 1831 in the Dutch East Indies. This experience later inspired his imaginative travelogue Reise nach Batavia (1841). Upon his return he worked for many years in the Prussian civil service, but his bitter criticism of bureaucracy and militarism in Die preussiche Bureaukratie (1844) caused such a furor that Heinzen was forced to flee, first to Belgium and then to Switzerland.

During his Swiss exile he became acquainted with, among others, Gottfried Keller, Conrad Ferdinand Meyer, August Adolf Ludwig Follen, Wilhelm Schulz, Ferdinand Freiligrath, Karl Grün, and Arnold Ruge. An indication of Heinzen's notoriety as a radical at the time is found in an 1847 letter of Meyer to Keller, in which he states: "Bei diesem Feste [a meeting of the Rosenbund in 1847] haben wir in effigie verbrannt: Feuerbachs Werke, Ruges Werke, Heinzens Schriften, Viktor Hugos 'Le roi s'amuse', Heines Schöpfungslieder und G. Sands sämtliche Romane. Das gab einen Rauch, Sata-

*Reprinted from German-American Studies 7 (1974): 107-29, by permission of the publisher.

nas fuhr aus!"[6]   Faced with expulsion from Switzerland as a *persona non grata* for his reputed leadership in the subversive activities of a Zürich Flugschriftenfabrik,[7] Heinzen used his connection with Wilhelm von Eichthal of the New York Deutsche Schnellpost to aid him in his emigration to the United States. Upon Eichthal's death in January of 1848, Heinzen became editor of his paper. In March of 1848, however, Heinzen felt compelled to return to Europe in order to take part in the imminent German revolution. When the second Baden revolt collapsed, Heinzen, after a short stay in London, returned to New York in 1850. From 1850 to 1853 he was the editor of five newspapers in succession, all of which failed because of his relentlessly radical outlook. The business offices of the last of these five papers, the Herold des Westens, were burned down in Louisville by opponents of Heinzen's steadfast pro-abolitionist position. Heinzen's next paper, the Pionier, was founded in Louisville in 1853, moved to Cincinnati, then to New York, and finally in 1859 to Boston, where it continued to be published until 1879, when it merged with the Milwaukee Freidenker. This paper remained the main forum for Heinzen's uncompromising social and political journalism until his death on November 12, 1880. If there is any consistency in Heinzen's eventful and colorful life, it is his outspoken and unrelenting tenacity throughout his literary career in advocating truth, liberty and justice, showing a total disregard for personal advantage and practical gain.

The neglect of Karl Heinzen as an author in his own right, apart from his role as a political and polemical bête noire in Europe and North America, is inherent in the few past investigations, which have also generated a number of errors regarding his literary output. In his article "Karl Heinzen: Reformer, Poet and Literary Critic,"[8] Otto P. Schinnerer grants only cursory attention to the prose works, the many pamphlets and newspapers, and makes no mention of Heinzen's autobiography, novel, and Lustspiele.[9] Although Schinnerer includes all three editions of Heinzen's collected verse (Köln, 1841; New York, 1858;[10] Boston, 1867) in an appended list of Heinzen's publications, he confines his rather uninspired consideration of Heinzen's verse to the first edition. On the basis of one early poem, "Ermannung eines jungen Poeten" (1827), he concludes that "we might almost regard Heinzen as one of the forerunners of Young Germany."[11] Notwithstanding any possible association of Heinzen with his Young German contemporaries, however, it should be pointed out that their self-styled prosecutor Wolfgang Menzel did not hesitate to laud the earthy appeal of Heinzen's poems in a review of 1842:

> So findet sich hier denn manches Gedicht, bei dem wir Freude haben, zu fühlen, dass es in schweren und leichten Stunden frei entstanden und nicht gemacht sey. Es weht darin ein Hauch des Lebens, bald ein rauher und kalter, bald aber ein zarter, von fremdartigen Düften trunkner Hauch, der uns überzeugt, der Dichter hat Wirkliches erlebt, er hat nicht bloss hinter seinem Fenster Phantasieblumen aufgekränkelt.[12]

Schinnerer mentions in passing that Heinzen was the "author
of a great number of epigrams,"[13] and that "he selected the satire
and polemic form of poetry as more congenial to his nature,"[14] but
no specific attention is granted to Heinzen's Amerikanische Epi-
gramme in Schinnerer's article. These epigrams were added to the
second edition of Heinzen's poems[15] and were especially important
in shaping his literary reputation among German-American contemporaries. After the second edition of 1858, Heinzen featured a column in his Pionier, entitled "Die Gedichte von K. Heinzen und die
Teutsche Kritik in Amerika,"[16] in which he reprinted recent reviews
of his poetry. The longest critique came from the St. Louis Anzeiger des Westens, whose editor at the time was Heinrich Börnstein,
While recommending the purchase of the volume, this review concludes, "Heinzen ist ein trefflicher Prosaiker mit einem markigen,
klaren Styl, aber Heinzen ist kein Dichter."[17] Most other review-
ers, however, voiced their preference for Heinzen's epigrams to the
rest of his poetry, which some criticized for occasional formal
flaws. Characteristic in its appreciation is the review of the New
York Familienblätter:

> Das Epigramm ist denn auch überhaupt die dem scharfen
> dialektischen Geist unseres Autors am meisten zusagende
> Form der Dichtung. Wir betrachten den 5. Abschnitt,
> welcher ausschliesslich kleine Gedichte und Epigramme
> enthält, als den interessantesten und gelungensten der
> ganzen Sammlung.... Etwas bitter, doch desshalb oft nicht
> minder treffend sind die beigefügten 'Amerikanischen Epi-
> gramme.' Der Autor geisselt unbarmherzig die Schwächen
> des amerikanischen sozialen und politischen Lebens; nach-
> dem er inzwischen seinem ganzen Grimme Luft gemacht
> und der modernen Musterrepublic ihr Sündenregister vor-
> gehalten, kann er doch schliesslich nicht umhin, ihr auch
> Gerechtigkeit widerfahren zu lassen.[18]

Carl Wittke's biography of Heinzen, Against the Current, de-
lineates his career from a historical rather than literary point of
view and thus contains neither a systematic nor a critical evaluation
of Heinzen as a literary figure Wittke recognizes, however, that
"Heinzen's literary ambitions were great ... he was not satisfied to
be known only as a journalist; he wanted recognition as a poet and
a playwright and as an author of books...."[19] Although Wittke informs us that "Heinzen regarded the Editoren-Kongress as the best
book he had produced in America," Wittke held that "its plot was insignificant and stupid."[20]

The complete title of this book is Der teutsche Editoren-Kongress zu Cincinnati, oder Das gebrochene Herz, and its preface explains that it is in fact a fictitious work, a satirical novel.[21] Although the preface also indicates that the novel had been printed earlier in one of Heinzen's newspapers, Wittke and others would have us
believe that it did not appear until 1872 in Boston. The Editoren-
Kongress had, however, been serialized as early as 1857 and 1858
in Heinzen's Pionier.[22] Even a cursory reading of this novel reveals

the striking similarity between its content and that of Heinzen's comedy Die teutschen "Organisten der Bildung" in Amerika. The reason for this is readily apparent when one considers that both works
originated at the same time, i.e., the late 1850's. The novel de-
picts the experiences of Editor Längst at a congress which meets in
various American cities for the purpose of improving the state of
journalism and culture among German-Americans. The preface to
the 1872 book edition confirms the obvious: Editor Längst really
represents "der Lange," i.e., Karl Heinzen, who is taking this fictitious trip with the high hopes of an "Organist der Bildung." The
subtitle, "das gebrochene Herz," foreshadows the sad outcome of the
story, while the ultimate disgust of Editor Längst is reflected in the
epigram "Teutsche Tonangeber in Amerika":

> Teutschlands Vertreter wollt ihr sein?
> O lasst euch diesen Irrthum nehmen!
> Teutschlands Vertreter sind allein
> Die Wen'gen, die sich eurer schämen. [23]

A good example of Heinzen's imaginative talent and prophetic intui-
tion, as well as of his concern about slavery and racial prejudice is
offered by the conclusion of his Editoren-Kongress. As in the Pionier serialization, one of Heinzen's favorite fictitious characters,
Julie von Berg, is called upon to complete the narration of Längst's
story, because he has been suffering from heart trouble since his
return from the itinerant congress. As his cardiac condition wors-
ens, she reports, a team of doctors decide to perform open-heart
surgery. Upon seeing the condition of his heart, they agree, however, that the only remaining solution is to attempt a heart transplant, using the hearts of several slaughtered men--Negroes of
course--to create a perfect donor heart. There is just one compli-
cation: "...der Patient wollte kein fremdes Herz im Leibe hab-
en,"[24] and thus the novel concludes with the patient's prejudice re-
sulting in his death. It would seem difficult to agree with Wittke
that his novel has an "insignificant and stupid plot."

     The same complex of critical ideas expressed in the novel--
the questionable quality of the language and content in German-American newspapers, the venality of many German-American intellectuals, the problems of American slavery, and women's rights--was also taking dramatic form in Heinzen's mind during 1858. Evidence
of this can be found in the Pionier of this year. However, before
we approach Heinzen's dramatic treatment of these ideas in his play
Die teutschen "Organisten der Bildung" in Amerika, a brief glance
at Heinzen's previous Lustspiele might here be indicated.

     Whenever Heinzen's dramas are mentioned at all, there
seems to be some confusion as to their number, correct titles,
places of publication, and present availability. As far as can be determined, Heinzen's first play was Doktor Nebel, oder: Gelehrsamkeit und Leben (Köln, 1841). According to Eitel Wolf Dobert, this
play has been lost.[25] Unknown to Dobert, at least one copy of it
exists.[26] In the past, critical reaction to Doktor Nebel has general-

ly been short and negative. Thus August Lewald in 1842 concluded:
"Das Theater ist nicht sein [Heinzens] Bereich und dieser Versuch
ein gänzlich verfehlter zu nennen."27 Similarly, Heinrich Kurz,
while showing some appreciation for Heinzen's poems, commented,
"Der bekannte K. Heinzen bewies in 'Doktor Nebel'..., wie weit
man es in Geschmacklosigkeit und Unsinn bringen könne."28 At
least one critic has felt this play to be of value; Michael Singer, editor of the Jahrbuch der Deutschamerikaner, wrote in 1918, "Das
Volkstück fand in dem radikalen aber vielseitigen Achtundvierziger
Karl Heinzen einen erfolgreichen Vertreter. Sein 'Dr. Nebel, oder
Gelehrsamkeit und Leben' verdiente ... dem Moder entrissen zu
werden...."29

Possibly another of Heinzen's early plays is Die Kölnische
Komödie (Köln, 1842). Wittke repeatedly notes that Heinzen wrote
"some satirical comedies"30 during the early 1840's, but he does
not name this work by its title. Several sources simply attribute it
to Heinzen.31 Although a copy of this work could not be located,
its full title can be identified as Die Kölnische Komödie, von Tante
Alhieri, oder getreue Beschreibung der Höllenfahrt des Hanswurst
und des Höllenzuges aus dem Kölnischen Karneval im Jahr 1842.32

On August 15, 1858, Heinzen offered for subscription the second volume of his collected works, which was to contain his Lust-
spiele.33 This volume did not appear until a year later, and although it was published in New York, Heinzen had already moved
with his Pionier to Boston.34 A second edition appeared (1872) in
Boston and included only two plays, Professor Irrwisch and Die
teutschen "Organisten der Bildung" in Amerika.35 The first and
longer of these satirical comedies, Professor Irrwisch, is interesting in a number of respects. One thing which Heinzen does not
mention, but which immediately becomes evident upon comparing this
play with Doktor Nebel, is that Professor Irrwisch is merely a re-
working of the earlier drama.36 The text has been altered to some
degree, but of the twelve characters, only the names of Dr. Nebel
and Dr. Feger have been changed to Dr. Irrwisch and Dr. Gift, respectively. A "Vorbemerkung" has also been added, in which Heinzen explains that this Lustspiel was originally conceived as the introduction to a planned comic novel called "Irrfahrten des Professors Irrwisch." Perhaps this explanation came in response to negative criticism of Doktor Nebel, or in anticipation of the major ob-
jection future critics might have to the play, namely its reliance on
monologues and dialogues rather than on action.37 Heinzen notes in
his autobiography that Professor Irrwisch is based on his experiences at the University of Bonn during the year 1827.38 This separates it in time and space from the second Lustspiel in the volume,
which grew out of Heinzen's career as a journalist in the United
States during the 1850's.39

Let us now turn to a fuller discussion of this latter play,
Die teutschen "Organisten der Bildung" in Amerika and its background. On September 5, 1858, a column appeared in Karl Hein-
zein's Pionier which was written in dialogue form and bore the

heading "Ein Beitrag zur teutsch-amerikanischen Originalliteratur."[40]   An obvious continuation of this column appeared in the September 19 issue with the title "Lesefrüchte aus dem Garten der N.Y. Staatszeitung." Six further articles[41] with this heading followed in the Pionier, but the initial dialogue form eventually gave way to prose letters.   The issue of November 7, 1858, brought the "Fortsetzung und einstweiliger Schluss" of the series.

The material in these columns, as well as the manner in which it is presented, very closely resembles in form and content the second act of Heinzen's play, "Organisten der Bildung," which appeared as the second Lustspiel in the 1859 edition of Heinzen's collected works.   Some of the newspaper columns begin with a stage direction: "Szene: Sanktum der 'N.Y. Staatszeitung'," "Sanktissimum der 'N.Y. Staatszeitung'," and finally, "Im eisenbeschlagenen Rhomboide der 'Staatszeitung'."[42]   In one instance the column also closes with "Der Vorhang fällt."[43]   Each of these columns contains a long conversation between a female editor, identified at first only as "die Patronin," and her assistants, variously referred to as "der dienende National-Geist," "der Lokal-Kopf," and "der Lokal-Verbrecher."   The subjects discussed range from slander (mostly of Karl Heinzen) and slavery, to German-American literature and foreign literary critics.   The author of these columns--obviously the editor of the Pionier, Karl Heinzen himself--only thinly disguises his purpose here, which is to present a dramatization of his disagreements over a wide range of subjects with the New Yorker Staatszeitung.   In the columns "die Patronin" is eventually identified as "Jakob Uhl's Wittwe."   This is the historical figure Anna Uhl, who became publisher and editor of the Staatszeitung upon her husband's death in 1852 and served as such until 1859.[44]

Heinzen's feud with this newspaper was also responsible for the somewhat unusual title of his comedy Die teutschen "Organisten der Bildung" in Amerika.   In the preface to the Editoren-Kongress,[45] (which, as explained above, had likewise been serialized in the Pionier during 1858), Heinzen informs us that it was the New Yorker Staatszeitung which had nicknamed him the "Organist der Bildung." It intended to imply by this cognomen that Heinzen, as the typical Forty-Eighter, was over-anxious to organize and educate all German-Americans socially, politically, and culturally, especially those who had come to the United States during the 1830's.   In order to understand the reasons for this personal literary feud, one must see it in the context of a general rift in contemporaneous German-American circles.   The editors of the Staatszeitung, like the editors of many other German-American papers, belonged to this latter group who felt confident that there was nothing wrong with the quality of their papers (even if every other word in them was an Americanism), nor with their social attitudes (even though they opposed abolition), nor with their right to speak as representatives of German culture in America (even though their papers did not show any interest in German literature, let alone its German-American branch).

This conflict was thus by no means limited to a personal feud

between Karl Heinzen and the New Yorker Staatszeitung during the
1850s and early 1860s. The split was so wide-spread among German-American newspapers of the day that the editors who had established themselves before 1848 came to be known as the "Grays,"
and those who had come after, as the "Greens."[46] The term
"Greens" arose because the older editors, those who had been in
America for at least twenty years in the 1850s, liked to refer to a
Forty-Eighter as a "Grünhorn." Besides their demand for higher
standards in journalism and their concern about German culture in
America, the Forty-Eighters also advocated such radical plans as
the establishment of a separate German state in the western United
States and the abolishment of the U.S. Presidency. Karl Heinzen,
however, wisely confined himself in his three-act "Organisten der
Bildung" to an exposure of two undesirable types of German-American editors.

      In the single lengthy scene constituting the first act, these
two editors are indirectly introduced through the conversation of two
men, Geissel and Streichling, at the former's inn. Geissel is a
Forty-Eighter, a writer-editor who has chosen to become an innkeeper because of the corrupt state of American journalism. His
enemies have labelled him the "Organist" or "Organisator der Bildung," and, true to his name, he is anxious to "whip into shape" at
least two of them. Streichling is a violinist, who has recently fled
from Germany (even his musical interpretations of Louis XVI's death
at the guillotine, he relates, could not elude the censors) and wants
to establish a reputation as a true artist in America. With his
somewhat hesitant help Geissel devises a plan which will force the
despicable editors of two rival papers to reveal publicly their true
natures.

      Act Two is divided into two scenes. The first scene is set
in the " 'Sanktum' des 'National-Hickory' " (176),[47] while the second
scene takes place in the " 'Sanktum' des 'Staats-Hickory'" (185).
The editor we meet first is Beutel. He can be described perfectly
by one of Heinzen's American epigrams, entitled "Der 'Graue' ":

> Ich bin schon zwanzig Jahr' im Land,
> Verlernte Sprache und Verstand,
> Drum soll kein Grüner sich erfrechen,
> Mir gegen die Sklaverei zu sprechen.[48]

The quality of his "Päper" becomes apparent when his assistant
Bengel informs him that the next edition will contain "... wie ge-
wöhnlich: ein Leitartikel über eine verbrannte Frau, ein Mann zu
Brei zermalmt, ein durchgegangenes Pferd, das 6 Menschen gekillt
hat, und ein Artikel gegen die Whigs..." (176). When Bengel asks
whether they should print a refugee's poem gratis, Beutel reveals in
his answer at once his ignorant attitude toward literature and his
bastardized German:

> Well, das wär' ein Büsiness, Gedichte umsonst aufzuneh-
> men! Das heisst, ich bin nicht ganz gegen die Gedicht-

> kunst: sogar Göthe und Schiller können ein Gedicht in
> mein Blatt setzen, wenn sie dafür bezahlen wollen, aber
> Käsch daun, das ist american fashion. Der 'National-
> Hickory' ist ein demokratisches Blatt, das soll so ein
> Grünhorn von einem Versemacher sich merken, und wir
> Demokraten sind praktisch. Was sagst Du, Tschali? (177)

The monetary significance of Beutel's name is demonstrated when
Draht, a tailor and father of six children, tries to collect the long
overdue payment for his work. Rather than part with any of his
ill-gained "honorariums" (most of which, we learn, he promptly
spends in nightly carousals), Beutel prefers to intimidate and threat-
en the tailor. First he asks questions like "Wie können Sie Grünhorn mir solche Dinge in meinem Sanktum sagen? Sind Sie ein
Demokrat?" (181) When this evasive technique fails, Beutel begins
to preach: "... ich sage Ihnen, dass ein Grüner an unsern gast-
lichen Gestaden erst etwas lernen muss, ehe er mitsprechen darf.
Ich bin schon zwanzig Jahre im Lande--" (182). Finally he threat-
ens to slander the tailor: "God däm! Jetzt ist es genug. Her
Grünhorn, in meinem nächsten Blatt werden Sie einen Artikel finden,
dass kein Mensch von der national-demokratischen Partei Ihnen
mehr einen Cent zu verdienen geben soll." (182)

There is also some attention given to politics, particularly
to an impending "Elekschen." Beutel's paper is supporting "Der
Fox" because he is a "Schentlemän" and his election will benefit the
paper. But this election is by no means a central theme in Heinzen's play, as it is, for instance, in Gustav Freytag's earlier Lustspiel, Die Journalisten (1853).

After Beutel's assistant becomes so disgusted with him that
he hurls him out the door, we meet the second editor, Schneider.
He has been in America only ten years (188) and in comparison with
Beutel is considered a " 'Soft', ein Weichschaaliger, ein Barnburner,
ein Jungamerikaner, ein Sozialist." (187)[49] His manner of speech
resembles that of a student of Hegel, and he boasts of his ability to
conceal his shrewd opportunism from his readers. On the ever
present issue of slavery, Schneider reveals his shifty editorial
stance as follows:

> Wir müssen immer eine Zeitfrage, z.B. die Sklavenfrage,
> benützen, um vor den Hunkern den Schein als Fortschritts-
> männer voraus zu haben, wir dürfen solche Fragen aber
> niemals bis auf das praktische Gebiet verfolgen, denn das
> verstösst gegen unsre Partei, untergräbt unser Büsiness
> und gleichzeitig die Kuppel dieser grossen Union. (187).

This editor is also inclined to publish "popular articles rather than
literary or cultural ones, whatever promises to attract more subscribers (188). As in the previous scene, an assistant, this one
named "Typus," is so revolted by his editor's lack of ethical principles that he throws him out the door.

Karl Heinzen   187

Act Three again takes place in Geissel's inn. The two editors, who have fallen for Geissel's trap and simultaneously exposed
each other in their newspapers, come to the inn demanding "Satis-
fäkschen." Geissel, whom they pretend to have never met before,
introduces himself: "Ich bin nämlich ein Philosoph und heisse Hag-
el." (199) He then succeeds in so confusing the editors with his
dialectical discussion of positives and negatives that they allow themselves to be whipped as just punishment for their corruption of the
German language (204). To add insult to injury, the whipping is
performed by a Negro, who has escaped from the South by the Un-
derground Railway and is heading for Canada. Geissel feels this is
particularly appropriate because Beutel and Schneider are two of the
anti-abolitionist German-American editors, "welche über Tyrannei
in Europa schimpfen und ihr in Amerika die Schleppe tragen." (205)
Geissel's position could best be described by these lines from Heinzen's "Teutsch-amerikanisches 'Volkslied' ":

                Nur Der ist Mensch, nur Der ist frei,
                Der jede fremde Sklaverei
                Hilft wie die eig'ne niederstreiten. 50

The ultimate humiliation comes when the editors learn that the Negro speaks "Dötsch" (207), which he learned from his German plantation master, and when Beutel finally finds out that his own sister
is going to marry the Negro (208). This situation thus recalls the
problems caused in the Editoren-Kongress when a Negro's heart was
to be transplanted into a white man's body. As a last punishment,
Geissel forces the editors to promise that they will give up their ed-
itorships and never begin another paper. When they ask whether
they could not simply reform, Geissel replies, "Wissen Sie denn
nicht, dass Sie die teutsche Literatur und die Sache der Freiheit
noch mehr schänden durch Ihre Gunst als durch Ihre Anfeindung?"
(210) The play ends as the editors circumvent their pledge to Geissel and exchange their papers together with their political positions.
When Schneider mildly protests about doing this, Beutel laconically
declares, "Nevermeind, es ist ja doch Alles eins." (213) This
sameness in the endeavors of two apparently hostile rivals is actually implied throughout the play by Heinzen's choice of names for both
editors. As they have been active in the same selfish pursuit of
material gain by all sorts of underhanded trickery, they are no better than swindlers, Beutelschneider.

In considering the critical reception of this play by various
German-American editors, many of whom were authors in their own
rights, one can begin to form an idea about the state of German-
American drama during the 1850s. Writing for the Anzeiger des
Westens, Otto Ruppius was the first German-American to review the
play. 51 His little-known interest in drama is apparent from his collaboration (1859-61) with another author and critic, Heinrich Börnstein, who had founded the St. Louis German stage in 1859. Ruppius' review is extremely negative; he supports his arguments by
selectively reprinting only the derogatory comments made about the
play by the Leipzig critic Hermann Marggraff. 52 A partial explana-

tion for Ruppius' malevolence is that he had been assistant editor of
the N. Y. Staatszeitung during the period of Heinzen's feud with the
paper,[53] and there can be no doubt that Ruppius considered slavery
an economic necessity for the South. [54] Another appraisal of the
play appeared early in 1860 in the N. Y. Demokrat[55] and came from
Adolf Douai. A German-American author, who had formerly been
assistant editor of the Pionier and had later broken with Heinzen,
Douai recognizes that Heinzen had made a noble effort to fill a gap
in German-American literature. He laments what he found most
Lustspiele of the day to be lacking in, "an Ideen, an edler zeitge-
mässer Tendenz, an Wahrheit der Charaktere, die in der Regel viel
zu stark karrikirt [sic] sind, und an Neuheit der Fabel," and concludes somewhat tepidly, "Es ist offenbar, dass Heinzen diese Män-
gel gefühlt und ihnen abzuhelfen gesucht hat. "

     In Germany, the first review of Heinzen's play was Hermann
Marggraff's three-page critique in the Blätter für literarische Unterhaltung, announcing: "In unserer lustspiellosen Zeit wird uns
plötzlich zu unserer Ueberraschung ein Lustspielgericht von Nordamerika aus servirt, und zwar durch keinen andern als durch Karl
Heinzen, den gefürchteten Redacteur des 'Pionier'.... "[56] Marggraff
lauds Heinzen's honesty, admires his defense of America's "schwarze
Brüder," and agrees with him about the generally deplorable state of
the German-American press and its readership, insofar as Marggraff is convinced that "Journalismus ist Ausdruck und Produkt des
Bildungszustandes eines Volks. "[57] His distress over Heinzen's un-
inhibited use of profanities as well as Heinzen's brutal treatment of
his "weisse Brüder" in the play is tempered by the conclusion, "er
meint es mit seinen Bestrebungen zur Besserung der Lage des
menschlichen Geschlechts ganz ernst und ehrlich. "[58]

     Whether the "Organisten der Bildung" had any significant
practical effects at the time is difficult to ascertain. In 1860 Karl
Weller, editor of the Leipzig Jahrbuch deutscher Dichtung, viewed
Heinzen not only as "der erste Pionier in der Gesteswildniss deutsch-
amerikanischer Cultur," but in many respects comparable and even
superior to Ludwig Börne:

          Heinzen ist seinem Charakter, seiner Anschauungsweise
          und selbst seinem Style nach ein auferstandener Börne--
          nur ist sein Gesichtskreis ein weiterer, ein viel mehr
          kosmopolitischer und radikaler, weil er eine viel grössere
          Fülle von Ideen und Verhältnissen an sich herantreten liess.

Weller attributed to him a marked improvement in German-American
journalism:

          [Heinzen] hat es erreicht, dass nachgerade jedes einiger-
          massen verbreitete deutsch-amerikanische Blatt sich eines
          erträglichen Styles befleissigt, nachdem er mit beissendem
          Spotte die yankeesirenden Verhunzung unserer edlen Mutter-
          sprache in den dortigen Journalen zehn Jahre lang gegeis-
          selt.... [59]

Undeniably, Heinzen's Lustspiel is of considerable socio-
historical interest today because it is basically the translation into
a dramatic art form of his active role in American affairs of the
1850s.   But, as the preceding analysis has attempted to demonstrate, it is also possible today to take issue with the 19th-century
critic who felt that Heinzen's Lustspiel was "in culturhistorischer
Hinsicht interessant, aber keineswegs erfreulich."[60]   This play contains a good deal of genuine humor which the modern reader can
still appreciate.   It merits rank and recognition as an original contribution to a select number of memorable satirical German comedies.   Over the last hundred years, far too many German playwrights have with a good deal of repetition and anachronism made
Johannes Gutenberg and Ulrich von Hutten exponents of modern journalism and its problems.   Heinzen's Lustspiel is comparable to the
few imaginative German comedies on the subject of journalism, like
Eduard Bauernfeld's Der literarische Salon (1836), Gustave Freytag's
Die Journalisten (1853), and Arthur Schnitzler's Fink und Flieder-
busch (1917).

Stimulated by his American comedy, German critical interest
in Heinzen was, however, short lived.   When Marggraff, in his
article "Characterstudien über die Deutschen in Deutschland und
Amerika,"[61] condemned Heinzen as a compulsive detractor of German Literatenthum, the editor of the influential Magazin für die Literatur des Auslandes, Joseph Lehmann in Berlin, came to Heinzen's
defense.[62]   Heinzen's Pionier recorded this dispute in a column
"Teutsche 'Kritik' hier und drüben"[63] and expressly invited further
exchange of views between German literati on both sides of the Atlantic.   "Wir sind ja doch alle 'teutsche Brüder'," he wrote, "bloss
getrennt durch ein wenig Wasser und ein wenig Polizei."[64]

Unfortunately, Heinzen's invitation met with no substantial response until twelve years later.   When in 1872 the Pionier printed
the anonymous epic Ein neues Wintermärchen.   Besuch im neuen
deutschen Reich der Gottesfurcht und der frommen Sitte von Heinrich
Heine, a caustic satire on the hollowness of the newly founded
Prusso-German Empire, readers immediately attributed it to Heinzen.   Paul Lindau's indignant review of it,[65] charging that Heinzen
had outdone Götz von Berlichingen in pugnaciousness and vulgarity,
prompted a repartee from Heinzen.[66]   After emphatically denying
authorship of the epic and thus refuting Lindau's personal invective
against him, Heinzen broached a larger issue: the frequently lacking or prejudiced reception of German-American works by 19th-cen-
tury Germany.   Heinzen linked this problem to an even larger perspective.   If German critics were to continue in their habit of ig-
noring as irrelevant, or even misinterpreting as unaesthetic, the only truthful works in their language, those written by freedom-loving
authors in forced or self-imposed exile, Germans would be enlight-
ened only too late.   Heinzen postulated that the future of a free Germany would lie in its close association with America, and prophe-
sied destruction for a smug and illiberal Germany, if not in the first
major war, then in the second.   In an arrogant rejoinder reflecting
the optimistic conceit of the Gründerjahre, Lindau dismissed Hein-

zen's warning as "wiederum eine schwarze Ausgeburt Ihrer Phantasie."[67]

Notes

1. From Heinzen's manuscript describing his expulsion from Bern in the winter of 1847. Nachlass Seidensticker, No. 25.6835, No. 90, Niedersächsische Staats- und Universitätsbibliothek, Göttingen.

2. "Am Empfindlichsten trafen mich die vernichtenden Beinamen. durch welch ich als öffentlicher Verbrecher gekennzeichnet wurde, und unter diesen zahlreichen, mit dem äussersten Aufwand von Geist ersonnenen Beinamen war keiner mehr geeignet, mich unter allgemeine Polizeiaufsicht zu bringen, als jener, den Inbegriff aller geistigen Unfähigkeit wie moralischen Verworfenheit bezeichende: 'Der Lange.' " From the preface to Heinzen's Der teutsche Editoren-Kongress (Boston, 1872), p. 3.

   Heinzen's American biographer, Carl Wittke, records that one of Heinzen's uncles was six feet five inches tall, and that Karl Heinzen was no exception to this family trait. Against the Current (Chicago, 1945), pp. 2-3.

   Although the above-mentioned preface seems to suggest that Heinzen was only known as "der Lange" in America during the years 1847-48 and 1850-1880, Gottfried Keller also refers to him thus in a line of his epigram "An Karl Heinzen," which was written as early as 1846:

   Du mit dem Kopfe voll Erbsen, o langer und redlicher Heinzen! Sämtliche Werke, ed. Jonas Fränkel (Bern und Leipzig, 1926-49), XIII, 357.

   Later, in these lines of his satire, "Der Apotheker von Chamounix" (Ibid., XV, 287), Keller again speaks of Heinzen as:

   > Jener lange Karl, der Heinzen,
   > Der seit vielen langen Jahren
   > Theoretisch Köpfe schneidet,
   >
   > Aber friedevollen Herzens
   > Noch kein Tröpflein Bluts vergossen,
   > Während schweigend die Tyrannen
   > Morden, dass die Erde raucht!

3. Gustav Adolf Zimmermann, Deutsche in Amerika (Chicago, 1892). p. xxx.

4. Hermann Marggraff, "Karl Heinzen als Lustspieldichter," Blätter für literarische Unterhaltung, vol. 6 (February 9, 1860), III.

5. Der Pionier (September 19, 1858), p. 3. Heinzen satirizes this appellation by the Staatszeitung when he puts the following words into the mouth of its female editor: "Das was man Schimpfwort nennt, wirkt nur dann, wenn es die verstärkte Bezeichnung einer Wahrheit ist; wenn Sie aber ein Pferd eine

Wanze schimpfen, wird es dadurch eine Wanze? Der Böse-
wicht vom 'Pionier' hört Sie mit lächelnder Miene alle Namen
der Naturgeschichte ablesen und wenn Sie zu Ende sind, sagt
er bloss: der Mensch scheint im Reich der Bestien gut zu
Hause zu sein. "

6. Emil Ermatinger, Gottfried Kellers Leben, Briefe und Tage-
bücher, I (Stuttgart und Berlin, 1924), 163.
    A clash over atheism in 1845 generated a number of liter-
ary works from these writers. Cf. Wittke, pp. 148-151;
Ermatinger, I, 157-163; the Fränkel edition of Keller's works,
XIII, 357; XIV, 341 ff., and II (II. Abteilung), 287 also adds
to the available knowledge about this religious conflict which
took literary form.
    Of primary importance for this study is the realization
that, as early as the 1840s, Karl Heinzen was already giving
literary form to his strong feelings on religion, politics and
the general social state of the society around him. Heinzen's
Gedichte (3rd. edition 1867, p. 228) include his sonnet "(An
den Zürcher Dichter G. Keller, Zögling und Schildknappen
Follens.), " which in turn provoked Keller's epigram quoted
above, his inclusion of Karl Heinzen in his literary satire,
and possibly also Keller's use of Heinzen as a model for the
atheist Peter Gilgus in this novel Der grüne Heinrich, as
Ermatinger suggests (I. 577). Keller continues to refer to
Heinzen in his letters until at least 1880 (Ermatinger, II,
252).
    Reprinted also in Heinzen's volume of poetry is Follen's
sonnet entitled "Einem Kaiserkandidaten (1846) 'An Karl Heinzen' " (p. 223). Several of Heinzen's sonnets to Follen, dated
1846 (pp. 223-228), with a note about their significance, as
well as a number of epigrams directed at Follen (pp. 182,
192, 193) are included as well.

7. Karl Glossy, "Literarische Geheimberichte aus dem Vormärz, "
Jahrbuch der Grillparzer-Gesellschaft, vol. 21 (1912), 95.

8. Jahrbuch der Deutsch-Amerikanischen Gesellschaft von Illinois,
vol. 15 (1915), 84-144.

9. Heinzen's non-poetic works are dismissed with the remark:
"Space will not permit a more comprehensive account of Heinzen's literary activities, but in order to convey a vivid idea
of the variety of his labors, a list of his publications is added
at the end of this paper. " (p. 120) On p. 143 Schinnerer
merely lists the Lustspiele as item No. 49. He fails, however, to indicate the date of publication, giving only Boston
as the place. In fact, they first appeared in New York (1859)
and only later in Boston (1872).

10. Not 1856, as Schinnerer (p. 143) claims. Heinzen's Pionier
contains the "Einladung zur Subskription" for this volume of
poetry on February 28, 1858 (p. 7), and the volume was not
available until June 27 of that year.
    Several other dates Schinnerer offers are inaccurate, e.g.,
1843 for Reise eines teutschen Romantikers nach Batavia.
According to the Literaturblatt of February 7, 1842 (No. 14,
p. 15), Wolfgang Menzel had reviewed this work prior to this

date. But conclusive proof that the Reise appeared in 1841
rather than in 1843 is found in C. G. Kayser's Neues Bücher-
Lexikon, Erster Theil (Leipzig, 1841), p. 413, where "Reise
nach Batavia. Köln, 1841. Boisserée" is listed. The British Museum General Catalogue of Printed Books, CI (London,
1961), 141, also dates it 1841.

11. Schinnerer, p. 110.
12. "Gedichte von Karl Heinzen," Literaturblatt, No. 14 (February
    7, 1842), 55. An interesting sidelight here is given by
    Heinzen in Erlebtes I, 331, where he states: "... bald
    vergiftete man aus Bosheit meinen treuen Begleiter, meinen
    Hund, der den glorreichen Namen Menzel trug...."
        Heinrich Kurz gives a similar positive judgment in Gesch-
    ichte der neuesten deutschen Literatur von 1830, 3rd. ed.
    (Leipzig, 1874), IV, 46: "Lyrische Poesie. Von dem bekann-
    ten Agitator Karl Heinzen... erschienen 'Gedichte' (Köln,
    1841), die nur zum Theil hierher gehören. aber unter diesen
    zeichnen sich mehrere durch Tiefe des Gefühls und Kraft des
    Ausdrucks aus...."
13. Schinnerer, p. 117.
14. Schinnerer, p. 114. Heinrich Rattermann in "Karl Heinzen,"
    Der deutsche Pionier, vol. 13 (1881), 5, expresses a similar
    opinion.
15. Usually only the third edition (Boston, 1867) is listed as "en-
    larged." The review of the New York Familienblätter (see
    fn. 18) reveals they were also included in the New York,
    1858 edition.
16. Pionier, vol. 5, No. 29 (July 18, 1858), p. 5 begins the column.
    It was continued in the issues of: July 25; August 1, 8, 22,
    29; and September 5, 1858. The review from the Anzeiger
    appeared in the July 25 issue, p. 6, and continued into the
    August 1 issue.
17. Ibid., (July 25, 1858), p. 6.
18. Ibid., (August 22, 1858), pp. 5-6.
19. Wittke, p. 142.
20. Ibid., p. 143.
21. (Boston, 1872), p. 4.
22. The January 3, 1858 issue of the Pionier contains this column,
    which begins: "Ich heisse Krüger und mein Name kommt von
    Krug, und es gäbe keinen Krug, wenn es kein Bier gäbe...."
    (p. 2). This corresponds exactly to page 281 of the Boston,
    1872 edition of the novel. The initial date of the column
    could not be determined at this time because the 1857 volume
    of the Pionier is presently missing from the Library of Con-
    gress. The column ends, however, on April 18, 1858 with
    the line "Gross bist du, Herr Jesus!" which is identical to
    the conclusion of the 1872 edition (p. 372).
23. Editoren-Kongress, p. 303. This also appears as an American
    epigram in the 1867 edition of Heinzen's poetry (p. 204).
24. Ibid., p. 346.
25. Deutsche Demokraten in Amerika (Göttingen, 1958), p. 109.
26. In the private collection of Professor Harold Jantz in Baltimore.
    The publishers were J. & W. Boisserée.

27. Europa. Chronik der gebildeten Welt, vol. 4 (1842), 585.
28. Op. cit., IV, 522.
29. "Deutsches Bühnenleben in Amerika," Jahrbuch der Deutsch-
    amerikaner, vol. 4 (1918), 227.
30. Pp. 23, 25, 143.
31. Dobert includes this work among Heinzen's "Andere Schriften,"
    p. 115; Schinnerer lists it as item No. 5, p. 142.
32. C. G. Kayser, Vollständiges Bücher-Lexikon, IX (Leipzig, 1848),
    520; also Wilhelm Heinsius, Allgemeines Bücher-Lexikon, X
    (Leipzig, 1848), 454, which gives the volume as 2 "Bogen,"
    i. e., 32 pages, and informs us that Ritzefeld was the pub-
    lisher.
    The Kölnische Komödie is not listed in the National Union
    Catalogue at the Library of Congress, and no review of it
    during 1841, 1842 or 1843 could be found. As far as could
    be determined there is no mention of the work in Heinzen's
    autobiography. Perhaps it is still available in a private col-
    lection, or reference to it can be found in the German maga-
    zines to which Heinzen was contributing at the time it was
    written.
33. Pionier, No. 33 (New York), p. 6.
34. Ibid., No. 33 (August 20, 1859), p. 6. The long delay in pub-
    lication is attributed to the length of the volume and its print-
    ing costs.
35. Dobert (p. 113) mentions only the first edition and distorts the
    title. In addition, the plot summary and one-sentence criti-
    cism offered by Dobert apply only to Professor Irrwisch.
36. Wittke mistakenly informs us that "Heinzen also wrote Lusts-
    piele, like Professor Irrwisch, Dr. Nebel, and several oth-
    ers, and published them in 1870." (p. 143) The date 1870
    is correct neither for Doktor Nebel (1841), nor for Profes-
    sor Irrwisch (1859; 1872), and Wittke seems to think that
    these are two different plays.
37. The "Vorbemerkung" reads: "Dieses Lustspiel hatte ursprüng-
    lich bloss die Bestimmung, als Einleitung zu einem (wegen
    Ungunst der Verthältnisse unbeendigt gebliebenen) komischen
    Roman, 'Irrfahrten des Professors Irrwisch' zu dienen. Auf
    Bühnengerechtigkeit wurde daher wenig Rücksicht genommen.
    Es bedarf wo[h]l keiner Bemerkung, dass die Häufung von
    Monologen im ersten Akt ein absichtlich angewandtes Mittel
    der Introduktion ist." (New York, 1859), p. 4.
    In light of the above, Wittke's criticism of Heinzen's come-
    dies, of which he mentions only Dr. Nebel and Professor Irr-
    wisch, seems unjustified: "The comedies could not possibly
    have been performed on the stage with success. They were
    practically all dialogue and no action... utterly lacking in
    taste, dramatic form, and understanding of the demands of
    the theater." (pp. 143-144).
    Dobert makes a similar mistake when he states that "Pro-
    fessor Irrwisch verrät einiges über Heinzens Technik als
    Bühnendichter." (p. 113).
38. Erlebtes, 1. Theil (Boston, 1864), p. 40.
39. Wittke (p. 143) generalizes about Heinzen's Lustspiele thus:

"They were attempts to write satire for the theater and attacked such favorite abuses as censorship, police, and bureaucracy and extolled the virtues of the revolutionary spirit." This description seems to relate only to Dr. Nebel and Professor Irrwisch as these abuses are not at issue in Die teutschen "Organisten der Bildung" in Amerika.

40. No. 36, p. 2.
41. Ibid., September 26; October 10, 17, 24 and 31; November 7.
42. Ibid., September 5; September 19 and 26; October 10.
43. Ibid., September 19, p. 3.
44. Karl Arndt and M. Olson, eds., German-American Newspapers and Periodicals, 1732-1955 (New York and London, 1965), pp. 399-400.
45. (Boston, 1872), p. 4.
46. Cf. Carl Wittke, We Who Built America (Ann Arbor, 1939), pp. 193-195.
      Franz Löher, Geschichte und Zustände der Deutschen in Amerika (Cincinnati und Leipzig, 1847), p. 456, gives an excellent description of the reputation of the Schnellpost, the Anzeiger des Westens and the New Yorker Staatszeitung during the late 1840s. The picture is anything but flattering for the Staatszeitung, which is referred to as the "Chorführer der Gemeinheit." Arndt-Olson (p. 399) confirm that this paper did not reach its highest standard of excellence until the editorship of Oswald Ottendorfer (1858-1900).
47. All further references to this play will be given in parentheses and apply to the 1859 New York edition.
48. Gedichte (Boston, 1867), p. 198.
49. For Heinzen's own dislike for "Junghegelianer" and their cowardly "Jungamerikaner" counterparts, cf. Erlebtes, I, 47.
50. Gedichte, p. 244.
51. See reprint in Pionier (April 12, 1860), pp. 1-2. For a discussion of Ruppius by Heinzen cf. Pionier (September 20, 1860), pp. 2-3.
52. This falsification is revealed in Pionier (September 20, 1860), pp. 2-3.
53. Arndt-Olson, p. 399, state that Ruppius was editor from 1856-57.
54. Cf., e.g., Otto Ruppius, "Amerikanische Zustände Nr. 2," Die Gartenlaube (1861), p. 622.
55. Reprinted in Pionier (April 12, 1860), p. 2.
56. Cf. fn. 4 above.
57. Marggraff, p. 111.
58. Ibid., p. 112.
59. Reprinted in Pionier (September 27, 1860), pp. 2-3.
60. Kurz, IV, 522.
61. First published in Marggraff's own Leipzig Blätter für literarische Unterhaltung, and reprinted in Magazin für die Literatur des Auslandes, No. 35 (August 29, 1860), p. 420.
62. "In der That sind Goltz und Heinzen selbst die besten Widerlegungen ihrer eigenen Behauptungen von der Engherzigkeit, Kurzsichtigkeit, Gemeinheit und Lüderlichkeit der Deutschen und des deutschen Literatenthums insbesondere, denn in

Beiden ist, bei aller Einseitigkeit und Verranntheit--der Eine
in konservativ-religiöse und der Andere in destructiv-atheist-
ische Ideen--ja, bei aller scheinbaren Lüderlichkeit, ein uni-
verseller Geist und die vollste Theilnahme für alles Mensch-
liche und Edle nicht zu verkennen." Ibid., and reprinted in
Pionier (September 27, 1860), pp. 2-3.

63. Pionier (April 12, 1860), pp. 1-2; (September 20, 1860), p. 2;
(September 27, 1860), pp. 2-3: "Mehr Kritik"; (October 4,
1860), pp. 2-3; "Noch Mehr Kritik."

64. "Mehr Kritik," Pionier (September 27, 1860), pp. 2-3.

65. "Deutsche Poesie in den Vereinigten Staaten," Die Gegenwart,
No. 15 May 4, 1872), pp. 235-237.

66. "Ueber Grobheit," Die Gegenwart, No. 22 (June 22, 1872), pp.
350-351.

67. "An den Redacteur des 'Pionier,' Karl Heinzen in Boston," Die
Gegenwart, No. 30 (August 17, 1872), p. 109.

17. KONRAD KREZ:
     POET BETWEEN CONTINENTS*

Hans E. Roemer

> Spät erklingt, was früh erklang,
> Glück und Englück wird Gesang.
> > --Goethe

To sing of man's afflictions has always been the mission of
poets. Immigrant poets in particular have embraced the sentiments
of both joy and sadness and perpetuated these ageless companions of
man. The dualism of their muse is cultivated by a sadness at being
separated from one's native soil and emboldened them to pay homage
to their new canton.

German-American poetry[1] is but one of the many artistic du-
alities which display an abundance of divided loyalties, the manifes-
tation of which is most prominent among those talented German
writers who through their participation in the 1848 revolutionary
movement were forced to flee their homeland. While some of these
exiles brought their battle to America and continued it through the
so called "politische Presselyrik," others reaffirmed their unshaken
patriotism in their writings in which they sought an almost mystical
affinity with the land of their birth.[2]

Konrad Krez (1828-1897) was one of the latter poets. Because
of his participation in the 1848 insurrection movement he was sentenced to death, but escaped to Switzerland and from there to France.
In 1850, he came to America and at first settled in New York where
he became a lawyer. Four years later he moved to Sheboygan, Wisconsin and assumed the office of District Attorney until the outbreak
of the Civil War. He participated in the war and reached the rank of
Brigadier General. Krez then settled in Milwaukee where he passed
away on September 9, 1897.

Like most German-American poets Krez's works are sentimental and romantic, and display a deep and sensual love for nature.
In his poetry he recalls the traditional values of his homeland; his
baroque conservatism serves as the mystical link between his newly
found home and his unreachable birthplace. Most striking in Krez's
poetry is the immutable link to the past and the emergence of an in-

---

*Reprinted from German-American Studies 3 (1971): 12-17, by per-
mission of the publisher.

timacy with his adopted homeland.   Aus Wiskonsin (1875) displays
the dual sentiments of the immigrant and the continuous growth of
the poet and stands at the forefront of German-American creative
literature.

Although Konrad Krez found a new and concordant life in
America, his incessant patriotism enticed him continually to laud his
lost homeland.   Aus Wiskinson contains some of his most soul-
stirring poetry appurtenant to this affaire de coeur. [3]   In "Heimweh"
Krez sings not only of the far-away land, but also of his spiritual
dependency upon his native soil.   The poem's mixed trochaic and
dactylic pattern is an old Germanic scansion which Opitz abolished
as barbaric. [4]   It is, however, this old Germanic folksong rhythm
which gives the poem its suscitation and emotional appeal.

HEIMWEH

Meiner Seele Feuer erlischt, der Tränen
Strom versiegt, es glüht das Gedächtnis, und die
Lust am Leben flieht, wenn ich deiner denke,
Heimischer Boden!

As can be seen in the first stanza of "Heimweh," the poet
truly sings, for the words and their part regular and part irregular
rime create not only passionate emotions, but also a soul-stirring
melody.   The poet-musician harmonizes thought, sound and rhythm
in order to communicate universality.   To be sure, it is Konrad
Krez the poet who sings of his native soil, but through his metaphor-
ical device he also expresses the universal lament of all men who
suffer expatriation.

A truly personal poem, however, is "An Mein Vaterland."
Here Krez sounds his intimate patriotism and esoteric nostalgia.

AN MEIN VATERLAND[5]

Kein Baum gehörte mir von deinen Wäldern,
Mein war kein Halm auf deinen Roggenfeldern,
Und schutzlos hast du mich hinausgetrieben,
Weil ich in meiner Jugend nicht verstand
Dich weniger und mehr mich selbst zu lieben,
Und dennoch lieb ich dich, mein Vaterland!

Not only does the poet cast a longing and lingering look at the
land of his forefathers, but he also recalls the days of his youth and
the aching void of his past.   It is a most sombre and solemn vocif-
eration of love, glory and sacrifice.   Most notable is the rhythm
pattern of his verse, for Krez uses a five-beat iambic verse with
feminine cadence, which is similar to the English heroic verse or
heroic couplet.   The verse is similar to that in Faust, but unlike
Goethe, who employs part regular and part irregular rime, Krez
uses pure rime only. [6]   The accented metre of the stanzas of this
patriotic song serve to unite sombre thought and emotional rhythm.

The genuineness of the exiled poet is avowed in "An mein Vaterland." Unlike Krez, Gottfried Keller and Hoffmann von Fallersleben employ trochaic metre in the four line stanzas of their patriotic poetry. Keller makes use of dissyllabic anacrusis in order to lift the beat of his hymn.

AN DAS VATERLAND

O mein Heimatland! O mein Vaterland!
Wie so innig, feurig lieb' ich dich!
Schönste Ros', ob jede mir verblich,
Duftest noch an meinem öden Strand!

Although this hymn displays the fierce love of the poet for the fatherland, it lacks the reverence of Krez's poem. Keller's poetry grows out of everyday reality and is rooted in post-romantic realism. Keller (who was not compelled to emigrate) is the naive lover who sings his emotions to his ever faithful beloved. Although Fallersleben was arrested for his "lyrical agitation" and sympathy with the cause of The Forty-Eighters, his punishment was less severe than that of Krez, for he was merely dismissed from his post at the University of Breslau. The patriotic overtones of Fallersleben's "An mein Vaterland" are strikingly similar to those of Krez's poem:

Treue Liebe bis zum Grabe
Schwör ich dir mit Herz und Hand;
Was ich bin und was ich habe
Dank' ich dir, mein Vaterland!

Nicht in Worten nur und Liedern
Ist mein Herz zum Dank bereit:
Mit der Tat will ich's erwidern
Dir in Not, in Kampf und Streit.

In der Freude wie im Leide
Ruf ich's Freund' und Feinden zu:
Ewig sind vereint wir beide,
Und mein Trost, mein Glück bist du.

Treue Liebe bis zum Grabe
Schwör' ich dir mit Herz und Hand;
Was ich bin und was ich habe
Dank' ich dir, mein Vaterland!

It is apparent that the theme and the sentiments of these three contemporary poets are concordant, but the metric pattern of Krez is different from that of Keller and Fallersleben. To be sure, Krez does very much favor the trochaic and dactylic line in his other works, but it is here, in "An Mein Vaterland," where he bolsters his pathos with the monotonous supportance of the five-beat iambic line.

It is characteristic of German-American poets that they reveal their divided loyalties in their works. Konrad Krez, like others, engaged in a continuous versification of his past, illuminating his eterne dependency upon his native soil as well as his great love for the land in which he was born.

However, like other immigrant poets, Krez has adopted his new country with the equal empressement with which he venerates Germany. Most notable perhaps is the new form in which he poetizes America. No longer does he adhibit to the measured rhythm of accented and unaccented syllables, but instead moves to the free form of the elegy and rhapsody. This metastasis is so lucid that one could conclude that the country which gave new liberty and independence to the man, also emancipated the poet. No longer bound by rime and rhythm, the poet uses unchained language in order to freely laud the treasures and sentiments of this pubescent, abundant and beautiful land.

But despite the new form and new theme, his love for nature remains singularly adamantine. In "Frühling bei New York" Krez offers a poetic view of an island having intercourse with surrounding green hills and clear water, crowned by a rejoicing sky. The language is fertile, the coinage uberous.

FRUEHLING BEI NEW YORK
(1854)

Lachend hat sich der Himmel gelagert über das Eiland,
Um das in Liebe vereint Hudson und Meer sich geschmiegt,
Schöner kann nicht der Äther gewölbt sein über Neapel,
Sonniger legt sich kein Strahl über das goldene Horn.
Frisch sind mit Gräsern bedeckt die Hügel am Ufer der
    Inseln,
Und es schmückt sich die Salzwiese mit saftigem Grün.
Zwischen dem Hickorylaub und Gewind wildwachsender
    Reben
Blicken die schimmernden Landhäuser am Ufer Hervor.
Da ist ein Busch, so laubig und kühl, und dort eine Hecke,
Heimlich und blütenbedeckt, aber die Nachtigall fehlt,
Um Gefühl in das Herz des lauschenden Horchers zu
    flöten,
Aber alles ist stumm, stumm wie das schweigende Grab.
Lerche, wo bist du? Hast du dein Lied hier verlernet?
    Vergebens
Seh ich zum Himmel hinauf! Hat dein melodisch Geschlecht
Keinen Verwandten herüber gesandt, um singend zu flattern
Über Amerikas höchstenglichten Fluren von Mais?

It appears that the sentiment of "Frühling bei New York" parallels the mood of the works of Klopstock, Schiller and Hölderlin.[7] These elegiac singers praised the beauty and revivification of nature while mourning a void. Krez also is sorrowing a void for he states "aber die Nachtigall fehlt," and proceeds to ask "Lerche, wo bist du?" Both birds are old world birds and the poet is pained by the lack of familiar enchantment in this earthly elysium.

Krez's lamentation appears to be rooted in the dualism of his love which subconsciously seeks to unite two continents and which at times reveals the veiled collation of the past and the present. Krez's poem "New Orleans" is, however, free of such an apposition. Again, nature provides the theme, and the verse is free flowing and unrestrained by metrical stresses. There are no reservations or past regrets, but only the emotions of love and admiration.

NEW ORLEANS

Herrliche Stadt, du Tochter der See und des Vaters der
    Wasser,
Wie die Göttin der Liebe, so spülten die Wellen ans Land
    dich,
Wo du gebettet liegst im Schoose des ewigen Frühlings.
Wie ein Mährchen erscheinst du dem nördlichen Fremdling
    der eben
Aus den blätterberaubten und schneeigen Ländern herab-
    kommt,
Wo ein düsterer Himmel auf rauchichten Städten sich lagert,
Wie verzaubert blickt er hinauf zu den silbernen Wolken,
Die in der Bläue des Himmels dahinziehn, blickt er zur Erde,
Wo die Strahlen der Sonne das Land und das Wasser vergolden.
Mitten im Winter begrüsst er das dunkle Laub der Orangen.
Und bewundert den herrlichen Baum mit den goldenen Aepfeln,
Den die duftende Blüte, die reife und reifende Frucht
    schmückt.
Staunend betrachtet er den vor den Häusern zur Zierde
    gepflanzten,
Aus den Stielen des Laubes gebildeten Stamm der Banane,
Deren Blätter wie flatternde Fahnen im Winde sich wiegen.
Fröhlich und heiter geniesst hier das Volk in glücklichem
    Leichtsinn,
Wie die Vögel im Wald, freiwillige Gaben des Himmels.
Lieblich ist es hier wohnen, und knüpften nicht Bande,
    die stärker
sind als die Gürtel der Erde, mich an das kalte Wisconsin,
Wo die Ceder wächst und der Zucker träufelnde Ahorn,
Möchte ich gern in den sonnigen Fluren von Luisiana
Eine Hütte mir baun, in dem Lande, wo niemals die Rosen
Müde werden zu blühn, wo die Feige wächst und die Myrte,
Und der spottende Vogel sein Nest ins Granatengebüsch baut.

"New Orleans" is truly an American hymn in which Krez abandons restrictions on form, rime and pattern and his endeavor to coarctate the span of two continents. Konrad Krez the poet has matured and has in fact become an American poet. The lines "Möchte ich gern in den sonnigen Fluren von Luisiana eine Hütte mir baun, in dem Lande, wo niemals die Rosen müde werden zu blühn" show perhaps best the deep affection which Krez now feels for his new homeland. No longer does he sing of beauty only, but he unequivocally desires to become a part of this noble culmination.

Cetainly, no account of Krez is complete without citing "Da waren Deutsche auch dabei." This poem lauds the puissant parity of German-American heritage, and the poet's pride of being German is fused with his pride of having become American. It is an account of the gifts of the old world to the new world, and of old world men contributing to the culture and destiny of the still infant land. The theme of this poem is also the essence of Krez's being. Honor your heritage, embrace your past, but pursue the new dawn.

DA WAREN DEUTSCHE AUCH DABEI

Als Bettler sind wir nicht gekommen
Aus unserem deutschen Vaterland.
Wir hatten manches mitgenommen,
Was hier noch fremd und unbekannt.
Und als man schuf aus dichten Wäldern,
Aus öder, düstrer Wüstenei
Den Kranz von reichen Feldern,
Da waren Deutsche auch dabei.

Gar vieles, was in früheren Zeiten
Ihr kaufen müsstet überm Meer,
Das lehrten wir euch selbst bereiten,
Wir stellten manche Werkstatt her.
Oh, wagt es nicht, dies zu vergessen,
Sagt nicht, als ob das nicht so sei,
Es künden's tausend Feueressen,
Da waren Deutsche auch dabei.

Und was die Kunst und Wissenschaften
Euch hier verlieh'n an Kraft und Stärk',
Es bleibt der Ruhm am Deutschen haften,
Das meiste war der Deutschen Werk.
Und wenn aus vollen Tönen klinget
Ans Herz des Liedes Melodei,
Ich glaub' von dem, was ihr da singet,
Ist vieles Deutsche auch dabei.

Drum steh'n wir stolz auf festem Grunde,
Den unsere Kraft der Wildnis nahm,
Wie wär's mit eurem Staatenbunde,
Wenn nie zu euch ein Deutscher kam?
Und wie in Bürgerkriegstagen,
Ja schon beim ersten Freiheitsschrei:
Wir dürfen's unbestritten sagen,
Da waren Deutsche auch dabei.

Notes

1. For an excellent sampling of the various themes to be found in German-American poetry, see Robert E. Ward, Deutsche Lyrik Aus Amerika. Eine Auswahl, The Literary Society

German-American Literature

Foundation, Inc. (New York, 1969).

2. For illuminating insight into the lives and works of the Forty-Eighters, see: Eitel Wolf Dobert, Deutsche Demokraten, die Achtundvierziger und ihre Schriften. (Göttingen, 1958); Carl Wittke, Refugees of the Revolution (Phila., 1952); A. E. Zucker, The Forty-Eighters (New York, 1950; 1957); Gottlieb Betz, "Die deutschamerikanische patriotische Lyrik der Achtundvierziger und ihre historische Grundlage," Ph.D. diss. (Univ. Pa., 1913).

3. Other volumes of Krez' poetry are: Dornen und Rosen von den Vogesen (Landau, 1846) and Gesangbuch (Strassburg, 1848).

4. Martin Opitz (1597-1639) insists on new forms for poetry in his Buch von der deutschen Poeterey (1624).

5. This poem won the first prize in Leipzig against a thousand contestants. "In justice to the poet, it should be said that he did not compose it expressly for the contest, for it was the spontaneous, heart-breaking plaint of a political exile, who loved his fatherland despite her faults and cruelty to him." See J. H. A. Lacher, The German Element in Wisconsin, (Milwaukee, 1925), pp. 44-45.

6. In Faust, Goethe alternates the four-beat and five-beat iambic line. The best example of the five-beat iambic line is the "Zueignung." It is composed of four elegiac stanzas using the Italian form (Octaveria, AB, AB, AB, CC). The verse, however, is five-beat iambic.

7. For bio-bibliographical data, see Franz Brümmer, Lexikon der deutschen Dichter und Prosaisten vom Beginn des 19. Jahrunderts bis zur Gegenwart, 8 vols. (Leipsig, 1913).

8. See F. Beisner, Geschichte der deutschen Elegie (Berlin, 1941), and W. Kayser, Geschichte der deutschen Ballade (Berlin, 1936).

18. CASPAR BUTZ OF CHICAGO:
     POLITICIAN AND POET*

Hildegard Binder Johnson

Part I

    The life data hitherto known about Caspar Butz are few, fre-
quently misleading and insignificant. He was spurred on by two
passionate interests, politics and poetry. In business he was not
very successful. He was probably the best known of all German-
American poets numerous among forty-eighters and his Gedichte
eines Deutsch-Amerikaners, published in Chicago in 1879, were
found in every German-American library. Caspar Butz deserves a
thorough investigation of contemporary newspapers, letters, and
sources for further biographical data and a sympathetic reading of
his poems.

    Butz was born on October 23, 1825, in Hagen, Westphalia,
the second son of an innkeeper who derived additional income from
fees for a toll bridge over the Volme river close to his home.
Against this simple background only the boy's more than ordinary intelligence explains his first expensive education in the Bürgerschule
of his town, where he learned Latin, French and Greek. After the
father's early death the boy had to leave school and was apprenticed
to a mercantile house which sent him as its representative to Belgium, France and Algiers in 1846 and 1847. The diaries of these
travels are lost. Upon his return Butz, who never was interested in
business, went to Leipzig to learn the booktrade and to attend lectures at the university.

    Butz was twenty-three when the German revolution broke out.
He was a radical from the beginning and became a close friend of
Friedrich Hecker. Butz's attempt to start a radical newspaper for
Westphalia was unsuccessful. In May, 1849, during the course of
political events which cannot be related here the Prussian government
called up troops to suppress civil revolts in Westphalia, also in the
town of Iserlohn, where Butz was a member of a Sicherheitsaus-
schuss on May 16 and demanded in radical speeches that the Prussian troops be withdrawn. By May 20 Butz was back in Hagen hid-
ing from the authorities. The family supplied him with money and
women's clothes and he escaped to London by way of Holland. In
September, 1849, he embarked on Le Havre for America the occa-

---

*Reprinted from American-German Review 12:6 (1946): 4-7; 13: 9-11,
by permission of the publisher.

sion of his first poem, published in the collection of 1879.   Bidding
a poetic farewell to Europe, he expressed his love for liberty and
his hopes for a free and united fatherland of the future.

Butz went straight to Detroit and got work in a fur dealer's
store.   His family sent a relative to keep house for him.   Butz expected another German revolution in the near future according to
letters to and from Hagen.   He planned to return to Germany as
soon as his five-year term of exile had expired.   But he was to see
Europe only once again for a short time in 1856 when he visited his
family in Cologne.   Before that he did not yet dare to visit Hagen.
The only memorable incident of this journey was his meeting with
Freiligrath and Kinkel in London which he commemorated in another
poem.   In Detroit, Butz became a friend of Christian Esselen and
contributed the introductory poem to the first issue of Atlantis, a
short lived philosophical journal of high standing published by Esselen.   All sources agree that Butz came to Chicago in 1854, where
he made his home until 1883.   Here he was first partner in the
firm of Butz and Schiffer, importers and dealers in hardware, later,
in 1858, a bankteller probably in the bank of his good friend Francis
A. Hoffmann.

In Chicago, Butz interested himself at once in German activi-
ties.   Together with Francis A. Hoffmann, Georg Schneider and
Ernest Prüssing he organized meetings for the erection of a German
House, which was completed in 1856.   The three story Gothic brick
structure, on the southeast corner of Indiana Avenue and Welles
Street, became the scene of the German Republican Convention of
May 14, 1860.   It burnt in the Chicago fire.   Burnt too were the
minutes for the years 1854 to 1871 of the German Immigrant Aid
Society, which Butz founded in 1854.   He was its president and
Francis Hoffman was its treasurer.   They employed an agent to ad-
vise German immigrants in Chicago.   The society lasted for seventy-
seven years and was one of the most successful and financially
sound of its kind.   Butz also was a popular speaker in the Chicago
Turngemeinde and participated in the campaign for Frémont in the
fall of 1854.   In short, Butz began life in Chicago as a typical forty-
eighter; a supporter of German activities, a Turner, a radical abo-
litionist and therefore a Republican.   Two years later he was one of
the three delegates from Chicago at the State Republican Convention
at Springfield, Illinois, on June 16.

From 1859 to 1866, Butz served as deputy clerk of the Superior Court of Cook County, a position that yielded a modest income and left him time for political activities.   In 1858 he was
elected as a Republican to the House of the Illinois legislature.   For
attending their meetings on forty-seven days and traveling five hundred miles he was paid $139.   He served on the immigration com-
mittee and helped to draft and pass "An act to protect emigrants and
for the encouragement of immigration to the State of Illinois."   On
one of these visits to Springfield, Butz met Abraham Lincoln but
was not, according to his own testimony, particularly impressed with
Lincoln's personality.

In the Republican campaign of 1860, Butz was an important
but not yet a major figure. The Germans who favored Seward more
than any other candidate could not press the latter's nomination but
were successful in defeating the nomination of Edward Bates of Missouri, the candidate whom they disliked most. This course was decided upon at the special German Republican Convention of May 14,
1860, where Butz as a delegate from Illinois was elected secretary.
He and Adolph Douai of Boston were to draft the resolutions that
would express the urgent concerns of the Germans. These were adherence to the Republican platform of Philadelphia of 1856, its
strict application against slavery, a pronouncement against the Massachusetts amendment, a recommendation of a homestead law and
admission of Kansas into the Union without slavery. Any candidate
who stood for these demands would be supported by the Germans
and by Butz. Butz voted for Lincoln.

Soon, however, Caspar Butz became disillusioned with the
new president; he particularly condemned Lincoln's emancipation
policy. As a strong opponent of Lincoln's administration he wel-
comed General John C. Frémont's declaration of August 31, which
freed the slaves of rebel planters in Missouri. On November 10,
1861, Butz attacked Lincoln publicly in vituperative speech at a
mass meeting of the Germans of Chicago in North Market Hall and
closed with a cheer for Frémont as the next president of the United
States.

He then started to prepare and in 1864 embarked on a very
ambitious journalistic enterprise, the publication of the Deutsch-
Amerikanische Monatshefte für Politik, Wissenschaft und Literatur.
The journal was conceived as a kind of Atlantic Monthly for the
German intelligentsia in the United States and had outstanding contributors, men like Reinhold Solger of New York, Friedrich Münch
of Missouri, Bayard Taylor of Boston, Karl Blind of London, Theodor Ohlshausen and Emil Prätorius of St. Louis, Adolph Douai of
Boston. Butz hoped to make the Monatshefte "a kind of international journal" which would "contribute toward the final victory of the
eternal ideas of liberty." The first issue made it very clear what
its editor meant to contribute first of all: the defeat of Lincoln and
the nomination of Frémont. This is proved in the two leading articles, "Lincoln" by Butz and "Missouri" by Prätorius. The next
number brought Butz's answer to many letters caused by the first
issue and proof of the division among the Germans into those for
and against Lincoln. The journal had more than three thousand subscribers after three months and reflects clearly the course of the
Frémont campaign of 1864, a very interesting chapter in the history
of German-American politics. Butz was its guiding spirit. Other
leading German-Americans, Carl Schurz and Gustav Körner, for instance, did not waver in their support of Lincoln. Butz had to fight
opposition close by, because the Illinois Staatszeitung supported Lincoln. The Frémont movement had its origin in Missouri; after the
first issue of the Monatschefte, Frémont movements started in the
East. By April, Butz had organized a Frémont club in Chicago.
A national convention was arranged for May 31 in Cleveland, where

Butz was one of four hundred delegates. Frémont was nominated
and Butz wrote in July that "if he was not going to be victorious
this time he still had the satisfaction of having gone into battle for
right and truth." The battle was lost.

In January 1864, Butz said in the Monatshefte that "the Germans will have the important, yes, the decisive word at the next
election" which was not a prudent statement. The fact that the Germans were the most important supporters of the Frémont movement
made it politically weak. But when the Republican Senators Wade
and Davis published a manifesto in the New York Tribune of August
5, many Republicans doubted Lincoln's chances for re-election.
They awaited the outcome of the National Democratic Convention on
September 1, in Chicago, before they would decide. At this occasion Butz, a member of the Central Frémont Committee of Illinois,
undertook a bold step. "The Wade-Davis Protest, a last Appeal to
the Democratic Party," an article by Butz, translated into English,
was distributed by him in pamphlet form among the delegates.
Among other strong statements, Lincoln's administration was called
a caricature of dictatorship. Frémont was strongly recommended
as the only candidate who would bring four hundred thousand German votes to the Democratic party. This single handed stroke
brought no result, the Democrats nominated McClellan and most of
the German vote stayed with the Republican Party and Lincoln.
Butz's most ambitious political adventure was a failure, but he
proved his political mettle by announcing in October 1864 that he
would vote for Lincoln under protest.

However, Butz was disillusioned. During 1864 he had published many political articles, poems, a lecture and excerpts from
two plays. During 1865 he contributed much less to the Monatshefte. After he visited Missouri and Friedrich Münch during that
summer his report of his journey sounded like a swan-song.

> Es gibt so wenige Lichtblicke im deutsch-amerikanischen
> Leben ... die geräuschvollen Turner und Sängerfeste sind
> nur ein krampfhafter Protest, nur ein Aufschrei der unter-
> drückten menschlichen Natur ... gegen das graue, poesie-
> lose Einerlei des hiesigen Lebens, gegen die Tretmühle
> des Tages.... Wir glauben nicht an eine Zukunft der
> deutschen Poesie in Amerika, ebenso wenig an eine selb-
> ständige Entwicklung des deutschen Lebens auf diesem
> Kontinent.... So lange die Einwanderung noch dauert ...
> wird man von der Macht der Deutschen in Amerika reden
> Die Zukunft ist deshalb doch nicht unser.... Wir müssen
> uns daran gewöhnen, dass es unsere Bestimmung ist, der
> grössten Republik der Neuzeit teilweise die entscheidende
> Richtung zu geben und das Ideal der Zukunft wenn auch
> wie der Gladiator im Circus nur sterbend zu grüssen.

Poetically he expressed the same thought in the dedication of his
volume of poems:

> Doch wohl das härt'ste Los auf Erden
> Ist hier ein deutscher Dichter sein.

On January 1, 1866, Rudolf Lexow, editor of the Belletristische Journal in New York, became editor of the Monatshefte, which ceased publication after June 1867.

   The position of deputy clerk at the Superior Court also came to an end in 1866 and Butz again turned to business. His brewery firm owned jointly with his brother-in-law was destroyed by the Chicago fire. Politically, Butz continued as a radical Republican during the campaign of 1868, favoring Grant. In 1870 he was elected as a Republican to serve on the Board of Commissioners of the Penitentiary of Joliet. His altruistic spirit wanted to improve the lot of the prisoners by organizing a library for them. As he often paid visits to prisons over weekends he was not in Chicago on October 9, 1871, when his home burnt down. Butz with his wife and youngest child which was prematurely born in the night of the fire, found shelter in the warden house of the penitentiary during the following winter, the older children lived with relatives. Later on the house was rebuilt on the old site.

   In 1872, Butz was joined by Carl Schurz and Gustav Körner in the opposition to re-election of the same president. They all attended the convention of Liberal Republicans in Cincinnati on May 2, 1872, where Johann Bernhard Stallo's home was the meeting place of all distinguished German politicians. All were disappointed in the nomination of Horace Greeley, and Butz and Hecker, the two radicals from Illinois, left the city without taking formal leave. Later on, Butz supported liberal Republicanism although he lost his position as inspector at the penitentiary on account of this support. He derived some income from editing the Westen, the Sunday issue of the Illinois Staatszeitung from April until November 1873. Soon, local politics demanded most of Butz's attention. The so-called "People's Party" was organized in May 1873 in opposition to the temperance movement. Under the leadership of Anton C. Hesing, German Republicans and Democrats fought together and were victorious in the Chicago election in the fall of 1873. Butz became chief deputy clerk for 1874 and 1875. In the next, also hotly contested campaign, he was elected city-clerk and re-elected in 1878. In 1879 he published his poems with the support of many friends and publishers because all manuscripts had burnt and the poems had to be gathered from former publications. His fame as a literary man probably earned him a call to New York where the editors of Puck, Keppler and Schwarzmann, asked him to become editor of a new monthly, Um die Welt. But conditions of work proved to be so unsatisfactory that Butz returned to Chicago very soon. His oldest and youngest sons had started a business in Des Moines, where the father joined them in 1883. He died there suddenly on October 19, 1885, shortly before his sixtieth birthday and was buried in Chicago according to freethinkers' rites. A little booklet titled Grossvater-Lieder, addressed to a little girl who died as a child of seven was published posthumously and is rare. Butz's political activities and personal history is closely associated with Chicago where his descendants, including one daughter, live to-day. His poetical genius is of nation-wide German-American significance.

Part II

In an appraisal of Butz, the poet, one must consider a fundamental problem of literature in exile. Language is kept alive by constantly changing speech and one may contend that nobody who leaves his country at the age of twenty-four can compose verses in his mother tongue thirty years later without betraying the estrangement from the living linguistic environment. Generally, this is true. But there are exceptions. Ferdinand Freiligrath, Germany's undisputedly greatest political poet of Butz's generation, left Germany at the age of forty-one and lived in England until 1868 when he returned to Germany. Nobody has said that Freiligrath's poetical language suffered perceptibly from his exile. Freiligrath was Butz's poetical idol--as Friedrich Hecker was his political hero. Both men had much in common. Some of the exterior circumstances in their lives were comparable. They did not finish their formal education and earned their living in exile by unappealing mercantile work. Their poetical tastes were similar too. Both liked to translate French and English poetry and much of their poetical material was found in ancient historical events and in lands far away. Political events of their time stirred both men to passionate songs demanding liberty and social justice. Both had a true understanding of the tragedy of emigration. Aside from their political songs both men were true lyricists. In all this Butz looked up to Freiligrath as his model and was to a certain degree his imitator. But he was also more than an imitator. His indignation at slavery, for instance, drove him to poetical outbursts which--while not as polished in form as the poetry of Freiligrath--were certainly his very personal creations. Butz's lyric poems were original in contents, often very simple and thus all the more genuine in tune.

Gustav Koerner, a well-meaning but by no means uncritical friend of Butz, said that Butz's poetry was "hardly inferior, if at all, to the best of Freiligrath's." Literary critics would disagree. Butz's political songs lack the clarity and strength that make many of Freiligrath's political poems convincing and give them a lasting character. Butz was not as gifted as his idol with respect to skillfulness in rhythm and certainty of word. He simply was the lesser poet. His genius was not fertilized by the contact with a congenial environment during the important period of its development. Freiligrath wrote many of his best verses before he emigrated as a mature man of forty-one years. Butz left the fatherland when he was twenty-four and the first poem in his collection was "Abschied vom Vaterlande," dated 1849. The publication of his poems thirty years later was only possible through the cooperation of many friends, newspaper publishers and correspondents who had preserved clippings or letters which contained some of Butz's verses. All his manuscripts were burned.

Butz often complained of the lack of interest of those at home in the fate of their sons far away in America. The ignorance in Germany of German-American poetry was appalling, indeed, and a few meagre anthologies around the turn of the century, particularly the more widely known but inadequate one by Georg A. Neef, could not remedy the negligence of many decades. Yet, among his contemporaries, Butz was better known than one might expect from his own words. Many well-known literary men in Germany read his volume and in the early eighties several German authors and publishers made efforts to arrange for a second publication of Butz's poems in Germany. Butz's early and unexpected death was partly responsible for the failure of their plan.

German literature in America has found little philological interest. While it is true that much of it hardly deserves to be called literature, a good deal is worth rescue from oblivion. In the same way, many of Butz's poems show all the marks of a Gelegenheitsgedicht, yet others can be enjoyed to this day. Anthologists of German literature--if they had not ignored the poetry by Germans outside the fatherland during the nineteenth century--might have considered them worth a quotation. Yet, again, the wider reading public in Germany could hardly have appreciated that ever present longing for the lost world and the defeated cause of German liberty. They could never have fully understood the fundamental problem in the life of a poet who emigrated. One has to undergo the same experience to understand. Only those German-contemporaries who were also exiles composed his really appreciative audience. Butz expressed his loneliness in a poem of August 11, 1879, thirty years after he had said the final good-bye to his country. A part of it may be translated as follows:

> Der Jugend darf sich kaum versehen
> Wer beiden Welten angehört;
> Die Eine wird ihn kaum verstehen,
> Die and're neue Weisen hört.
> 'S ist ein gewalt'ger Schritt im Leben,
> Vertauschen seiner Heimat Land;
> Die alte kennt nicht unser Streben,
> Ganz heimisch nie wird dieser Strand.

> Nur wer ihn mitthat kann uns richten,
> Nur wer ihn mitthat kann verstehen;

Many of Butz's poems were liked by his German contemporaries because these songs were born out of experiences that they had had, because these poems expressed indignation and grief where they had felt them; in short, because they were special messages for them. There are some poems though which contain an all-time human message at least for those--and their number is great--who sometimes long for the country or village which they left long ago and which seem so very far away. Little things, the appearance of a sparrow before his window, the unexpected ring of church bells may startle Butz's homesick soul to sing. He was sentimental; but

quite apt to insert kindly sarcasms like the one about the sparrow
which "of course, being a German, would appear in the old uni-
form." Or he might reveal freethinkers' tendencies by warning this
country to beware of the purpose for which church bells are rung.

Any American of German birth who occasionally likes to
read a book in his native tongue can appreciate the charm of a poem of 1852 where Butz describes the gratifying experience of sub-
merging into the old lost word by reading poems by Annette von
Droste-Hülshoff on a rainy Sunday traveling on the Mississippi:

> Ich hab', wenn auch in der Kajüte Raum,
> Doch in Westfalen Sonntag heut gehalten.

Butz's mother became eighty years old in 1876. He had not seen
her for about twenty years and of his poem to her two lines may
be quoted thus:

> Für mich hat nie Dein Alter zugenommen,
> Du bist für mich noch immer fünfzig Jahr;

Do we not all remember beloved ones as we saw them at our last
farewell?

Many of the forty-eighters died early after unsuccessful struggles in America. Christian Esselen and Georg Hillgärtner, journalist and lawyer in Chicago and Missouri, who stood by Butz in every
political fight and died forty years old in 1865, were among the
friends and comrades whose deaths Butz mourned in his poems.
The grief about the steadily widening gaps in the ranks of old fight-
ers and comrades, the feeling of the futility of their high ideals
found simple expression in "Unsere Todten."

> Es is so still geworden
>   In unsrer lauten Schaar;
> Zersprengt in West' und Norden
>   Ist sie seit manchem Jahr.
> Sie schafft und gräbt im Sande
>   Der unfruchtbaren Zeit
> Baut im Gedankenlande
>   Den Dom der Herrlichkeit.

Like all forty-eighters Butz was hostile to church organizations. He hated Puritanism and stupid piousness. But the complete
negativism often coupled with snobbish atheistic arrogance exhibited
by many Germans of his generation was not his attitude. He was
ready to call the unprivileged children together for a Christmas celebration "in the name of Him whose great heroic deed was to die for
the happiness of mankind," in the name of "the mild spirit of
Christ." His "Poetic Notes to Doré's Illustrated Bible," no longer
accessible, are said to have shown a deep religious feeling. Here
and there it breaks through in his poems.

He shared the cosmpolitanism of all forty-eighters. The exe-
cution of a printer in Havana, the misery of the proletariat in
France, the tragic political fate of Poland, the revolution in Hungary, the deliverance of Italy from Austria,--whenever and wherever
men rose and died for the cause of freedom and social justice their
cause was his and Butz's heart cried out in a song. John Brown's
death and the fate of the slaves in the United States stirred him to
passionate verses without restraint as to the selection of scenes or
language. As a political singer Butz has a certain directness and
swiftness in his verses that make the flowery and bombastic phrases,
so frequent and painful in political poetry, at least quite bearable.
Many German exiles wrote political poems, it was their favorite and
rather inefficient form of political action. When compared with these
poems Butz's superiority is evident because of the absence of artificial allegories and word-mannerisms.

In spite of all his criticism of the American republic and the
shortcomings in American life as he saw them Butz was deeply convinced that hope for progress of mankind could only be found here.
He asked his countrymen to come and be welcome if they wanted to
help in building up "a work, perhaps of good to Germany too some
day." His spirit surged with German victories in 1870 and 1871.
He was among the first to speak on behalf of the fatherland in need
in July 1870 and protested in January 1871 against the shipment of
arms from the United States to France. The past seemed forgiven
and forgotten and he begged the fatherland to permit its exiled sons
to participate in the national rebirth. But Butz was never swept
away to acceptance of the social and political structure of the German Empire after the war. Political success did not dull his critical spirit or feeling for the underprivileged as it dulled them in others.

This final turn to simple love of mankind, to positivism and
cooperation re-occurs in Butz's poetry, religion and political activity. Butz was absolutely honest; he was impractical and impetuous,
but very talented and always genial and likeable. In his later years
his verses and his prose often sound disappointed and reflect increasing loneliness and disillusion. But one force kept him alive.
The pride in having always fought for liberty, be it in vain in Germany, be it with success in America, and in having participated in
the fight for the deliverance of the world's greatest country from its
curse, slavery. No matter how often he refers to his "old age" to
the historian he was one who stayed young until he died at sixty.
Essentially he was a happy man, thoroughly German in background
and cultural tastes and a good American citizen, if participation and
self-sacrifice in the service of every public and national issue during a lifetime means good citizenship.

19. ERNST ANTON ZUENDT: PROFILE OF A GERMAN WRITER IN THE MIDWEST*

Robert E. Ward

... In the history of American literature the largest body of non-English writing is in the German language. It remains then for literary historians to tap this great reserve of literature, a significan portion of which dwells upon themes which are not merely American or German, but uniquely German-American. Here are to be found all of the diverse experiences of the individuals who carried the cultural values of their homeland to a foreign, often hostile environment in which they were assimilated.

When the current wave of German-American studies reaches its crest, one particular literary talent will most certainly be rediscovered. Ernst Anton Zuendt (pseud., "Ein Heimathloser") has been included in nearly every major reference work on German-American literature.[1] Born Ernst Anton Zuendt Freiherr von Kenzingen at St. Georgenberg near Mindelheim, Bavaria on January 12, 1819, Zuendt early renounced claim to his title and ancestral estates as the son of an Austrian count to follow his personal convictions which brought him to America. The demise of his father who had served in the Bavarian militia against Napoleon came early in Zuendt's life. The Zuendts had been masons in the 16th and 17th centuries until the Bull of 1763 was issued by Clement XII. Zuendt's ancestors on the maternal side of the Zuendt family included Baroness Freyburg-Eisenburg von Ranau, a guest at the wedding of Marie Antoinette and Louis XIV of France. Educated at the Hollaendische Institut in Munich, young Zuendt qualified to enter the university there where he pursued studies in philosophy and law, spending his leisure hours cultivating his interest in the muses.[2] At the age of twenty-three he published Lukretia, which he translated from the French of Francois Ponsard, and his first volume of poems, Einsame Stunden. Two years before his emigration he published Die Gambsenjaga, an alpine sketch accompanied by song and dance, and Rienzi, der letzte Tribun, which he modelled after Milford's tragedy.

In 1856 he departed from Germany with his wife (Johanna, née Ammann) and two sons for Green Bay, Wisconsin where he founded and edited the Green Bay Post. Ten months later he moved with his family to the German Athens of America--Milwaukee. There Zuendt earned a modest income as a private tutor. Before

*Reprinted by permission of the publisher from Grand Prairie Historical Bulletin 14:1 (1971): 1-6.

accepting a teaching position in the public schools, he served as director of the Stadttheater, editor of Gradaus,[3] and as a staff member on the Herold and Banner. In 1864[4] he made the acquaintance of Willibald Winkler[5] with whom he coedited the Milwaukee Theater Kalender. Later that year he departed with his family for St. Louis where he worked for three years on the staff of the Westliche Post. From 1868 to 1876 he taught in the public schools of Jefferson City, Missouri and translated French and German war dispatches for St. Louis newspapers, and continued to write creative literature. His best known original tragedy, Jugurtha, appeared in 1871 in his collection, Lyrische und dramatische Dichtungen, which was published at the press of F. B. Meissner in St. Louis.[6] In the preface to this collection Zuendt says this drama reflects the similarities between the Roman and young American Republics. Also included in the collection is Galilei, his translation of Francois Ponsard's play in alexandrine verse, which he had rendered into iambic pentameter in May 1868 while residing in Jefferson City. The poems in this volume treat a variety of American and German figures and events: Abe Lincoln, U. S. Grant, Thomas Paine, Barbarossa, Schiller, Guttenberg, and the opening of the German Apollo Theater in St. Louis in 1871. Zuendt's translations of "The Star Spangled Banner," "Yankee-Doodle" and poems by E. A. Poe, Horace, and others point to his literary versatility. This work was followed in 1874 by the comedies, Im Olymp and Die Eis-Fee, and his second volume of verse, Amerika (1876).

Upon returning to St. Louis, where his uncle Wilhelm E. Zuendt was vice president of The First National Bank, Zuendt assumed the position of translator for the city tax department. Plagued by prolonged illness and misfortune, Zuendt nonetheless continued writing. In 1875 he published a play, Dornroeschen which was followed in 1879 by his Gesammelte Gedichte,[7] Lasst uns Frieden haben, and Columbia am Rhein. An ardent Republican, Zuendt lost his position when the Democrats took office in city hall. In 1886 his verse story, Die Perle. Eine romantische Erzaehlung[8] appeared and in the same year he returned briefly to Milwaukee, then went to Minneapolis where he edited the Freie Presse until 1889 when he joined the staff of a German newspaper in Helena. In the following year he retired to live out his remaining years with his son, daughter-in-law, and nine grandchildren in Jefferson City. Before his death there on May 1, 1898 the Freidenker Publishing Company in Milwaukee published his collected poems and his tragedy, Jugurtha in one volume entitled Ebbe und Fluth.[9]

An enthusiastic supporter of the Turner movement in America, Zuendt contributed poetry and prose to leading Turner publications including the Jahrbuch der deutsch-amerikanischen Turnerei and the Deutsch-Amerikanische Turner-Kalender. Zuendt founded the Schiller Club from which the West St. Louis Turnverein was spawned. His "Lincoln-Hymne" became so popular that it was set to music by O. Schmal and was sung by Turner choirs in St. Louis and Illinois at celebrations commemorating the twentieth anniversary of Lincoln's death. Zuendt's "Lied eines Deutsch-Amerikaners" is

perhaps his best known poem.   The poem earned him the first prize
from over two hundred entries at a Turner-sponsored German-
American poetry contest.   On January 12, 1894 his play, Rienzi,
der letzte Tribun, was performed at the Germania Theater in St.
Louis and was followed by a banquet celebration at which he was
crowned with laurels as a German-American poet.   Congratulations
came to him from home and abroad, and five years later, in 1899,
a monument to his honor was erected in Jefferson City.

Several of his belletristic writings appeared in Konrad
Nies'10 monthly, Deutsch-Amerikanische Dichtung, Deutsch-Ameri-
kanisches Magazin, and in E. Steiger's early anthologies of German-
American poetry.11   Zuendt's poems also appeared in Stimmen der
Freiheit, edited by Conrad Beiswanger, and one act from his tragedy,
Jugurtha was included in Johannes Scherr's Bildersaal der Literatur
published in 1888.

Ernst Anton Zuendt was in every sense a genuine representative of German-Americanism.   Faithful at once to the cultural heritage of the land of his birth as well as to his adopted homeland, he
sought to transplant those values which would contribute to the ethnic character of American society.   His artistic treatment of the
German element's role in the American Civil War will be of interest to scholars and students of American literature and history as
they seek to assess the great body of literature created by the German-Americans, and therewith add another chapter to the annals of
German-America.

Notes

1.   See Josef Nadler, Literaturgeschichte der deutschen Stämme,
     Vol. IV (1928); Henry A. Pochmann, "The Mingling of
     Tongues" in Literary History of the United States, Vol. II
     (1948); K. K. Klein, "Auslanddeutsches Schrifttum" in Real-
     lexikon der deutschen Literaturgeschichte, eds. P. Merker
     and W. Stammler, Vol. IV (1931).   See also the bio-biblio-
     graphical sketches by Ludwig Fraenkel in Allegemeine
     Deutsche Biographie, Vol. XLV (1900); Martin Drescher in
     Die Glocke (Chicago, 1906); Franz Bruemmer, ed., Lexikon
     der deutschen Dichter und Prosaisten vom Beginn des 19 Jhds.
     bis zur Gegenwart (1913); Wilhelm Kosch, ed., Deutsches
     Literatur-Lexikon (1959).
2.   In Munich Zuendt became a personal friend of Hermann Lingg
     (1820-1905), popular German writer of novels, dramas, and
     poetry.
3.   Zuendt edited the periodical for nine months after the resigna-
     tion of its former editor, Otto Ruppius (1819-1864), popular
     German novelist and Forty-Eighter who spent ten years in ex-
     ile in America until his pardon by the Prussian government.
4.   Winkler (1838-1871) was also a German journalist, poet, and
     writer who spent several years in America.   Most of his
     works deal with the American and German-American culture.

5. In the same year his fourth child, Adelbert K. Zuendt was born in St. Louis. Mrs. Adelbert Zuendt (née Emilie Doerner) died at the age of 105 years in Little Rock, Arkansas on December 16, 1967. On her 103rd birthday she received a citation from the American Legion Auxiliary there for having sold more liberty bonds than anyone else in Arkansas during the Second World War. Her son Robert Ernst Zuendt died on December 24, 1965 at the age of 82 in North Little Rock, Arkansas. Robert E. Zuendt was survived by a stepson, Charles E. Carter of Texarkana, Texas, a stepdaughter, Mrs. E. Frances Lehmann of Little Rock, a brother Fritz Anton Zuendt of North Little Rock, a stepgrandchild, two great-grandchildren and four great-great grandchildren.

6. A later edition was published by Friedrich Roeslein in Milwaukee in 1879.

7. In addition to lyric poetry, this volume also contains Aschenbroedel, Die Gambsenjaga, Die Eis-Fee oder: Die gefrorene Hand, and Dornroeschen. Copies are to be found at: German Society of Pa. in Phila., Cleveland Public Library, Duke Univ. Library, Univ. of Cincinnati Library, and the Univ. of Pa. Library.

8. Published by H. Rauth in St. Louis. Copy at Univ. of Cincinnati Library.

9. Contents: Im Licht; Dornrosen; Daheim; An Turnerkreisen; In Memoriam; Jugurtha; Columbia am Rhein, Zeitbild in einem Akt; Aus anderen Sprachen; Am Abschluss den Freunden. Copies at libraries of Univ. of Cincinnati, Wisconsin, German Society of Pa. in Phila.

10. Nies (1862-1921) is perhaps the best known of the German-American writers. See Robert E. Ward, "Konrad Nies, German-American Literary Knight," German-American Studies, III, 1 (1971).

11. Steiger compiled, edited, and published Heimatgruesse aus Amerika (N.Y., 1870), and Dornrosen. Erstlingsblüten deutscher Lyrik in Amerika. See also G. A. Zimmermann, Deutsch in Amerika (Chicago, 1892, 1894) for more of Zuendt's poetry.

20. WILLIAM MUELLER, WRITER*

Wilma Guyot

It has been thirty years since my grandfather, William Mueller, died in Heppenheim, Germany. Yet, when I leafed through several volumes of his newspaper articles recently I could almost see him again in a well worn jacket, with a cap on his head, and in his hand a crude cane which he had whittled from some sapling, ready to set out on one of his long, exploratory walks.

I remember him only as an old man with silky white hair, a full beard and mustache, fair smooth skin, and clear blue eyes, which looked guilelessly out into the world. He was gentle, yet determined, a man of physical and moral courage, not easily perturbed, with a fair and unbiased judgment about people and events, and a meticulous adherence to regularity. His meals, his walks, his hours of repose, the time set aside for writing and study followed at precise intervals.

We were living in an apartment on Central Park West, New York, when Grandfather came home one evening at dusk, went into his room, exchanged his heavy gold watch for a nickel-plated one and went off again into the park. Years later Mother heard through a friend that he had been attacked that day by two ruffians, but that he had pushed them aside with great force, gone home quite unconcerned, and had then returned to the park to continue his walk.

Very soon after this episode we rented a farmhouse in the northern Adirondacks for the summer. My father, Theodore Spiering, who was a violinist and conductor, took his pupils along for summer instruction. That farm was a paradise for Grandfather. It was surrounded by overgrown fields and neglected orchards, and at the rear of the property was a stand of virgin trees stretching out into the country beyond. Every afternoon, after his hour of rest, Grandfather would disappear into the fields and woods, and each evening would return with some flowers, plants, or insects to be sorted and examined.

The white-haired man faded from my mind when I came upon a photograph of him as a youth of twenty-one, a soft bowler tilted at a rakish angle on his head, and a theatrical black cape thrown over his shoulder. In this garb he had arrived as an immigrant in New York in 1866.

*Reprinted from American German Review 28:3 (1962): 14-15, by permission of the publisher.

With a diploma from the Teachers' Seminary in Bensheim,
Hesse, in his pocket and three years of teaching experience to his
credit, he went to Indianapolis, where a position at the Seidensticker
German-American School awaited him. His stay, however, was
short, for members of a school commission from Cincinnati, on the
lookout for young talent, offered him a head mastership at the Twentieth District School in that city, and in the fall of 1869 William
Mueller and his young bride of a few weeks moved to Cincinnati.
Here their two children were born, and Grandfather taught for three
years. After passing the Ohio state teachers' and principals' examination, he became principal of the Fifteenth District School.
Meanwhile, his wife, who had studied singing at the Institute of Music in Stuttgart, held positions as soloist at a synagogue and in a
Methodist church.

The couple's days were not only given to their respective positions. Grandfather, who was a gifted writer and poet, wrote many
articles, novels, plays, and poems. Although he spoke and wrote
English very well, his literary contributions were mostly in German.
A novel, Leida, appeared in the Belletristische Journal in 1870. A
humorous poem, Schabiade, came out in book form in 1871. In
1882 a book of lyric verse was printed in Switzerland, and in the
same year a prize was awarded him for his comedy, Im Gelobten
Land. The play received his initial performance at the Germania
Theater in New York on December 29, 1882. So skillfully were the
German-American characters portrayed, and so humorous were the
episodes depicted, that the comedy was a great success and was
performed in every American city having a large German population.

While William Mueller was devoting much of his free time to
writing and to the German Literary Club of Cincinnati, which he had
helped to found, his wife had many concert engagements. She sang
at the Maenner Verein concerts, appeared at the May Festival, and
several times when an itinerant opera company stopped at Cincinnati
and a performer was indisposed, she was asked to substitute.

In 1886 the editor of Puck--A German comic paper in New
York--died and William Mueller was asked to fill his place. He
left his active, yet peaceful life in Cincinnati behind and moved to
New York, where, upon taking over his new job, he was thrust into
a frenzy of activity. Every week he had to grind out poems, articles, skits, and short stories, while the printing presses hammered
relentlessly above his head. The pressures of work affected his
health adversely, and after only two years at Puck he had to give
up the position, and go abroad with his wife.

The years in Germany, however, were not idle ones for him,
for he was a regular contributor to several German papers in the
United States including the New Yorker Staats-Zeitung, the Cincinnati Volksblatt, and others. The couple returned to New York when
Grandfather was able to resume the daily routine at Puck. But
times were changing: new interests, new political trends emerged.
And so, on August 19, 1898, the German Puck was published for

the last time. For some years after that William Mueller was director of the German-American School of the Nineteenth Ward in
New York.   Later he returned to Europe and headed for the Bergstrasse, that delightful section of Germany between Darmstadt and
Heidelberg.   At his birthplace in Heppenheim he and his wife bought
a house and settled down.   Here Grandfather spent many hours in
the tower room writing.   He could look down upon the medieval
town below, and see the steep, red-tiled roofs, the high chimney of
the Half Moon Inn on which a stork nest perched, and the narrow,
cobble-stoned streets.   On clear days the spires of Worms cathed-
ral were visible in the distance.   The fruit trees whose myriads of
blossoms make the Bergstrasse so famous in the early spring could
be seen everywhere.   In that tower room many books were written
and many lectures prepared to be given in various cities of Germany.
Among the books were: Religiöses Leben in Amerika, published by
Eugen Diederichs, 1911; Amerikanisches Volksbildungswesen, published by Diederichs, 1910; and several short biographies, including
Schurz, Astor, and Franklin.   Deutsch-Amerikaner und der Krieg
was written and published after World War I.

The variety of subjects on which William Mueller wrote is
both astonishing and impressive: music, history, politics, art,
philosophy, psychology, and religion.   His style was clear-cut and
logical, and he wrote in an interesting and compelling manner.

After my grandmother died in 1909 Grandfather sold his
house and boarded in the little town.   He continued his studies and
literary pursuits; his walks in the beautiful countryside and woods
were a great solace to him.   When the war began, he returned to
America and remained until 1924.   Then the peace and quiet of his
native town and the picturesque natural surroundings beckoned once
more, and he returned to spend his last years in a home run by
Franciscan sisters.   He died in 1931, at the age of eighty-six.

It was not so much what he taught or wrote that made his
long life one of value: it was what he was.   Brought up a Roman
Catholic, he revered and studied all the great religions, and was
tolerant of every belief.   To build stronger cultural relations between Germany and America had been the purpose of his endeavors.

"Let our German traditions, our soul qualities, and our cultural heritage be used in giving our best efforts and our most ear-
nest work for the enrichment of the life of the New World."   That is
what he wrote and what he stood for.

Süsse Beute

Wenn ich in frischer Morgenluft
Durch Wald und Wiesen schweife,
Geschieht es wohl, dass ich den Duft
Von jungen Blüten streife.

Es bleibt der Tau im Buchenhag
In meinen Locken hängen.
Die Brust lebt mir von Amselschlag
Und hellen Lerchenklängen.

Und alles trag' ich mit nach Haus,
Duft, Tau und Lerchengrüsse
Und winde es zum Liederstrauss
Für dich, du Holde, Süsse.

Wilhelm Müller

21. THE WRITINGS OF ALBERT WOLFF*

Lynwood G. Downs

Among the books in the library of the Minnesota Historical
Society is a small volume entitled Literarischer Nachlass ("Literary
Legacy") by Albert Wolff (St. Paul, 1894). In this unpretentious
book, published a year after the author's death, are to be found selected poems, speeches, and a novel by a man who was probably
the first German-American poet and novelist of Minnesota.

As a student of theology, Wolff participated in the revolution
of 1848 in Germany, was captured, sentenced to death, had his sentence commuted, and finally was allowed to go into exile. After arriving in St. Paul in November, 1852, he found employment in the
confectionery shop of Renz and Karcher. On November 19, 1855,
Friedrich Orthwein began the publication of the Minnesota Deutsche
Zeitung, the first German newspaper in Minnesota, and Wolff became associated with the venture. Just when and in what capacity
he served has not been ascertained, since unfortunately none of the
early issues of the paper have come down to us. When Orthwein
severed his connections with the paper, Wolff joined him in publishing the Thalbote at Chaska and the National Demokrat in St. Paul.
In 1864 Wolff was for a short time the editor of the New Ulm Post,
successor to the ill-fated New Ulm Pionier, but he soon relinquished
this post to join the staff of the Minnesota Staatszeitung of St. Paul,
with which he remained until his death in 1893.

In the early years of Wolff's connection with the Staatszeitung,
almost every issue contained one of his poems. Some were merely
bits of doggerel concerned with local political affairs, or expressing
gratitude for the donation of a keg of beer by a local brewer, or
commemorating the raising of the roof on a friend's new dwelling.
Frequently, as the selection published in his Nachlass attests, the
poems were more pretentious in character. The section headings
in the volume are, in translation, "Freedom and Fatherland," featuring principally the Civil War and Minnesota's part in it; "Love and
Marriage," their joys and sorrows; "Ballads," "Varied Poems,"
"Translations from the Low German of Klaus Groth," "Travel Pictures," and "Epigrams." Typical of the poems dealing with Minnesota during the Civil War period is the "Marching Song of the Minnesota German Squadron," composed on November 2, 1861, and intended to be sung to the tune of "Zu Mantua in Banden."

*Reprinted from Minnesota History 27 (1946): 327-29, by permission
of the publisher.

Since Wolff was not only a poet, but an orator much in demand at German celebrations and ceremonies, it is fitting that five
of his orations are printed in the Nachlass. Among them is one delivered at the dedication of the flag of the St. Paul Turnverein on
May 26, 1860, and another given at the laying of the foundation for
the statue of Hermann in New Ulm, on June 14, 1888. The volume
includes also a brief history of Minnesota in German, dated 1859;
and an article on the opening of the new stock exchange in Bremen,
Germany, on July 10, 1870--an event that Wolff witnessed while
serving in the seaport as immigration commissioner from Minnesota.

The remainder of the volume is given over to "Otakte, der
Vieltödter" ("Otakte, the Killer of Many"), a novel about the Sioux
Outbreak of 1862. The story is that of a mulatto who was harshly
treated by slaveowners in New Orleans. He vows vengeance on the
whites, flees northward, and joins a Sioux tribe in Minnesota,
marrying the daughter of the chief. With the aid of an English
agent, who supplies money and arms, and of a Confederate spy, he
instigates and leads the uprising of 1862. The scene of this improbable story ranges from New Orleans to Fort Garry in the Canadian Red River Valley. Historical personages, such as General Sibley, Little Crow, and Other Day, are introduced, and such actual
places as Fort Ridgley, the International House in St. Paul, and the
Dakota House in New Ulm tend to add verisimilitude to the intricate
plot, but the story remains fantastic and improbable. Wolff liked to
display his knowledge of Indian customs and lore, supplementing the
references in the text with copious footnotes. The novel first appeared in Kohlmann's Literaturblätter, a short-lived literary journal
published in Oshkosh, Wisconsin.

It is known that some of Wolff's works were published in
book form during his lifetime. When the Athenaeum, the German
theater of St. Paul, was dedicated on November 11, 1859, the centennial of Schiller's birth, Wolff was the orator of the day. His
speech was printed and the Germans of Minnesota were urged to purchase copies as souvenirs of the occasion. In 1867 a volume of poems, Vermischte Gedichte ("Assorted Poems") is said to have appeared. Thus far neither of these publications has been found by the
writer. Any information concerning them or any other early German literary publications in Minnesota will be greatly appreciated.

It is not to be inferred that Wolff's works set a high literary
standard, or that they are important contributions to German-American literature. They do, however, throw light on a phase of Minnesota history which needs further exploration--the cultural life of the
state's pioneer Germans.

22. KARL KNORTZ, INTERPRETER OF AMERICAN LITERATURE AND CULTURE*

Horst Frenz

Karl Knortz--teacher, editor, critic and translator--deserves to be known on the roster of German-born Americans who have made their contributions to the cultural life of this country and have succeeded in interpreting American culture to foreign audiences. To judge from the list of publications, he was one of the most prolific German writers in the United States during the end of the nineteenth and the beginning of the present century.

Born in Garbenheim, Rhenish Prussia, on August 28, 1841, Knortz attended the Royal Prussian Gymnasium in Wetzlar and studied philology and philosophy at the University of Heidelberg. In 1863 he came to the United States and, between 1864 and 1874, taught in Detroit, Oshkosh, and Cincinnati. For a short period of time, from May 1873 to February 1874, he was editor of the well-known Der deutsche Pionier, which he tried to transform into a predominantly literary magazine. His efforts were apparently not appreciated, for in 1874 he gave up the editorship. From Cincinnati he went to Indianapolis and edited a German daily newspaper the Indiana Deutsche Zeitung. In 1882 he moved to New York City and devoted his time to critical and creative writing. For thirteen years, from 1892 to 1905, he lived in Evansville, Indiana where he was superintendent of German instruction in the public schools of that city. From then on to his death in 1918 he led the life of a free lance scholar and writer in North Tarrytown, New York.

His first publication, Märchen und Sagen der nordamerikanischen Indianer (1871), was followed by a number of studies of the mythology and civilization of the American Indians. He wrote a short history of the colony of Rappists in Pennsylvania, an account of the community of the Inspirationists in Iowa, and a book on Robert Owen and his Weltverbesserungsversuche. The problems of the German language, literature and culture in the United States he discussed in such works as Der Kindergarten und seine Bedeutung für die Erhaltung des Deutschthums im Auslande (2nd. ed., 1895), Die plattdeutsche Litteratur Amerikas (1897), Das Deutschtum der Vereinigten Staaten (1898), Nachklänge germanischen Glaubens und Brauchs in Amerika (1903), Deutsch in Amerika (1906). He published numerous books on folklore and education, and between 1898 and 1909, wrote

*Reprinted from American-German Review 13:2 (1946): 27-30, by permission of the publisher.

three interesting essays on Nietzsche ("Friedrich Nietzsche und sein
Uebermensch," "Nietzsches Zarathustra," and "Friedrich Nietzsche,
der Unzeitgemässe"). In a hitherto unpublished letter, dated June
21, 1888, Nietzsche had given Knortz a brief but valuable analysis
of his own works.

Much of Knortz's writing was designed to interpret American
life and letters to German-speaking people. He wrote about capital
and labor in this country, analysed the religious life, and published
several sketches of life in the United States as he saw it. Amerikanische Lebensbilder (1884) and Deutsches und Amerikanisches
(1894) contain probably his most interesting descriptions of some of
his American experiences. Of his strictly literary works might be
mentioned an essay on Washington Irving in Tarrytown (1909). In
Brook Farm and Margaret Fuller (1886) he discussed the interest of
the New England Transcendentalists in Kant, Jacobi, Schleiermacher,
and Herder, and showed Margaret Fuller's appreciation of German
writers, particularly of Goethe. In 1898, Knortz published a sympathetic study of Thoreau (Ein amerikanischer Diogenes) whom he calls
the Anarchist des Idealismus. Thoreau's religion, according to
Knortz, consisted in

> Selbstveredlung, Selbstachtung, Reinheit der Seele und des
> Körpers und in der Fernhaltung alles Kleinlichen und Un-
> edlen.

In his discussion of Thoreau's affinity with foreign thinkers and poets, Knortz drew an interesting and, I believe, original parallel
with the peasant-poet Christian Wagner (1835-1918) from Warmbronn
in Württemberg. In their philosophical and religious beliefs Thoreau
and Wagner appear to have much in common.

In 1879, Knortz wrote a study of Longfellow which contains
valuable information on the American poet's reputation in Europe and
particularly in Germany, and cites foreign essays on and translations of the works of Longfellow, "des zum populärsten Dichter der
Neuzeit gewordenen Amerikaners." Longfellow's poems he characterized as "sein subjectives Glauben, Hoffen und Lieben," and continued:

> Seine Muse hat den Duft des Morgens in den Locken und
> ihr Gesicht ist vom Geisterhauche aus romantischen Fel-
> senruinen angeweht. Wohin er sieht, sieht er mit dem
> Auge des Dichters und die Landschaft nimmt stets den
> Ausdruck seiner Stimmung an. Sein Ausdruck ist stets
> kurz und treffend und das Metrum stets mit bewunderungs-
> würdigen Feingefühl gewählt. Besondere Originalität wird
> man bei Longfellow vergeblich suchen.

Knortz's translations of such poems as "Elisabeth," "Hiawa-
tha," "Evangeline," and his version of the Brautwerbung des Miles
Standish are somewhat inferior to those by Adolf Strothmann and
Friedrich Spielhagen; he obviously did not have the poetic powers of

a Freiligrath. He tried his hand at almost every important American poet--Emerson, Whittier, Holmes, Lowell, Poe, Stoddard, Taylor and others--and, to gather from the number of translated poems, apparently worked in a hurry. Knortz was most successful with his renderings of Whitman's verse in which he equalled many other translators and even surpassed Freiligrath.

That Knortz was able to grasp the whole field of American literature, he proved in his Geschichte der nordamerikanischen Literatur (Berlin, 1891). H. Houston Peckham, in the South Atlantic Quarterly of 1914 (XIII, 38), called the history "a work which for comprehensiveness, accuracy, and appreciativeness compares favorably with any of our own text books on American literature." In these two volumes, Knortz speaks of Oliver Wendell Holmes as "der lachende Philosoph Amerikas ... ein echter Gemüthsmensch, der sich mit den Fröhlichen freut und mit den Traurigen weint" and of Bayard Taylor as "der gewandte Reiseschriftsteller, Dichter und Vermittler deutscher Literatur und Ansichten in Amerika." Emerson is called "ein Priester der Humanität, der sich für alle Freiheitsbestrebungen warm begeisterte und der stets den Mutn hatte, seine Ansichten frei und offen, ohne sich um das Urteil des Publikums zu bekümmern, auszusprechen" and Poe "ein seltener Originaldichter ... der Dichter der inneren Zerrissenheit, des aller Hoffnung baren Pessimismus." Of Bryant he says: "Er war der erste wirkliche Dichter, den dieses Land hervorbrachte und an Geist und Begabung hat ihn bis jetzt keiner übertroffen. In seinem Schaffen war er stets selbständig."

Comparing him with Longfellow, he makes this interesting comment:

> "Während der fast ausschliesslich receptive Longfellow in
> seinen Gedichten hauptsächlich an das Gemüt appelirt,
> wirkt Bryant vorherrschend auf den Verstand seiner Leser;
> Longfellow schrieb für das Herz, Bryant hingegen für den
> Kopf, und in diesem Umstande ist auch die grössere Popularität des ersteren zu suchen. Bryant ist vom Scheitel
> bis zur Zehe Amerikaner, Longfellow hingegen Weltbürger.

That Knortz was a discerning critic, he showed in his estimate of Walt Whitman. He saw in him the poet of the future and the spokesman of democracy. I do not know of a passage that better expresses Whitman's place in the world than the following words in the Geschichte:

> Whitman ist ein Fortschrittsmann und Humanitarier vom
> reinsten Wasser; er ist ein Sänger und ein Kämpfer für
> die Verwirklichung der höchsten Ideale; er besingt den
> Krieg gegen alle überlieferten Formen unseres geistigen
> und politischen Lebens und der Schauplatz dieses Krieges
> ist die ganze Welt, auf der er Jeden zu einem mutigen
> Kämpfer erziehen will. Er tritt kühn auf und ist sich
> seiner Bedeutung vollkommen bewusst. Er ist der einzige
> Dichter, der einer wahrhaft demokratischen Weltanschauung

huldigt; er predigt daher auch echt amerikanische Tugenden,
wie Ausdauer, Fleiss, Mässigkeit, Freiheit und Fort-
schritt.   Für ihn ist das Alte vergangen und er fordert nun
Jeden zum Mitstreben auf, dass Alles neu werde.   Jede
Arbeit, die nicht auf einer humanen Basis ruht, dünkt ihm
zwecklos.   Mit den vergangenen feudalen Verhältnissen und
Ansichten der Vorzeit hat er nichts zu tun; er fusst auf
den sozialen und politischen Umständen der Gegenwart und
wirft von dort aus seinen Seherblick in die Zukunft.   Da
er nun so dem gesammten Zunftwesen energisch und rück-
sichtslos den Fehdehandschuh hinwarf, darf es uns nicht
Wunder nehmen, dass derselbe von zahlreichen Dunkel-
männern aufgenommen wurde.   Nur langsam, sehr langsam
hat er sich Bahn gebrochen, aber sich in dem einmal ges-
teckten Ziele nicht irre machen lassen.

Anyone interested in the development of Whitman's foreign
reputation cannot ignore Knortz's general interest in Whitman, his
translations and critical essays.   In 1880, Knortz published together
with Dickman a collection called Modern American Lyrics which,
peculiarly enough, did not include Whitman.   For this omission the
collection was severely criticized by at least one German literary
critic.   Two years later, Knortz is corresponding with Whitman and,
in 1883, the American poet acknowledged the receipt of the translations of "Cradle Endlessly Rocking" and other poems.   From then
on, he considered it one of his main tasks to make Whitman better
known in the German-speaking countries.   He published an essay on
Walt Whitman, der Dichter der Demokratie in the New Yorker Staatszeitung which appeared, as a monograph, in Germany in several editions during the eighties and nineties.   An abbreviated version of
this essay was translated by Alfred Forman and Richard Maurice
Bucke for In Re Walt Whitman, 1893.   Here he defends the American poet against the charge of obscenity, praises his songs of brotherhood and love, and makes every effort to excuse what he considers his occasional offenses against the code of so-called good taste,
against metrical and grammatical conventions.   He calls Leaves of
Grass Whitman's flesh and blood, his heart and soul and concludes
with the following statement:

> Als Aesthetiker hat er sich das Schöne zum Ziel genom-
> men; als Philosoph sucht er nach Wahrheit; als Ethiker
> strebt er das Gute an; als Demokrat will er allen Men-
> schen Freiheit und Freude bringen.   Whitman ist ein urei-
> genes Genie, ein moderner Titane.

In the appendix to the second edition of Walt Whitman, der
Dichter der Demokratie (1899), Knortz printed a number of Whitman's poems such as "Das Lied von der Holzaxt" and "Nächtliche
Wanderung."   As an example of Knortz's renderings published in
this volume I should like to quote "Sehnsucht" which shows Whitman
as the poet of one world.   His lines are as timely today as they
were at the end of the last century.

SEHNSUCHT

Bekümmert und voll Sehnsucht jetzt
    einsam für mich sitzend,
Scheint es mir, als ob es andre
    Menschen in andern Ländern
    voll Kummer und Sehnsucht gäbe.
Es scheint mir, als könne ich hinüber-
    blicken und sie erkennen in
    Deutschland, Italien, Frankreich,
    Spanien,
Oder weit weg in China, in Russland
    oder Japan, sprechend andre
    Sprachen.
Es scheint mir, dass, wenn ich diese
    Menschen kennte, ich mich zu ihnen
    hingezogen fühlen würde, wie zu
    den Menschen meines Landes.
O, ich weiss, wir würden Brüder und
    Liebende sein;
    Ich weiss, ich würde glücklich
    mit ihnen werden.

In the same appendix Knortz printed thirteen letters which
Whitman wrote to him between 1882 and 1887. This correspondence
is interesting, for it shows that Whitman was pleased with the efforts of his German-American critic to obtain a wider international
audience for the American poet and, by sending him his writings and
material written about him, even encouraged Knortz in his undertaking. Whitman was also extremely interested in the project of a German translation of his work and reveals his anxiety over this matter
in several of his letters.

For a number of years the Irishman T. W. Rolleston had been
working on a German translation of Leaves of Grass. Since Whitman
had great faith in Knortz's ability as a translator and in his literary
judgment, the latter was asked to collaborate. In one of his letters
to Knortz, Whitman expressed the wish to see Knortz's Representative German Poems, a collection of German poems printed parallel
with the English translations, in order to consider it as a pattern for
the German edition of his works. However, Knortz was unable to
find a publisher who would print the English and the German text.
After much delay, Grashalme appeared in Zürich in 1889, not a complete translation of Leaves of Grass, as Whitman wanted it to be,
but a selection. It is somewhat difficult to ascertain the extent of
Knortz's work on this publication. He served as an editor and may
have contributed a few translations of his own. Knortz wrote a preface and Rolleston an introduction, which he closed with the following
interesting letter from Whitman, the original of which has been lost.
Since W. S. Kennedy (in Fight of a Book) has reconstructed Whitman's
letter from the translation, I shall quote it in English: "I approve of
your attempt to translate certain of my poems into the German tongue.
Indeed, arrogant as the statement may seem, I had more than my own

native land in view when I was composing <u>Leaves of Grass</u>. I
wished to take the first step toward calling into existence a cycle of
international poems.   The chief reason for being of the United States
of America is to bring about the common good will of all mankind,
the solidarity of the world.   What is still lacking in this respect can
perhaps be accomplished by the art of poetry, through songs radiating from all lands of the globe.   I had also in mind, as one of my
objects, to send a hearty greeting to these lands in America's name.
And glad, very glad, should I be to gain entrance and audience
among the Germanic peoples." The Zürich edition has often been
considered the beginning of a real Whitman movement in German-
speaking countries.   For more than a decade it was the only important German translation of <u>Leaves of Grass</u>, and through it kindred
minds became acquainted with the work of the American poet.   The
nature of Whitman's influence upon some of his followers Knortz has
discussed in <u>Walt Whitman und seine Nachfolger</u> (1910).

Many of Knortz's publications--too numerous to be listed here
--deal with the exchange of political, social and religious ideas between countries and investigate the impact of the culture of one country upon that of another.   In this essay, I have been interested chiefly in his achievements as interpreter of the vast field of American
literature and culture and in his efforts at establishing a foreign
audience for Whitman and other American writers.   This work alone
should assure him recognition by the student of comparative literature and particularly of American-German relations.

23. ROBERT REITZEL, A. T. (1849-1898)*

Erwin F. Ritter

"Robert Reitzel, the editor of the Armer Teufel, stands pre-eminent among German-American authors."1 For fourteen years his thought-provoking essays and his stirring lyrics fascinated the readers of his weekly, the most widely circulated German literary journal ever published in America. As a lecturer he exerted espe-cially great influence in the Freien Gemeinden of this land. But his words on liberty and beauty were welcome wherever people gathered to hear them. An avid propagandist for freedom--reli-gious, moral, social--but also a dedicated artist, Reitzel left the force of his personality on all that he wrote, said or did.

Born in the turbulent days of the revolution, on the 27th of January 1849, Reitzel grew up in Weitenau (badischer Schwarzwald) where he cultivated a lifelong hatred of monarchies and bureaucra-cies. The night he was born, the police searched the Reitzel home for a participant in the revolution, the brother of Reitzel's mother, to whom his father had tried to refuse shelter for fear of losing his position as a schoolmaster. His mother, however, persuaded Reit-zel's father to give protection to her fugitive brother. The mother also gave the child the name of Robert, in memory of Robert Blum, a hero of the people, who was executed in the revolution of 1849. The incompatability of the parents caused much of the unhappiness of his early childhood. The father, an insignificant schoolmaster, believed in not sparing the rod; yet a great deal of sunshine was dif-fused during these early years by his mother, a woman of fine char-acter who stirred the poetic imagination of the boy. Reitzel drew a striking picture of this poor consumptive woman who slaved in the wretched schoolhouse: "Es war ein recht hässliches altes Haus, aber ich habe doch darin die glücklichsten Stunden verlebt, und die dort sich mühte und sich grämte und den Tod sich holte--das war meine Mutter."2

In the Gymnasium this precocious, self-willed boy, to whom poetry meant more than his daily routine of dull lessons, proved to be a trial to his teachers, and was ultimately expelled. Neverthe-less, he did reach the University of Heidelberg, registering for his-tory and philosophy. As the son of a poor schoolmaster, theology was about the only area of study open to him, stipends being avail-able only to students of divinity. Theology, however, was to pre-

*Reprinted from German-American Studies 5 (1972): 148-62, by per-mission of the publisher.

occupy him very little, except for reading the Bible as an exercise in
prosody and poetic imagery. He preferred to spend his time reading the
works of the romanticists, such as Heine, Eichendorff, Brentano, etc.
and began writing verse on the themes of love, wine, revolution, and
freedom. He was one of six students who met regularly during those
days, swearing not to rest until Germany had become a republic. Twenty years later, two of these revolutionaries were dead, one had become
a teacher, another a pillar of the orthodox church, and still another was
prominent in governmental circles. The only one still dedicated to his
revolutionary ideals was Reitzel.

It was customary for young men in that period, who had
failed to establish themselves as professional men in Germany, and
whose position in society forbade their doing manual labor, to go to
America to survive or perish. Hence in 1870, when Reitzel's financial resources were exhausted, his father advised him to try his
fortune in the United States. His account, Abenteuer eines Grünen,
tells of the pleasures and hardships he met in America. Much has
been said about the hardships of the lateinische Bauern in America,
but even harder was the lot of the lateinische Vagabunden, or poet-
tramps such as Reitzel and Martin Drescher. These university-
trained men had to put up with hunger, the hardest and most menial
sort of labor, persecution by the police, and actual imprisonment.
After his arrival on the Eastern seaboard Reitzel tramped in Pennsylvania for a while and then began seeking winter employment. In
Baltimore he went begging for work with an empty stomach until he
seriously thought of ending his life. One day he crossed the path of
a Reverend Pister who told the starving immigrant that the most logical thing for him to do was to pass an examination before the Board
of the German Reformed Church and to take charge of a congregation.

In 1871 Reitzel was appointed minister of the German Reformed Church in Washington. About a year later he married; this
marriage proved to be unhappy and ended in a separation. As a
clergyman, however, Reitzel could not have done his work more
conscientiously. There were vague dreams of bringing together science and religion, of initiating a reformation of the church on a
grand scale, of becoming even another Luther or Calvin in the nineteenth century. But he was to become a martyr to these personal
aspirations. He met with so many discouraging failings in his congregation, of people who called themselves Christians, that he de-
spaired entirely of the traditional modes of Christianity. Moreover,
his convictions were not orthodox enough for the Church Board, who
decided to give him the alternative of returning to more orthodox
views or seeking another position. Reitzel chose the latter.

His unflagging enthusiasm for social issues, his love of truth
and freedom, although these had precisely caused his clerical dismissal, won for him many friends in other German-American circles. For the next several years he traveled through most of the
states of the Union as a lecturer on literary and social topics. Because of his spirited eloquence many came to regard Reitzel as the
ablest German-American speaker, if not the German-American

spokesman. To enable Reitzel to broaden his influence, his Michigan friends decided to found a newspaper for him in Detroit. The year in which this newspaper was founded was 1884, and Reitzel was to edit it until his death in 1898. As an editor and journalist Reitzel had inadvertently stumbled upon his real calling.

By naming the journal Der arme Teufel Reitzel had in mind history's disinherited geniuses, e.g., Feuerbach, Schiller, Lessing, and even Christ; but especially a chance acquaintance with a Norwegian itinerant inspired him to view the quintessence of his armer Teufel as follows:

> Sein Weib starb im ersten Jahre des Glücks und mit ihr sein Interesse an allem, was sonst die Menschen ihr Teuerstes nennen. Er wurde zum ruhelosen Wanderer; aber, merkwürdig, wo immer die Standarten der Freiheit erhoben wurden, da hat ihn auch sein Schritt hingeführt.... Seine wenigen Bedürfnisse deckt er entweder durch zeitweilige Arbeit als Schriftsetzer oder aber durch freiwillige Gaben, welche ihm gute Menschen darbieten. Dieser Mann hat seit langen Jahren nicht mehr in einem Bett geschlafen, 'aber,' erzählte er mir, 'wenn ich so des Nachts an irgend einer Landstrasse liege, unter irgend einem Baum, und ich sehe die Sterne blinken und höre die Winde sausen, so kommt es mir vor, als ob ich der glücklichste Mensch sei, ich fühle mich als einen Teil dieser grossen unendlichen Welt, und von jenen Sorgen, wie sie die andern Menschen plagen, kann ich mir kaum mehr einen Begriff machen.

> Das ist gewiss ein armer Teufel! und wenn wir bei der Taufe unsrer Zeitung an ihn dachten, so war es, weil er zwei Eigenschaften gewissermassen verkörpert, die einem echten armen Teufel nicht fehlen dürfen, nämlich erstlich die vollständige Unabhängigkeit von allen Verhältnissen, welche die Urteilskraft beeinflussen können, und zweitens die idealistische, tatkräftige Liebe zur Freiheit.[3]

About half of Reitzel's journal was filled with original contributions, most of them written by the editor himself. Some of his collaborators were: Bruno Wille, John Henry Mackay, Karl Henckell, Michael Georg Conrad, and Karl Heinzen. With the efforts of these collaborators, and also by means of his own critical evaluations of such authors as Goethe, Uhland, Heine, Seume, Boerne, Reuter, etc., Reitzel was to educate the German-American. But not only German authors; also Hawthorne, Whitman, and especially Shakespeare, were celebrated by him in most original and trenchant essays.

Like Karl Heinzen, another German-American journalist, Reitzel felt the poet ought to be a man of the people, but not necessarily a socialist as Heinzen believed. He felt the nature and function of poetry to be social and not political. His ambition was to

bring great literature closer to the hearts of every member in society, but he found this task increasingly difficult among German-
Americans, whom he considered to be falling away from their native
tongue and its cultural ideals in an endeavor to become rich over-
night. [4]

For a time, it can be said, Reitzel did become a socialist,
only because of his aversion to the smug bourgeoisie and their oppression of the laboring class. His indignation toward prevailing social ills often found in him anarchistic expression, but his independent temperament would not allow him ultimately to become a rapid
follower of any social or religious cause: "Wie mir die Christen
am Christentum, die Socialdemokraten am Socialismus, die Anarch-
isten am Anarchismus die Freude verleidet haben, so gehts mir
jetzt auch mit den Individualisten."[5] Any flagrant injustice, however, aroused in him an immediate response. At the time when
popular opinion found it impossible to believe that the death sentence
passed against the men involved in the Chicago Haymarket Affair
would be carried out, Reitzel foresaw the revenge that capitalism
would exact and tried to arouse the working class to action in order
to save their leaders from the gallows.[6] But in spite of all he
tried to do, four of the men were executed. His poem "Zum neuen
Jahr 1888" recounts his disillusionment with the laboring class who
were too terrified to do anything for the victims of the Haymarket incident: "Es war wie immer,/Es blieb beim Alten,/Wir haben uns
Alle/Recht brav gehalten."[7]

Reitzel, the social battler that he often was, signed himself
also as Reitzel the lover--both being for him the main expressions
of his character, as is revealed in a stanza of the poem "In Sturm
und Drang": "Wenn mich in dem Kampfgewühle/Tötlich scharfe
Hiebe trafen,/War mein letzter Frohgedanke:/Bei der Liebe darfst
du schlafen."[8] His deepest love, however, was the social cause:
the advancement of humanity towards greater enlightenment and liberty. The essay "Erste Liebe" touches upon this very theme:
"Wohlauf ihr wackeren Paladine! da ist eine Dulcinea, für die es
der Mühe wert ist, in den Kampf zu gehen: die Menschheit. Wenn
ihr nur recht in die verliebt seid, dann findet sich leicht das soci-
ale Heilmittel...."[9] This twofold expression of Reitzel's personality contains much of Heinrich Heine's own Weltanschauung, and odd-
ly enough, Reitzel's own literary style in prose and poetry is even
reminiscent of that past master of German letters. Max Baginski,
the editor of the Reitzel collection, draws a notable parallel between
the two poets: "Mag daran herumbosseln, dies und das mildern,
das Charakteristische verschweigen, in milder Vergebung wegen der
aussergewöhnlichen Persönlichkeit beide Augen zudrücken--für den
engen Rahmen des hurrahpatriotischen Bardentums bleibt Reitzel eine
zu glänzende, gigantische Erscheinung, wie Heine in Reichsdeutsch-
land zu unnahbar und zu gross bleiben wird für Gartenlauben-Schrei-
ber, Regierungsrate, schwache Poeten und nationalliberale Stadt-
verordnete."[10]

The final years of Reitzel's life, as Heine's, were spent in

bed with a lame back. It was hard for Reitzel, the active individual he was, to be tied down helplessly by his affliction. But while
he increasingly became imprisoned by his body, his unyielding spirit
struggled to be free. From his Luginsland or Matrazengruft, as
Reitzel referred to his couch that was set before a window, he was
to prepare many an essay and poem for the outside world.

Six months before his death Reitzel became acquainted with
the poet Martin Drescher, and their friendship was to be important
for Reitzel's journal. His intimate conversations with Drescher
made Reitzel select his friend as his successor in the work of Der
arme Teufel. For two years Drescher did so very ably, but financial difficulties finally put an end to the publication.

Reitzel's general disposition during his remaining years was
cheerful. Whenever friends visited his sickroom it became the
scene of a joyous occasion with wine and song. An autopsy was to
reveal that all of the poet's organs were diseased--lungs, kidneys,
liver--all but his heart. According to a statement by the poet's
physician, Reitzel died of tuberculosis, a condition he had inherited
from his mother. The disease attacked the spine, causing paralysis
in his lower limbs. Karl Schmidt, a Detroit businessman, offered
Reitzel his summer home, Villa Weidenlaub, on Lake Orion in Canada when his condition began to worsen. This lovely spot became
the poet's retreat for his final years. Death came on April 1, 1898
after Reitzel's forty-ninth birthday, but not at the villa as he had
hoped. At his request his friends had his body cremated and then
met together at Lake Orion to celebrate his memory over wine cups.
He had envisioned such a gathering in a dream account: "Die Tote
am Orionsee."11

Concerning his own life and its achievements Reitzel was from
time to time pessimistic. All of his idealism and his aspirations for
a liberated mankind seemed to have exerted very little influence over
his contemporaries. In the resigned strains of the poem "Zuletzt"
he voiced this disillusionment: "Die sanfte Schwermut ... flüstert
dir ins Herz das kühle Wort, /Das aller Weisheit letzter Trost, /
Dass man die Sterne nicht begehrt, /Und dass man arm dahinfährt,
wie man kam."12

* * * *

On December 6, 1884 Reitzel announced the program of a new
journal, Der arme Teufel, in a short lyric poem entitled "Für Freund
und Feind":

> Mir bleibe fern der Unkenchor der Heuchler,
> Mir bleibe fern, wer lächelt stets und witzelt,
> Mir bleibe fern, wen nur Gemeines kitzelt,
> Mir bleiben fern die Händler und die Schmeichler!

. . . .

Ich lob mir leichte, lustige Gesellen,
Die gerne sind, wo volle Becher winken,
Und gern der Schönheit an den Busen sinken,
Doch die auch, wenn zu Kampf die Hörner gellen

Begreifen unsrer Zeit gewalt'ges Ringen,
Im Herzen heil'gen Zornes Springquell tragen,
Der Freiheit ihre Schlachten helfen schlagen--
Und köstlich Herzblut ihr zum Opfer bringen. 13

In German-American letters Reitzel remains an anomaly. His life
was an integral part of a movement in the '80s known as Jüngstdeutschland, a socialistically tainted naturalism: two tendencies
which were not necessarily related, but which competed for the imagination of German writers during the '80s and early '90s. No serious writer of this period was left untouched by these trends.
Jüngstdeutschland was an inevitable reaction to what had gone before
in art, as well as a social protest against the economic conditions
of the times. Both the social and the literary movements developed differently with each author, many of whom survived the age to
go on to literary fame. The writers most closely related to Reitzel
and with whom he must be grouped were Karl Henckell, John Henry
Mackay, Bruno Wille, and Reinhold Maurice von Stern. All were
contributors to Reitzel's Armer Teufel.

For a subscription of $2.50 per year (five cents a copy) to
Reitzel's journal the German-American could read a journal similar
in its social outlook to Die Gesellschaft, which was founded two
months after Reitzel's publication. Reitzel frequently quoted from
this sister journal in Munich for which he wrote several essays. Upon his death the Gesellschaft lauded Reitzel's work in an article
which appeared in its twelfth issue.

Indeed, Der arme Teufel was much more provincial than Die
Gesellschaft, to which all of the great literary figures of the day
contributed. The social and literary spectrum of Der arme Teufel
was, therefore, not nearly as wide, and its main interest was more
revolutionary than aesthetic: the fight against the church and the ideals
of the Aufklärer were emphasized much more in Detroit than in Munich.
Nonetheless, it is this distinctness that makes Reitzel's publication
something uniquely German-American, and it ought to be valued especially for this reason. Both journals do have, however, the same
iconoclastic enthusiasm for social change, and their format at least
was similar: short stories, poems, plays, reviews, political, literary, and religious essays, correspondence with readers, and theatrical and musical notices.

It cannot be said of Reitzel that he had a truly great influence
over German-Americans. During his lifetime he was never able to
enlist a large body of followers from among the German-American
community. His influence failed for two reasons, namely: his attacks on religion made impossible any contact with Kirchendeutsche,
who were far more orthodox than their cousins in Germany, while

234 German-American Literature

his ridicule of philistinism lost for him the sympathy of many free-thinkers who would have readily forgiven the poet's lack of piety. Thus his followers were a select and small circle of authors, socialists, anarchists, and Bohemians--anything but the Prominenten of acceptable society. After his death, various Armer Teufel clubs were formed in Toledo, Pittsburgh, Cincinnati, St. Louis, and other places. Just how extensively Reitzel influenced German-American culture is difficult to estimate, "but wherever Reitzel carried the message of the world's best literature, he brought the very finest, and his influence might be said to have been deep rather than broad."14

Another importance of Der arme Teufel is that it leads German-American publications in the number of contemporary German poets it introduced to the public. Though the paper was by nature radical, its literary standard was far from being narrow. It was fortunate for the journal that Reitzel's literary taste was truly cosmopolitan and that he possessed a fine appreciation of the classics, combined with a keen eye for newer works of lasting value. The greatest service to the journal was his gift for literary criticism.

Reitzel addressed himself to Germans in their language and dealt, therefore, mostly with German literature. But his knowledge of literature was by no means confined to the writings of one nation; he was aware, for example, of the greatness of Walt Whitman. To both Reitzel and German critics of the Gesellschaft Whitman was America's greatest poet, whom Reitzel heralded as a mediator in international peace and a prophet of a freer humanity. He also reviewed and reprinted in the Armer Teufel a vast number of contemporary works. Poems by one hundred and eighty-one modern German writers appeared in his publication, about a tenth of them written for the Armer Teufel, many translated from English and French, and about sixty poems were penned by the editor himself. Of the thirty leading contributors, eleven were German-Americans, a fact which shows that the journal was truly a cultural phenomenon of German-American art. "Never before nor since has there been such a representative German-American belletristic and aesthetic journal."15

Yet it was Reitzel's own critical talent that did much more for the spread of interest in the best of German and foreign literature than merely his printing of poems and stories. Week after week he reviewed some German author or a particular work, and discussed both in sensitive, vivid, and generous fashion. He took a great deal of pride in this work and it must be said "that it is a unique cultural act in America."16 He had an unpretentious drive to bring great literature to the public which was his abiding belief as a man of letters: "... ich meine, es gebe keine schönere Aufgabe als das ewig Schöne und das ewig Wahre, das was die Dichter in ihren Liedern verkörpert, so viel als möglich in unserm alltäglichen Leben heimisch, so viel als möglich dem arbeitenden Manne, der arbeitenden Frau zu eigen zu machen."17

The importance of Reitzel's labors can, in conclusion, best be evaluated by those who were closest to his journalistic efforts. Amalie von Ende in an essay appearing (May, 1899) in the Literarisches Echo had this to say: "Reitzel founded his Armer Teufel, this precious enfant terrible of German-American journalism, an organ which swore allegiance to no 'ism' whatsoever, but which for a period of fourteen years tossed week for week its flaming torch into the camp of philistinism.... It is an achievement which is not sufficiently recognized, that it was Reitzel who introduced the German-American public to Liliencron, Wille, Mackay, Henckell, Bierbaum, Wedekind, Keller and many others...."[18] Max Baginski, the editor of Reitzel's collected writings, offered the following comment: "Reitzel hatte sicher sehr schätzbare Qualitäten, mit welchen auch das Deutschtum schlechthin sich glänzend drapieren könnte. Seine Genialität, seine ausserordentliche Begabung, vor allem sein Stil stehen unübertroffen da unter den deutsch-amerikanischen Schriftstellern."[19]

In a study of German-American poets to be found in Singer's Jahrbuch für 1917, Martin Drescher writes: "Unbestritten war Robert Reitzel unter deutsch-amerikanischen Schriftstellern der letzten Jahrzehnte der grösste Stilist; er war auch einer der gedankenreichsten. Souverän wie der grosse Virtuose sein Instrument herrscht, beherrscht er die deutsche Sprache. Für jede Empfindung, die auf ein Menschenherz eindringen kann, fand er mit bewunderswerter Feinheit das treffende Wort.... Er war vornehmlich ein Dichter in Prosa, dessen Skizzen und Schilderungen, dessen Erinnerungen und Bekenntnisse nicht so bald vergehen. Aber auch von seinen Versen können manche sich getrost den besten Erzeugnissen der deutsch-amerikanischen Literatur an die Seite stellen."[20]

A final incentive to further research Reitzel's singular literary productivity was made by Rudolf Rieder: "Robert Reitzel als Dichter der besten deutschen Prosa in Amerika und der anerkannte Literaturvermittler seiner Gemeinde von Anhängern verdient mehr Beachtung, als ihm bis jetzt zugekommen ist; das freisinnige Element der deutschen Einwanderung zu kennen ist Pflicht des amerikanischen Historikers."[21]

Notes

1. Adolf Eduard Zucker, Robert Reitzel (Philadelphia; Americana-Germanica Press, No. 25, 1917), p. 9. Cf. also Johannes Gaulke, "Robert Reitzel," Das literarische Echo, IV (1901-02); Edna Fern, "Robert Reitzel, ein deutsch-amerikanischer Heine," Deutscher Vorkämpfer, II, 5 (1908), 25-26; P. E. Werkshagen, Robert Reitzel. Seine Persönlichkeit und seine Weltanschauung (Champaign, Ill., 1908).
2. Robert Reitzel, Des armen Teufels gesammelte Schriften, ed. Max Baginski (Detroit, 1913), I, 25.
3. Op. cit., III, 10-11.
4. Robert Reitzel, Mein Buch (Detroit, 1900), p. 166ff.

5. Op. cit., pp. 299-300.
6. Reitzel, Gesammelte Schriften, III, 112.
7. Reitzel, Mein Buch, p. 419.
8. Reitzel, Gesammelte Schriften, II, 31.
9. Reitzel, Mein Buch, p. 33.
10. Reitzel, Gesammelte Schriften, I, 10.
11. Op. cit., III, 199.
12. Op. cit., II, 49.
13. Ibid., 10.
14. Zucker, op. cit., p. 58.
15. Ibid., p. 73.
16. Loc. cit.
17. Reitzel, Mein Buch, p. 116.
18. Zucker, op. cit., p. 55.
19. Reitzel, Gesammelte Schriften, I, 10.
20. Zucker, op. cit., p. 56.
21. Rudolf Theodor Rieder, Ein Bild Robert Reitzels und des armen
    Teufels aus seinem Verhältnis zur Litteratur (Diss.: University of Wisconsin, 1918), p. ii.

24. MARTIN DRESCHER:
    A GERMAN-AMERICAN POET*

Frieda Voigt

Around the turn of the century there was quite an extensive
German-American literature deserving of attention and study, since
it expressed the sentiments and impressions of an important segment
of this country. Half a century ago the second largest ethnic group
in the United States was the German, a fact that two world wars have
tended to almost obliterate....

Among the German-American poets who wrote between 1880
and 1920 there probably was none who surpassed Martin Drescher,
nor could we find a better representative of the genre "German-
American." Born in 1863 in Mark Brandenburg, Drescher came to
America in 1891 because of family disruptions following his failure to
attain a university degree or to establish himself professionally.
Friendless and penniless, the young man, like Dreamer Hans of fairy
tale lore, sought to find his fortune in the New World. New York
did not put out the red carpet for the countless emigrants who came
over so hopefully, but Drescher managed to survive the first weeks
in a cheap hotel by pawning his gold watch and ring, a good suit and
other items that attested to his family's affluence. Down to his last
dollar, he was forced to find work, but he lasted only two days as
dishwasher in a restaurant. Other failures followed: as book salesman in Brooklyn, as bartender in Baron's saloon, as sewing machine
salesman. Once, after he had hopped freighters a while, he was arrested in Harrisburg and fined two dollars or twenty days on a vag-
rancy charge and he had to take the prison sentence. In Philadelphia
the luckless Drescher sold shoe polish and insect powder, but failed
even in such lowly ventures. The utter loneliness and hopelessness
of those years are ably recounted in his prose biography Vom Sturm
Gepeitscht (Lashed by the Storm), published in Germany in 1913.
The sub-title "Skizzen und Geschichten aus einem Zigeunerleben"
(Sketches and stories from the life of a gypsy) reveals his realization
of failure by the epithet "gypsy," a name he applied to himself with
bitter humor.

From New York and Philadelphia the wind of poverty and failure swept him westward, ever searching for work and security. His
experiences helped him toward a firm philosophy of life, as one illustration confirms: during a forced stay in a midwestern poorhouse he

*Reprinted from the Canadian Modern Language Review 22 (1966):
37-39, by permission of the publisher.

observed with deep concern and horror that negroes were badly mis-
treated and generally discriminated against.   He determined then
and there to fight intolerance and injustice wherever he found it.   In
Cincinnati he had the chance to express his views while employed as
a newspaper reporter--to be sure without salary, but with adequate
bed and board, assuring a welcome refuge from the storm.   Yet
this interlude was of brief duration, due to Drescher's resistance to
conformity and mediocrity.   He bummed his way to Chicago where
a new chance to settle down was offered him.   The Freie Gemeinde
(Free Thought Society) employed him as teacher for their children--
again without salary, but he felt grateful to be given the chance to
meet "his kind" of people.   His predecessor had impressed the community with strong tirades against Catholicism and for world revolution, so when Drescher chose to inculcate his young charges with informative facts about nature and the laws of evolution, the parents
relieved him of his voluntary duties and again the young idealist was
an outcast.   Fortunately, the editor of a German Labor newspaper
recognized the ability of the young man and employed him on a trial
basis.   At last Martin Drescher had found his niche and there followed the happiest period of his life when he became editor of the
Chicago Arbeiterzeitung.   While he had frequent adversities and never
attained even a semblance of affluence, yet he was never again friendless or homeless, indeed he achieved an enviable popularity and
some fame as a literary figure.

      In his poetic works Martin Drescher attains full stature as an
exponent of the German-American intellectual class.   He retained his
mother tongue from choice as chief medium of communication, but in
other respects "melted" into the American way of life and culture.
The recurring motif of yearning for the scenes of childhood is to be
understood not as dissatisfaction with the new homeland but simply as
the nostalgic reminiscence of the past, a romantic trait common to
most Germans.   In Martin Drescher's poems (Gedichte, 1909) we
find some lyric passages that can be designated as excellent as are
the freely translated poems of Edgar Allan Poe.   This writer considers several poems to be among the best ever written by a German
in this country and thus when considering the field of German-American literature we must do justice to this man, who today would be
grouped with our beatnik writers, since he was a social and political
non-conformist who spoke for the under-privileged classes.

      Probably one poem stands out as the best Martin Drescher
wrote and deserves our attention.   He called it "Bettelleut" (Beggar
Folks) and considered it his favorite.   It was this writer's privilege
in her early childhood to hear Drescher recite these stirring verses
to friends, towering on his long legs, completely carried away by
the dramatic tragedy of the tale of love in a tenement.   Yet the stark
realism of the situation is glowingly offset by the joy of shared love,
so that the effect was truly startling for young and old listeners, especially when the poet himself unashamedly wept over his verses.
(Ernest L. Meyer in Bucket Boy (1947) describes such an evening
with Drescher.)   Many years have passed since I was first impressed by this poem but it has not lost its appeal, nor has another

of his own favorites: "Stille Nacht" (Silent Night), in which he has captured the nostalgic experience of the immigrant at Christmas time, when the lights of the Tannenbaum transport him to his childhood and his German home. The secret of Martin Drescher's poetic strength lies in his strong emotional feelings expressed in simple but beautiful verses. For his fellow men, especially the poor, the uprooted, the deprived, he has a message of understanding and love. He stands far in the foreground of the group of German writers whose works were published in America in the decades preceding and following the turn of the century.

25. HEINRICH ARMIN RATTERMANN: GERMAN-AMERICAN POET, 1832-1923*

Fred Karl Scheibe

On October 14, 1832 one of the finest citizens in German-American circles was born as the son of a carpenter in Ankum, near Osnabrueck, in the northern part of Germany. When Heinrich Armin was eighty years old and reminiscing, he wrote:

> O fondest place where I was given birth
> From which the fates coerced my early going:
> Yet, Ankum, my faith in thee keeps flowing,
> E'en in this so strange and distant earth.
> (Translated by Fred Karl Scheibe)

When Heinrich was fourteen years old he left the village school. To his teacher Moellenbrock, who was a great inspiration to young Heinrich, he set a fine poetic monument which ends with the line, "Dir, Heinrich Moellenbrock, hab' ich's zu danken!"

In 1845 the Rattermann family (formerly Rathermann) emigrated to America. It took two long months on the "Hermitage" to cross the Atlantic. On October 14th they landed in Baltimore with the other 128 passengers. The family went directly to Cincinnati, queen of the West. Heinrich could not continue his studies because his father, a very practical German, said that the boy should help earn his keep. He was fortunate enough to meet the wife of his employer who took the bright boy under her wing and taught him to read and write English. In America he worked as a butcher, laborer in a brickyard, and waiter. Heinrich preferred his job as a waiter in Louisville since it enabled him to make fruitful acquaintances with educated Germans.

An aunt of his discovered his talent for drawing and promptly sent him to art school. When his father heard of this he strongly disapproved and Heinrich had to discontinue his art studies. Soon thereafter, however, his father died and Heinrich, being the eldest of three children, had to provide for them. He had learned to work with hammer and plane and had no difficulty in obtaining a good job as a carpenter. While providing for his charges he put a small amount of his wages into savings and when he had accumulated enough money, he registered at a business college where he

*Reprinted from German-American Studies 1:1 (1969): 3-7, by permission of the publisher.

studied accounting and related subjects.   A few years later, after
having worked successfully as an accountant and business advisor,
he became the founder and director of the "German Mutual Fire Insurance Company of Cincinnati," a position he held for the remainder of his life.   He also studied law and conducted a legal practice
for several years.

As editor of the monthly magazine Der deutsche Pionier[1]
Rattermann came into personal contact with well-known German-
American poets.   Among these were Theodor Kirchhoff, Kaspar
Butz, Conrad Krez, Ernst A. Zuendt and Gustav Bruehl, Heinrich
Armin also made friends with physicians, naturalists, statesmen,
and artists.   Because of his fondness for music he became one of
the founders of the North-American Saengerbund and organized many
great music festivals.

When Johann Bernhard Stallo, Cincinnati philosopher, lawyer,
and statesman accepted the post of ambassador to Italy, Rattermann
lost his best friend and advisor.   It was Stallo who had taught him
how to collect and organize historic material.   Heinrich made long
trips to gather historical data, writings, and letters pertaining to
German immigration.   A. B. Faust and a host of others have used
Rattermann's historical collections as a basis for much of their research.   It is interesting to note that Rattermann considered himself
a collector of historic materials and not a historian since he felt he
did not possess the ability to organize the collected materials into
a meaningful presentation.   Nevertheless, Rattermann's investigations were vital and we thank him today for his important efforts.
Among the noted historians who have recognized Rattermann as a
leading researcher in the field of German-American studies are Otto
Lohr and A. E. Zucker.[2]

Rattermann was a passionate fighter for the use of the German language in Cincinnati's public schools.   The German element
at that time was so strong in this city that anyone who spoke
against the "Zweisprachensystem," i.e., that English and German
were to be taught on equal terms, would have had little chance to
be elected to public office.

It seems to be somewhat presumptuous on the part of certain
literary critics to describe the poetry of Heinrich Armin Rattermann
as dead, sentimental, and unfeeling.   Of course, if one approaches
his poetry purely from the standpoint of a modernist, we may well
come to accept these conclusions.[3]   It is important to study a poet
from within the period in which he lives and consider the influences
to which he was exposed.   Time and space are very important here.
Rattermann was born when the literary movement known by the name
of "Junges Deutschland" made its appearance and with it began the
epoch of journalism.   Romanticism which, in its narrower sense,
had come upon the German scene with the publication of the literary
journal Athenaeum in 1798 was coming to a close and a new generation projected a different Zeitgeist.   This development, however,
took time.   Several literary movements ran parallel to one another.

242   German-American Literature

Grillparzer, Kleist, and Hebbel could not entirely break away from
the influence of the classic poets, mainly Goethe and Schiller. Nevertheless, a new dawn had risen and revolutionary literary movements in the latter part of the past century made their disturbing
and challenging appearance.

These movements, which dealt with heredity, poverty, insan-
ity, revolt against authority, sex, and many other themes, were but
little understood by the German immigrant groups in America. Even
great writers such as Zola, Strindberg, Ibsen, Hauptmann, Wedekind and many others were not accepted, nor were they understood
by the Rattermann immigrant generation. Even in Germany, for example, one critic called a play (Familie Selicke) by the Naturalists,
Holz and Schlaf, a comedy of animal sounds. Had Rattermann lived
thirty years or so longer and had he viewed Gerhart Hauptmann's
plays, from Vor Sonnenaufgang to Der Bogen des Odysseus, I believe
that he would have revised his judgment of some of the leading modern poets. In Rattermann's epic "Vater Rhein," sonnet No. 50, he
writes:

>   A doll should never be a wedded wife
>   Of a German man, for whom he's pining;
>   It is the equal partner whom he's alining,
>   Who shares with him the joys and grief of life.
>   (Translated by Fred K. Scheibe)

It should be obvious that Rattermann was familiar with Hen-
rik Ibsen's A Doll's House in which the right of a woman to be the
equal partner of her husband is defended, and Rattermann believed
in the integrity of that right. Indeed he was modern in his political
and social reasoning.

True, Rattermann wrote in the style of the middle of the 19th
century, but, then, this would be quite normal for a German immigrant in America. Heinrich believes in the classical form of poetry.
He writes:

>   Jedoch Gedanken
>   in Formenschranken
>   Zusammen ranken...
>   (Vol. 4, page 126)

In other words, one's thoughts should harmonize and be cast within
the limits of rhyme and meter. His greatest and perhaps most beautiful work is his epic "Vater Rhein" which is written in 130 sonnets.
Some of these are very beautiful and contain true poetic feeling and
expression. Thirty-eight years of Rattermann's life were devoted to
this work of love; of course, with lengthy interruptions. "Vater
Rhein" relates the history of this great stream. Poetic unity is
achieved by "Vater Rhein" himself who presents us with a kaleido-
scopic picture of its varied history. In the fifth sonnet the poet refers to Walther von der Vogelweide's poem "Unter der linden an
der heide":

> Away, my wanderlust won't let me stay
> Through mountain ranges eagerly departing,
> From rocky cliffs the bearded pines are smarting
> As if they knew that I was on the way.
>
> Here Vaduz anchored on a palisade
> Where courage bold and sweetest love were searching,
> Encourage castle-maiden's coy emerging:
> With loving heart knight Ulbricht wooed the maid.
>
> From far away we hear the rumors flying
> In Bozen land we hear a bridal cooing:
> "Under the linden tree upon the meadows."
>
> Her reddened cheeks with pious shame are vying
> When "Frauenlob" seeks death in raptured wooing,
> Dame Venus plots to lure him in the shadows.
> (Translated by Fred Karl Scheibe)

In the fourth volume of Rattermann's works, which contains his aphorisms, we find his contemplations on reason and knowledge, literature, poetry, history, art and aesthetics, love and justice, statecraft and politics, as well as citizenship and its responsibilities.[4] There is enough material here for someone to write a series of enlightening articles.

It is most unfortunate that volumes 13, 14, and 15 have remained unpublished. Rattermann tried to obtain financial assistance from German-Americans as well as the German government, but to no avail. Rattermann in his old age could be called a tragic character, although this did not deter him from striking out against fate and doing whatever he could to finish as much of his collected works as possible. It was at this difficult time when his eyesight was failing him and his hearing caused him difficulties. He had the plates for the above mentioned volumes melted down in order to finish printing at least twelve of the planned fifteen volumes. The loss to our generation is great.

Rattermann reminds one of Hans Sachs, the Nuremberg shoemaker, meistersinger, and poet. He was despised, laughed at and quite forgotten until Goethe honored him by writing a fine article on him and employing his "Knittelvers" (with some variations) in his "Urfaust." The great German-American bard sings no more, nevertheless, every decade that passes will add to his fame.

Notes

1. In 1868 Rattermann and several of his colleagues founded the Deutscher Pionier Verein. In 1879 the first issue of Der deutsche Pionier appeared. Rattermann edited it from 1874 to 1885. The magazine comprised 500 to 600 pages annually and ran for eighteen years. In it appeared historical es-

244 German-American Literature

says, biographies, original poetry, literary criticism, sketches, discussions on music, politics and social events as well as editorials.

2. In his illuminating article, "Heinrich Armin Rattermann--German-American Poet and Historian" (The American German Review, Oct. 1939, 13-15), Zucker compares Rattermann's work to that of the great historians Justus Moeser and Leopold von Ranke.

3. See H. Willen's stark criticism in his doctoral dissertation, H. A. Rattermann's Life and Poetical Work (University of Pennsylvania, 1939). Sister Mary Spanheimer qualifies Rattermann as one of the most talented of the German-American poets. See her doctoral dissertation, Heinrich Rattermann, German-American Author, Poet and Historian, 1832-1923 (The Catholic Univ. of America, 1937).

4. Rattermann's collected works are: Volumes I and II: Oden, Balladen und vermischte Gedichte; Vols. IIIa and IIIb: "Spaetherbst-Garben." Denksprueche und Raetsel in Prosa und Versen; Vols. VI and VII: "Bluethen und Stachelfruechte." Epigrammatische und Satyrische Dichtungen; Vol. VIII: Denkreden und Vortraege (Contains "Shakspeareana," "Musiker- und Kuenstler Biographien"); Vol. IX: Denkreden und Vortraege aus der deutschen Literaturgeschichte von Opitz bis Geibel; Vols. X-XII: Deutsch-Amerikanisches Biographikon und Dichter-Album der ersten Haelfte des 19. Jahrhunderts; Vol. XVI: Abhandlungen, Vortraege und Reden. An extra volume was also published under the title: Nord-Amerikanische Voegel in Liedern.

26. KONRAD NIES, GERMAN-AMERICAN LITERARY KNIGHT*

Robert E. Ward

With the advent of World War I, German-American institutions were dealt a deadly blow from which they have never recovered. Today the paucity of journalistic and literary publications in the German language in America hardly echoes the enormous amount of German-American writing which took place prior to the death of the author known as "der deutschamerikanisch Klassiker": Konrad Nies (pseud., Konrad von Alzey). One of German-America's most prolific writers, Nies turned to spiritualism during the last few years of his life "heartbroken over the catastrophe which involved the land of his birth and the land of his adoption."[1] On the grounds of his "Waldnest," overlooking San Francisco Bay, Nies erected a monument to the muses which he illuminated with multi-colored lights. Here, in the summer house which his friends had purchased for him in 1914, Nies worked vigorously, completing his last volume of poetry which, long delayed on account of the war, reached this country from Germany shortly after the poet's demise. How tragic that he should suffer further from his arrest by federal officers who claimed he had constructed his illuminated monument for the purpose of signaling German U-boats in the San Francisco harbor.[2] But then, this was just one of the many misfortunes suffered by this German-American literary knight throughout his thirty-eight years in his adopted homeland. Beset by money-problems during most of those years, Nies moved from place to place, like a medieval troubadour seeking to earn his way through creativity in the field of literature. Had he been born perhaps a half century earlier, he might have enjoyed the success he so earnestly desired. German-American literature achieved its most favorable receptance during the period from 1830 to 1880, after which it waned sharply until it succumbed almost completely with the outbreak of the "war to end all wars." Noble attempts to revive it have since failed, and today only the Exil-Literatur of the post 1933 period receives the favorable attention of most noted scholars.

As a teacher Nies had little patience with his students, preferring instead to write and edit. Of the paucity of major German-American writers included in the literary histories of Spiller, Nadler, Engel, Bartels, Klein, Kindermann, and others, Nies is consistently recognized as the most versatile. During his thirty-eight

*Reprinted from German-American Studies 3 (1971): 7-11, by permission of the publisher.

years of literary activity in America he published hundreds of poems, wrote essays, monographs, reviews, Novellen, sketches, and
plays. He founded at least one literary society,[3] took part in the Balti-
morer Blumenspiel of 1904 (at which he won first prize),[4] contributed to
German and German-American anthologies, newspapers and periodicals,[5]
gave lectures on literature, acted on the German and German-American
stage, and founded the famous periodical, Deutsch-Amerikanische Dichtung which he edited from April 1888 to its demise in April 1890.

Ever since early childhood, Konrad Nies was interested in
literature and the theatre. He was born in Alzey in Rheinhessen on
October 10, 1861 where he later attended the Realschule. In Worms
he continued his education at the Gymnasium, in Leipzig at the The-
aterschule. On February 26, 1880 he gave recitations from Goethe's
Faust and Schiller's Wilhelm Tell; on May 22 and June 3, 1881 he
appeared with the actor, H. Curschmann (Brüning) in several farces
and comedies on the German stage. After a short stay in Dresden
he began his formal acting career. In 1882 he played Hamlet on the
stage in Darmstadt and undertook a series of engagements in Chemnitz, Speyer, Dortmund, Aachen, Kaiserslautern and Mühlhausen i.
Elsass. On December 17, 1882 Nies directed and acted in the performance of his monodrama, Konradin von Hohenstaufen. Perhaps
unhappy with the rather mediocre response to his acting, Nies decided to give his talents a try on the German stage in America. On
August 28, 1883 he arrived in Hoboken, then proceeded to Columbus
and Cincinnati where he gave his second performance of Konradin
von Hohenstaufen. From the Queen City he travelled in 1884 to Buffalo, Milwaukee, and Omaha where he appeared on the German-
American stage. Interrupting his acting career to study English and
German at Duane Academy, a branch of Denison University in Ohio,
Nies then entered the employ of the Freidenker Publishing Co. in
Milwaukee where in 1886 he met with Otto Soubron to discuss the
publication of a monthly periodical which would serve to bring attention to German-American literary endeavor. Noting that in the past
the term "German-American literature" had been applied to all German writings written by authors residing in America regardless of
the content of their works, Nies sought to publish prosaic and poetic
contributions including translations of English-language works which
dealt primarily with the American experience. In doing so he hoped
to attract the support of American as well as German-American
writers.[6]

Nies proceeded to Omaha and in 1887 his Novelle, Die Volk-
ersfiedel appeared in print. That same year he consulted several
German-American writers including H. C. Bechtold, Max Hempel,
E. A. Zündt, Karl Knortz, and Theodor Kirchhoff, who pledged to
support his literary monthly. Although Nies had expected support
from German-American organizations such as the Turners and especially from the great many teachers of German around the country,
he found little interest on their part. With a limited number of subscribers and advertisers to finance his venture, he set up an office
at 843 South Seventeenth Street in Omaha where he designed and edited in collaboration with Hermann Rosenthal in New York the first

number of Deutsch-Amerikanische Dichtung which appeared in April
1888. Rosenthal joined him as co-editor of the monthly when the
first number of the second volume appeared in April 1889. The
cover to the first issue carried Nies' editorial note:

> Wenn wir es wagen, in unserer vom krassen Materialis-
> mus beherrschten Zeit und einem der Poesie so ungünsti-
> gen Lande wie Amerika eine der Dichtkunst gewidmete
> Zeitschrift herauszugeben, so geschicht dies zunächst mit
> dem Wunsche, in unserem Blatte der seither heimathlos
> herumirrenden deutsch-amerikanischen Dichtkunst endlich
> einmal ein festes Heim und den deutsch-amerikanischen
> Poeten ein Organ zu schaffen, das dazu dienen soll, die
> sich in ihrer Vereinzelung zersplitternden literarischen
> Kräfte zu sammeln und durch gegenseitige Anregung und
> fachmännische Kritik fördernd auf das wahre Talent zu
> wirken, den anmassenden Dilettantismus aber, wie er sich
> häufig in unserer Tagespresse breit macht und die deutsch-
> amerikanische Poesie der Gefahr der Verflachung aussetzt,
> zu bekämpfen.

Late in 1888 Nies moved to Newark, Ohio where he continued to publish his monthly while teaching German at the local high
school. Despite a most promising response from some 300 readers,
the magazine lasted only two years and brought Nies near to financial ruin. Of the over 100 contributors to Nies' periodical, only a
few were able to transcend the epigonistic crutch upon which most of
them leaned.[7] Apart from the disconcerting lack of interest in the
arts in America during the period of Nies' activity, another barrier
stood against this pioneer publication. Whereas Nies stubbornly refused to consider controversial works on social, religious, and political questions, most of the contemporary German-American periodicals did not.[8] Rosenthal, who marketed the D-AD in New York,
apparently realized that the periodical would have to appeal more to
the general German-American reading public and their social organizations rather than to only a select group of poets and poetasters in
order to increase the income from subscriptions.[9] Unlike the popular Kalender and Jahrbücher, Nies' publication was almost solely
devoted to creative literature, essays, book reviews, and cultural
notes. Early in 1897 Rudolf Cronau corresponded with Nies concerning the establishing of a successor to D-AD, but later that year
abandoned the idea.

Although disappointed at the failure of D-AD, Nies pursued
his goal to promote interest in German-American literary endeavor
by writing a repertoire of lectures, six of which he presented in
St. Louis in 1889: "Deutsche Dichter von heute," "Deutsch-ameri-
kanische Dichtung," "Aus dem Buche der Poesie," "Das Glück im
Lichte der Dichtung," "Amerikas deutsche Dichter," and "Unsere
Zeit im Spiegel der Dichtung" which was later published in the
Rheinische Volksblätter (March 5, 1895). In 1890 he travelled ex-
tensively, delivering thirty-six lectures in the East, New England,
Colorado, Alabama, Texas, and the Middle West. His unpublished

manuscript, "Sommertage in San Antonio, Texas" was probably composed during his stay in Texas. Exhausted from his teaching, lecture trips, and writing, and still suffering asthmatic attacks, Nies sought a drier climate with a trip to California early in 1893, then a stay in the Catskills before moving with his family to Palenville, New York. In 1894 the family again moved--this time to St. Louis where Nies first taught at the "Toensfeldt Institut," then at the "Viktoria-Institut," a private school for girls which he and his wife directed. While in St. Louis he contributed poems and weekly articles to the Westliche Post.

Despite his ailing health Nies continued to teach and write. In 1891, one year before he resigned from his teaching post in Newark, Ohio, he published his own volume of poems (Funken) with a financial assist from Rosenthal in New York. The book reached a second edition in 1901.

In 1898 C. Witter in St. Louis published Nies' Deutsche Gaben. Ein Festspiel zum Deutschen Tag, and in 1900 the second edition of Deutsche Gaben as well as the author's Rosen im Schnee. Ein deutsch-amerikanisches Weihnachtsspiel in vier Bildern. These works were followed by Im Zeichen der Freiheit (1902) and Die herrlichen Drei. Festspiel (Nordamerikanischer Turnerbund: Indianapolis, 1904) which reached a second edition in 1905. In the same year Nies published his second major collection of poems, Aus westlichen Weiten (Grossenheim, Leipzig, New York) and departed for a lecture tour in Germany. While abroad in 1906 he met Olga Khripunowa, a Russian noblewoman with whom he travelled to Italy, Egypt, Palestine, and Greece. This brief affaire de coeur eventually led to the author's estrangement from his wife.

Although he earned a considerable amount of money during his lecture tour in Germany, Nies returned to America almost penniless. His wife's excessive demands as terms of their divorce and Nies' extravagant spending brought the author again to the brink of bankruptcy. Shortly after his return to America in 1907 he completed a Novelle, Im Schatten der Höhe and in the same year (1908) he departed for Denver where he edited the Denver Demokrat and later the Colorado Herold. 10 But his strong desire to promote the appreciation of German literature in America did not cease, and so, with his manager, Adolf Leon, he made a "Konrad Nies Tournee 1913-1914," presenting the following lectures in various German-American centers: "Ein Abend bei deutschen Dichtern," "Aus dem Buch der Poesie," "Deutsche Dichter in Amerika," "Das Glück im Lichte der Dichtung," "Die Mission der Poesie," "Das Freiheitsjahr und die Freiheitsdichter Deutschlands 1815," "Einkehr bei Friedrich Schiller," "Auf geweihten Staetten," and "Kalifornien und seine Schönheiten." The following year (1915) his "Stimmen der Höhe," which Nies considered his best poem, appeared in the New York Staatszeitung. On January 23, 1916 he published his first article in the Colorado Herold and continued his agitation against the war with Germany which he had begun with his first war poem, "Ein Brudergruss," written in August of 1914. Although this political agitation

cost him his position as editor of The Colorado Herold, Nies continued to lament the war, writing his last war-poem in May, 1920.
In "Zum Rettungswerk" he calls for assistance to his defeated homeland.   Characteristic of his later poetry is a strong note of pessimism and fear of growing old.   Death claimed this literary knight of German-America on August 10, 1921 in San Francisco's German Hospital.   In accordance with his last wishes, he was cremated. Shortly after his demise his wife received a shipment from W. Haertel in Leipzig of her husband's last volume of poetry, Welt und Wildnis. Gedichte aus vier Erdteilen in which are recorded the many sufferings and experiences of a man whose many talents and travels were directed toward literature as an art.   The life of Konrad Nies mirrors the tragedy of the German-American who so desperately sought to retain his cultural heritage in a foreign environment.   His works are a tribute to his dedication and a monument to a bygone era when German-America was an integral part of the American scene.

The following is a previously unpublished sonnet taken from Nies' Nachlass.   The sonnet was one of Nies' favorite forms of poetic expression.

BEIM MAIWEIN

Frau Anna Levi[11] zur freundl. Erinnerung an den
huebschen Abend des 2. Mai 1895.

Waldmeisterduft weht aus krystallner Schale,
Drin übermüth'ge Rheinweingeister ringen,
Er will vom jungen Wald die Botschaft bringen
Dass uns die Welt im Maienglanz erstrahle.

In neuen Träumen blüht mit einem Male
Die Stunde auf. Der Frohlust Knospen springen.
Ein Koboldchen mit bunten Falterschwingen
Trinkt, neckisch uns zum Elfenbachanale.

Die Gläser klingen. Maienzauber spinnen.
Waldmeisters Gruss hat es uns angethan;
Des Alltags kleine Sorgen, sie zerrinnen.

Weit schwillt die Brust in junger Blüthen Bann
Und will sich kühn ein kurzes Glück gewinnen
Voll Elfenspuk und tollem Märchenwahn.

Notes

1.   Georg Sylvester Viereck, "Konrad Nies, a Knight of the Blue Flower," The American Monthly, XIII, 7 (Sept. , 1921), 201. Viereck, Friedrich Michel, E. A. Baruch, Hermann Alexander, Emil Praetorius and other popular German-American writers stood by Nies during those trying last years of his life. Nies'

long correspondence with Friedrich Karl Castelhun and Theodor Kirchhoff, if uncovered and studied, would provide further insight into the nature and extent of German-American
creative literature.

2. See C. R. Walther-Thomas' doctoral dissertation, "Konrad Nies,
    ein deutsche Dichter in Amerika" (Univ. Penn., 1933).   Cf.
    also Ernst Rose, "German-American Literature" in Cassell's
    Encyclopedia of Literature, 2nd ed. (N.Y., 1970); Dictionary
    of American Biography; "Ein deutsch-amerikanischer Dichter,"
    Der Türmer, XXIV (1921); Fritz Erckmann, "Konrad Nies,
    ein vergessener Alzeyer Dichter," Sonderdruck der Rhein-
    hessischen Volksblätter (Alzey, Jan. 18, 1933).

3. Nies invited his supporters to join a society which he founded as
    "Der Verein für deutsche Literatur und Kunst in Amerika."
    The first membership list of the society appeared in the last
    issue of the periodical. Nies is listed as the poetry editor,
    Rosenthal as the prose editor, Georg J. Edelheim as the fi-
    nance secretary and editor of the "Vereinsbeiträge" section.
    Listed as members are several prominent German-American
    authors, including Hermann Alexander, Hugo Andriessen, Her-
    mann Behr, Pedro Ilgen, Georg Juraschek, Marie Raible,
    Hugo Scheller, Moritz Wiener, and others.

4. His poem, "Die Rache der Wälder" received first prize.

5. Nies contributed to Die New York Staatszeitung, Deutsch-ameri-
    kanische Dichtung, Der deutsche Vorkämpfer, Rheinische
    Volksblätter, Puck, Frank Leslie's Rundschau, Die Westliche
    Post, Belletristisches Journal, Colorado Herold, Der Frei-
    denker, Hausbuch, ein Halbmonatsschrift für deutsche Dichtung,
    and other periodicals. Sixteen of his poems appeared in the
    latter publication. Several more appear in the following an-
    thologies: G. A. Zimmermann, Deutsch in Amerika (Chicago,
    1892; 1894); Das Baltimorer Blumenspiel (Baltimore, 1904);
    G. A. Neeff, Vom Lande des Sternenbanners (Ellenville, N.Y.,
    1905); Max Heinrici, Das Buch der Deutschen in Amerika
    (Phila., 1909); Irving T. Sanders, Aus ruhmreicher Zeit,
    deutsch-amerikanische Dichtungen aus dem ersten Jahre des
    Weltkrieges (N.Y., 1915); Anthologie deutsch-amerikanischer
    Dichtung (N.Y., 1925-26); Robert E. Ward, Deutsche Lyrik
    aus Amerika. Eine Auswahl (N.Y., 1969).

6. Cf. "Rückblicke und Ausblicke," D-AD, XI-XII (1888), 114. Max
    Nordau wrote to Nies that the main reason German-American
    writers were not yet appreciated in Europe was that they had
    no central literary organ in which they might publish their
    works. Nordau notes that German-American literature would
    have difficulty in gaining an American reading public because
    of the anti-cultural trend in "the land of the almighty dollar."
    See D-AD, I, 3-4 (1888), 35.

7. Of the 241 original poems by 94 poets published in D-AD, twenty-
    two were composed by Nies. Included in the various issues
    are book reviews, essays, sketches, cultural notes, German
    translations of English and foreign poems, biographical ar-
    ticles, short stories, Novellen, sayings, and aphorisms.

8. Nies' disagreement with Robert Reitzel's comments on the role

of contemporary literature led to a short controversy between
the two writers which ended in the ninth number with Nies
calling the latter a genuine poet and fanatic nihilist. His reply addressed to F. K. in Detroit is strongly worded: "Man
kennt R. R. überall zur Genüge und weiss, dass er nur zu
bereit ist, selbst mit der schmutzigen Waffe der Gemeinheit
gegen denjenigen zu kämpfen, der das Wohlgefallen an den
unsauberen Schimpfereien und anarchistischen Phantastereien,
die immer mehr und mehr das einzige Element bilden, in
dem sich R. R. noch wohl zu fühlen scheint, nicht theilt . . . .
Wie ewig schade, bei solchen Geistesgaben und solcher Gem-
üthsfülle:--solche charakterlose Zaunenhaftigkeit!" Reitzel
was the editor of Der arme Teufel.

9. In a letter to Cronau in March, 1897, Nies wrote:
Als Redakteur der D-AD hatte ich vielen moralischen Erf-
olg, und selbst drüben hat mir die Kritik das beste Zeug-
nis ausgestellt. Das Blatt würde wohl heute noch bestehen,
hätte man es in Neu York nicht in den Dienst der flachen
Vereinsmeierei stellen wollen. Diesem Vorhaben wider-
setzte ich mich aufs Entschiedenste und sah schliesslich
lieber, dass das Blatt einging.

10. Nies has been credited with editing Der Flaneur in Omaha in
1885-1886, but this is disputed. See Karl J. R. Arndt and
May E. Olson, eds., German-American Newspapers and Periodicals 1732-1955 (Heidelberg, 1961).

11. The Levi family owned a haberdashery and were neighbors of
the Nies family in Alzey. Young Nies was often given ribbons
and bright colored materials from their stock which he used
when he and other children from the neighborhood played
"Theater" in a barn nearby. I am indebted to Mrs. Marie
von Aiken of Vineland, N.J. who kindly sent me the original
copy of this poem in Nies' own handwriting.

27. THE LITERARY ACTIVITY OF GEORG EDWARD*

Karl-Heinz Stoll

Georg Edward was born Georg Daniel Eduard August Andreas Geilfuss in Giessen on Dec. 13, 1869. His father was a well-to-do businessman who after the completion of his graduate studies in chemistry passed his "Staatsexamen" in pharmacy, later taking over his father-in-law's building supplies company. Georg hardly knew his mother who died when he was only five years old. His fondest recollection of her is that she sang folk songs and told him fairy tales.[1] After her demise the four children, among whom Georg was the eldest, were raised by an aunt; during their vacations they often stayed with relatives in Darmstadt.

At the age of six Georg entered the "Volksschule," at ten the "Gymnasium." As a student he pursued only those subjects for which he had a particular interest. Not formal schooling, but his father's library opened the world of literature to Edward, for it was there that he made his first acquaintance with Goethe, Schiller, Herder, Klopstock, Wieland, Eichendorff, Lenau, Arnim, and Fouque. At the age of nine he wrote his first verse. The poems of the "Gymnasiast" display an early talent for the lyric as well as the epic in his preference for the "Lied" and the ballad. His "kleine Gedichte" of this period are reminiscent of Heinrich Heine's poetry. Edward founded a literary club which consisted of about twenty young writers, painters, and composers most of whom were fellow students. They met every Saturday afternoon, drank coffee and read to each other what they had written. The fruit of this activity comprises two large volumes which today are in the hands of the chairman's descendants. One of them, entitled Die gebildete Kaffeeschwester, contains humorous contributions, the other, Die literarischen Blaetter, serious ones.

At the age of sixteen Edward fell in love with an English girl who in a few weeks made him sufficiently acquainted with her native tongue to enable him to translate several poems. Two of the translations (a Scottish ballad and the "Song of the Shirt" by Thomas Hood) were published in the Magazin fuer Literatur in Dresden. Edward also translated Robert Burns and Lord Byron. The shortness and vicissitude of the Scottish ballads in particular fascinated him.[2] A great number of poems were subsequently composed while Edward was attending the "Gymnasium" in Mainz. They were published in the Goslar magazine, Literarische Blaetter. Five of the contributors to

*Reprinted from German-American Studies 1:1 (1969): 17-32, by permission of the publisher.

this magazine wrote an anthology entitled Symphonie; of their poems only Edward's received a favorable response from the critics. The Frankfurter Zeitung printed his essay "Die altschottischen Volksballaden" which included examples of translations; the Muenchner Allgemeine Zeitung carried his portrait of the Danish author Jens Peter Jacobsen, the first such study ever written in German.

In the meantime Stefan George had taken notice of the young author. He even visited Edward in Giessen[3] and found his writing worthy of publication in his Blaetter fuer die Kunst. In 1892 Edward's poems "Mittagsstille" and "Des Friedens Land" were published in this magazine, in 1893 a translation from Swinburne, "Eine Ballade vom Traumland," and in 1894 the poems "Fruehling" and "Ungesprochene Worte." Edward never really liked George; the break came when George displayed his high-browedness toward friends of Edward's who on one occasion had joined the two writers in a hotel restaurant. Around this time Edward entered into a friendship with the writer Alfred Bock, the owner of a mill in Giessen. His son, Dr. Werner Bock was a particularly close friend of Edward's and the two sought each other's company almost daily. Bock had to leave Germany in 1939; after the war he lived in the Tessin. Edward considered his friend's poems among the best that have been published in recent years. Through the Bocks Edward made the acquaintance of Karl Wolfskehl. Wolfskehl owes to Edward his introduction to the works of Stefan George in whose circle he later was to become so very much involved. He remained Edward's friend until his death in New Zealand.

Edward's father was displeased with his son's literary activities, maintaining that they were of no avail and urging him to go to the university so that he might join the fraternity of which he himself had been a member. The young author, however, had little interest in studies and fraternities and consequently, there was almost daily friction between him and his father which finally erupted into a violent argument whereupon the son left home. Edward went to Frankfurt where he hoped to establish a connection with a newspaper. Claar, the manager of the Frankfurt playhouse, offered him a position as a dramaturgist. The actor Diegelmann, however, warned him that the job would be "suicidal," whereupon Edward declined. Although Edward was accepted by none of the Frankfurt papers, the editors supplied him with letters of recommendation. With these he traveled to Darmstadt, Augsburg, Munich, and Stuttgart, but nowhere was he given a position. In Stuttgart he received a telegram from Dr. Mamroth of the Frankfurter Zeitung informing him that the Bremen Weser Zeitung was looking for a correspondent to cover the Chicago World Exhibition and that Mamroth had proposed Edward be the one. A few days later Edward was on his way to Antwerp from where he departed in May, 1893 for New York on the Red Star steamboat "Westernland." In Chicago he lived in the quiet suburb of Rogers Park with an English family who made him feel at home to the extent of permitting him to have two dogs, several canaries and parakeets. After the World Exhibition came to an end, the Weser Zeit-

ung asked Edward to continue working for them and arranged for his
articles to be printed also by the Neue Zuericher Zeitung and the
Hamburgischer Correspondent.   He remained a newspaper correspondent until November, 1923.

During this time the Deutsche Dichtung in Berlin published
Edward's "Die Jagd im Ettrickforst," which the then famous novelist Wilhelm Hertz praised very highly, comparing Edward to Theodor Fontane. [4]   The poem was reprinted in 1897 when the best poetry of the young Georg Edward was collected in the beautifully printed 165-page volume Balladen und Lieder. [5]   A revised edition of
this collection was published in 1903. [6] In it only a few of the poems which appeared in the first edition are included, the others being new.   The majority of the ballads are set in a Germanic, Nordic
world, mostly English or German, often medieval.

Although the author had been residing in the United States for
ten years when his second edition appeared, not a single reference
to the American scene occurs in it (nor in the first edition, for
that matter).   One of the four subdivisions in the second edition is
called "Heimat und Fremde." it contains twenty-two poems, a few
of which can already be found in the first edition, but "die Fremde"
in these poems hardly seems any further away than in Theodor
Storm's lyrics or in the "Wanderburschenlyrik" that was so popular
in the nineteenth century.   Edward seems to have written "Ein Abschied" with the melody of perhaps the most popular one of these
songs in his ear: Wilhelm Mueller's "Am Brunnen vor dem Tore."

EIN ABSCHIED[7]

Nun wird es still und traurig
In Heide und Geheg,
Eiskalte Nebel suchen
Sich durch das Tal den Weg--
Und ich muss alles lassen,
Was mein war lange Zeit,
Und wandern muss ich, wandern
Gott weiss allein, wie weit.

Das Muehlrad ist zerbrochen,
Im Winde knarrt das Tor,
Und auf dem stillen Teiche
Verfault der Kahn im Rohr;
Die Blumen sind verdorben
Schon lange vor der Zeit,
Die Welt wie ausgestorben,
Und jeder Pfad verschneit.

Am Wege draussen liegen
Zwei Graeber unterm Schnee--
Da muss ich noch vorueber,
Wenn ich nun wandern geh:
Da grab ich aus dem Grunde

Mir eine Handvoll Sand,
Die will ich mit mir tragen
Hinaus ins fremde Land.

Und eine mag wohl weinen,
Weil sie verlassen blieb--
Doch morgen, ach, schon morgen
Herzt sie ein ander Lieb--
Dann ist mir nichts geblieben,
Und alles still und leer--
O Gott, mein Gott, dann habe
Ich keine Heimat mehr!

Edward's "Vagantenlieder" as well as his ballads and love
songs are very romantic. Many deal with the wonders of nature,
with meadows, gardens, rye fields, forests, flowers, asps, genista,
grass, with butterflies, birds, cats, larks, swans, deer, and with
the moon, the sun, and the stars.

LIED

Die Rose, die Deine Hand mir gab
In der froehlichen Zeit, im Mai,
Die ist laengst verwelkt und ihr Duft verweht,
Und der Fruehling ging vorbei.

Das Laub vermodert am Wegesrand
Und das raschelnde Gras verdorrt--
Nur heimlich in meines Herzens Grund
Blueht noch immer der Fruehling fort.

Dort singt noch immer die Nachtigall,
Dort gehen die Winde sacht,
Und der Flieder hinter dem Gartenzaun,
Der duftet die ganze Nacht.

Und ich wahre mein Herz vor Sturm und Frost
Und vor Alter und nagender Pein,
Und ich warte der Rosen, die
     dort bluehn,
Dass sie heimlich und still gedeihn.

Mein Herz ist an Schoenheit und
     Glueck so reich,
Wie ein ewiger sonniger Mai--
Und Dir bring' ich die
     bluehenden Rosen all,
Wenn Dein Fruehling dereinst vorbei.

All of the poems focus on the action of balladic stories or the joys
and longings of love; nowhere does the author try in the least to offer a criticism of modern problems or a didactic "message." He
seems to have written poetry for its own sake. Most of the poems

sound as if they had been composed several decades earlier; none of
them has been influenced by the fact that in the Europe of 1903 Naturalism was in its hey-day and Impressionism was gaining ground.

This symptom is not typical of Edward alone, but of large
parts of German-American writing in general. Nineteenth century
German-America often seems like an antedated Germany transplanted
in another country. American life and literature as well as the
latest European trends influenced the writers but little. The development of most German-American authors seems to have come to a
standstill the moment they left Germany.

Edward did not particularly like Chicago but he loved his occupation. On occasion he spoke before various audiences such as
one at Northwestern University in Evanston where he soon made the
acquaintance of some of the professors, in particular that of James
Taft Hatfield. This well-known historian of German literature had
tea with him every Thursday and constantly urged him to accept a
position at Northwestern, stating that he would speak on his behalf.
Edward refused until one night in 1900 Hatfield came to him in great
excitement and asked him to teach a class for another professor who
had suddenly been taken very ill. This time Edward could not decline, because the ailing professor was also one of his friends. And
thus he entered the teaching profession in which he remained until
the end of World War I. From 1911 on he lived in Evanston, Illinois. He describes the city's beautifully old-fashioned Puritan atmosphere in the second chapter of his novel, Komoedie des Lebens. [8]

Edward was one of the main speakers at the celebration which
Virginia State University held in 1909 in commemoration of the 100th
birthday of its famous student, Edgar Allan Poe. He talked about
the great admiration this American writer enjoyed in Germany and
was so successful that his photograph was printed in several Rich-
mond[9] papers and his lecture was published in The Book of the Poe
Centenary. [10] Furthermore, the University's president offered him
a summer school teaching position which he gladly accepted because
of his preference for Virginia over Illinois. During his first summer there he fell in love with the beautiful Lillie Bowman from Wil-
mington, North Carolina who was seventeen years his junior. They
married a few months later (in 1910), and the following summer
they travelled to Germany by way of Canada and England. Edward's
father was delighted with his beautiful daughter-in-law, who could not
speak a word of German. The young couple visited a number of
large cities including Berlin, Munich, and Frankfurt. In Munich
they spoke with Karl Wolfskehl at whose home they met with the
Darmstadt author Else Leuchs (a friend of Friedrich Gundolf) and also with Stefan George who had just arrived from Italy. George made
fun of the German-American writers and called Viereck an arrogant
fool. Edward and his young wife returned to America in September.
From New York Mrs. Edward went to see her parents and in her
first letter to her husband she complained about the reception she
had received by her relatives who had called her a liar when she
told them how beautiful Europe was.

The war years were a difficult period for Edward. At the beginning, when America had not yet entered the war, he tried to speak in behalf of Germany, but he met only with animosity. His wife proved loyal, his students behaved well, although on one occasion they wrote "Deutschland unter alles" on the blackboard. Edward disregarded this mischief and consequently the words remained there for several months. Edward's subsequent dismissal shortly before the armistice brought his university career to an end. The Edwards sold their house and went to live with the Bowmans in North Carolina. The subtropical climate there was unbearable to Edward and, being German, he met with great hostility. He and his wife returned to Chicago, took up residence again with the same English family, and Edward resumed his occupation as a journalist which he had never completely abandoned but had tried to keep secret.

One day the multi-millionaire, William S. Mason, offered him a position as a private librarian. Mason already owned a large Benjamin Franklin collection which he intended to present to the American people in order to make sure the public would recognize that Franklin had been "the greatest American who ever lived." For twelve years Edward held this position, with four girls and a young man as his assistants, traveling all over the United States to various book auctions. In the meantime, his wife had taken ill with multiple sclerosis and had to remain bed-ridden and paralyzed for two years until her death in 1928. Three years later Edward returned to Germany. His employer had lost millions of dollars during the depression and so he gave his Franklin Library to Yale University rather than bear the costs of housing and enlarging it. Edward sold his own valuable 6000-volume library to Northwestern University. After his return to Germany Edward no longer followed a profession, but lived a rather secluded life (with his 4000-volume library) writing a considerable number of poems, stories and novels. Before his death on July sixteenth of this year (five months before his hundredth birthday) he contributed several unpublished poems to the first selective anthology of German-American poetry, Deutsche Lyrik aus Amerika, published by the Literary Society Foundation in New York. 11

Characteristic of all of Edward's writings is their remoteness from the literary fashions of the time they were written. If his youthful poetry had already been little influenced by contemporary fashions and strife, his stay in America had meant a further loss of contact with the mainstream of German literature for which he did not compensate by an assimilation of American influences. 12 That, however, his gift as a writer did not wither in the foreign soil like that of so many other German-Americans, but that he transformed his disadvantage into the virtue of a timeless gracefulness, is Edward's great personal achievement. Even among his recent poetry we find those beautiful, simple "Lieder" that remind one of the best German Romanticism has created.

KLEINES LIEBESLIED

In meinem stillen Herzen
Ist eine Rose erblueht,
Luftige, duftige Traeume
Huschen durch mein Gemuet.

Ueber die blauen Berge,
Ueber das gruene Revier
Fliegen meine Gedanken,
Fliegen hinaus zu dir.

Weil du nicht ahnst, wie mein Herze
Heimlich sich sehnt und glueht,
Leg' ich mit wortlosen Gruessen
Dir meine Rose zu Fuessen,
Ehe sie welkt und verblueht.

A new note in the poetry of his old age are his frequent allusions to separation, illness, death and eternity.

WER FRAGT NACH MIR,
WENN ICH GESTORBEN BIN?

Wer fragt nach mir, wenn ich gestorben bin?
Das Gras wird ueber meinem Huegel wehen
Und Sterne werden nachts darueber stehen
Und Wolken gleiten lautlos drueber hin.

Und Frieden weit umher. Kein Laermen dringt
Zu mir hinab und stoert mir meinen Schlummer,
Nur eins erbittert mich und macht mir Kummer,
Dass ich's nicht hoere, wenn die Drossel singt.

His prayers have a profound, unpretentious beauty.

TAEGLICHES GEBET

Herr Gott, der du die Zuflucht aller bist
Die einsam sind und schwer am Leben tragen,
Goenn' ihnen eine kurze Gnadenfrist,
Damit sie stille sind und nicht verzagen.

Sie schleppen sich dahin mit ihrer Last
Und Tag fuer Tag ist es dasselbe Leben,
Und Tag fuer Tag kein Ruhen, keine Rast,
Du aber, Herr, Kannst ihnen Freude geben.

Lass' frei von Kummer ihre Herzen sein
Und trage sie empor auf deinen Armen,
Lass' alle Wesen ohne Schmerzen sein,
Der du die Liebe bist und das Erbarmen.

New in the poetry created during the second half-century of
Edward's life is his tendency to deal with contemporary problems.
Frequently he expresses his skepticism about modern technology and
praises natural life. Here, too, he reminds one of a romantic author when he contrasts the city with its bad morality, its dirt, noise,
and high prices to the comforting and soothing joys of nature and
rural life.[13] Often in this context Edward refers to America: big
cities with their disadvantages are, if anything, even worse in the
New World.

> Nun sind wir endlich in der grossen Stadt,
> Die mehrere Millionen Menschen hat,
> Wo hohe Haeuser in die Wolken ragen
> Und wo die Menschen schwer am Leben tragen.
>
> Und alles rennt umher und laermt und schreit
> Und niemand goennt sich nur ein Weilchen Zeit
> Denn alle haben sie nur eins im Sinn:
> Erfolg und Geld und bleibenden Gewinn.
>
> Sie hatten grade einen Feiertag,
> Revolver hoert man krachen Schlag auf Schlag,
> Die Nebelhoerner draussen in der Bucht,
> Die stimmen ein und heulen voller Wucht.
>
> Und Autos hupen ohne Unterlass,
> Man merkt, der Bloedsinn macht den Leuten Spass,
> Am tollsten aber treibt es doch die Jugend,
> Auch hierzulande kennt sie keine Tugend.[14]

Also new in Edward's poetry is the abundance of exotic themes
which occur only occasionally in his early writings.

MARTINIQUE

> Schwarze Lilien auf goldenem Grund,
> Palmen und Pinien mit silbernen Zweigen,
> Zwoelf Musikanten, die floeten und geigen,
> Dahinter ein Vollmond, rosig und rund--
>
> Zwoelf Musikanten floeten und geigen,
> Ein Maedchen tanzt zu der Melodie,
> Sie reckt die braunen, gelenkigen Glieder
> Und hebt das Kleid bis zum seidenen Knie:
>
>> "O Land, wo die purpurnen Stroeme sind,
>> Wo das Blut wie Wein in den Adern kreist,
>> Wo die Liebe kommt wie der Sommerwind
>> Und das Glueck sich nicht bangt und nicht
>> Suende heisst--"
>
> Zwoelf Musikanten floeten und geigen,
> Kraushaarige Koepfe nicken zum Takt,

Das Maedchen tanzt geschmeidig und nackt,
Eine schwarze Lilie auf goldenem Grund--
Die Maenner sitzen und schauen und schweigen,
Und der Mond grinst herunter, gluehend und rund.

Edward's first stories were written at the beginning of the
second half century of his life. Die Insel Antilla, eine Sommerge-
schichte[15] was composed by the fifty-year-old author as the fruit of
his stay at the home of in-laws in North Carolina. Since then,
works in prose have comprised the greater part of his writing. He
has composed thirty-four novels, only four of which have been printed, and forty-nine stories, a large number of which has appeared
in newspapers and periodicals.[16]

The poem quoted above, "Martinique," stems from the novel
Passatwind,[17] Edward's most poetic work in prose. It is full of exotic charm; the harmony of nature pervades it as a secret stream.
The action is centered around the beautiful daughter of a planter.
With but a few exceptions Edward's stories portray such delightful
young women of exciting beauty and animal-like innocence.[18] The
heroine of Die chinesische Sklavin (1940) has legally been free for a
long time, but she stays with her rich master because the thought
of freedom is alien to her mentality. Even after her enforced liber-
ation through a defender of justice, who tries to explain to her the
joys of personal liberty, she returns to her master in the Chinese
section of Chicago despite the fact that often he beat and kicked her.
Die Gazelle is a seductive negress with ravishing beauty. She loves
Elmer, a young negro, but is raped by a brutal, relentless white
farmer. Finally she manages to find her way back to Elmer who in
utter despair at the thought of his lost love is in the act of com-
mitting suicide. Die Flucht aus Cayenne narrates the flight of
brave young Lucien Jusserand from the French penal colony. In the
jungle he meets a beautiful negress who takes him over the river
that separates Cayenne from Brazil, but they are captured by the
girl's father who returns Lucien to the colony. Belatedly the father
learns that the prisoner had lied to him about his name and that
Lucien was the man who many years before had saved his daughter's
life. Der Hafen von Mombasa contrasts the healthiness and morality of native customs with the grotesque, devastating results of mission work. The story is centered around the love of a white salesman in colonial Africa for a tribesgirl. In Die kleine Tai Yue und
der Fischhaendler a Dutch-American fish merchant falls in love with
a Chinese girl in a San Francisco teahouse. He marries her, but
is too coarse to understand her fine poetic nature. Because he also
does not bother to learn her native tongue, she tricks him into being
the messenger between her and her lover, a young Chinese student,
with whom she eventually runs away. The last sentence of the story
humorously gives the lesson.

Ja, ja, wenn einer die Sprache seiner Frau nicht versteht!
wiederholte der Ladensbesitzer, zwinkerte lustig mit den
schwarzen Schlitzaugen und leerte sein Glas Reiswein bis
zur Neige.

Moschusrose deals with the tragic relationship of a colonial officer
with a Chinese slavegirl. Again the European's lack of understanding for local customs leads to catastrophic consequences for the native.   The destructive influence of the white man is again visible in
the brutal actions of two slave hunters in Tropenzauber.

All of the tropical stories take place in a mostly peaceful
colonial atmosphere.   The natives are the innocent, moral, good
characters; the Caucasians are only good when they show empathy,
when they change their way of thinking in order to understand the
natives.   In most cases they do not bother to do so and therefore
destroy natural harmony and innocence.

Apart from his prose form, the contents and themes of Edward's later works stand in great contrast to the creations of his
youth.   Most obvious are the scenery and the characters.   Whereas
the action of the early poetry usually takes place in North European
countries with Nordic characters, Edward now writes about the
Americas and even more frequently about exotic people and countries.

Although the novel Wenn die Wasser toben is set in different
surroundings (a small German city) the main characters and the
problems are the same as in Edward's other stories.   The novel begins with the return of a young German, Gerd Scheffauer to his
hometown after a decade-long stay in America and a trip around the
world.   His first impression of the old German town is that hardly
anything has changed in the decade he has been away: "alles machte
einen kleinlichen, beschraenkten Eindruck."   In his welcome toast,
the young man's father frowns upon the "looseness" of American
customs and laws and expresses his hope that his son will find his
way back to the decent way of life practiced by the family.   This
bourgeois self-righteousness repulses Gerd who recognizes that his
father's "buergerliche Ehre und buergerliche Moral" are nothing but
a superficial facade for a man who had sowed his wild oats when
young and who now is grasping for an excuse to justify his loss of
inventiveness and enterprising spirit.   Gerd Scheffauer's attitude toward the narrowmindedness of the society he stems from seems to
parallel that of Edward himself:

> Das Schwerfaellige, Eigenwillige und Anmassende das er
> frueher an sich hatte, war laengst bei ihm verschwunden,
> er hatte gelernt, dass das Leben etwas unbeschreiblich
> Vielseitiges und Verworrenes ist und die Menschheit sich
> aus Millionen von Wesen zusammensetzt, deren Eigenart
> ebensolviel Gutes aufzuweisen hat, wie die Eigenart des
> Volkes, dem er entsprossen war.   Er war mit allen
> moeglichen Nationen und Rassen in Beruehrung gekommen
> und hatte gelernt, jeder einzelnen Gerechtigkeit widerfahren
> zu lassen.   Fuer den engherzigen Standpunkt von Menschen,
> die nie ueber das Weichbild ihrer Heimat hinausgekommen
> waren, besass er laengst kein Verstaendnis mehr.

Throughout the story the hero revolts against the narrow prejudices
of his hometown and contrasts them with the pleasant freedom of
American cities where no one troubles his neighbor with idle gossip.[18] The story ridicules the conservative bourgeoisie of the little
German town who complain: "Die Verwilderung der Sitten, die bei
uns eingerissen ist, stammt geradeswegs aus Amerika."

Gerd is skeptical about America, too, especially so far as
female attempts to lighten his pocketbook are concerned:

> Die vier Maedchen, die er zu Gaste hatte, erinnerten ihn
> an die huebschen amerikanischen Maedchen, die zuweilen
> mit ihm in Neuyork zu Abend gespeist hatten.   Aber weiter
> ging der Vergleich nicht, denn die klugen Amerikanerinnen
> nutzten ihn aus, waehrend die deutschen Maedchen nicht
> einmal an eine solche Moeglichkeit auch nur dachten.   Es
> war der Unterschied zwischen zwei Welten.

The hero falls in love with the charming blonde beauty Asta,
contemplates marrying her, but then receives a letter from Jarifa,
a young lady who had become his mistress during his stay in North
Carolina and had later joined him in New York.   Gerd moves out of
his parents' house into an apartment and rents the next-door apartment for Jarifa.   His mistress is another one of Edward's exotic
ladies: she was born on an island in the Gulf of Mexico as a poor
fisherman's daughter.   Gerd possesses no prejudices:

> ... er freute sich darueber, dass fuer ihn die Menschen
> einfach Menschen waren und dass er sich nicht fuer besser
> hielt als die Angehoerigen fremder Rassen und Farben.
> Er kannte keine Vorurteile, deshalb besass er jenen Reich-
> tum an Erfahrung und jenes Verstaendnis fuer die Schoen-
> heit und Vielseitigkeit des Lebens, die den Leuten ewig
> fremd bleiben muessen, die sich in Ueberheblichkeit und
> Beschraenktheit ueber andere erhaben fuehlen.

We are told that Jarifa looks strikingly different from the German
townspeople.   The novel leaves us, however, in the dark about her
exact race.   In the stories that do tell us that the heroine is Chinese, African, Negro, South American Negro, etc., the race is in-
cidental and generally is alluded to as "non-European" or "native."
These characters are usually more types than individuals; Edward's
interest seems to be more concentrated upon the action and the
"message" of his stories than upon character-drawing.

As in the narratives, the unsophisticated young lady is superior to the European who is hampered by a thousand limitations
and conventions:

> ... das Seltsame dabei war, dass er immer das Gefuehl
> hatte, dass Jarifa unabhaengiger, freier und vielseitiger sei
> als er, weil ihre Herkunft ihr nicht die Beschraenkungen
> auferlegte, die ihm durch Herkommen, Erziehung und

Vorurteile auferlegt waren. Eine dunkle Ahnung sagte ihm,
dass sie ihm trotz allem ueberlegen sei, weil sie sich
nicht gebunden fuehlte und keine Ruecksichten zu nehmen
brauchte, waehrend er neimals vergessen durfte, wer und
was er war.

Gerd's illicit relationship meets with great resistance and en-
mity from his family, friends, and acquaintances with the exception
of Asta. In order to fight the impudence of their prejudices he marries Jarifa. Even after the marriage, however, the young lady is
socially ignored and constantly harassed. The impending crisis finally reaches its most acute stage when out of a dispute over his
wife, Gerd receives a challenge to a duel with a local lawyer. Jarifa is afraid that her beloved Gerd might be killed and feels guilty
that she should be the source of so much trouble for him. She voluntarily ends her life by taking poison. Even this tragic event is
received by the community with further malicious gossip. Gerd
takes Jarifa's ashes to her native island, then goes on a world trip
until he finds peace in India. In the end he comes back to Asta and
they leave together for a foreign country.

Edwards' technique of narration is a straightforward narrative
report of action and dialogue. He seldom delves into the deeper
thoughts and feelings of his characters and he uses modern tech-
niques such as the indirect interior monologue and stream-of-con-
sciousness only sparingly. Edward does not work from an outline,
rather the structure of his works develops naturally from spontaneous beginnings. The clarity and profundity of his message is mir-
rored by the clear and straightforward language. Nothing that he has
ever written appears forced or artificial. He draws the world as he
has experienced it, allowing the problems to emerge organically
from the flow of the narration.

The "message" of Edward's prose works is the same as that
of his later poetry: he stresses the Rousseauesque idea that nature
is good and beautiful, civilization is bad and corruptive. In Wenn
die Wasser toben as in all of his exotic stories the native girl possesses a pure heart and is elevated above the narrowminded, vicious
Europeans. Western civilization overcomes by means of its brutal-
ity and malice. It destroys natural innocence, beauty, and purity.
Edward fought vigorously the self-righteousness and prejudices of
Europeans and Americans who look down upon other races. His stories and novels show a deep natural humor, a great heart, and a
great knowledge of the world. The most obvious influence that his
long stay in the United States had upon Georg Edward seems to have
been the acquiring of a wider viewpoint, a greater understanding for
human beings of other races and customs than his own, a more intense feeling for the necessity of human tolerance and understanding.

Notes

1.   Most of the biographical facts reported in this article stem from

special information which Georg Edward kindly supplied in his
extensive correspondence with the "Society for German-American Studies. "

2. The popular ballad "Edward, Edward" from Percy's Reliques of
Ancient English Poetry (translated by Herder and Platen;
Heine borrowed a line for his "Die Grenadiere") may have
had some influence upon the change--or rather, the simplifi-
cation-- of the author's name which became official in 1903.

3. Cf. G. Edward, "Stefan George in Giessen," Hessische Heimat,
VII (1964).

4. From this time on the magazine printed Edward's poems until it
ceased publication after its 35th volume.

5. Georg Edward, Balladen und Lieder, Verlag Baumert & Ronge
(Grossenhain und Leipzig, 1897).

6. Balladen und Lieder, 2. vermehrte Aufl., Concordia Deutsche
Verlags-Anstalt (Berlin, 1903).

7. This poem was subsequently reprinted in G. A. Neef, Vom Lande
des Sternenbanners (Ellensville, N.Y., 1905), Das Buch der
Deutschen in Amerika, ed. Max Heinrici (Philadelphia, 1909),
and Robert E. Ward, Deutsche Lyrik aus Amerika (N.Y.,
1969).

8. The manuscript of this novel is in the possession of the Society
for German-American Studies.

9. The city in which Poe had grown up.

10. University of Virginia, 1909.

11. Op. cit.

12. Edward's conservative attitude in poetry is expressed most ex-
plicitly in Das Schwanenlied (Bruehlsche Universitaetsdruckerei, Giessen, 1964, pp. 28-29).

13. Especially in Das Schwanenlied, pp. 18-19, 16-17, 40-41, and
in: "Das Zwanzigste Jahrhundert (Amerika)" in Dreizehn
Gedichte fuer Gustel Wagner zum Geburtsag am 14. April
1967, Bruehlsche Universitaetsdruckerei (Giessen, 1967), pp.
17-30.

14. Das Schwanenlied, pp. 46-47.

15. Printed by the Hamburger Nachrichten in 1923.

16. After his ninetieth birthday Edward deposited fifty of his unpublished novels and narratives with the Stadtbibliothek Fried-
berg. Some of the titles are: Weisse Schatten (13 exotic
stories), Die Seele Aethiopiens, Sklavenblut, Der Eidechsen-
bruch, Bis an den Abgrund, Die Dschungel, Juanita Marquina,
Der Oktavone, Der Garten vor der Stadt, Der Hellseher, Ora
Dabney, Hochsommer, Die Santa-Maria-Plantage, Schloss
Falkenstein.

17. Drei-Masken-Verlag, Muenchen und Berlin, 1928; English version: The Naked Island, 1929.

18. Edward's negress-figures bear striking similarities to Theodor
Storm's character Jenni (Von Jenseit des Meeres, 1867). In
his article, "Storm and Sealsfield" The Germanic Review,
VII (1933), 178-182, L.A. Shears points to the influence of
Sealsfield's Pflanzerleben und die Farbigen on Storm. It is
interesting to note that Storm's Jenni is the only one of his
exotic types who is not characterized in a negative fashion.

See Robert E. Ward, <u>The Theme of Foreignness in the Works</u>
<u>of Theodor Storm</u>, Diss. (Vanderbilt University, 1967).   All
of Storm's other foreigners and half-foreigners of the "southern type" disturb the lives of his North German heroes.
Conversely, Edward has his foreign-types suffering under the
"achievements" of Western civilization.

28. GEORG SYLVESTER VIERECK: AN APPRECIATION*

Ludwig Lewisohn

Among the many more or less exotic literary phenomena to which our peculiar social conditions have given rise, no other is so interesting, or of such intrinsic value as the poetry written by German emigrants in their new homes beyond the sea. From the time when the first German settlers came to Pennsylvania to the present day, there has never been a time when men and women of German birth, living in the United States, have not yielded to this singularly unselfish impulse of song. Singularly unselfish, for they had at the best but little hope of any audience; of visible recompense for their work none at all. And from their work it would be possible to form a small anthology of really admirable German verse. But it is only within very recent years that German-American poetry can show work that no longer permits itself to be neglected. I do not speak of the work of such men as Dr. Ernst Henrici, of Baltimore; or Professor Hugo Münsterberg, of Harvard. They had established a reputation before, in riper years, they came to America. It is the poetry of two men--Konrad Nies, of St. Louis, and George Sylvester Viereck, of New York, the author of the present collection-- that deserves, or rather demands, the attention and appreciation of those of us who understand the language in which they write. The more so, as the fate of the German poet in America is not without elements of pathos. His audience here is of the smallest; the fatherland, with its plethoric literary market, will hardly heed him. Influences of many kinds are against him, and Nies created a phrase of tragic truthfulness when he called German-American poetry "Roses in the Snow."

Nies is the older poet, and in some respects the more accomplished. But Viereck is not only the more modern, but likewise offers the almost unparalleled phenomenon of a poet who has formed himself exclusively on the literary traditions of one language, and yet is compelled, in creative work, to use another. He is, therefore the only real German-American poet, and deserves our attention not only on account of the high intrinsic value of his best work but because he offers a significant illustration of the strange possibilities of our American civilization.

All these peculiarities of his fate and fortune--his early re-

---

*Reprinted from Georg Sylvester Viereck, Gedichte. (New York: Progressive Printing Co., 1904).

moval from the land of his birth, his indebtedness to English poetry,
and the ultimate possibility of his becoming a poet in that language
to which so many profound sympathies attract him--all these things
Viereck has embodied in an English sonnet which shows that he has
a mastery over that language attained by no other German-American
poet.   This self-interpretative sonnet it will be well to quote:

> Beyond the sea a land of heroes lies,
>   Of faery heaths and rivers, mountains steep
>   O'ergrown with vine; her memory I shall keep
> Most dear; her heritage most dearly prize.
> But lo, a lad I left her, and mine eyes
>   Fell on the sea-girl mistress of the deep,
>   When first my boy's heart heard as in a sleep,
> The choral walls of rythmic beauty rise.
>
> O, lyric England, thee I call mine own,
>   With lyre and lute and wreath I come to thee,
>   Thine is the realm of song as of the sea,
> And thy mouth's speech is heard from zone to zone.
>   Turn not in scorn thine ivied brow from me,
> Who am a suppliant kneeling at thy throne.

Georg Sylvester Viereck was born in Munich, December 31,
1884.   His father is a late member of the "Reichstag," who has
done much since his residence in America to promote cordial relations between the two countries; his mother is an American lady, a
native of California.   In Munich young Viereck attended a public
school, and, after removal to Berlin in 1895, a gymnasium.   Late
in the year 1897 his father took up his residence definitely in America.   He now began to write verse which was almost from the beginning unusually adequate in regard to perfection of form.   It will
be seen then that Viereck has passed those years of his life which
really count in his artistic development on this side of the Atlantic.
He is now a student at the College of the City of New York.

It may seem strange at first sight that one should concern
himself seriously with the life and poetry of a lad who has not yet
completed his twentieth year.   I do not hesitate to do so in view of
his extraordinary maturity, and of the high and strange quality of his
best poetic work.   With this, too, his personality is in accord.
Something elfish and weird there is about him; an atmosphere like
that of some exotic flower.   It needs the subtlest sympathy to penetrate to the essential humanity that lies hidden, to recognize the mature and serious artist in this defiant, engaging, and at times irri-
tating boy.   A slight affectation of cynicism and of worldly wisdom
sits not ungracefully upon him, but one forgets and forgives it easily
enough in view of the passionate sincerity of his best poems.   For
of one thing there is no doubt.   Viereck has lived these poems of
his.   He is no callow youth who embodies unutterable nothings in
flowing verse.   His experience of life is extremely narrow in range,
but within certain limits it has been intense.

The only German influence that came to Viereck was that of
Heine.   But that influence faded soon enough, and the poems written
under it do not count.   Next came Poe, and for some time the young
poet adapted Poe's artistic effects with great delicacy to the needs
of the German language.   But it was Swinburne who struck the fire
from him, and through whose saner work he came in touch with the
great traditions of English poetry.   Rossetti influenced him slightly,
but profoundly and enduringly the poignant pathos, the plangent ten-
derness of the singer of the "Ballad of Reading Gaol." In a word,
then, Viereck is a member of the decadent school of English poetry,
who, by a strange play of fate, uses the German language.

Let me hasten to add that I use the word decadent in no de-
tracting sense, but merely to indicate a certain literary atmosphere.
Catullus was a decadent, and so, in many respects, were Heine and
Shelley; and to give to the word a merely opprobrious sense is entirely uncritical.   For all that, the limitations of this kind of poetry
and its defects, both of which Viereck shares to the fullest extent,
are obvious.   The best and greatest poetry deal largely, sanely and
nobly with man, nature and human life.   Decadent poetry deals in-
tensely and often with unforgettable charm, but often too with a deplorable lack of sanity and measure with certain small segments of
the great arch of human life, segments which do not face the stars,
but are in the shadow of the earth.   But after all, we of the earth
are earthy.   Passion has its supreme rights, and to have added
a new and striking note to the large chorus of human passion is
Viereck's praise and the excuse, if such be needed, for speaking of
his poetry.   I shall here concentrate attention upon a limited group
of Viereck's poems; those, namely, in which his originality comes
out most clearly, and which illustrate the formal perfection of his
work at its best.   The English renderings of certain passages which
follow are my own.

"Hadrian" is indubitably the first poem to be noted.   In it
Viereck does homage to the spirit of Greek life and art.   The emperor is weary of splendor and power.   One thing alone can solace
him, "love immortalized by art." And hence they bring to him the
marble statue of the dead Antinous.   All things will pass away, but
this endures.   Thou, says the emperor:

> Thou in the realm of marble and of song
> Livest forever.

And the young poet adds an epilogue in honor of universal loneliness,

> Whether the star of beauty has arisen
> In Greece or Galilee.

It is easily said, but the weight of twenty Hebraic centuries is not
to be cast off by a word.   The old conflict reappears, embodied with
a richness of poetic effect, a subtle harmony of color and sound
which no translation can give.   Thus in "Confession" the life of the
senses has lost its Greek joy and freedom, and has become an evil
siren:

        I know of an odorous palm-forest,
            Filled with mysterious murmurings,
        Where in the glow of the crimson West
            A brilliant song bird sobs and sings.
        He sings a song that makes mad the soul,
            Makes heavy the heart within our breast,
        And who this evil song has heard
            Forever forfeits peace and rest.

Nor does Viereck stop here.   The pendulum swings back through the
whole arc.   What is in some respects his most impressive poem is
essentially a prayer that the scarlet flower of love be slain.   I will
not do "Maria Hilf" the injustice of rendering any part of it into English.   The heavy lines are like hammer-blows; they rise once or
twice to a tragic strength, a terrible directness of expression which
I do not know where to parallel in their own kind.

            Ich bin ans Kreuz geschlagen,
            Ans Kreuz der bösen Lust,
            Durch all die bösen Wunsche
            In meiner eignen Brust.

Once again Viereck embodied the great conflict in a prayer before a
symbol of Christian faith.   "Before the Cross" is hardly less powerful and tragic than "Maria Hilf," even though it ends with a note of
peace.   I translate a single stanza:

            O give me of Thy body's bread,
                And of Thine awful wine,
            That in the grasp of bitter dread
                I may not ever pine.

            Roses of blood I bring to Thee,
                My heart it craves for grace,
            O Jesus of Gethsemane
                Turn not from me Thy face!

But there is no salvation.   The strange mystery of passion symbol-
ized in a dumb idol which stands in a gray temple, in a dim far
land, shall remain.   The idol is without mercy.   Kings in the splendor of their purple, priests in the robes of holy offices--all are pil-
grims to that shrine and its idol.

            Thus shall it stand for evermore,
                Until the fateful trumpet's call,
            When all the lands and oceans o'er
                The twilight of the idols fall.

In all these poems Viereck universalizes the facts of his own experience, and thus they acquire a significance somewhat greater than
those in which he is more narrowly himself.   He has few poems on
the triumph of love, unless it be "Liebesnacht," a powerful study in
elemental passion.   His poetic imagination is essentially sombre, and

in hardly any other poem does he strike so gentle a note as in the
tender regret of "Die rote Blume." This poem is interesting, furthermore, for the admirable technical skill with which it makes the
somewhat unbending German flow in a liquid meter. It is easily
adapted to English translation, and I may therefore give two stanzas:

It was in the days, in the days of the roses,
    When under thy kisses my sorrow was sped;
Now Autumn blossoms the field encloses,
    And Autumn blossoms enwreath our head.
And love and rejoicing and May are dead,
And the world is windy and waste and wide;
    The days of the roses have long since fled,
And the scarlet flower of love has died.

We two of the honey of love have eaten,
    Have drunk deep draughts of the gold sunshine;
But the key of the grove we were wont to meet in,
    Where bloomed that flower as red as wine,
    Is lost in some magical land divine,
No refuge our love has, no place to abide,
    In our grove dwells the Autumn 'mid woodland and vine,
And the scarlet flower of love has died.

"When Idols Fall," in which Viereck returns to his note of
tragic regret, cannot be disfigured by translation. Certain it is that
no other poet of his years has ever expressed with such passionate
sincerity one of the deepest and most frequent tragedies of human
life. The idols of our hearts fall into the dust; the halo with which
our love crowned them fades into the light of common day, and yet,
love cannot die. It is the old cry of Catallus:

Nunc te cognovi: quare etsi impensius uror,
    Multo mi tamen es vilior et levior.

But in Viereck's poem the cry deepens. It is an arraignment at the
judgment bar of love, and a condemnation--no less beautiful than
tragic. "Die Sphinx" is a large and rich symbolic expression of
those mysterious elements in human life which attract Viereck, and
which he interprets always with the power that comes of real insight. "Das Lächeln der Sphinx" is a sustained exercise of subtle
fancy, full of a weird transfiguration of common things; and in
"Prinz Carneval" a sad and serious thought gives weight to the swift
movement of bacchic verse.

In his most recent poems Viereck returns to the fruitful practice of using his own experience as a mere symbol for the universal
experience of mankind. Of these poems the most remarkable and
sustained is "Aiogyne," the eternal woman. The lover and his mistress are alone, and he speaks:

We are alone, are quite alone,
    Under the heavy canopy;

> Only the crimson light far-thrown
> From the dim lamp gleams fitfully.
> Now passion's rites have all been paid,
> Lean back in silence, gently, thus--
> Until my dreaming eyes have strayed
> O'er your white beauty luminous.

And as he gazes upon her mysterious beauty, she becomes to him in
that weird mood the eternal woman, good and evil, though oftener
evil than good.   It was she who penitent dried the Lord's feet with
her fragrant hair, but it was also she of whose monstrous sins the
world rings.

> Es tobte wilde Liebesgier,
> Heiss unter deines Busens Schnee,
> Du nahmst beim Horn den weissen Stier,
> Denkst du noch dran--Pasiphaë?

She was Herodias and Messaline, but the eternal years have left her
body faultless in beauty and her mystery unsolved.

> What nameless lust, what stranger woes
> Once moved thee I will not recall--
> Thine everlasting beauty glows
> More argent than the first snowfall.
> Lean back in all thy loveliness,
> Mine eyes would on thy beauty feed;
> A fool who would thy secret guess,
> And who has guessed it, poor indeed!

This poem is especially remarkable for the concrete historical imagination displayed in it, for the stately simplicity of its form, and
for that which is at all times a distinguishing characteristic of Viereck's poetry--rich and sonorous vowel-music.

Viereck's technique is at all times admirable.   Nothing could
be better than the effects of tragic solemnity which he extracts from
the simplest of German lyric meters, or his adaptations of difficult
and involved English forms.   But in truth, young as he is, he has
devoted himself to his art with great sincerity, and mature single-
ness of purpose.   And not the least service that he has rendered it
is his excellent translation of the "Ballad of Reading Gaol."   Art is
to him the great liberator from the trammels of material life, and
in his imagination it is art that gives a soul to the world's history.
I may translate a single stanza from his dithyrambic poem "Die
Kunst":

> Upon the scene a sightless singer stands,
> Who Ilion sings--
> From Hellas and the Latian shore
> The sacred echo rings.
> In crimson splendor bursts the flame immortal, high and higher,
> For Sappho sings on Lesbos' strand, Catullus strikes his lyre.

> But from the depth of the ages
> Song does not rise alone;
> Before mine eyes a vision
> Blooms of the Parthenon;
> Visions of deathless marble
> Wrought by the hand of man,
> I see the argent limbs that were
> Beloved of Hadrian.

The defects of Viereck's poetry I have already indicated, in speaking of the school to which he belongs. The best poetry cannot be written without a far profounder realization of the beauty and terror, the splendor and solemnity of the external world; without a keener consciousness of those great issues of human life and destiny which transcend even love. But within his own limits Viereck is a true poet. He has originality, he has power, he has imagination, and his extreme youth gives his talents large possibilities of development.

29. THE LAST CINCINNATI GERMAN POET:
HEINRICH H. FICK*

Don Heinrich Tolzmann

Between 1840 and the advent of World War I Cincinnati was
a mecca for German-American culture. German immigrants and
their American offspring succeeded in transplanting German culture
to America and in creating a unique hybrid culture called German-
America or Little Germany. Little Germany was a community in
which German customs, traditions and language were maintained with
Teutonic precision. German-America attained its cultural zenith before World War I and reached its greatest fruition in Cincinnati.
It was so Germanized that every state had consular representation
in the Queen City. [1]

When Heinrich H. Fick arrived in Cincinnati in the 1860s he
found an impressive German-American community. There were
German newspapers (Der Christliche Apologete, Das Volksblatt, Der
Volksfreund, Freie Presse, Die Morgenpost), forty-one German
churches, seven German bookstores, three German-American private
libraries (Turngemeinde, Männerchor, and Arbeiterbund collections)
and the public library stocked a German collection which by the
1880s numbered 10,000. [2] German singing societies abounded: the
Männerchor, the Harugari-Männerchor, the Helvetie-Männerchor and
the Cincinnati-Sängerbund. And then there was "Over the Rhine"
where "everything is German and even the American discards his
formality and envelops himself in German Gemütlichkeit." [3] Here in
1859 the Turners had built the Turnhalle, a central point of social
life considered "a mighty fortress of German-American culture." [4]
In "Over the Rhine" one found the Arbeiter-Halle, the Männerchor-
Halle, Heuck's, Schickling's and the other German theaters, Wiel-
ert's Pavillion and "everywhere it is gemütlich in 'Over the
Rhine'." [5]

Alongside the fun and frolic of "Over the Rhine" blossomed
some serious attempts at establishing German-American literature.
Ohio had already been the home of two famous German authors:
Nikolaus Lenau and Friedrich Gerstäcker. [6] The Cincinnati Germans
were inspired to write. More volumes of German-American prose
and poetry were written in Cincinnati than in any American city.
There were scores of authors: Christian Burkhalter, Clemens Hammer, Adolf Bauer, Johann Bernhard Stallo, Gustav Brühl, Gotthard

*Reprinted from the Journal of German-American Studies 11:1
(1976): 1-16, by permission of the publisher.

Deutsch, Friedrich Hassaurek, Friedrich Hecker, Constantin Grebner, Franz Pauly, Oskar Braun, Phillip von Gemmingen--the list is
almost endless.[7] However, German-America's greatest poet and
scholar, Heinrich A. Rattermann, towered over them all. He had
co-founded the German Literary Club of Cincinnati on November 27,
1877, with Wilhelm Müller and Emil Rothe to further German-American literature.[8] German-American art thrived here also. W. J.
Baer, John Hauser, Henry F. Farny, Leopold Fettweiss and others
painted, sculpted and created in Zinzinnati.[9] When Fick arrived in
1864 he found a thriving and stimulating German-American community.

          Heinrich Hermann Adolf Fick was born August 16, 1849, in
Lübeck, Germany, where he attended the internationally known
Grossheimsche Schule. Here he developed an intense interest for
language, history and literature.[10] In 1864, three years after the
death of his father, Fick immigrated to New York where he had
been offered a position in his uncle's business. He then moved to
Cincinnati to engage in a similar business venture as a salesman.
Dissatisfaction with the business world caused him to enter the
teaching profession after successfully passing the entrance exams.
In 1870 he was appointed as a teacher of German and taught at an
elementary school. Because of his artistic talent he also gave art
instruction. Fick gave tremendous impetus to the art program in
the public schools. In 1872 an art exhibit was sent to the Vienna
Exposition and the report of the Commissioner of Education ex-
claimed that Cincinnati "had gained an enviable reputation in this
branch."[11] By November, 1878, Fick had been appointed Superintendent of Drawing, a position he held until 1884. Under Fick's su-
perintendency a knowledge of drawing was made one of the qualifica-
tions for a regular teacher's certificate. In 1884 he published <u>Pen-
cil And Brush; An Introduction to the Elementary Principles of
Graphic Representation</u> for the use of students and teachers in Cincinnati's schools.

          In 1884 Fick moved to Chicago where he wrote for the Chi-
cago German press and gave private instructions in German and art.
In Chicago he met and courted a highly-educated German teacher,
Clementine Barna. After their marriage they established a German-
English school with Louis Schutt. The school became well-known
and attracted pupils from across the Midwest. Fick soon became
the director of the school, but returned to Cincinnati in 1890 because
of a dispute with Schutt. He then studied at Ohio University and
earned his Ph.D. degree in 1892. From that year until 1901 Fick
was the principal of the Sixth District School, from 1901 to 1903 he
was Assistant Superintendent of the Public Schools of Cincinnati and
from 1903 until 1918 Supervisor of German for the Public Schools.[12]

          Fick became nationally known for his contributions to the
teaching profession. He was elected seven times to the presidency
of the National German-American Teacher's Association which had
its central office in Milwaukee at the German-American Teachers'
Seminary.[13] The Teachers' Seminary was a four-year college that

educated students to become teachers of the Germanic languages and
literatures. It stemmed from the Annual Convention of the National
German-American Teacher's Association where Fick, as secretary
of the Convention, helped to lead the move to establish a German-
American teacher's college.

The Teacher's Association was formed in August, 1870 in
Louisville by 117 teachers of German.[14] The activities of the Association "were marked by significant discussions of pedagogical
problems and the publication of a journal of high quality."[15] At the
1874 Detroit Convention Adolf Douai, Mathilde Anneke, Fick, and
others pushed for the creation of the German-American college which
finally opened in 1879 in Milwaukee as the National German-American Teachers' Seminary. Fick played a leading role in the creation
and direction of the Seminary. For forty years, until 1918 when
the anti-German hysteria of World War I caused it to close, Fick
was a member of the administrative board of the Seminary. As
president of the Teachers' Association, Fick devoted great attention
to building up the Seminary's curriculum and staff. Many of the nation's German teachers were educated at the Milwaukee college before World War I.

The high quality German-American educational journal issued
by the Teachers' Association was Fick's creation. He was co-editor
and then editor-in-chief for a total of thirty-five years of the Erziehungsblätter. It was the organ not only of the German-American
Teachers' Association but also of the German Teacher's Association
of Ohio. According to Karl Arndt, "This journal had some excellent
goals. It proposed to advance the interest of German language
teaching and the welfare of German teachers, promote German methods of developmental teaching, and to get rid of prison-like discipline, dry textbook instruction, insufficient salaries of teachers, and
to abolish annual elections of the teaching force."[16] The journal
was the forerunner of the present day Monatshefte für deutschen Unterricht, a publication of the German Department of the University of
Wisconsin. The First World War brought the Seminary to a temporary halt and it re-surfaced after the war as a unit of the German
Department of the University of Wisconsin. This heritage can be
traced directly to Fick.

Fick was quite well known among the teachers of German in
Cincinnati. As the Supervisor of German from 1903-18 he worked
closely with two Cincinnati teachers' groups: the German High
School Teachers' Association and the German Teachers' Association
of Cincinnati.[17] The German High School Teachers' Association met
every month for discussions and lectures on German language and
literature. Fick lectured and announced news of interest from the
school board. The German Teachers' Association also met monthly
for a program of music, song, lectures and discussions. All teachers of German in Cincinnati belonged to this association as did any
party interested in German instruction in the schools. Fick's presence and influence in both of these groups was all pervasive. Before the World War there were over two hundred and fifty German

teachers in the public schools of Cincinnati.[18] Fick's pedagogical
methods became known as the "Cincinnati Plan" and were introduced
in other public school systems in the U.S.   The plan consisted of
bi-lingual instruction at the elementary school level.[19]

There was an obvious need for instructional materials for this
German teaching program and Fick provided them.   He authored five
books for children studying German.   These books were widely used
in Ohio and other public schools in the U.S.   They contained poems,
stories and folk tales in an easy-to-read format.   Fick's German
language children's magazine was called Jung-Amerika and was published from December, 1901, to May, 1906, by Gustav Mueller in
Cincinnati.   It appeared monthly during the school year and contained
prose and poetry by Fick and his wife.   It also contained many items
written on Ohio and Cincinnati themes by such Cincinnati German authors as Rattermann, Constantin Grebner, Emil Kramer, Hermann
von Wahlde and others.   The children's magazine, hence, became a
vehicle of expression for German-American authors.[20]

German-American literature has "never had a Schiller, a
Goethe, a Lessing or a Heine."[21]   Nevertheless, some high quality
verse and prose were composed by Cincinnati German authors.
Fick swiftly acquired a reputation as one of the leading German-
American authors.   His poetry book, for example, found its way
"into many German-American homes."[22]   His poems were printed
on a regular basis in the various German papers in America.   Alfred Gorowicz wrote, "He belongs decidedly to the best German-
American poets."[23]

Fick belonged to that sublime group of sages who had united
to form the German Literary Club of Cincinnati.   This club aimed
at furthering German-American literature through lectures, writing
and publication.[24]   Over 1,700 meetings were held from 1877 to
1927 and the leading German-Americans spoke at some of them:
Udo Brachvogel, a New York German poet (1892); Dr. Julius Goebel,
chairman of the German-American Historical Society (1907); and Dr.
Kuno Francke, curator of the Germanic Museum at Harvard (1907).
Fick delivered many lectures and had a poem for almost every occasion.   On March 26, 1906, he gave the main speech at a special
service held to mourn the death of Carl Schurz.   Between the years
1878 and 1897 Fick gave fifty lectures on such various topics as:
"German-American Newspaper Names (Nov. 8, 1891)," "German-
American Original Poems (Nov. 30, 1892)," "A Stepchild of Our
Time: German-American Poetry (Oct. 25, 1893)," and "Poems By
Robert Reitzel (Nov. 21, 1894)."[25]   Most of Fick's lectures had already appeared as articles in German-American journals.

Another Cincinnati German group to which Fick belonged was
the German Pioneer Association of Cincinnati, a group of Cincinnati
Germans dedicated to preserving the documents and history of German-Americana for future generations.[26]   In its long history (1868-
1930s) the group had more than four thousand members.   The Association's journal Der Deutsche Pionier is considered the central

storehouse of information on German-Americana in the last century.
The Pioneer Association, like the Literary Club, met monthly to
discuss German-American history and culture.   Dr. Fick gave numerous talks at meetings of the Pioneer Association.   On April 6,
1899, he lectured on Theodor Kirchhoff, a California German poet,
and was then unexpectedly named honorary member of the Pioneer
Association.   Dr. Fick was also an honorary member of the Literary Club and the Cincinnati Turngemeinde.   Even after World War I
Fick continued to be quite active in the Pioneer Association.   On
March 4, 1922, he spoke on German-American dialect poetry.   An
observer wrote "It was a rare enjoyment to listen to the talk of a
skilled speaker, who himself is a giant amongst Columbia's
poets."[27]   The reports of the Pioneer Association, Vorstandsberichte,
carried Fick's poems until 1931.[28]   The poetry book In Freud und
Leid (1914) carried a selection of Dr. Fick's poetry.   A commentator said of the book: "These are the pearls of German-American
poetry.   Although many of these poems were already known to us,
we could not lay down the book until we had read it from beginning
to end ... it is pure gold--this collection.   It should not be missing
in any German family."[29]

Fick's poetry was so popular that he was invited to read his
poems at various German-American celebrations: at the Luther Celebration in the Music Hall (Nov. 4, 1883), at the Central Ohio Sängerfest in Springfield (June 17, 1884), at the Annual Convention of the
National German-American Teachers' Association (1889), at the German Teachers' Association of Cincinnati (April 23, 1898), at the
Turnverein in Indianapolis (August 27, 1899), the Cincinnati Turngemeinde (March 22, 1903) and at many other fests and occasions.[30]
The one poem of Fick's which was published repeatedly in the German-American press and in Germany was his "Das Lied, das meine
Mutter sang."[31]   It is a poem which is almost untranslatable and in-
comprehensible to the reader unfamiliar with German-American culture before World War I.

German-American literature is a neglected dimension of German literature.   It is an expression of an intellectual position in
which old (German) and new (American) cultural values unite to form
a new synthesis and as such offers a unique viewpoint on American
life.   German-American art is created by the artist in whom these
cultural values have attained a remarkable equilibrium.   A German-
American author writes from the perspective of his German-American world.   Cincinnati was a center for German-American culture.
Here the literature of a German-American poet could be defined, re-
fined, accepted or rejected.   The author grappled with the problem
of the synthesis of two cultural realms and the resultant hybrid cultural offspring: German-America.   The poems written by Cincinnati
German authors are crystallizations of their attempts at articulating
this new synthesis.   Fick was the greatest local proponent of this
new culture.   The following two poems demonstrate this.

DAS LIED, DAS MEINE MUTTER SANG

Früh von der Heimat musst' ich wandern,
Vom Elternhause lieb und traut;
Mich trieb's von einem Ort zum andern,
Ich hörte fremder Sprache Laut.
Doch in des Lebens regem Treiben,
Das seine Fesseln um mich schlang
Wird mir vor allem teuer bleiben
Das Lied, das meine Mutter sang.

WAHRT DEUTSCHES WESEN

Ach, immer selt'ner trägt zu diesen Fluren
Des Deutschtums beste Kraft der Wanderstab;
Doch rastlos müh'n die feindlichen Naturen
Der Widersacher gegen uns sich ab.
Nun gilt's, zu wahren schon errung'ne Güter,

Wenn nicht das Erbe sich verlieren soll,
Euch, die ihre standet als getreue Hüter
So oft des Wächters warnend Wort erscholl,
Euch tönt mein Ruf.

    The high point of Fick's career occurred in 1916 at an event
which could also be considered the zenith of German-Americana. On
May 16, 1916, in the Music Hall the seventy-fifth anniversary of the
introduction of the German language into the public schools of Cincinnati was celebrated with pomp and circumstance.   Dr. Heinrich
Fick, the chief architect of the German language program in Cincinnati, was the main speaker.   Every seat in the Music Hall was
filled.   On stage was an eight hundred member children's choir singing such songs as: "Der Mai ist gekommen," "Droben steht die
Kapelle," and "Ade, du lieber Tannenwald."   The oldest Cincinnati
German teacher, Marie Eichner, was presented with a bouquet of
flowers as was Dr. Fick who was seated on stage.   Then the program began with several regal organ selections played by Emilie
Borger-Weissmann.   Several songs were then sung by the Männerchor der Vereinigten Sänger.

    After these preliminaries W. Wienecke, President of the Ger-
man High School Teachers' Association of Cincinnati, spoke passion-
ately about the need to preserve the German language in Cincinnati.
He said that he wanted "to make the cultural values of the German
people accessible to our children.   That is our holy duty...."[32]
Under the direction of Gustav Clemens the children's choir sang
several more German folk songs.   The long program heightened the
excitement and solemnity of the occasion.   Dr. R. J. Condon, Superintendent of the Public Schools, gave a statistical overview of German instruction in Cincinnati since 1840.[33]   Then another solo was
sung: "Herzensfrühling" by Lillian Wuest.   After this Mayor George
H. Puchta spoke of the role of the Germans in Cincinnati's history:
"The influence of the Germans in this city through their splendid

congenial language..., their industry, thoroughness and ability for acquisition, their patriotism and love for home and friends, their inclination for music and art, their German culture have contributed so much to the present greatness of Cincinnati that so long as the Queen City exists the fame of the noble character of its German citizens will stand forever."[34]

Again the children's choir entertained and this time they sang Dr. Fick's well known poem "Das Lied, das meine Mutter sang." Dr. Fick then spoke about the history and meaning of German instruction in Cincinnati.[35] A silent audience listened "with true reverence" in a state of exultation as Fick spoke. He spoke "with a far sounding voice in a wonderful way."[36] It was the apex of Fick's career as a German-American teacher, poet and scholar. After his speech, some school choirs sang more German songs: "Sehnsucht nach dem Frühling," "Aus der Jugendzeit," "Die Lorelei," and "America." After the program the audience milled around in the foyer where Fick and Emil Kramer had arranged a display of seventy-eight pictures of the older Cincinnati German teachers. On May 21 a special dinner was held at the Gibson House to bring the celebration to a close. Dr. Max Griebsch, Director of the German-American Teachers' Seminary in Milwaukee, spoke as did Dr. Gotthard Deutsch of Hebrew Union College.

Germany's esteem in America deteriorated rapidly with the advent of World War I, and, as stated by Robert E. Ward, "... German-American institutions were dealt a deadly blow from which they have never recovered."[37] The German language was declared illegal in twenty-six states and German-Americans were unjustly persecuted.[38] It was a harsh blow to a man who had devoted his whole life to German instruction and to German-American culture. Dr. Fick did not, however, harbor any bitterness. He even censored German books during the World War for the public school system. And during the 1920s he kept active in German-American life, but after 1925 he withdrew "almost entirely" from public life. The other leading Cincinnati German, Heinrich A. Rattermann, died in 1923. With Fick's retirement and Rattermann's death the Cincinnati Germans lost two intellectual leaders. Dr. Fick spent his last years at the homes of his daughters in Indianapolis and in Chicago where he died March 23, 1935. He spent his last years creating archives and a library for future students of German-Americana.

Fick had written incessantly on German-American and Cincinnati German literature for many publications. In his last years he collected all his articles and put them together into several scrapbooks, the value of which is inestimable. The four volumes of his Ausflüge ins romantische Amerika (Cincinnati, 192..) contain Fick's articles about his travels across America. His Wir in Amerika (Cincinnati, 192..), also four volumes, is a mine of information about Cincinnati German scholars, teachers, authors and poets. A most valuable volume for literary studies is his Deutsche Dichter und Dichtung in Cincinnati (Cincinnati, 192..) which contains all his articles on the Cincinnati German poets. In 1924 he wrote his autobiography on Cincinnati German life entitled <u>Im Rahmen von sechs Jahrzehnten</u>, a one hundred and thirty-two page manuscript. For the study of German-American literature his <u>Bibliographie der deutsch-amerikanischen Schönliteratur</u> (Cincinnati, 192. .) is of great value. It is the only bio-bibliographical handbook of German-American literature in existence and contains data on three hundred and seventy-eight authors. In it Fick inserted numerous autographs, pictures and letters from dozens of German-American poets. [40]

Because of his position in the German-American community Fick personally knew most of the German-American authors of his time. He, therefore, amassed a library of their works which is one of the largest in the U.S. These rare volumes and materials were acquired for the University of Cincinnati Library in the early 1930s by Dr. Edwin Zeydel. [41] In 1974 this library officially became the H. H. Fick Collection of German-Americana and contains about 1,000 volumes of prose, poetry, manuscripts and literary periodicals. In it are most of the Cincinnati German imprints. The collection is a permanent monument and tribute to a man and his culture. [42]

THE WORKS OF H. H. FICK

A. Books and Monographs

1. Die Fürbitte der Unschuld, Erzählung, n.p. 1872.

2. Die Pflege des Schönheitssinnes in der Erzählung. Cincinnati: Rosenthal, 1880.

3. Was soll die Jugend lesen? Vortrag. Chicago: Franz Gendele Printing Co., 1880.

4. Aesthetic Culture. Cincinnati, 1881.

5. Lessing, der Bahnbrecher des deutschen Dramas. Cincinnati, 1881.

6. Eins aber ist noth. Milwaukee: Doerflinger, 1882.

7. Karakter und Gemüthsbildung der Jugend. Cincinnati, 1882.

8. Die Poesie in der deutschamerikanischen Schule. Cincinnati: Rosenthal, 1883.

9. Emanuel Geibel. Cincinnati, 1884.

10. Pencil and Brush: An Introduction to the Elementary Principles of Graphic Representation. Cincinnati: W. E. Dibble, 1884.

11. Die Pädagogie unserer Dichtergrössen. Milwaukee: Freidenker Publishing Co., 1885.

12. Does the American Common School Meet the Educational
     Needs of the People? Chicago, 1886.

13. Dance of Death: A Dissertation. New York: Lithographic
     Publishing Co., 1887.

14. Zur Verlobungs-Feier von Fryde B. Huck und Augustus H.
     Vogel. Oktober 23, 1887. Chicago, 1887.

15. Columbia und Germania: Festspiel aufgeführt bei der Ein-
     weihung des Schulgebäudes des Deutsch-Englischen Schul-
     vereins von Chicago. Mai 1888. Musik von G. Katzen-
     berger. Chicago, 1888.

16. Gedankenperlen, gesammelt und nach Stufen geordnet. Mil-
     waukee: Freidenker Publishing Co., 1890.

17. Die deutsche Muse in Amerika. Cincinnati, 1893.

18. Gruss euch Turnern: Festlied. Cincinnati, 1898.

19. Prolog: geschrieben für das Jubiläum, gelegentlich des
     goldenen Jubiläums der Cincinnatier Turngemeinde.
     November 1898. Cincinnati, 1898.

20. German Contributions to American Progress. Boston, 1902.

21. Die deutsch-amerikanische Dichtung. Milwaukee: Herold
     Publishing Co., 1903.

22. Silbernes Jubiläum Konzert des Cincinnati Liederkranz.
     Programm. Cincinnati, 1911.

23. German Taught with Success in American Public Schools.
     Philadelphia: National German-American Alliance, 1911.

24. Neu und Alt: ein Buch für die Jugend. New York: Amer-
     ican Book Co., 1911.

25. Hin und Her: ein Buch für die Kinder. New York: Amer-
     ican Book Co., 1913.

26. In Freud und Leid. Cincinnati: O. G. Muehler, 1914.

27. Hier und Dort: ein Buch für die reifere Jugend. New York:
     American Book Co., 1916.

28. Ich und Du: ein Buch für die Kleinsten. New York: Amer-
     ican Book Co., 1916.

B. Undated Works

29. Der deutsche Unterricht in amerikanischen Schulen: ein
     Förderer der idealen Entwicklung; Der deutsche Unterricht
     in den öffentlichen Schulen von Cincinnati. Bielefeld, n. d.

30. National deutsch-amerikanischer Lehrerbund, gegr. 1870.
     Cincinnati: American Book Co. , n. d.

31. Festspiel: Karneval der Nationen. n. p. , n. d.

C. Scrapbooks and Manuscripts

32. Ausflüge ins romantische Amerika. 4 vols. Cincinnati,
     192...

33. Bibliographie der deutsch-amerikanischen Schönliteratur.
     Cincinnati, 192...

34. Deutsche Dichter und Dichtung in Cincinnati. Cincinnati,
     192...

35. Im Rahmen von sechs Jahrzehnten. Cincinnati, 1924.

36. Wir in Amerika. 4 vols. Cincinnati, n. d.

Notes

1. For the history of the Cincinnati Germans, see Max Burgheim,
    Cincinnati in Wort und Bild (Cincinnati: M. & R. Burgheim,
    1888); Armin Tenner, Cincinnati Sonst und Jetzt (Cincinnati:
    Mecklenborg & Rosenthal, 1878); and Deutsch-Amerikanischer
    Stadtverband, Deutscher Vereins-Wegweiser (Cincinnati: Aug.
    B. Gorbach, 1915).
2. Tenner, pp. 76-77.
3. Tenner, p. 81.
4. Tenner, p. 82
5. Tenner, p. 82.
6. See Heinrich A. Rattermann, "Friedrich Gerstäcker: Reise-
    schriftsteller und Novellist, " Gesammelte Werke (Cincinnati:
    Selbstverlag, 1912), vol. 12: 67-80, and his "Nikolaus Len-
    au mit besonderem Bezug auf seine amerikanischen Gedichte, "
    Gesammelte Werke (Cincinnati: Selbstverlag, 1911), vol. 11:
    401-42.
7. For the history of Cincinnati German literature see Heinrich H.
    Fick, Deutsche Dichter und Dichtung in Cincinnati (Cincinnati:
    n. d). Collection of articles by Fick. Located in the Fick
    Collection of German-Americana, University of Cincinnati
    Main Library.
8. See Hermann Barnstorff, "Der Deutsche Literarische Klub: Ein
    geschichtlicher Ueberblick, " Cincinnati Freie Presse: Illus-

trierte Beilage (Nov. 6, 1927), pp. 2-6.
9. See K. L. Stoll, "Deutsche Werke im Kunstmuseum," Cincinnati Freie Presse: Illustrierte Beilage. (Nov. 6, 1927), pp. 43-48.
10. See Max Griebsch, "H. H. Fick," Monatschefte für deutschen Unterricht, 27 (1935), 191-94.
11. John F. Shotwell, A History of the Schools of Cincinnati (Cincinnati: School Life Co., 1902), p. 176.
12. William Coyle, Ohio Authors and Their Books: Biographical Data and Selective Bibliographies for Ohio Authors, Natives and Residents 1796-1950 (Cleveland: World Publishing Co., 1962), p. 204.
13. Carl Wittke, Refugees of Revolution (Philadelphia: University of Pennsylvania Press, 1952), p. 308.
14. Wittke, p. 308-09.
15. Wittke, p. 308.
16. Karl J. Arndt and May E. Olson, German-American Newspapers and Periodicals, 1732-1955: History and Bibliography (Heidelberg: Quelle & Merzer, 1965), p. 677.
17. Deutsch-Amerikanischer Stadtverband, p. 48-49.
18. See Monatshefte, 27 (1935): p. 147.
19. Griebsch, p. 192.
20. Arndt, p. 447.
21. Heinrich H. Fick, "Die deutsch-amerikanische Dichtung," Monatshefte, 4 (1903-04), 272.
22. See Monatshefte, 27 (1935), 147.
23. A. Gorowicz, "Ein deutsch-amerikanischer Poet," p. 2 (A Dresden, German newspaper clipping in the Fick Collection).
24. See Hans Haupt, "Deutsche Gelehrte und Schriftsteller," Cincinnati Freie Presse: Illustrierte Beilage (Nov. 6, 1927), p. 7.
25. On Fick's lectures, see Geschichte des Deutschen Literarischen Klubs von Cincinnati, Ohio: Erinnerungsschrift für das zehnte Stiftungsfest 26. Nov. 1887 (Cincinnati: Rosenthal, 1887), p. 52-53, and also Vorträge gehalten im Deutschen Literarischen Klub von Cincinnati: Festgabe zum 20. Stiftungsfest (Cincinnati: Rosenthal, 1897), pp. 9-11.
26. Heinrich A. Rattermann, "Die erste Anregung zur Gründung des Deutschen Pionier-Vereins von Cincinnati," Gesammelte Werke (Cincinnati: Selbstverlag, 1912), vol. 16, 367-72.
27. Deutscher Pionier-Verein: Vorstandsbericht (1921-22), p. 20.
28. Fick's poems were dedicated to German-American pioneers.
29. Turner-Leben, vol. 1:3 (January, 1915), 10.
30. The German Literary Club named Fick Honorary President in 1927 for his contributions to German-American poetry.
31. See H. H. Fick, In Freud und Leid (Cincinnati: Muehler, 1914), p. 10. The poem was first published in Der Deutsche Pionier. (June, 1878).
32. See Das Hilfswerk und Cincinnatis deutsche Vereine, 2. Ausgabe (Cincinnati: A. B. Gorbach, 1917), p. 12.
33. See H. H. Fick, "Deutsch in Cincinnati," Erziehungsblätter, 17 (1915), 203, and also his "Die Einführung des deutschen Unterrichts in die öffentlichen Schulen von Cincinnati am 7. Sept. 1840," Erziehungsblätter, 16 (1915), 203-10.

34. Das Hilfswerk und Cincinnatis deutsche Vereine, p. 14.
35. Das Hilfswerk, pp. 16-21.
36. Das Hilfswerk, p. 15.
37. Robert E. Ward, "Konrad Nies, German-American Literary
    Knight," German-American Studies, 3 (1971), 7.
38. See Carl Wittke, German-Americans in the World War (Colum-
    bus: Ohio State Archaeological and Historical Society, 1936).
39. For a picture of Fick censoring German books see G. A. Dob-
    bert, "The Cincinnati Germans, 1870-1920: Disintegration of
    An Immigrant Community," Bulletin of the Cincinnati Histori-
    cal Society, 23 (1965), 241.
40. This bibliography contains letters written by Konrad Nies. See
    footnote 37. Dr. Ward's Dictionary of German-American Cre-
    ative Literature, 1675-1975 will replace this work.
41. See Helga Slessarev, "In Memoriam--Edwin H. Zeydel," Monat-
    shefte, 66 (1975), 152.
42. For the content of the Fick Collection of German-Americana see
    Robert E. Ward, "The German-American Library of H. H.
    Fick: A Rediscovery," German-American Studies. 1 (1969),
    49-68; 2 (1970), 2-29. For information on the creation of the
    special collection see "Collection of German-Americana Es-
    tablished," Candid Campus (University of Cincinnati, May 29,
    1974); also "The University of Cincinnati Is Celebrating,"
    LJ/SLJ Hotline (June 17, 1974), p. 5.

30. OTTO OSCAR KOLLBRUNNER,
    SWISS-AMERICAN POET, 1895-1932*

Linus Spuler

   March 26, 1955 would have been Otto Oscar Kollbrunner's
sixtieth birthday. However, for more than twenty years the poet has
rested in the quiet cemetery of his native village of Hüttlingen in the
Swiss canton of Thurgau. On March 14, 1932, his life came to an
end, a life which had been one of endless struggle and nervous restlessness, a life which seemed to have been a chain of indefinite
longings for the faraway blue horizon of foreign lands, and of home-
sickness for the familiar village where he had spent his childhood.
Death cut off suddenly the line of development of this poet who had
not yet been able to find his way and who was full of inner conflicts
and contrasts. In his own country and in German-American communities in the New World, Kollbrunner had established a modest reputation; however, soon after his untimely death his name was forgotten and only a few remembered the unassuming artist. Yet his work
is worth being known in wider circles since it shows poetic crafts-
manship in building a finely chiseled frame for contents full of moving humanity and originality.

   Otto Oscar Kollbrunner originated in a poor but sound farmer's environment. Since his early boyhood he liked to go his own
way and investigate whatever could bring him in touch with the unknown world far away from his village surroundings. Nobody believed that this dreamy and eccentric young man who secretly wrote
poetry would ever be able to make a living. He enrolled in a
teachers' college but could not adjust to the strictness and discipline. An attempt as an apprentice in a publishing house was not
successful either. In 1913 Kollbrunner boarded a steamer for New
York. This was to rehabilitate him in the eyes of the village people who had looked down on him with wondering disdain. Kollbrunner hoped to get rich in the States within a few years and he also
wanted to gather experience and impressions. However, fate interrupted his plans, for he had to stay in America after World War I
broke out. He underwent all the hardships of the life of a lonesome
immigrant. Nobody in Switzerland knew that the young man in the
metropolis on the Hudson had to earn money by working as a spit-
tooncleaner, a dishwasher and in other odd jobs. Nobody knew that
as a tramp he crossed and re-crossed the States in all directions
and actually became a beggar. At the end of 1917, at last, with the

*Reprinted from American German Review 21 (1955): 9-11, by per-
mission of the publisher.

help of an influential protector, he obtained a job in a firm in New
York.   Later, he became an official in the Swiss consulate there.
In 1922 he was able to start his voyage back home for which he had
been longing all these years.   By this time he was known and ad-
mired in the Swiss colony as the poet of deeply felt nostalgic songs.

Unfortunately, the situation in the old country was not such
that he could settle down and so, after a few months, he was forced
to return to the States.   He worked as a business man and as a
secretary in different positions, but in his spare hours he wrote poetry with tireless inspiration.   He wrote about the fascinating city
of New York, about his wanderings on the sea and along the road;
he expressed his loving admiration for nature and everything created; he described his distant homeland, constantly missed, in the
most tender words; he analyzed his own subtle thought and feelings
and not only molded them into poetry but he also wrote short stories
in a picturesque and colorful prose.   Many of his literary products
were published in the Amerikanische Schweizer-Zeitung, of which he
became an editor in 1926.

Two years later, shocked by the sudden death of his wife
whom he had married in 1922 and who, although she never understood the artistic aspect of his personality, had been his unfailing
support, he left New York and returned to Switzerland for good.
Even there he could not regain mental balance.   In vain his mother,
whose understanding love had guided him during his darkest years,
tried to comfort him.   Again the old restlessness came over him
and pushed him now to far, then to near places of his own land and
of foreign countries.

In this period Kollbrunner wrote some of his most beautiful
poems reflecting impressions of seemingly unimportant objects of
daily life.   In the early spring of 1932 a heart attack ended this disturbed existence and broke off the development of a still improving
poet.

Oscar Kollbrunner, insofar as he can be reckoned among
them, has his own special place among German-American poets; he
ranks highest in artistic means of expression and his attitude toward
his subjects.   His credo read:

> Ich liebe die Welt...
> Ich presse jede Blüte ans Herz,
> Die der Odem der Winde streift.
> Alles Schöne, das Bläue und Licht begreift,
> Ziehe ich niederwärts
> In die Seele, in der es zum Liede reift....

In verses which are reminiscent of Walt Whitman Kollbrunner exult-
ed in life and expressed his zest for existence.   Though he certainly had his roots in the world of the neo-romantics, yet he stood
firmly on the ground of a realistic estimation of the majestic phenomenon of life.   He was shown the way by the imagists of America

with their plastic, colorful and suggestive language. This Swiss poet, after having overcome the first, almost horrifying awe, let himself be carried away by the strong pulsation of New York; the gigantic city seemed to catch and digest every recent cultural movement and every new event. He created his own linguistic and technical instrument in order to reflect his impressions and wild visions
of the American metropolis, and this made it possible for him to
picture them in his poems in a way that no other German-language
poet ever had done before. In Kollbrunner's works a heroic city
rises, real and imposing with himmelanwuchtenden Handelskathedral-
en, huge and whimsical. Bewildered and dismayed, the poet's intuitive mind sensed that the metropolis of our time is a current symbol of "mammonism." This is clearly shown in his "Manhattan-
sonnet":

>   Granitgequadert stösst bei Meer und Masten
>   Der Mammoniten Zion zackig auf.
>   Den Horizont machtprahlend abzutasten,
>   Stürzt Stein und Eisen kerkergrau hinauf.
>
>   Der Himmelshöhle Riesenstalagmiten
>   Sind leichenstarr der Decke zugedreht,
>   Und alle sind aus einem Rumpf geschnitten,
>   Und alle sind des Goldes Fluchgebet.
>
>   Und Klamm an Klamm sind Gassen hier und
>   Strassen,
>   Die abermillionen Menschen fassen,
>   In der Giganten schmalen Schlund geklemmt.
>
>   Ein Babelvolk durchkitzelt ihren Rachen,
>   Und manchmal fratzt um Stein und Turm ein Lachen,
>   Wenn ahnungslos es durch den Abgrund schwemmt.

Sometimes Kollbruner's language is like a tower of piled up rocks;
at other times it reflects the poet's wrestling and struggling for the
exact expression. Plastic depiction is shown in the poem "Wolken-
kratzerbau," verses which for the greater part move on with difficulty and awkwardness, a witness to the gigantic struggle to master
reality and impressions with the tools of language.

>   Wittern und Schnuppern von stählernen
>   Riesengiraffen,
>   Hälse und Krahnen, die gier und gefrässig nach
>   Beute sich straffen;
>   Kalk und Sand und Eisen packen die lüsternen
>   Mäuler,
>   Palmenblättergerupfleicht sind ihnen Balken und
>   Pfeiler;
>   Steinerne Klötze spucken sie teilnahmslos in die
>   gähnenden Rachen
>   Nilferdplumper Maschinen, die sie zu Marmeln
>   verkrachen. . . .

Steingewordene Brandung von Schöpfergedanken,
Deren Zinnen die wehenden Wolken umschwanken,
Deren Aufsturz die ewigen Felsen tragen:
Morgen schon wird dich der Schrei nach dem
    Mammon durchschlagen!
Doch in dir selber erstarrt, wird für Zeiten und
    Zeiten
Weder ein Schmerz noch ein Lächeln dein Antlitz
    umgleiten.

In the beginning Kollbrunner shrank from New York-Babel, this steinerner Wahnsinn kühnster Träume, where mankind becomes a slave to the frantic effort to create a gigantic over-dimensional world.   However, it did not take long till he was under the influence of New York's equalizing power.

Und wer weiss?
Es kommt die Zeit, es kommt die Zeit,
Wo ich selber zum Stein erstarre,
Wo ich Geschäftsmann werde,
Amerikaner.
Und mit einer Maurerkelle
Helfe ich auch in den Himmel hineinbauen,
Ihr vertikalen Städte von Babel.

Soon the resistance to adjustment changed into enthusiasm, for Oscar Kollbrunner saw in New York the place where loftier things were awaiting him, where he could give full scope to his talents and his own personality.

New York...
Du bist der Stahl, geschmiedet aus dem Erz,
Das sich von Alteuropa trennte;
Du bist das ewige Geborenwerden,
Bist unbeugsam empor sich lebendes,
Mit Geist und Faust sich selbst zum Himmel
    hebendes
Gewaltsam grösstes Wunderkind der Erden.

Dann......., wenn ich
Hin in den Tag von Stadt und Strassen stürme,
In Lärm und Hatz und Wolkenbaugetürme,
Dann bist du mein im Wahnsinn deiner Träume--
Dann schweift die Phantasie nach Wolkenzinnen;
Den Babelturm des Glückes zu beginnen
Bin ich bereit--bis an des Himmels Bäume.

Dann fühl' ich mich der Kraft geboren werden,
Bin unbeugsam empor mich lebendes,
Mit Geist und Faust mich selbst zum Himmel
    hebendes
Kind dieser Riesenbabelstadt der Erden.

Though he is aware of the depressing power of the metropolis the poet recognizes it as the stimulating source of a climax in
adventures and happiness, as the touchstone for those whose inner
life is strong and sound and who can stand up to this "Babel." The
city is a concentrated expression of energetic enterprise; it is not
only condemned, but it is blessed as well because of its majesty;
it gives the individual an undefined grandiose feeling of life-conscious-
ness and lifts him into an atmosphere of higher potentialities. Shortly before the last return to his home country Kollbrunner published
the following poem:

DER ZEIGEFINGER......

Ich habe mich emporgeliebt zu dir,
Manhattan, erst nach langen Schicksalsjahren--
Es mussten tausend Blitze in mich fahren,
Eh' ich es voll begriff, dein Machtgebahren,
Ehe dein Stein zum Tönen kam in mir.

Dann aber hat der junge Emigrant,
Der Tag für Tag mit Hader dich verkündet
Als Stätte, die die Gier nach Gold gegründet,
Sich endlich im Erlebnis dir verbündet,
Und dich in Wortgewittern festgebannt.

Als ich mich einmal ganz in dir verlor,
Fiel alle Hässlichkeit von deinen Gliedern;
Ich hämmerte in klanggeschwellten Liedern,
Dein triumphantes Ragen zu erwidern,
Die These meiner Liebe an dein Tor.

Du warst der Zeigefinger einer Hand,
Auf der sich goldnen Westens Schätze häufen,
Auf deren Fläche Mais und Weizen reifen,
Und deren Finger nach dem Süden greifen
Und nach des Nordens strömereichem Land.

Zum Zeigefinger einer neuen Welt,
Zum Machtsymbol, ins Uebermass geraten,
Zum Willensausdruck der geeinten Staaten,
Zum Denkmal jungen Volks und neuer Taten
Warst du graniten vor die Welt gestellt.

Zu Memnonssäulen wurde dein Gerag,
Zur goldnen Wahrheit ward die graue Lüge,
Zu Obelisken ward dein Steingefüge,
Licht sprang in deiner Sphinxgesichter Züge
Und du wardst mein an einem grossen Tag.

Oscar Kollbrunner, who has been characterized as the "poet
of passionate, hard words, of boastful welding of ideas and glitter-
ing obtrusive adverbs," also wrote silent, contemplative poetry to
the whisper of the microcosmos. While focusing the spotlight of im-

pression on his own soul he found mysterious, inscrutable depths
which could be excavated only with the help of metaphors and symbols.   Unfortunately, the poet's untimely death interrupted this process.

> Und willst du meiner Seele Traum verstehen,
> Soll, wenn es dunkel wird in meinem Kreise,
> Die Seele dein auf meinen Wegen gehen,
> Vor meiner Sehnsucht Häusern soll sie stehen
> Und leise klopfen, so wie Nachtwind leise.
>
> In die Gelasse tiefster Dämmerungen
> Will ich sie dann zum Fest des Traumes führen;
> Dort soll sie mich mit seltner Lust verspüren
> Und, wenn die Quellen in mir aufgesungen,
> Verzaubert stehen vor kristallenen Türen.

Still, in some of his poems Kollbrunner gave us essential explanations of his visions.   We stand fascinated before the crystal doors
of his domain and gratefully receive what he was able to present us
in his book, Geschenk der Stille: wonderful poems in a contemplative mood.   However, we also get a hint of what the poet might have
gone on to tell us from "Hinter der Dämmerung":

> Das ist die Stunde, wo es stiller wird
> In meinem Kreise, denn die Schatten weben
> Am dunkeln Netz der Nacht und spinnen leise.
>
> Das ist die Stunde voll geheimer Weise,
> In die des Traumes Regenbogen beben...
> In meiner Stube ist der Tag verblasst.
>
> In tiefe Vasen versickert alle Helle nun,
> Gedämpften Tons, durchschimmernd mit
>   geheimnisvollem Glast
> An aller Dinge Dunkelheit zu rühren
> Mit einem letzten Nach-den-Dingen-spüren,
> Und dann gleich mir in tiefer Nacht zu ruhn.

Oscar Kollbrunner published two volumes of poetry: Wolken-
kratzer und Schweizerheimweh, Ernst Kuhn, Biel, Bern, 1925; and
Geschenk der Stille, Huber, Frauenfeld, Leipzig, 1929.   He also
published two volumes of short stories, Treibholz and Die Schenke
des Mister Bucalo, both Huber and Co., 1927.

31. DORA GRUNEWALD: REMINISCENCES*

Erwin F. Ritter

Whenever Milwaukee German-Americans assembled in fellowship during the troubled times of World War II, the spirited voice
of Dora Grunewald was sure to be heard as a part of the program
for that day.   Her presence usually marked the cultural highlight of
the day's activities: her words always evoked nostalgic recollections
in the hearts of her countrymen toward the historically rich legacy
of the German nation.   In her own way she rekindled and recalled
for her audience the humanistic ideals of the Humboldtean educational system known to every German school child.   Such was the value
of her own verse at these occasions which expressed the sentiments
dear to Germans at a time when their national allegiances were being sorely tried.   From her poetic themes Germans could derive a
needed consolation and pride in their homeland which reassured them
that the political tragedy of the moment was but a passing one.

Born in Hanau, near Frankfurt on December 31, 1895, Dora
Grunewald is the eldest of a family of three daughters.   Her father
was an architect whom she describes as "a studious and nature-lov-
ing man."[1]   Both of her parents shared a particular love of poetry
and nature.   Able to read when she was three years old, word-
rhyming came to her early as a mode of self-expression.   Because
of the nature of the father's profession, the family often moved:
Dresden, Chemnitz, Offenburg, and lastly Braunschweig.

After finishing her formal education, Dora Grunewald attended
a business college for a year, worked another year in an attorney's
office, and then studied for the next four years at Teachers' Prepar-
atory College at Rothenburg/ Fulda.   From 1918 until 1922 she taught
in a small country school in the province Hesse-Nassau and for a
time in Hanover.   Deciding to take a leave of absence from her position in Hanover, Dora Grunewald came to Milwaukee, her present
home.   In Milwaukee she was to meet her future husband, thus ending her teaching career in Germany.

With the birth of a son, now a professor of finance and business administration at Michigan State-East Lansing, she devoted all
of her time to her family.   Nevertheless, she pursued during these
years the study of languages and continued to write verse during her
leisure hours.   Her poems were regularly printed in German-Amer-

*Reprinted from German-American Studies 7 (1974): 5-12, by per-
mission of the publisher.

ican newspapers. She also attended classes at the University of
Wisconsin-Milwaukee and Marquette University where she studied
Latin, Italian, Spanish, Portuguese, French, and Russian. Ultimately, she was awarded an M. A. in German from Marquette University
in 1960. While taking courses at these universities, Dora Grunewald substituted in practically all of the Milwaukee area high schools
until she received a permanent position at Washington High School.
Here she taught Spanish, German, and Ancient History until her retirement in 1968. Even before grade school foreign language instruction (FLES Programs) became popular, Mrs. Grunewald conducted German classes for thirty-two years at one of the Milwaukee
Freie Gemeinden centers. It was as a grade schooler that the
writer of this article received his first formal introduction to German at one of these Saturday morning sessions. Still active at the
present, Dora Grunewald continues to offer regular evening classes
in Italian, Spanish, French, Russian, and English-for-the-foreign-
born at the Central YMCA in Milwaukee.

By her own admission, Dora Grunewald is a nature poet. Nature is the main theme and interest of her verse. In the "Fore-
word" to her Gedichte she explains the underlying intent of her collection of poems which in its inspiration resembles the Goethean
Weltanschauung, especially the poet's views of man and nature during the classical years at Weimar which were to become the inherit-
ance of the German Romantics, and the legacy of German Idealism:
"Die Gedichte dieses kleinen Buches sind der tiefsinnigen Liebe zur
Natur entsprungen. Der Mensch ist ein Teil der Natur, und nur in
enger Verbindung mit ihr kann er rein, wahr und glücklich bleiben.
Ich habe das selbst an mir erlebt. Draussen, in freier Gottesnatur,
fern von der grossen Stadt, fällt so vieles Hässliche vom Menschen
ab. Er denkt und fühlt freier, und die Seele bekommt Flügel. "[2]

Poetry has been a way of life for Dora Grunewald, and as she
confesses, her "greatest joy. "[3] Before her husband passed away,
the Grunewalds used to spend weekends at their lake cottage at Bark
Lake near Milwaukee. Each time they returned from the lake to
their home in the city, she brought along a poem or two which had
been inspired by being close to nature. The small collection of her
verse entitled Gedichte is but a sampling of the verse she has written over the years. In a year or so Mrs. Grunewald intends to
have a second volume of verse published. At the present, however,
her poems appear almost weekly in the Milwaukee Herold, a German-American newspaper printed in Omaha, Nebraska. Thus she
continues to enjoy a special talent that has given so much meaning
to her life.

If nature is the thematic material (Stoff) of Dora Grunewald's
verse, then the message (Inhalt) of her poems reflects the moral
presence of the Creator in the universe. The seasonal moods and
nature's phenomena are a source of inexhaustible joy to her:

Wenn der Schnee zergeht
und der Lenzwind weht,

> ist mein Herz so froh,
> so hoffnungsvoll, so frei.
>
> Wenn die Sonne glüht,
> und die Rose blüht,
> jauchz ich auf in tiefer,
> voller Sommerlust.
>
> ....
>
> Ist zur Winterzeit
> alles eingeschneit,
> staunt mein Auge
> ob der weissen, hehren Pracht.
>
> Mögen Blitze glüh'n,
> schwarze Wolken zieh'n,
> immer, Erde, bist du, ach
> unendlich schön. [4]

> Der Winter floh, es kam der Frühling,
> und nun die gold'ne, heisse Zeit,
> So reihen Jahre sich an Jahre,
> wie liegst du, Jugend, ach so weit!
>
> Bald naht der Herbst, die Früchte reifen.
> Es eilt die Zeit, sie steht nie still.
> Sie zieht mich mit in Risenschritten.
> Wie lange wohl? Nun, wie Gott will. [5]

Yet that joy which pervades the poetess' celebration of nature is always closely linked with the deeper awareness of the Divine Presence:

> Es zucken Blitze, Donner grollen.
> Ich sage leis ein fromm Gebet.
> Nichts hat Bestand in allen Welten.
> Nur ewig Gottes Geist besteht. [6]

> Durch deine Träume
> wehet der Hauch der Ewigkeit. [7]

> Jahre kommen, Jahre gehen,
> Und ich ziehe meine Bahn,
> Folgend ewigen Gesetzen,
> Doch das Aug' glänzt sternenan. [8]

> Gott der Welten: voller Inbrunst
> nennt mein Mund den Namen dein. [9]

The solace that comes to man in returning to a natural setting where he can once more be responsive to musing about the origins of life, makes the return trip to his "civilized" life style increasingly

difficult.   This recurrent motif echoes Dora Grunewald's devotion to
nature:

> Es brennt die Sonne aufs weisse Gestein,
> es flimmert die Luft im Mittagsschein
> Die Menge jagt in wilder Hast,
> die grosse Stadt kennt keine Rast.
>
> . . . .
>
> Da sitzt verträumt an der Mauer Rand
> ein alter Mann; mit blasser Hand
> wehrt er dem grellen Sonnenlicht.
>
> . . . .
>
> Und Stunde um Stunde er starrt und träumt,
> ihn eilet nicht, er nichts versäumt,
> und niemand ruft ihn, volle Liebe bereit:
> Die grosse Stadt hat keine Zeit.[10]

> Das ist die grosse Stadt,
> die steinerne Stadt,
> die keine Seele hat,
> wo die Menschen sich drängen
> durch der Strassen Engen,
> sich mühen und plagen,
> das Glück zu erjagen,
> zu erhaschen das Geld,
> das ihre Sinne gefangen hält.
>
> Doch tief drinnen im Herzen
> brennen heisse Schmerzen.
> Da rührt sich ein Sehnen
> nach Licht und nach Sonne,
> nach Reinheit, nach Wonne,
> nach Atmen in freier Gottesnatur.[11]

The stylistic format of Dora Grunewald's verse is undoubtedly rooted in the tradition of the Volkslied: the words are direct,
the message clear, the prosody and melody simple and unadorned.
Poems which exemplify the folk element in her verse are those which
reflect upon the cultural adjustment experienced by the German in
a strange land.   These poems single her out as a distinctively German-American poetess and endeared her to the generation of the war
years:

> Lang, lang ist es her,
> seit ich kam übers Meer
> in das neue Land,
> das ich Heimat genannt.

Ich strebt' voran mit Herz und Hand,
schuf mir ein neues Heimatland.
Die Jahre flohen schnell dahin
Es jagt der Mensch nach Glück, Gewinn.

Viel Ängste gab's und Sorg' und Plag',
an Mühen reich war jeder Tag.
Es wuchs das Haus, der Freunde Zahl,
und Liebe lacht beim vollen Mahl.

Doch oft, in tiefer Abendstund',
wenn selig schweigt der Kindermund
und still die müde Hände ruh'n
von all des Tages em'sem Tun,

die Seele fliegt ins Heimatland,
dort, wo das Vaterhaus einst stand,
und träumt und denkt der holden Zeit.

O Kinderland, wie liegest du weit!
O Eltern traut, o Jugendglück!
was einstmals war, kehrt nie zurück.

Der Morgen graut, der Tag beginnt.
Heiss mir im Aug' die Träne rinnt
Fahr wohl, fahr wohl mein Kinderland!
Es ruh' auf dir des Glückes Hand![12]

Was ist das schönste Lied auf Erden?
Das Lied, das einst die Mutter sang
als ich daheim bei ihr gesessen,
ihr süsses Lied ins Ohr mir drang.
Was ist so teuer meinem Herzen?
Der Mutter Sprache, Mutter Laut,
die sie mit frommen Eifer lehrte
dem Kind, das gläubig ihr vertraut.
Was ist der schönste Platz auf Erden?
Der Ort, wo meine Wiege stand,
wo ich der Jugend Traum gelebet,
geleitet an der Mutter Hand.

Nie könnt' der Heimat ich vergessen,
sie machte stark mich, fromm und gut.
O Heimatsprache, Heimaterde,
mögs stehen du in Gottes Hut.[13]

To the German-American immigrant the aforegoing nostalgic expressions denote a cultural void that evokes nostalgic reminders. To the native of this land such sentiments are often received unfavorably--based on a lack of appreciation for the cultural ties which are strongest in the lingual development of the child. Dora Grunewald's verse voices the immigrant's indelible romance with the language of childhood: the only cultural legacy that most stubbornly

resists Americanization. The unpublished poems, "Muttersprache"
and "Amerika und Deutschland," summarize this very human plight
of the German-American: his deep gratitude toward the land of his
adoption, and his lingual privation which is his deepest awareness
of all that we conveniently label Heimweh:

> Amerika und Deutschland,
> zwei Länder gross und schön!
> Wer hätt' in allen Zeiten
> je Fein'res wohl gesehen?
>
> Und als in schwersten Zeiten
> es arm, verlassen stand,
>
> Amerika, du Grosse, gabst
> helfend ihm die Hand.
>
> Kunst, Denken, Fühlen, Wissen
> tauscht ihr mit'ander aus.
>
> . . . .
>
> Amerika und Deutschland,
> zwei Länder kühn und schön,
> mög' eurer Freundschaft Bande
> nun nimmermehr vergeh'n.
>
> Mög' Weisheit stets Euch leiten,
> in schicksalschwerster Zeit
> zum Heile aller Völker
> für jetzt und Ewigkeit.[14]
>
> Die Sprache ist ein Heil'ges Erbe,
> uns von den Vätern anvertraut,
> dass wir getreulich hüten, pflegen
> der Kindheit Lieder süssen Laut.
> Wo du auch immer mögest weilen,
> in fremdem Orte, fernem Land:
> Die Muttersprache sei dir heilig,
> gewalt'ger Schätze Unterpfand.
> Und bist allein du, und verlassen,
> drängt dich die Welt in irrem Lauf,
> so falte still die müden Hände,
> schau gläubig du zum Himmel auf.
> Dann in der Muttersprache Lauten
> formt sich in dir ein fromm Gebet,
> der Kindheit Zauber liegt darinnen,
> ein Glaube, der im Kampf besteht.
> O Muttersprache, schönstes Erbe,
> das Gott uns in der Wiege gab.
> O pflege sie, sie sei dir heilig
> dein ganzes Leben bis zum Grab.[15]

In conclusion, what can be recorded of Dora Grunewald's life and verse? From her verse which is the record of her life we know she treasures a lifelong communion with nature, she raises her voice in pious gratitude for the gift of life, she nourishes an abiding love of the language and the land of her birth. She writes of a Germany known in her childhood, a Germany that has seen many changes, but whose cultural richness endures in the hearts of those who have made a home in foreign lands. In her recollection and praise of this Germany, the cultural Germany which transcends time and survives with each succeeding generation, she truly can be termed a patriot viewing the lasting qualities of her heritage in a foreign context. Such a literary disposition is, in essence, the ledger of German-American literature. Yet beyond the national traits of Dora Grunewald's poetry and life one senses notes of a deeper admission: her work conveys a happiness that can only come from personal contentment, a mystery in every land and age.

Notes

1. Biographical material has been taken from Mrs. Grunewald's correspondence of July 16, 1972 with the author of this study.
2. D. Grunewald, Gedichte (Milwaukee, 1967), p. 3.
3. Grunewald-Ritter Correspondence.
4. "Wenn der Schnee zergeht," Gedichte, p. 9. Hereafter only titles from this work will be cited.
5. "Sommerandacht," p. 20.
6. Loc. cit.
7. "Schlummerlied," p. 39.
8. "Sehnsucht," p. 45.
9. "Leise senkt die Nacht sich nieder," p. 47.
10. "Stadtbild," p. 78.
11. "Die grosse Stadt," p. 86.
12. "Fernes Gedenken," pp. 42-43.
13. "Heimatsprache, Heimaterde," p. 83.
14. "Amerika und Deutschland" (1972).
15. "Muttersprache" (1972).

32. A CONVERSATION WITH JOHANNES URZIDIL*

David Berger

Johannes Urzidil, the Prague-born author, is one of
the many outstanding German writers who settled in
the United States during the period of Nazi rule in Europe. Though he continues to write in German he
chooses to remain in this country. Urzidil was a
close friend of Franz Kafka and Franz Werfel. Among
Urzidil's best known books are Die Verlorene Geliebte,
for which he received the Charles Veillon prize, Das
grosse Halleluja, and the recently published Da geht
Kafka. He has also received the "Literaturpreis der
Stadt Köln" and the "Grossen Oesterreichischen Staats-
preis für Literatur."
I recently conducted the following interview with Mr.
Urzidil, which was broadcast by many American University radio stations as part of the Germany Today series.

Berger: It seems obvious that a transplanted writer has to
overcome far more complex problems than a painter or composer.
Would you comment on some of the problems a foreign author faces
in this country?

Urzidil: Of all the creative artists transplanted to a new
country, the writer certainly has the most difficult lot. For he is
basically dependent upon his native language. Even if he acquires
a good command of the new language, he still lacks the psychologi-
cal advantage of having absorbed the ideas associated with phenomena simultaneously with their names, as every child does with his
mother tongue. This incidentally is also a reason why even the best
translations lack absolute authenticity. For instance, you will have
noticed that the most remarkable exiled German language fiction
writers and playwrights, who came to this country during the 'thirties and 'forties, continued to write in their native German. This
was true for Thomas Mann, Heinrich Mann, Carl Zuckmayer, Hermann Broch, Fritz von Unruh, Bert Brecht, Franz Werfel, to mention only the most famous ones. Musicians or painters, however,
can present their works directly without the interfering medium of
language, and therefore are in a much better position to reach new
audiences than writers.

*Reprinted from American-German Review 32:1 (1965): 23-24, by
permission of the publisher.

Berger: What are some of the more specific problems an exiled writer has to cope with?

Urzidil: His main problem, and of course the most difficult one, is to preserve carefully his own creative language. At the same time he should not hesitate to make some useful acquisitions from the new language and its style, which represent the new life which surrounds him. After all, the language of a writer is enhanced and enriched by the events and activity confronting him. But he must avoid affecting his native style and the structure of his native language through the intrusion of elements which belong structurally to the new language. To maintain this kind of balance is an almost overwhelming task. Another of the exiled writer's problems is to learn to love the new country and people and, at the same time, not to exaggerate this love but to maintain a rational attitude. He should not act like a blind lover, who prefers to see only the beautiful and positive aspects. Such blind love would not serve his own writings nor would he make a useful contribution to his adopted country and its people.

Berger: There have been cases in which writers have exiled themselves voluntarily. I am thinking of the American exiled writers of the '20s. Today there are a number of German writers who lived or now live in foreign countries. Would you comment on that?

Urzidil: I do not really believe that a writer exiles himself voluntarily. The American writers of the '20s were not exiles in the proper sense. They came and left freely. There is always a profound reason for living and creating abroad, for example, a desire to gain distance. This gives a writer the opportunity to discover new and clearer perspectives. He feels as if he were looking through an inverted telescope watching the objects seemingly farther away, of smaller dimensions but incomparably clearer. The German, Austrian and other writers of our time, including those who seemingly exiled themselves, still acted under moral or political pressure or both, and thus became real exiles, as if they had been driven out by physical force.

Berger: I assume that it is far more difficult for a German author to live in New York than, say, in Paris.

Urzidil: In a way it might be more comfortable to live in Paris. But New York, although tiresome, offers many more and greater opportunities. It is not only the larger, it is, indeed, the true and real metropolis. Paris, in all its beauty and attractiveness, is a national capital. New York is supernational, the center of converging ideological powerlines from all continents. At the same time it is intrinsically American, because all America is omnipresent here. It is always modern, always new, always exciting. In New York, the writer may lack the coffee houses, the boulevards and the literary circles of Paris, but that lovable Paris of Puccini's La Bohème has passed long ago. New York has the greatest possible concentration and accumulation of nations, religions, races, and so-

cial strata of all kinds. It offers good luck and bad luck, success
and trouble. I would never exchange it for any other city, for after almost a quarter of a century residence, I feel like a real New
Yorker. And for that matter, I doubt very much that, after 25
years, I could feel like an old Parisian or Londoner.

Berger: What then are the tangible advantages of living in
New York for a foreign language author?

Urzidil: Well among others, New York offers excellent library research facilities, including the availability of the Library of
Congress. Since I am primarily a fiction writer I also find that
New York is an inexhaustible source of unusual individuals, occurrences and ideas. But I should like to stress one special point. An
exiled foreign language writer can hardly expect to become an influential force in his adopted country. Some of his ideas may command respect, but he can hardly influence the style and the literary
language there. But by publishing his works in Europe, in Germany,
Switzerland and Austria, as I am doing, he can act as a mediator
between different cultures. At times he will interpret the American
scene more soberly and fairly than even a very competent American
writer who might overestimate certain actualities and misjudge some
paramount American virtues.

Berger: Don't you feel at times cut off from your publishers
and colleagues in Europe?

Urzidil: Not I, personally. I receive a steady stream of letters and books from my publishers in Europe, my editors and many
literary friends. And, of course, I get messages every day from
European readers of my books, people whom I personally do not know
at all. I conduct my literary conversations by mail, which, admit-
tedly, is slow, but solid and reliable.

Berger: From your living in the U.S. for 25 years, I assume that your books must have acquired an American slant. Your
book Goethe in Böhmen which was published in 1962 would be different if it had been written in Vienna or Paris.

Urzidil: The American experience, as indeed the Anglo-Saxon
experience and by this I mean the literary one, makes for a more
realistic presentation of subjects and ideas. This, I feel, is the advantage a foreign language writer enjoys in New York, or in the USA.
A book which might turn out to be rather abstract if conceived and
written in Vienna or perhaps Paris, might become more drastic and
more lifelike if written in America. And this I consider eminently
beneficial.

Berger: During World War II, I knew a number of European
writers who meticulously avoided any contact with American literature, in order to preserve their national purity, so to speak. Do
you attempt to isolate yourself from American literary influences?

Urzidil: Not at all. On the contrary, I am profoundly impressed by Thoreau and Hawthorne and I love the great lyrical poets, Whitman, Dickinson, Jeffers, Edna Millay, Frost or Marianne Moore. For my personal pleasure I translated many verses of these poets and even published a translation of Hilda Doolittle's fascinating book By Avon River. I like Thomas Wolfe and much of Faulkner and, indeed, many theoretical works, for example, those by Van Wyck Brooks, whose Makers and Finders and especially whose Flowering of New England are some of my most beloved American works. I am deeply grateful for all these literary experiences. But they do not affect my own style and I still remain entirely independent as a writer in German.

Berger: Now I would like to ask you a purely theoretical question: if you had the improbable choice of being either an American or a German writer, which would you prefer?

Urzidil: Indeed, there is nothing to prefer. You might as well ask a birch tree whether it would prefer being an oak. Each has its special merits and mission in life. I am by descent and by my work an Austrian writer, and the German language is the nutritive element of my existence. Living in this country affords me the privilege of conceiving of all human problems in more than one way. But above all, in America I can remain faithful to my own language. This, it seems to me, proves more than anything else the maturity of the culture of this country.

Berger: Thank you, Mr. Urzidil.

33. ERNST WALDINGER: AN AUSTRO-
    AMERICAN POET*

Robert Kauf

The poet Ernst Waldinger, an American citizen residing in
Saratoga Springs, where he is chairman of the German department
of Skidmore College, recently received two notable Austrian literary awards: Theodor-Körner-Preis in 1958, and Preis der Stadt
Wien für Kunst, Wissenschaft und Volksbildung in 1960. Waldinger
was born in Vienna in 1896, and lived there until his emigration to
the United States in 1938. His first critical recognition came, interestingly enough, from America, when in 1926 Ludwig Lewisohn
published an essay in The Nation (later reprinted in Lewisohn's Of
Cities and Men) about the then practically unknown young Austrian
poet. Today he is much less known in America than in Austria,
where his work soon gained, and has maintained to this day, the
favor of critics and fellow poets such as Josef Weinheber, who wrote
an essay about him in 1933. In the same year, the University of
Vienna honored its alumnus--he holds a Dr. phil. in Germanics--
with the Julius-Reich-Preis.

Waldinger's poetry springs from the soil of Austrian literary
tradition which, although it probably has more in common with German literature than just the language, as another prominent contemporary Austrian writer asserts, still differs enough from the latter
in many of its tendencies to warrant a brief discussion. The literature of Germany tends toward radicalism: it seeks to penetrate to
the essence of things and places other considerations, such as form,
tradition, and intelligibility, secondarily. Austrian literature on the
whole more skeptical, is less passionate in its search for essence,
is more reluctant to part with meaningful traditions, and values form
and lucid presentation. It is also, as a rule, less esoteric and
more "middle-brow" than German literature. The dangers arising
from such leanings are stagnation and shallowness. In the past,
however, Austrian literature has not only been able to avoid these,
but has even been successful in initiating new literary trends, notably that of Expressionism, which began there around 1910, though it
reached its zenith and its extremest form in Berlin about ten years
later.

Waldinger's early poetry, too, is influenced by Expressionism, as the following poem, which appeared in an early anthology,
clearly shows:

*Reprinted from American-German Review 27:6 (1961): 11-3, by per-
mission of the publisher.

Der Mensch der Städte

Du läufst dir nach, doch du erreichst dich nicht,
Enteilst dir jäh und kannst dir nicht entfliehn,
Wie eine Mücke taumelst du ums Licht
Und lässt dich locken und ins Dunkel ziehn,
Du würgst den Schrei, doch der zeigt ungeschrien
In deinem wahnzerklüfteten Gesicht
Die wilde Klage deiner Ungeduld:
O meine Schuld, o meine grosse Schuld!

Ob du die Türme blind ins Blaue wagst,
Ob du dich rasend nun im Netz der Strassen,
Ein selbstgefangnes Tier, ins Irre jagst,
Die Sorgen, die sich in die Stirne frassen,
Die Furien, die noch immer nicht vergassen,
Sind ewig da, in allem was du sagst,
Bleibt dein Bekenntnis, nimmer eingelullt:
O meine Schuld, o meine grosse Schuld!

Du flüchtest in die Arbeit, in den Dampf
Aus den Ventilen, ins Gekreisch der Feilen,
Dein Pult nicht, nicht dein hämmerndes Gestampf
Kennt Frieden, Ruhe und des Glücks Verweilen,
Es hetzt dich über der Gedanken Meilen,
Im Leeren krümmt dich nur der gleiche Krampf,
Und gnadenlos verzeiht dir keine Huld:
O deine Schuld, o deine grosse Schuld!

Für die Minute kaufst du nur dich los,
Wenn dein Gewissen du mit Wein betrügst,
Wenn trunken du in deines Weibes Schoss
Für neue Saat, für neue Sünde pflügst,
Wenn du im Wald dich träumerisch belügst,
Schweift Sehnsucht wipfelwärts aus Busch und Moos--
Der Tag, ein grauer Richter, weist verschrullt:
Auf deine Schuld, auf deine grosse Schuld!

Wir alle, arme Menschen in der Stadt,
Wenn einer seinen Blick zum Himmel hebt,
Und keine Bleibe, keine Hoffnung hat,
Vergeb uns Gott, wenn irgendeiner lebt,
Dass Angst am Klöppel unsres Herzens klebt,
--Wir sind nur Kranke und vom Fieber matt--
Hör uns gestehn, unendliche Geduld:
O unsre Schuld, o unsre übergrosse Schuld!

Typical of Expressionism is the poem's dynamic and pathetic language, its imagery, and its mood, which is one of metaphysical anguish due to the threatened destruction of man's human spirit by the Big City (a favorite Expressionist symbol for industrial civilization); atypical of it, but typical of Waldinger and his Austrian background, is that the form remains intact, in spite of the intensity and immedi-

acy of expression, which reminded the poet Richard von Schaukal of
the verse of Louise Labé, the sixteenth century French poetess.

Although Waldinger soon abandoned Expressionism which, because of its tendency toward the chaotic and irregular, he must have
found uncongenial, he did not embrace the all-too-matter-of-fact poetry of the Neue Sachlichkeit, which predominated in the literature of
the early thirties.   By 1934, he had found a literary style of his
own and also a poetic purpose, which he sets forth in the poem "Die
Gestalt ist gerettet," the first poem in Die Kuppel, his first published volume of verse.

Die Gestalt ist gerettet

Hat mich der Gott der Unterwelt beschworen,
Aus allen Kratern, aus der Glut der Hölle
Die Schlacke nur zu holen, das Gerölle
Porphyrner Worte mit zerrissnen Poren?
Die Verse, die das Chaos einst verloren,
Das mir die Lava aus den Händen quölle?
Und zahlten wir dem Fährmann unsre Zölle
Und ziehn nur Schatten aus den Stygschen Toren?

Kein Nebelftzen hängt an meinen Worten,
Wenn alle anderen Arme auch verdorrten,
Und Hohn von allen Wänden widerhallt,

Ich will den Meissel in den Marmor hau'n,
Mag spiegelnd die gerettete Gestalt
Den Himmel fangen und sich selbst beschau'n.

Unlike many of the other writers of his generation who, deeply
troubled by the threat to human values brought about by the man-
made hell of industrial mass-civilization, sought to destroy all existing culture in order to create an entirely new order from the result-
ing chaos, Waldinger seeks to stem the de-humanizing tendencies of
much of modern life by inculcating into his reader an awareness of
the great traditions of Western civilization.   One of its important
concepts is the ideal of Gestalt, which Waldinger defines as "the humane synthesis of emotion and reason."   By upholding Gestalt, the
poet defends civilization.

Concern with the preservation of Western civilization perme-
ates Waldinger's work: in the face of rising anti-humanism he reminds his readers of the traditional humane ideals; and to counter-
act the decline of discipline in thinking, writing, and living, which
to him is an indication of a new barbarism, he strives in his poetry
toward ever increasing simplicity, lucidity, and precision.   This
article places him ideologically and formally outside the main stream
of contemporary letters with its fascination for hopelessness, despair,
and nihilism and its stylistic predilection for the obscure and absurd.
As a lyric poet from Austria he should however be little concerned
with his isolation knowing that the old and strong literary tradition

of his former homeland attaches little value to literary fashions and
-isms; and he will probably agree with Siegfried Melchinger, who
recently reminded his readers that man has not ceased to express
his sorrow through tears and his joy through laughter, and that
therefore also in lyric poetry that which is immutable and eternal
is more essential than that which is new....

PART VI

GERMAN-AMERICAN LITERATURE TODAY

34. CONTEMPORARY GERMAN-AMERICAN LITERATURE: 1970-76

Don Heinrich Tolzmann

For the first time since World War II, German-American literature blossomed in the 1970s. Authors again united in various literary and historical societies, published journals and volumes of prose and poetry. The great body of German-American literature was rediscovered by literary critics in the old and new worlds. Poets talked seriously about a "Blütezeit" of German-American belles lettres. Libraries began to collect German-American publications and 1976 saw an unprecedented number of conferences and symposia on German-American culture.

Several German-American literary and historical societies exist which coordinate contemporary literary endeavors. The Society for German-American Studies (Cleveland, Ohio) is perhaps the most significant organization dedicated to the study of the German element in the Americas. It publishes an excellent Journal of German-American Studies which contains original German language poetry, reviews, essays and articles. The Association of German Language Authors in America (Cincinnati, Ohio) is the largest literary society for German-American authors. It publishes the Zeitschrift für deutschamerikanische Literatur, a journal with original German-American prose and poetry and news of interest to German-American authors. The Association sponsors short story and poetry contests and publishes occasional volumes of poetry by members of the Association. These two organizations appear to be the central literary-historical societies for German-American literature, but there are several other significant groups with special areas of interest and concentration.

The Literarische Gesellschaft von Chicago and the Literarischer Verein (New York, New York) sponsor lectures and discussions on German literature and culture, and the Literary Society Foundation, Inc. (New York, New York) aids schools and libraries with grants and German-language publications. There are several historical societies which focus on various aspects of German life in the Americas. The American Historical Society of the Germans from Russia (Greeley, Colorado) is mainly concerned with the history of the Russian-Germans in America. It publishes a Work Paper with articles and bibliographical information on the Russian-Germans. The two oldest German-American historical societies are the Society for the History of the Germans in Maryland and the

Pennsylvania German Society. The former publishes The Report:
A Journal of German-American Studies and the latter issues a quarterly journal, Der Reggeboge, and also an annual yearbook. Another
Russian-German organization is the North Dakota Historical Society
of the Germans from Russia. The Swiss-American Historical Society publishes a very fine Newsletter with articles, reviews and bibliographies. There are also some small localized historical societies. The Cincinnati German Historical Society limits itself to the
preservation of historical data on the Germans in the Greater Cincinnati, Ohio area. The Georgia Salzburger Historical Society is
concerned with the history of Georgians of Salzburger background.
The addresses of these societies can be found in my German-Americana: A Bibliography (Metuchen, N.J.: Scarecrow Press, 1975).

There are a number of other journals and newspapers which
the student of German-American literature should consult. Klingsor,
published at the State University of New York-Buffalo, contains some
fine German-American poetry, as does Lyrica Germanica: Journal
for German Lyric Poetry (Rutgers University) and the Schatzkammer
der deutschen Sprachlehre, Dichtung und Geschichte (University of
Texas-Arlington). German-American original poetry is published in
these three journals and also in the Journal of German-American
Studies and the Zeitschrift für deutschamerikanische Literatur. Two
newspapers of importance are the Aufbau (New York) and the New
Yorker Staats-Zeitung und Herold. Both carry German-American
literature and contain reviews of the publications of German-American authors. The Staats-Zeitung publishes the extremely valuable
column of Gert Niers entitled "Deutschamerikanische Literaturnach-
richten." This has news of interest from German language authors
in the Americas.

Two excellent anthologies of German-American literature have
been compiled by Robert E. Ward: Deutsche Lyrik aus Amerika
(New York: Literary Society Foundation Inc., 1969) and Nachrichten
aus den Staaten. Deutsche Literatur in den USA (Hildesheim: Olms
Presse, 1977). Both contain valuable biobibliographical data on contemporary German-American authors. Another fine anthology, this
one concentrating on Austro-American authors, is Mimi Grossberg's
Oesterreichisches aus Amerika: Vers und Prosa (Wien: Bergland
Verlag, 1974). These three anthologies provide an overview of
contemporary German language writing in America.

There are several libraries which contain strong holdings in
German-American literature: the H. H. Fick Collection of German-
Americana at the University of Cincinnati, the Max Kade German-
American Document and Research Center at the University of Kansas, the German Society of Pennsylvania in Philadelphia, and the Robert E. Ward Collection of Americana Germanica at the Western Reserve Historical Society in Cleveland. Students interested in pursu-
ing their research in German-American literature should turn to these
collections for resources. There are many other libraries with German-Americana, but these are the main repositories of German-
American literature. The student of contemporary German-American

German-American Literature

belles lettres should examine the following works which have been
produced since 1970:

Robert E. Ward, Unser Geist. Youngstown, Ohio, 1971.

Mimi Grossberg, Gedichte und kleine Prosa. Wien: Bergland Ver-
    lag, 1972.

Don Heinrich Tolzmann, Handbuch eines Deutschamerikaners: Ged-
    ichte. Gordonville, Pa.: Kinsinger, 1973.

Maria Berl-Lee, Schaumwein aus meinem Krug. Wien: Bergland
    Verlag, 1974.

Mimi Grossberg, Die K.U.K. Armee in der österreichischen satire.
    Wien: Bergland Verlag, 1974.

Dora Grunewald, Was ist Poesie? Vortrag. Milwaukee, 1974.

Margarcte Kollisch, Unverlorene Zeit. Gedichte und Betrachtungen.
    Wien: Bergland Verlag, 1974.

Peter Lindt, Schriftsteller im Exil. Zwei Jahre deutsche literar-
    ische Sendung am Rundfunk in New York. 1944. Nachdruck:
    Nendeln: Kraus, 1974.

Elisabeth Mayer, Deutschsprachige und die deutsche Sprache in Mich-
    igan. Kalamazoo, Michigan, 1974.

Georg Rath, Fabeln. Peru, Nebraska, 1974.

Georg Rath, Klänge der Seele. Peru, Nebraska, 1974.

Anna Reichrath, 20 Jahre Donauschwaben in Cincinnati. Cincinnati,
    Ohio, 1974.

Carrie Seib, Gedichte der Höheren Kraft. St. Louis: Eden Publish-
    ing House, 1974-75. Vol. 1-2.

Stuart Friebert, Nicht hinauslehnen. Gedichte. München: Delp-
    Verlag, 1975.

Russell W. Gilbert, Bilder un Gedanke. Breinigsville, Pa.: Penn-
    sylvania German Society, 1975.

Peter Heller, Menschentiere. (Sonderheft der Lyrik und Prosa).
    Buffalo, New York, 1975.

Peter Heller, Prosa in Versen. Darmstadt: Bläschke Verlag, 1975.

Lisa Kahn, Klopfet an so wird euch nichts aufgetan. Darmstadt:
    Bläschke Verlag, 1975.

Don Heinrich Tolzmann, Abschied. Cincinnati, Ohio: Im Verlage
    des Verbands deutschsprachiger Autoren, 1975.

Franzi Ascher-Nash, Gedichte eines Lebens. Darmstadt: Blaeschke
    Verlag, 1976.

Franzi Ascher-Nash, Essays aus jüngster Zeit. Beckingen: Literar-
    ische Union, 1976.

Christiane Seiler, Der knallrote Hahn. Cincinnati, Ohio: Im Ver-
    lage des Verbands deutschsprachiger Autoren, 1976.

    Students interested in locating books and articles on German-
American literature should consult German-Americana: A Bibliography (Metuchen, N.J.: Scarecrow Press, 1976), pp. 103-86. This
work also contains a chronological list of German-American literature
from 1700-1974 (pp. 133-58).

PART VII

CONCLUSION

Christian Esselen's review of the first anthology of German-
American poetry, Conrad Marxhausen's Deutsch-Amerikanischer
Dichterwald (1856), remarked that "Such a collection should treat
preferably American themes--it should include none of the old Ge-
fühlsduselei of German romanticism--it should rather attempt to
catch the poetic content of American life, of this young vigorous
country...." According to him, German-American literature should
be a "poetry of progress, of development." And it did, indeed,
capture the essence and spirit of American life from a perspective
that was uniquely German-American. As LaVern Rippley notes in
his recent history, The German-Americans (Boston: Twayne, 1976,
p. 171), "publications in German provided the German element in
the United States with the means by which their immigrant experiences could be shared and a sense of identity maintained."

Future studies of German-American literature will bring
greater understanding not only for the German element, but also to
our pluralistic society. There are many treasures awaiting discov-
ery: dramas, novels, novellas, poetry, etc. This book is a tribute
to the German-American author and his work, a neglected dimension
of American historical and literary studies.

Don Heinrich Tolzmann

312

INDEX

ndex 321